Jolene

1

Democracy and New Media

Media in Transition

David Thorburn, *series editor*

Edward Barrett, Henry Jenkins, *associate editors*

New Media, 1740–1915, edited by Lisa Gitelman and Geoffrey B. Pingree, 2003

Democracy and New Media, edited by Henry Jenkins and David Thorburn, 2003

Rethinking Media Change: The Aesthetics of Transition, edited by David Thorburn and Henry Jenkins, 2003

Democracy and New Media

Edited by Henry Jenkins and David Thorburn
Associate Editor: Brad Seawell

The MIT Press
Cambridge, Massachusetts
London, England

This book was set in Perpetua by Graphic Composition, Inc.
Printed and bound in the United States of America.

Library of Congress Cataloging-in-Publication Data

Democracy and new media / edited by Henry Jenkins and David Thorburn ; associate
editor, Brad Seawell.
       p. cm. — (Media in transition)
    Includes bibliographical references and index.
    ISBN 0-262-10101-7 (hc. : alk. paper)
    1. Democracy. 2. Communications — Political aspects. 3. Information society — Political
aspects. 4. Information technology — Political aspects. I. Jenkins, Henry, 1958– II. Thorburn,
David. III. Seawell, Brad. IV. Series.

    JC423 .D43 2003
    320'.01'4—dc21

                                                                            2002043243

10 9 8 7 6 5 4 3 2 1

Contents

Series Foreword

David Thorburn, *editor*
Edward Barrett, Henry Jenkins, *associate editors*

New media technologies and new linkages and alliances across older media are generating profound changes in our political, social, and aesthetic experience. But the media systems of our own era are unique neither in their instability nor in their complex, ongoing transformations. The Media in Transition series will explore older periods of media change as well as our own digital age. The series hopes to nourish a pragmatic, historically informed discourse that maps a middle ground between the extremes of euphoria and panic that define so much current discussion about emerging media—a discourse that recognizes the place of economic, political, legal, social, and cultural institutions in mediating and partly shaping technological change.

Though it will be open to many theories and methods, three principles will define the series:

- It will be historical—grounded in an awareness of the past, of continuities and discontinuities among contemporary media and their ancestors.
- It will be comparative—open especially to studies that juxtapose older and contemporary media, or that examine continuities across different media and historical eras, or that compare the media systems of different societies.
- It will be accessible—suspicious of specialized terminologies, a forum for humanists and social scientists who wish to speak not only across academic disciplines but also to policymakers, to media and corporate practitioners, and to their fellow citizens.

Democracy and New Media
edited by Henry Jenkins and David Thorburn

The essays in this volume capture something of the complexity and disagreement in current discourse about the politics of cyberspace. Some contributors offer us front-line perspectives on the impact of emerging technologies on politics, journalism, and civic experience. What happens when we reduce the transaction costs for civic participation, or increase access to information, or expand the arena of free speech? Other contributors place our shifting understanding of citizenship in historical context, suggesting that notions of cyberdemocracy and online community must grow out of older models of civic life. Still others expand this conversation to consider the global flow of information and to test our American conceptions of cyberdemocracy against developments in other parts of the world. How, for example, do new media operate in Castro's Cuba, or in post-apartheid South Africa, or in the context of multicultural debates on the Pacific Rim? Some contributors examine specific sites and practices, describing new forms of journalism or community organizing. Some voices here are deeply skeptical; others are optimistic. For some writers the new technologies endanger our political culture; for others, they promise civic renewal.

Most of the papers on which these chapters are based originated in series of public forums and conferences hosted at MIT from 1998 to 2000 under the title "Media in Transition." Funded by the John and Mary R. Markle Foundation and organized by the MIT Communications Forum, these events aimed to nourish a broad civic conversation about the political impact of new media technologies. The essays have been revised for this book.

The editors wish to thank Barbara Thorburn for her rigorous editorial help.

Democracy and New Media

1 Introduction: The Digital Revolution, the Informed Citizen, and the Culture of Democracy

Henry Jenkins and David Thorburn

Snapshot: American Democracy, circa 2000

Many political commentators predicted that networked computing might be the decisive factor in the election of 2000. By November 2000, 64 percent of all voters were Internet users and 90 percent of Americans on the Internet were registered voters.[1] The Web would offer, these commentators claimed, the least costly and most effective means of reaching likely voters. How did such predictions turn out?

- Steve Forbes became the first individual to announce his presidential candidacy on the Web.

- Arizona became the first state to allow online voting in its presidential primary.

- Bill Bradley established records in raising campaign contributions on his Web site.

- The presidential nominating conventions were Webcast for the first time.

- Both George W. Bush and Al Gore deployed their Web sites to issue "e-buttals" critiquing the other side's performance in the presidential debates. In some cases these responses were posted while the debate was still taking place. Traffic to these sites was so heavy following the debates that the Bush Web site crashed.

- The Markle Foundation's Web, White and Blue cyberdebate site featured daily exchanges among six presidential candidates in response to questions submitted by Internet users.[2]

- Campaign staffs used computer modeling and extensive polling data to map their strategies, hour by hour, precinct by precinct, allowing rapid shifts of resources. In one of the closest elections in American history, both major parties believed they knew down to the last dangling chad how many votes they could expect in each district of each contested state.

Yet despite such signs of change, some commentators expressed disappointment, convinced that the public was not yet ready to participate in the cyberdemocracy they had envisioned. Jonah Seiger, cofounder of Mindshare Internet Campaigns, spoke of his disillusionment: "The evolution of the Internet and politics is going to happen a lot more slowly than people expect."[3] A Pew Research Center study found that only 18 percent of Americans had used the Internet to learn about the candidates.[4] On the other hand, in an election that was decided by a few thousand votes, such numbers could have had an impact on the outcome. Of those whom Pew identified as seeking candidate information online, 43 percent said the Web had influenced their final decision. Fifty percent of Internet users under the age of thirty said the Net had affected their vote, a finding that suggests a generational shift in political culture.

But maybe these disappointed observers were looking in the wrong places, searching for some decisive moment that would embody the new power of digital media—the contemporary equivalent of Roosevelt's "fireside" chats on radio or the Kennedy-Nixon debates on television. Such events, of course, were emblematic of the old "consensus" media of broadcasting, systems defined by a few monopoly networks and limited access to the channels of communication.[5] These events were important, in part, because they enabled candidates to address directly a significant portion of the electorate. The current diversification of communication channels, on the other hand, is politically important because it expands the range of voices that can be heard in a national debate, ensuring that no one voice can speak with unquestioned authority. Networked computing operates according to principles fundamentally different from those of broadcast media: access, participation, reciprocity, and many-to-many rather than one-to-many communication.

We will not discover a single decisive moment when the Internet emerges as a force in our national politics. Instead, digital democracy will be decentralized, unevenly dispersed, even profoundly contradictory. Moreover, the effects some have ascribed to networked computing's democratic impulses are likely to appear first not in electoral politics, but in cultural forms: in a changed sense of community, for example, or in a citizenry less dependent on official voices of expertise and authority.

We must recognize that "democracy" itself is a disputed term. Is democracy a particular structure of governance or a culture of citizenship or some complex hybrid of the two? How much power must shift to the voters to justify the argument that society is becoming more democratic? How much of our current understanding of democracy is bound up with the concept of the "informed citizen"?[6] In an era of networked computing, we are starting to see changes not only in how politics is conducted, but in what counts as politics. Consequently, it may take some time to discern the full influence of the Internet on American civic life.

Still, certain political events of the recent past offer some contradictory clues about what online democracy may look like. If we wish to locate a moment when the nation's attention turned to cyberspace, we might choose the 1998 release of the Starr Report.[7] The creation of Thomas, the Library of Congress Web server, in 1995, had been one of the great idealistic achievements of the early history of cyberspace: All government documents, speeches, committee hearings, reports, and even, in some cases, drafts of reports would be made available to the public free on the Internet. Coupled with C-SPAN, which provided live or recorded television broadcasts of congressional debates and committee sessions, Thomas would permit the public to follow the tangled paths through which legislative proposals became law.[8] Yet these noble expectations were mainly disappointed. Thomas's resources were largely unused until the presidential sex scandal and the impeachment hearings seized the nation's attention. Following a story first publicized by the online journalist Matt Drudge, more than twenty-five million citizens downloaded the Starr Report and another two million downloaded President Clinton's grand jury testimony in the first two weeks of their availability on the Web. Americans wanted access to governmental information, but perhaps not the kind the idealists had imagined.

Again, if we search for an instance in which online campaigning changed the outcome of an election, we might consider fall 1999, when Jesse Ventura, former World Wrestling Federation wrestler and Reform Party candidate, was elected governor of Minnesota.[9] Prior to his surprising victory, Ventura received far less broadcast and print coverage than his Republican and Democratic opponents. Commentators explained his election mainly as a negative vote against the established political parties. Yet there is good reason to believe that his campaign succeeded in part because it made effective use of the World Wide Web to reach a new constituency. The major party candidates, for the most part, conceived their Web sites as glossy brochures, full of smiling pictures and vague slogans. Ventura's site, on the other hand, offered detailed position papers, and more importantly, constructed an online community that connected his supporters to the campaign and to each other. In a series of polls, *Wired* found that "netizens"—registered voters with e-mail access—were fiscally conservative and socially libertarian. Yet neither party was likely to nominate a candidate with this mix of views.[10] Ventura actively appealed to these netizens, bringing record numbers of younger voters to the polls and dramatizing the changed fortunes of third parties in the digital age.

Here is another salient example of the Web's power to influence the electoral process: the Ralph Nader "vote-swapping" campaign of 2000.[11] Recognizing that Nader could not win the presidential election, his campaign developed a strategy calculated to enhance his percentage of the national vote, thus improving the Green Party's chances of receiving federal matching funds in the next presidential election. Gore voters in heavily Democratic states like Massachusetts were encouraged to trade their votes on the Web with Nader supporters in more closely contested states, such as Florida, California, or Oregon. Ultimately, 15,000 vote swaps were logged, with some 1,400 Nader supporters in Florida agreeing to vote for Gore. These "Nader traders" incited sharp controversy; some commentators deplored what they saw as the "Napsterization" of American politics, whereas others suggested that such vote swapping valuably enlarged the role of third parties in national elections.

To illustrate how the Web may grant visibility and influence to alternative political perspectives, we might document the rise of independent media centers during the 2000 protests in Seattle against the World Trade Organization.[12] Indymedia.org acted as a clearinghouse for publicizing the goals of the protesters, posting first-person reports, photographs, sound recordings, and digital video footage. These digitally savvy activists linked their own documentaries via satellite to a network of public-access stations around the country, developed their own Internet radio station, and published their own newspaper, available on their Web site to readers around the world. What began as a tactical response to a specific protest has become a self-sustaining, volunteer-run news organization with outposts in Belgium, Canada, Czechoslovakia, England, France, Italy, and Mexico. These independent media centers have become a central force in a worldwide campaign against what the activists perceive as the evils of globalization.

Conversely, critics who have argued that more information in circulation does not necessarily result in a more informed citizenry could cite the debate in fall 2000 in the New York senatorial campaign between Rick Lazio and Hillary Clinton. Responding to a reporter's question, both candidates strongly opposed pending legislation that would tax e-mail to provide financial support for the federal postal service.[13] The following day, they discovered that the so-called bill was an Internet hoax, though the reporter—and the candidates—on the nationally televised debate had mistakenly believed it to be genuine.

As these examples suggest, the World Wide Web is already a powerful influence on many aspects of American political life: on the public's access to government documents, on candidates' communication with their constituencies, on voters' behavior in elections, on political activists' efforts to circulate their message, and on the topics that enter into national debates among candidates. Not everyone would agree, however, as to whether that influence is positive or negative, even in the specific instances described above, or as to whether technological change adequately explains such social and political developments.

Challenging the Myth of Inevitability

In his famous 1974 monograph *Television: Technology and Cultural Form,* Raymond Williams challenges widespread popular and scholarly notions of technological determinism (the belief that new technologies have an intrinsic, autonomous power to shape and transform society). Instead, Williams argues, we must understand the emergence of new technologies, and in particular new communications systems, as a result of complex interactions among technological, social, cultural, political, legal, and economic forces.[14] Different cultures and different political regimes will exploit nascent technologies in radically different ways, as a comparison of the early history of television in Britain, the United States, and Nazi Germany dramatically illustrates. Moreover, not only are notions of technological determinism historically mistaken, they are politically and morally dangerous, because they assume we are powerless to shape new media in socially beneficial ways and powerless to resist their pernicious effects. Paul Starr strongly agrees: "*A priori,* little can be said about the net effects of new media. When a new medium strikes an 'old regime,' the political effects depend on both the technology and the regime and on the decisions, both technical and political, that shape the new medium and the institutions that grow up around it."[15] Williams's research suggests that the introduction of a new medium will engender debate about political culture but cannot by itself significantly alter the society in which it appears. Instead, the new medium generates an extended negotiation or contestation among competing forces—some emergent, some well-established; some encouraging change, others resisting it; some publicly visible, others operating covertly. The impact of new media, in Williams's model, is evolutionary, not revolutionary.

Williams's powerful argument confutes what one might call the rhetoric of inevitability: the assumption that the introduction of networked computing will inevitably lead to a more democratic society. In "The Laws of Cyberspace," Lawrence Lessig, a sharp critic of technological determinism, offers a summary of such utopian faith: "Cyberspace is unavoidable, and yet cyberspace is unregulatable. No nation can live without it, yet no nation can control behavior within it. Cyberspace is that space where individuals are, inherently, free from control by real space sovereigns."[16]

Such rhetoric sees freedom and democracy as inevitable consequences of digital technology, sometimes going so far as to imagine the withering away of the nation-state in favor of direct democracy.[17] For example, in his notorious "Declaration of Independence for Cyberspace," John Perry Barlow proclaims that national governments have no authority over online communities: "Governments of the Industrial World, you weary giants of flesh and steel, I come from Cyberspace, the new home of Mind. . . . You have no sovereignty where we gather. . . . Cyberspace does not lie within your borders. Do not think that you can build it, as though it were a public construction project. You cannot. It is an act of nature and it grows itself through our collective actions."[18] In a manifesto that claims a global perspective yet draws only on American political traditions, Barlow describes computers as liberating us from the dictates of national governments. For Barlow, the battle has already been won and the outcome has been determined; it is absurd for government even to attempt to regulate this new "tribe" of the "Mind."

One might contrast Barlow's blithe assumption that the "revolution" has already been won with Pierre Levy's more nuanced account of the emergence of a culture of "collective intelligence."[19] For Levy, this new information culture, defined by its high degree of participation and reciprocity, exists alongside such established structures of power as the multinational corporation and the nation-state. Levy sees these political and cultural structures as sometimes complementing, sometimes opposing each other. For Levy, the world of "collective intelligence" is an "attainable utopia," but not a condition already achieved.

Lessig reaches a similar, if more pessimistic conclusion: "The world we are entering . . . is not a world where freedom is ensured."[20] Forms of control and regulation, Lessig writes, are already embedded in the operational codes that govern our interactions in cyberspace; we already accept without thought a series of invisible constraints on digital associations and transactions that have never been publicly debated. Unless we understand this antidemocratic potential of cyberspace, Lessig says, we are likely to "sleep through the transition from freedom into control."

Lessig is one of a number of recent writers calling on technologically literate citizens to ensure a broader public debate about the political impact of new media. Langdon Winner, for example, urges computer professionals to take civic responsibility for their work and insists that the general public should have a part in the creation and deployment of new technologies. "Right now it's anyone's guess what sorts of personalities, styles of discourse, and social norms will ultimately flourish" in our digital future, Winner says. "Industrial leaders present as *faits accomplis* what otherwise might have been choices open for diverse public imaginings, investigations and debates. . . . If we're asking people to change their lives to adapt to new information systems, it seems responsible to solicit broad participation in deliberation, planning, decision making, prototyping, testing, [and] evaluation."[21]

In *Technologies of Freedom* (1983), Ithiel de Sola Pool established a framework for this debate about communication technologies and democracy: "Freedom is fostered when the means of communication are dispersed, decentralized, and easily available, as are printing presses or microcomputers. Central control is more likely when the means of communication are concentrated, monopolized, and scarce, as are great networks."[22] At a time when the mainframe computer was seen as an emblem of bureaucratic control, Pool envisioned a decentralized and participatory media environment. The emergence of home computers, he predicted, might strengthen democratic culture, enabling citizens and grassroots organizations to circulate their ideas more widely than ever before. But he also recognized that such an outcome was not inevitable: "The characteristics of media shape what is done with them, so one might anticipate that these technologies of freedom will overwhelm all attempts to control them. . . . [Technology] shapes the structure of the battle, but not every outcome. While the printing press was without doubt the foundation of modern democracy, the response to the flood of publishing that it brought forth has been censorship as often as press freedom. In some times and places the even more capacious new media will open wider the floodgates for discourse, but in other times and places, in fear of that flood, attempts will be made to shut the gates."[23] Moreover, Pool said, new media are often perceived as versions or extensions of their ancestor technologies and are subjected to regulatory schemes that limit or undermine their progressive potential. The conservative force of these regulatory schemes will often blunt the radical transformations predicted at the time of the technologies' first introduction.

The most useful accounts of the political impact of new media balance excitement about these emerging communications technologies with an awareness of the social, economic, political, and cultural forces that shape their deployment. In the early 1990s, many writers believed networked computing would revitalize the public sphere. Throughout the twentieth century, theorists had warned that urbanization and increased mobility would weaken the fragile social ties upon which American democracy depended.[24] Now, writers were insisting that the American public hungered for community and predicting that cyberspace would give birth to a new civic culture.

Jürgen Habermas's ideal of the public sphere set the terms for this argument: "Access to the public sphere is open in principle to all citizens. A portion of the public sphere is constituted in every conversation in which private persons come together to form a public. They are then acting neither as business or professional people conducting their private affairs nor as legal consociates subject to the legal regulations of a state bureaucracy and obligated to obedience."[25] The public sphere, Habermas argued, is the site where deliberations about important civic concerns occur and the public consensus takes shape. Habermas blamed the rise of modern mass media for privatizing civic life and turning citizens into consumers. Critics have suggested that Habermas underestimated the barriers to participation in this historic public sphere.[26] Economic factors, for example, determined which citizens would have access to a printing press; social factors determined which citizens could exert influence at town meetings. The democratic ideals of the earlier public sphere were compromised by the disenfranchisement of women, minorities, and the poor. Similarly, the promise of a new public sphere depends on whether technical, economic, and cultural barriers to full participation—the so-called digital divide—can be overcome.[27] Network computing offers potential resources for community building, yet how those resources are used depends on whether society embraces the civic ideals essential to a viable public sphere.[28]

Some writers cite evidence that online communities are embracing those civic virtues. Julian Dibbel, for example, has described the passionate debates that occurred as multiuser domains (MUDs) and other online communities struggled to develop strategies for dealing with dissent and antisocial conduct.[29] Online communities offer participants a chance to experience civic affiliation or personal empowerment and thus nourish ideals of citizenship.[30] But others have argued that immersion in these virtual worlds may simply displace what would be more productively deployed in real-world political action. These skeptics express alarm over the vulgarity, triviality, and aggressiveness of online interactions and see virtual communities through a glass darkly, as enclaves isolating participants from opposing perspectives.[31]

Howard Rheingold, the journalist who coined and popularized the term "virtual community," is far from a technological utopian. Rheingold argued that online citizens needed to educate themselves in order to "leverage" the emerging forms of political and economic power enabled by new media: "The technology will not in itself fulfill that potential; this latent technical power must be used intelligently and deliberately by an informed population. . . . The odds are always good that big power and big money will find a way to control access to virtual communities; big power and big money always found ways to control new communications media when they emerged in the past."[32] In the early 1990s Rheingold saw a need to defend virtual communities against political and economic forces that would coopt or corrupt them. A decade later, the economic colonization of cyberspace is still recognized as a serious threat to this participatory culture; activists are calling for the establishment of a "public commons" to ensure the survival of the grass-roots social and political experiments Rheingold and Dibble documented.[33]

Which Digital Revolution?

The utopian rhetoric predicting an imminent digital revolution is simplistic and often oblivious to complex historical processes. But its tenacious, diverse history is instructive and significant. For one thing, such pervasive talk about revolutionary change implies some fundamental dissatisfaction with the established order. Even if we believe that the concept of a digital revolution is empty rhetoric, we still must explain why a revolution, even a virtual one, has such appeal. A surprising range of thinkers on the right and the left have used the notion of "the computer revolution" to imagine forms of political change. Examining the rhetoric of digital revolution, we may identify a discourse about politics and culture that appears not only in academic writing or in explicitly ideological ex-changes, but also in popular journalism and science fiction. This rhetoric has clear polit-ical effects, helping to shape attitudes toward emerging technologies. And even if such discourse is not an accurate measure of the impact of new media, it may nonetheless nourish serious discussion about core values and central institutions, allowing us to envi-sion the possibility of change. Utopian visions help us to imagine a just society and to map strategies for achieving it.

For some writers on the left, the rhetoric of "digital revolution" registers their disillu-sionment with earlier fantasies of revolutionary change following the fall of communism. In a return to Frankfurt School categories, some left intellectuals have cast capitalism as an irresistible force and media consumption as its most powerful tool for manufacturing consent. In contrast, some younger left intellectuals have found the "digital revolution" to be a revitalizing fantasy, the promise of an alternative media culture.[34] At the same time, the rhetoric of revolution has been appropriated by the right, with Newt Gingrich and George Gilder, among others, advocating a "Republican revolution" that would "get the government off our backs" and return decision making to the local level.[35] Still oth-ers have seen computers as paving the way for a new economy, an entrepreneurial "revo-lution" that would allow smaller, leaner new companies to rise to the top of corporate America. The introduction of networked computers, it has been said, will transform all aspects of our society, changing industry, government and social life, altering the ways in which artists circulate their work and money flows through the economy. All institutions will have to be "reinvented" in response to these new technologies. The rhetoric of the digital revolution thus has allowed disillusioned left intellectuals, a newly emboldened right, ambitious entrepreneurs, and many other interest groups to see themselves as on the cusp of vast historical change.

Such a climate has enabled political alliances that would have been inconceivable a decade earlier.[36] Both the left and the right distrust monopoly broadcasting and embrace the promise of a more dispersed and participatory media, although they would surely disagree, in the end, about the society they hope will emerge from the "digital revolution." Some communitarians see the Web as an instrument for social cohesion, for cybercommunities, whereas conservatives and libertarians use distributed computing as an emblem of decentralized antifederalism. Yet such alliances are fragile and problematic. One can divide these digital revolutionaries by posing basic questions. Which is the greater threat to free speech: government censorship or corporate ownership of intellectual property? Which is the greater danger to privacy: government surveillance or massive corporate databases of consumer information? In other words, if this is a digital revolution, what are we rebelling against?

There is powerful irony in the fact that both the left and the right initially understood computer networks in opposition to bureaucratic control because so much of the initial research had been funded by the military and had occurred at the Rand Corporation. The original governing fantasies, closely linked to the nuclear fears of the Cold War, were dystopian, not utopian. The government wanted to ensure "minimum essential communication" and thus preserve "second-strike" capability. A distributed system was essential so that it could operate even if central nodes were destroyed. What was envisioned was not a broad-based participatory medium, but a system restricted to government officials and the military high command in their bunkers; access was extended only reluctantly to the research scientists who were helping to transform this Cold War vision into a practical reality. One legacy of this bureaucratic understanding of the Internet is embedded in the metaphor of the "information superhighway," allegedly coined by Albert Gore as a tribute to his senator father, who had helped to promote the interstate highway system following World War II. Describing this new information space as a "superhighway" implies that it is a federal project, a stark contrast to the libertarian fantasy of an "electronic frontier" that should remain forever free of government intervention.

Current notions of cyberdemocracy took shape amid the heated debates of the Vietnam War era. Frederick Turner has shown how publications such as *Wired* and *Mondo*

2000, digital communities like the Well, and organizations like the Electronic Frontier Foundation took root in the political culture of San Francisco, a center for many 1960s countercultural movements and subsequently a seedbed for the new digital economy.[37] Many writers, including Stewart Brand, Timothy Leary, Howard Rhinegold, Alvin Toffler, and John Perry Barlow, shifted easily from the agrarian countercultural style associated with the *Whole Earth Catalog* to the cyberutopian and consumerist values promoted in *Wired,* helping to define the popular representations of digital technologies. Ironically, whereas the early counterculture had been emphatically anticorporate, the rhetoric of the cyberculture was coopted by digital entrepreneurs who transformed utopian longings for participatory culture into pitches for high-tech commodities. One of the most influential commercials of the personal computing era, Apple's "1984" campaign, represented the home computer as a tool of liberation directed against an impersonal Orwellian bureaucracy.[38] At the same time, this easy linkage of political and corporate fantasies deepened the skepticism of other leftists who understood the computer through the filter of Frankfurt School theories of mass culture as yet another manifestation of corporate control over American civic life.[39]

In an influential essay, "Constituents for a Theory of the Media," Hans Magnus Enzensberger described the student movement's embrace of a participatory model of communications in opposition to the corporate monopoly systems of the movies and television. Enzensberger's critique centered on the absence of reciprocity in mass media, their reliance on one-to-many modes of communication. Television, he warned, "does not serve communications but prevents it."[40] Enzensberger documented the emergence of the underground newspaper, grassroots video production, people's radio stations, and other forms of independent media production and distribution, seeing them as the birthplace of a new political culture. But these "do-it-yourself" media never offered a serious alternative to commercial systems. The regulatory and policy decisions governing UHF and cable television, for example, marginalized local access content and granted priority to commercial broadcasters.[41] Similarly, although the reduced cost of photocopying enabled the production of grassroots zines, there was no viable system for distributing such materials to a significant reading public.[42]

For some, the failure of these earlier participatory media intensified skepticism about networked computing. But for others, cyberspace appeared as the second coming of participatory media; the Web, these hopefuls proclaimed, would be a world with no center, no gatekeepers, no margins. The new cyberculture would be a bulwark against the concentration of commercial media, ensuring access to alternative perspectives. Such countercultural impulses shaped, for example, the online community's early resistance to unsolicited advertising messages and their insistence on free expression and strong encryption to protect privacy. The legacy of this construction of computing can be seen in the cyberpunk movement in science fiction, which often depicts hackers as activists at war with powerful media corporations,[43] or in the culture jammer movement, which aims to block the signals of commercial media in order to open channels for alternative messages,[44] or in the open-source movement, which pits the grassroots collaborators of Linux against the concentrated power of Microsoft.

Two slogans of the 1960s may help us to understand this distinction between old and new media. The first is Gil Scott Heron's song "Will the Revolution Be Televised?" The answer, in 1968, was clearly "No." A narrow pipeline controlled by corporate media was unlikely to transmit dissenting ideas or images. The counterculture communicated primarily through alternative media: underground newspapers, folk songs, posters, people's radio, comics.

But in 2003, if we ask whether the revolution will be digitized, the answer is "Yes." The Web's low barriers to entry ensure greater access than ever before to innovative, even revolutionary ideas. Those silenced by corporate media have been among the first, as Pool predicted, to transform their computers into printing presses. This access to the World Wide Web has empowered revolutionaries, reactionaries, and racists alike. It has also engendered fear in the gatekeeper intermediaries and their allies. One person's diversity, no doubt, is another person's anarchy.

Now, consider the second slogan, which students in the streets of Chicago chanted at the network news trucks: "The whole world is watching." Whatever the difficulties, the students knew that if their protests were broadcast via ABC, CBS, and NBC, they would reach tens of millions of viewers. Is there any place on the Web where the whole world is watching? The Web is a billion people on a billion soapboxes all speaking at once. But who is listening? The old intermediaries are still in place, not likely to wither away any time soon, so long as they command national and international audiences and thus retain their power to deliver commercial messages to millions.

Online activists were quick to recognize the value of that first slogan but slow to realize the importance of the second. At its most excessive, the rhetoric of the digital revolution envisioned a total displacement of centralized broadcast media by a trackless web of participatory channels. Netizens spoke of the major networks, for example, as dinosaurs slinking off to the tar pits as they confronted the realities of the new economy. The decline of the dot-coms makes clear, however, that such predictions were premature.

The power of movies and television to speak to a vast public is immensely greater than the diffused reach of the new media, through which many messages can be circulated but few can ensure a hearing. This dramatic reversal of economic fortunes suggests that similar arguments for the decline of powerful governmental institutions in the face of cyber-democracy may be equally premature and simple-minded.

Notes

1. Jim Buie, "Internet Proves to Be Powerful in Political, Legislative Battles" (2001), available online at <http://www.cybersavvycitizen.com/campaign2000.htm>. See also William Benoit and Pamela J. Benoit, "The Virtual Campaign: Presidential Primary Websites in Campaign 2000," *American Communication Journal* 3, no. 3 (2000), available online at <http://acjournal.org/holdings/vol3/Iss3/rogue4/benoit.html>.

2. Markle Foundation, "Web, White & Blue 2000" (2000), available online at <http://www.webwhiteblue.org/>.

3. Aaron Pressman, "Analysis: Internet Lessons for Campaign 2004," *Industry Standard* (November 15, 2000), available online at <http://www.cnn.com/2000/TECH/computing/11/15/campaign.2004.idg/index.html>.

4. The Pew Research Center for the People and the Press, "Youth Vote Influenced by Online Information" (2000), available online at <http://www.people-press.org/online00rpt.htm>.

5. On the concept of consensus narrative, see David Thorburn, "Television Melodrama," in *TV: The Critical View,* ed. Horace Newcomb (New York: Oxford University Press, 2000), 595–608, and "Television as an Aesthetic Medium" *Critical Studies in Mass Communication* 4 (1987): 161–173.

6. On the role of the flow of information in defining our sense of belonging to nation-states, see Benedict Anderson, *Imagined Communities: Reflections on the Origin and Spread of Nation States* (London: Verso, 1991). For a history of how the concept of the "informed citizen" shapes debates about American democracy, see Michael Schudson, *The Good Citizen: A History of American Civic Life* (New York: Free Press, 1998).

7. CBS MarketWatch, "Starr Report Cost Business Millions" (October 5, 1998), available online at <http://www.websense.com/company/news/features/98/100598b.cfm>.

8. Stephen Frantzich, *The C-SPAN Revolution* (Oklahoma City: University of Oklahoma Press, 1996). On Newt Gingrich's vision for Thomas, see John Heileman, "The Making of the President, 2000," *Wired* 3, no. 12 (December 1995), available online at <http://www.wired.com/wired/archive/3.12/gorenewt.html>.

9. For an insider perspective on the Ventura Web campaign, see Phil Madsen, "Notes Regarding Jesse Ventura's Internet Use in His 1998 Campaign for Minnesota Governor" (1998), available online at <http://www.jesseventura.org/internet/netnotes.htm>. Ventura's success was built on the foundation of many years of work in Minnesota promoting cyberdemocracy. For background on this earlier work, see G. S. Aikens, "American Democracy and Computer-Mediated Communication: A Case Study in Minnesota" (1998), available online at <http://www.aikens.org/phd/>.

10. Jonathan Katz, "The Digital Citizen," *Wired* 5, no. 12 (December 1997), available online at <http://hotwired.lycos.com/special/citizen/>.

11. Scott Harris, "Nader Traders May Have Affected Outcome in Florida," *Industry Standard* (November 17, 2000), available online at <http://www.cnn.com/2000/TECH/computing/11/17/nader.traders.help.gore.idg/index.html>. For a fuller overview of the movement, see the materials assembled at <http://voteswap.com/>.

12. <http://www.indymedia.org>. On the use of the Web for grassroots activism, see Robert Rhoads, *Freedom's Web: Student Activism in An Age of Cultural Diversity* (Baltimore: Johns Hopkins University Press, 2000).

13. Daniel Sieberg, "Debate Gaff Over E-mail Hoax Raises Red Flag for Some," CNN, Oct. 11, 2000, available online at <http://www.cnn.com/2000/tech/computing/10/11/web.politics>.

14. Raymond Williams, *Television: Technology and Cultural Form* (New York: Schocken, 1974).

15. Paul Starr, "The New Media and the Old Regime," paper presented at the Democracy and Digital Media Conference, Massachusetts Institute of Technology (Cambridge, October 8, 1998).

16. Lawrence Lessig, "The Laws of Cyberspace (1998), available online at <http://www.lessig.org/>.

17. For an overview of these debates, see Lawrence K. Grossman, *The Electronic Republic: Reshaping Democracy in the Information Age* (New York: Penguin, 1995).

18. John Perry Barlow, "Declaration of Independence for Cyberspace" (1996), available online at <http://members.aye.net/~hippie/barlow/barlowci.htm>.

19. Pierre Levy, *Collective Intelligence: Mankind's Emerging World in Cyberspace* (New York: Perseus, 2000). For an overview of Levy, see Henry Jenkins, "Interactive Audiences?" in *The New Media Book,* ed. Dan Harries (London: British Film Institute, 2002).

20. Lessig, "The Laws of Cyberspace." Lessig explores these ideas in more depth in his books *The Future of Ideas: The Fate of the Commons in the Digital World* (New York: Random House, 2001) and *Code and Other Laws of Cyberspace* (New York: Basic Books, 2000).

21. Langdon Winner, "Who Will We Be in Cyberspace?" *The Network Observer* 2, no. 9 (September 1995), available online at <http://dlis.gseis.ucla.edu/people/pagre/tno/september-1995.html#who>.

22. Ithiel de Sola Pool, *Technologies of Freedom: On Free Speech in an Electronic Age* (Cambridge: Harvard University Press, 1983), 5.

23. Ibid., 251.

24. For a contemporary example of this argument, see Robert D. Putnam, *Bowling Alone: The Collapse and Revival of American Community* (New York: Touchstone, 2001).

25. Jürgen Habermas, "The Public Sphere," in *Media Studies: A Reader,* ed. Paul Marris and Sue Thornham (New York: New York University Press, 2000), 92–98, at 92. For a useful application of Habermas, see Mark Poster, "Cyberdemocracy; The Internet and the Public Sphere," in *Reading Digital Culture,* ed. David Trend (London: Blackwell, 2001), 259–271.

26. For a useful account of the debates surrounding Habermas's public sphere concept in contemporary media theory, see Lisa Cartwright and Marissa Sturken, *Practices of Looking: An Introduction to Visual Culture* (Oxford: Oxford University Press, 2001).

27. Pippa Norris, *Digital Divide: Civic Engagement, Information Poverty and the Internet Worldwide* (Cambridge: Cambridge University Press, 2001); Benjamin M. Compaigne, *The Digital Divide* (Cambridge: MIT Press, 2001); Brian Kahin and James Keller, eds., *Public Access to the Internet* (Cambridge: MIT Press, 1995); Alondra Nelson, Thu Linh Thu, and Alicia Headlam Hines, eds., *Technocolor: Race, Technology and Everyday Life* (New York: New York University Press, 2001); and Beth E. Kolko, Lisa Nakamura, and Gilbert B. Rodman, eds., *Race in Digital Space* (New York: Routledge, 2000). On struggles to overcome the gender gap in access to these technologies, see Susan Hawthorne and Renate Klein, eds., *Cyberfeminism: Connectivity, Critique, and Creativity* (Sydney: Spinifex, 1999); and Lynn Cherney and Elizabeth Reba Weise, eds., *Wired Women: Gender and New Realities in Cyberspace* (Seattle: Seal, 1996).

28. This question of how we inculcate civic virtues into our children is a recurring question in the literature on democracy: See, for example, David Buckingham, *The Making of Citizens: Young People, News and Politics* (New York: Routledge, 2000); and Don Tappscott, *Growing up Digital: The Rise of the Net Generation* (New York: McGraw-Hill, 1999). For historical antecedents of this question, see Henry Jenkins, "'No Matter How Small': The Democratic Imagination of Doctor Seuss," in *Hop on Pop: The Politics and Pleasures of Popular Culture,* ed. Henry Jenkins, Tara McPherson, and Jane Shattuc (Durham: Duke University Press, 2002), 189–210.

29. Julian Dibbel, *My Tiny Life: Crime and Passion in a Virtual World* (New York: Owl, 1999).

30. For an overview of these debates, see Steven G. Jones, *Cybersociety: Computer-Mediated Communication and Community* (Thousand Oaks, Calif.: Sage, 1995); and Peter Ludlow, ed., *High Noon on the Electronic Frontier: Conceptual Issues in Cyberspace* (Cambridge: MIT Press, 1996).

31. Cass Sunstein, *Republic.com* (Princeton: Princeton University Press, 2001). For critical responses to the book, see *Boston Review* (June 2001).

32. Howard Rheingold, *The Virtual Community: Homesteading on the Electronic Frontier* (Cambridge: MIT Press, 2000), 8.

33. Lawrence K. Grossman and Newton Minnow, *A Digital Gift to the Nation: Fulfilling the Promise of the Digital and Internet Age* (New York: Century Foundation, 2001).

34. For examples of a wide range of perspectives on these questions, see David Trend, ed., *Reading Digital Culture* (London: Blackwell, 2001); and Andrew Herman and Thomas Swiss, eds., *The World Wide Web and Contemporary Cultural Theory* (New York: Routledge, 2000).

35. George Gilder, *Telecosm: How Infinite Bandwidth Will Revolutionize Our World* (New York: Free Press, 2000), and *Life after Television* (New York: W. W. Norton, 1994).

36. For one perspective on these political realignments, see Virginia Postrel, *The Future and Its Enemies: The Growing Conflict over Creativity, Enterprise and Progress* (New York: Touchstone, 1999).

37. Frederick Turner, "From Counterculture to Cyberculture: How Stewart Brand and the *Whole Earth Catalog* Brought Us *Wired* Magazine," Ph.D. diss., Department of Communication, University of California, San Diego (forthcoming). See also Thomas Streeter, "'That Deep Romantic Chasm': Libertarianism, Neoliberalism and the Computer Culture," in *Communication, Citizenship, and Social Policy: Re-thinking the Limits of the Welfare State,* ed. Andrew Calabrese and Jean-Claude Burgelman (London: Rowman & Littlefield, 1999), 49–64.

38. For background on this advertisement, see Ted Friedman, "Apple's 1984: The Introduction of the Macintosh in the Cultural History of Personal Computers" (1997), available online at <http://www.duke.edu/~tlove/mac.htm>.

39. Robert McChesney, *Rich Media, Poor Democracy: Communication Politics in Dubious Times* (New York: New Press, 2000).

40. Hans Magnus Enzensberger, "Constituents of a Theory of the Media," in *Media Studies: A Reader,* ed. Paul Marris and Sue Thornham (New York: New York University Press, 2000), 68–91, at 69–70.

41. Thomas Streeter, "Blue Skies and Strange Bedfellows: The Discourse on Cable Television," in *The Revolution Wasn't Televised: Sixties Television and Social Conflict,* ed. Lynn Spigel and Michael Curtin (New York: Routledge, 1997), 221–242.

42. Steven Duncombe, *Notes from Underground: Zines and the Politics of Alternative Culture* (London: Verso, 1997).

43. For an overview of the cyberpunk movement, see Larry McCaffrey, ed., *Storming the Reality Studio: A Casebook for Cyberpunk and Postmodern Science Fiction* (Durham: Duke University Press, 1992).

44. Mark Dery, *Culture Jamming: Hacking, Slashing and Sniping in the Empire of Signs* (Open Magazine Pamphlet Series, 1993), available online at <http://web.nwe.ufl.edu/~mlaffey/cultjam1.html>. For elaboration on the concept of culture jamming, see also Gareth Branwyn, *Jamming the Media: A Citizen's Guide for Reclaiming the Tools of Communication* (San Francisco: Chronicle, 1997); and David Cox, "Notes on Culture Jamming" (2000), available online at <http://www.sniggle.net/Manifesti/notes.php>.

I *How Democratic Is Cyberspace?*

2 Technologies of Freedom?

Lloyd Morrisett

In the United States much of our freedom, as we understand it, is defined and protected by the Bill of Rights, and especially the First Amendment to the Constitution: "Congress shall make no law respecting an establishment of religion, or prohibiting the free exercise thereof; or abridging the freedom of speech, or of the press, or the right of the people peaceably to assemble, and to petition the Government for a redress of grievances."

The opinion in the 1963 case of *The New York Times versus Sullivan,* begins with two great commentaries on this amendment:

> The First Amendment, said Judge Learned Hand, "presupposes that right conclusions are more likely to be gathered out of a multitude of tongues, than through any kind of authoritative selection. To many this is, and always will be, folly; but we have staked upon it our all."
>
> Mr. Justice Brandeis . . . gave the principle its classic formulation:
>
> "Those who won our independence believed . . . that public discussion is a political duty; and that this should be a fundamental principle of the American government. They recognized the risks to which all human institutions are subject. But they knew that order cannot be secured merely through fear of punishment for its infraction; that it is hazardous to discourage thought, hope and imagination; that fear breeds repression; that repression breeds hate; that hate menaces stable government; that the path of safety lies in the opportunity to discuss freely supposed grievances and proposed remedies; and that the fitting remedy for evil counsels is good ones. Believing in the power of reason as applied through public discussion, they eschewed silence coerced by law—the argument of force in its worst form. Recognizing the occasional tyrannies of governing majorities, they amended the Constitution so that free speech and assembly should be guaranteed."

When the First Amendment was formulated, passed by Congress, and later ratified by the states as part of the Bill of Rights, the means of exercising First Amendment freedoms were face-to-face discussion, sending and receiving letters, and printing and reading newspapers. Distance and time might have been obstacles to exercising those freedoms, but size of population was not thought to be a factor. When the first Federal Congress convened in March 1789, the population of the United States was approximately four million. It is highly unlikely that the framers of the Constitution imagined that the passage of 200 years would bring a population of 250 million, and even more unlikely that they thought about how changing technologies would interact with freedom and the exercise of First Amendment rights.

Technology and Habits of Mind

There is a forceful interplay between society and its technologies. Society creates technology, but society is also created by technology. As Daniel Bell points out, Marx said in *Capital* that "in changing the technical world, Man changes his own nature."[1] If human nature is partially the result of a society's technologies, it becomes crucial to examine technology, both to ascertain the effects of technological history and to attempt to infer the consequences of technological decisions on the future development of society.

There is no question that the dominant communications technologies of the twentieth century have been the printing press, radio, television, and the telephone. All of us have been shaped by these technologies and by our use of them. They have been, in Ithiel Pool's phrase, "technologies of freedom." They have made knowledge available, opened our minds to events around the world, and in the case of the telephone, extended our means of conversation. One does not need fully to accept Marshall McLuhan's aphorism that "the medium is the message" to agree that both technology and its content have human consequences. Books, newspapers, radio programs, and television shows differ among themselves, but all involve the transmission of information and knowledge from a central source to many people. It is the economies of scale that this wide dissemination affords that make them so cost effective. An hour of prime-time television programming may cost more than $1 million to produce, but when the cost is amortized over millions of people, the cost per person is minuscule. The rights to a book may cost millions of dollars, but the title can be sold for $25 a copy. With a book, newspaper, television show, or radio program, we receive the communication via a one-way street. Although it may stimulate our thoughts, arouse our emotions, or cause us to act, we are described as "readers," "listeners," or "viewers."

Although reading, listening, and viewing all can involve thought and learning, because no conscious thought, response, or action may be required, they can also be highly passive activities. All of us have had the experience of reading a page and being unable to remember what was being discussed, or even a single word. On one level, our eyes process the words, but our minds are elsewhere. The stereotypic "couch potato" sits gazing mindlessly at the television set, thinking hardly at all. Nevertheless, certain techniques can greatly increase the likelihood of thought.

For example, questions can be introduced, with the audience or reader invited to think of answers; anomalies can be created that invite resolution; moral dilemmas can be introduced with no immediate solution. These devices, however, depart from the normal conventions of the media. The absence of thought may be due to the lack of thought-provoking content, or possibly to hypnotic involvement, with no time taken for reflection. Whatever the cause, I think it can be fairly argued that the technologies of broadcast communications and the printing press, on balance, favor the passive reception of information and entertainment.

I am not arguing against the value of reading, listening, and viewing. They are vital skills, skills that can open the doors of culture and education. It is rather that the technologies with which these skills are usually associated favor passive reception over active thought. Among the skills of information reception, reading has a special place. The proficient reader has access to knowledge that is denied to the less-skilled reader. The written word remains the storehouse of the world's wisdom and knowledge. Therefore, a special problem with television is that it has tended to displace reading in many young people's lives. If there were no difference in content between books and television, that displacement in itself might not be very important. The problem is that reading opens the door to symbolic thought, and without that skill the citizen is severely handicapped. The corollary skill of writing also has special cultural value: A means of ordering and communicating thought, the discipline of writing is a powerful antidote to sloppy thinking.

There are certainly many exceptions to my generalization that, on balance, the technologies of broadcast communications, including the printing press, favor the passive reception of information and entertainment. Many books stimulate thought and even demand it; yet many others simply provide escape and diversion. Newspapers can similarly stimulate thought but often only provide diversion. In his classic study "What 'Missing the Newspaper' Means,"[2] Bernard Berelson acknowledged the "rational" uses of the newspaper in providing news and information. At the same time, he noted that reading the newspaper often becomes a ceremonial, ritualistic, or nearly compulsive act for many people. Individual television and radio programs, such as *Bill Moyers' Journal, Nightline, Fred Friendly's Media and Society,* and others, may cause people to think, but few people would argue with Newton Minow that these are exceptions and not the rule. Finally, it is significant that we are called the "information society"—not the thinking society, not the deliberative society, not the society of reason and rationality.

The telephone is different. It is primarily a technology for conversation. Except when listening to a recorded message, people most often use the telephone to talk with each other. In this sense, the technology of the telephone favors active participation rather than the passive reception of information and entertainment. The limitation of the telephone in stimulating thought and deliberation, however, is that there is pressure for immediate response. In a telephone conversation, you seldom hear someone say, "Give me a few minutes to think about that." He may say, "I'll call back soon with some thoughts," but during the conversation itself, silence is likely to provoke the question, "What are you doing?" Perhaps some people using the telephone equate time with money and when using the telephone think their bill is increasing; or in the absence of visual cues about the other person's feelings, people may simply feel uncomfortable with telephone silence. Whatever the reason, the technology of the telephone, although involving activity, favors immediacy of response over deliberative thought.

The need for time for deliberative thought was brought home to me on a visit to Japan. In the early 1970s, several of us went to Japan to discuss the production of a Japanese version of *Sesame Street*. With two colleagues from the United States, we met with the management of a Japanese television network. None of the Americans spoke a word of Japanese, so naturally we had translators at the meeting. We would discuss an issue in English, and our comments would be translated into Japanese. Our Japanese counterparts would reply in Japanese that would be translated into English. Only after the meeting ended did we discover that all the Japanese present spoke perfectly good English. Whatever else the translation accomplished, it provided time for the Japanese to think over their comments before making them. They had time to think and deliberate—a distinct advantage in negotiation!

A Benevolent Tyranny

The communications technologies that have permeated our lives—the printing press, radio, television, and the telephone—have brought enormous benefits. They have been technologies of freedom. They have made information and entertainment available to the masses at a very low cost per person. The telephone has made conversation at a distance commonplace, and the costs of such conversation is steadily decreasing. Being able to talk from New York to someone in California for ten cents a minute or less would have been unimaginable fifty years ago. Yet with all their advantages, these technologies have also exercised a benevolent tyranny over us. They have favored passive reception of information and entertainment over thoughtful reaction, and the telephone has favored immediate response over considered and deliberative response.

What I am describing as a "benevolent tyranny" would be judged more harshly by others. Many observers of our political system decry its dependence on television advertising and the techniques of mass marketing. The presidential debates, arguably the only political events that are somewhat designed to stimulate thought, have not yet been institutionalized. In the 1992 campaign, it is notable that Ross Perot's "infomercials" drew large audiences. Designed in part as teaching vehicles, they were very different from the normal campaign advertisements. Other critics are very concerned about a concentration of media ownership, which may consequently narrow the range of ideas to which the public is exposed.

I believe that we are fortunate indeed that the tyranny has been benevolent and that, despite the resulting decline of the habits of mind that are associated with reason and rationality, we have remained a constitutional democracy. Although demagogues such as Father Charles Coughlin and Joseph McCarthy saw the potential for power and tyranny in our mass communications, they were not in a position to dominate our institutions. Conditions were very different in Nazi Germany: Adolph Hitler and Joseph Goebbels saw that rationality was the enemy of National Socialism and dictatorship and that modern mass communications (radio and newspapers) offered unlimited power to displace reason through the use of propaganda. In Hitler's view: "What luck for governments that people don't think. Thinking may be done only when an order is given or executed. If this is different, human society could not exist."[3] Goebbels, who carried out a program of propaganda and the displacement of reason, would "see that the press be so artfully organized that it is so to speak like a piano in the hands of the government, on which the government can play."

As human beings, we are extremely adaptable to the conditions in which we find ourselves. For those who live at sea level, the sudden transition to life in the mountains at 8,000 feet usually brings some discomfort, shortness of breath, and perhaps a headache. But for almost everyone except those with respiratory incapacity, adaptation is complete within a few weeks in the mountains. Life on a farm with relatively few human contacts, living in harmony with the rhythms of the days and seasons, seems normal to the farmer. Yet most people who grow up on farms are able to adapt to the frenetic life of the city.

And so we have adapted to the benevolent tyranny of our communications technology. Apart from a few holdouts, we have eagerly become compulsive consumers of information, viewers of television, and radio listeners. The decline of study, analysis, reflection, contemplation, and deliberation—the mental habits of reason and rationality—has gone largely unnoticed. We have adapted to the conditions that we and our technologies have created.

New Technology, New Freedom

In the dawning years of the twenty-first century, the great story of communications technology is the growth of computer communications. Headlines announce the emergence of online services and corporate changes and acquisitions that involve these services. Underneath these headlines there is another, more important story. Internet traffic is growing at a staggering rate. A recent estimate is that Internet traffic is doubling in volume every hundred days. Despite all the publicity surrounding new proprietary Internet services, the major use of the Internet is for e-mail and its close relations: bulletin boards, chat rooms, list-servs, and newsgroups. Just as the printing press, then radio, and finally television were technologies of freedom in their times, computer communications and e-mail can be a technology of freedom now. Just as those earlier technologies of freedom carried with them dangers to freedom, so does and will the Internet.

The way will soon be open for Ross Perot's "electronic town halls" to become a fixture of our national scene. More easily than ever before, a politician will be able to leap over normal governmental processes and take important questions directly to the public, raising all the dangers of national plebiscites. Unless regulated to ensure time for education and judgment, with all sides having a fair chance to be heard, plebiscites could be determined by demagogic rhetoric and inflamed momentary passions. Properly designed plebiscites could have the advantage of greatly increased citizen involvement in national policy. As potentially almost everyone will be able to participate, public decisions on questions of importance could be taken as mandates for political action. Even though it might not have any legal standing, surely an overwhelming national vote by this means on a question of importance would have compelling weight with any political leader. Tendencies toward plebiscitary democracy are already evident, and technological progress will accelerate them.

Citizen initiatives are another form of freedom, but the use and misuse of citizen initiatives illustrate both the advantages and dangers of plebiscites. In California (and at least twenty-two other states), the initiative gives people the right to place on the ballot legislation and amendments to the state's constitution and obtain a statewide vote. The idea behind the initiative is to allow people a means of expressing their political will in the face of legislative inaction or the opposition of special interests. The problem is that in California the ballot has become so loaded with complex initiatives that it seems to discourage people from going to the polls rather than motivating them to express their judgment. Outcomes seem more often to depend upon the effectiveness of political advertising than on the carefully weighed choices of an educated citizenry. The apparent limitations and failures of the initiative process suggest the dangers inherent in the new electronic technology: manipulation may be substituted for education and advertising for careful information gathering; debate and deliberation may be overridden by the adrenaline of an immediate reaction; and minority opinions and objections can be lost in the voice of the crowd.

Enhancing Democracy: Six Requirements

The failures of the initiative process, the problems of plebiscites, and the dangers of propaganda and demagoguery suggest the characteristics that are needed to define democratic uses of new interactive information technologies and the Internet and make them true technologies of freedom. At least six important features must be taken into account: access, information, discussion, deliberation, choice, and action. Perhaps the most important requirement is access.

Access

The experience of the last few elections, the meteoric rise of Ross Perot, and the popularity of the talk show and call-in format in television and radio all show the hunger of citizens for access to their leaders and to means for expressing their own opinions and judgments. Provision of such access, however, does not necessarily mean that citizens will take advantage of it; not all citizens take advantage of their voting rights. Fewer than 50 percent of eligible voters participated in the 1996 presidential elections, and even fewer participate in primaries and most local elections. The importance of the availability of the vote cannot, however, be exaggerated. Imagine the public's wrath if someone decided to begin restricting voting rights rather than extending them, as has been the historical trend since the founding of the republic. A well-designed national system of interactive information technology for consideration of important issues could be expected to be similarly treasured, but not necessarily universally used. It is this problem of access for a growing and diverse population, dispersed over a very large geographical area, that makes a national system of interactive information technology civically useful. If well designed, such a system could counter divisive trends and help bring the nation together.

Information and Education

A vital part of any deliberative discussion is the provision of relevant information. In the discussion of any issue, people enter the conversation with widely differing experience and information about the issue. Take the issue of health care. Many citizens understand that severe problems exist in our present system of financing and distributing health care; many are dissatisfied with managed care or see that their own insurance costs are rising rapidly; others know that they are uninsured or underinsured; and older people may worry about Medicare and Medicaid cutbacks. Surveys show, however, that relatively few citizens have a thorough understanding of the forces that drive medical costs and the alternatives for provision of care that have been tried in the United States and around the world. Any general public discussion of health care must find ways to allow more citizens to be thoroughly informed about the issues and problems. Otherwise, debate will be based upon opinion rather than fact, prejudice rather than knowledge. A system of interactive information technology need not itself contain the vital information. References could be made to other sources of information ranging from reference material in libraries to documentaries on television. In fact, the national media would naturally be expected to carry much of the relevant information in any national discussion of an issue.

Discussion

Information technology can stimulate discussion not only between citizens and their leaders, but among the citizens themselves. Although radio and television broadcasting has been a superb means for the dissemination of entertainment and culture, news, and sports, a broadcast is a transmission from a central source to an audience. Not only is there usually no feedback from the audience to the source, but the audience typically receives the broadcast in individual isolation. Broadcasting, as a technology, does not naturally stimulate discussion among the people who receive the broadcast.

Networked computers offer quite a different model. Whether through computer conference or electronic mail, networked computing encourages people to communicate with one another. The experience of highly networked communities, such as Carnegie Mellon University or the nationwide SeniorNet organization, shows that when people are connected over a computer system, they tend to communicate more broadly and intensively than without the system. The evidence is very clear that computer conferencing tends to reduce isolation rather than increase it. To discuss civic issues, people need easy ways to enter such discussions. Anecdotes tell of the local barbershop as one place where citizens have naturally gathered to talk with each other. Electronic technology can be used to provide a modern-day equivalent of the barber shop, connecting citizens with each other all across the nation and with their leaders.

Deliberation

Any interactive communication system must provide the means for deliberation, that is, the careful consideration of an issue and the likely consequences of decisions. For deliberation to occur, provision must be made for the presentation of various sides of a question and attention given to different approaches to outcomes. The great issues of our time—such as health care, the improvement of the educational system, the functioning of the economy, or political reform—are extremely complex and cannot be deliberately considered in any brief period of time. Work by the Public Agenda Foundation, over many years, has shown that even after issues have been clarified, it usually takes at least six weeks, with a concentrated educational campaign, for people to deliberate about a problem and come to a reasoned judgment. In many matters, the time would be much longer, and it would not be unexpected if a year or even several years would have to be devoted to deliberative consideration before certain types of problems become clarified in the public's mind. The implication for a system of interactive information technology is that whatever is done must be an ongoing process. There could be repeated uses of the system on a single topic, for example, a series of debates about health care lasting several months. The computer conference is an alternative model for such a deliberative system. In a computer conference, people have access to questions, facts, and opinions and can take their time about when they are ready to give their own opinion. Input can be made at any time, and the ongoing output of the system can be studied until someone believes he or she has something to say.

Choices

Discussion and deliberation are sharpened when participants understand that choices among alternative courses of action must be made. The managers of an interactive system devoted to electronic democracy need to organize the process so that choices are the outcome. Responsible government is not merely a means of educating the citizenry, but it is also a process of making choices that shape the future of society. With some deliberative dialogues, the possible choices may be clear from the beginning; this might be the case if the issue involves the deployment of limited resources among various desirable ends. How should limited resources be allocated to health care, education, and scientific research, for example? In this case, the rough nature of the alternatives is clear, even though much would need to be learned about the consequences of choices and the details of proposals. With other types of issues, it is likely that the nature of the choices themselves would emerge only during the deliberation. No one has any easy answers as to how to revive decaying central cities, and it is likely that reasonable public choices can be developed only during the course of extensive deliberation. If actions are to be taken, however, choices must be made, and in the development and application of a system for electronic democracy, citizens should understand that one of the major purposes of the dialogue is to inform the making of such choices.

Action

Why should citizens enter into the hard work of education, discussion, deliberation, and choice? They must understand that when they go through that hard work, their choices and judgments will be used. Many people agree that the responsible choices and judgments of citizens are important but debate how they should be used. Some believe that it will be enough if citizens understand that the elected representatives listen to their choices and take them into full account in legislative and executive action. Others believe that it is vital that the final choices of a well-conducted national deliberation have the essential force of law. This is, of course, what the initiative process was supposed to accomplish. National initiatives may be part of our future freedoms. Absent national initiatives, it might be suffcient to know that clear national choices resulting after a period of substantial deliberation would, by their very nature, have a compelling effect on legislators and national executives. It is hard to see how a legislator could be expected to be reelected if he or she failed to take into account the clear will of his or her constituency. As there is relatively little experience in many of these areas, however, it may be necessary to experiment with several models of electronic democracy.

The authors of the *Federalist Papers,* when they argued the case for the American experiment, were well aware of two great questions about politics and human nature. One question was whether there could be a viable democratic republic in an extended geographical area with a heterogeneous population. The other was whether human beings are capable of peacefully and deliberately defining and shaping their own futures, or whether the future will inevitably be determined by power and accident. The growth of population and the advance of science and technology sharpen our appreciation of the importance of these two questions. The geographical size of the United States is far beyond that imagined by any of the founding fathers. The population growth has far exceeded what anyone expected a hundred years ago. At the same time, science and technology have greatly increased the power available to rule populations by force. Science and technology can also be applied to allow the American experiment to become more effective, however, to engage citizens in responsible discussion and deliberation about their future; to enable the nation to make choices and shape its destiny more effectively; and to give elected representatives confidence that they can do their work based on an educated citizenry working with, rather than in opposition to, government. Electronic information technology will be used for political purposes. Whether it is used for demogoguery or democracy, the choice is ours.

Acknowledgments

Much of the material in this chapter is drawn from two of my essays, "Electronic Democracy," and "Habits of Mind and a New Technology of Freedom," both in *Collected Essays,* ed. Lloyd N. Morrisett (New York: Markle Foundation, 1998). The title of the chapter is borrowed, in part, from Ithiel de Sola Pool, *Technologies of Freedom* (Cambridge: Harvard University Press, 1983).

I am indebted to many people for the thought and work that helped form the essays and this chapter. I would particularly like to thank Jeffrey Abramson, Paul Aicher, Gary Arlen, Christopher Arterton, Benjamin Barber, Amitai Etzioni, Charles Firestone, James Fishkin, Siobhan Nicolau, Norman Ornstein, Gary Orren, Erik Sandburg-Diment, William Schneider, Deborah Wadsworth, and Daniel Yankelovich.

Notes

1. Daniel Bell, "Social Science: An Imperfect Art," *The Tocqueville Review* 16, no. 1 (1995): 13.

2. Bernard Berelson, "What 'Missing the Newspaper' Means," in *Communications Research,* ed. P. F. Lazerfield and F. Stanton (New York: Harper, 1948–49), 111–129.

3. Richard Abraham and Alexander Kerensky, *The First Love of the Revolution* (New York: Columbia University Press, 1987), 22, 25; quoted in Benjamin Barber and James David, *The Book of Democracy* (New York: Prentice Hall, 1995), 312.

3 Which Technology and Which Democracy?

Benjamin R. Barber

To talk without polemic or misunderstanding about the relationship between the new technologies and democracy, we need to ask these key questions: Which technologies? And indeed, which democracy? For both of these terms have plural referents. I will take a stab at these perplexing definitional questions, but first, I need to offer four rather extensive caveats that raise some central problems about the promise of the new technologies.

Four Caveats

First, I want to emphasize that I am not a technological determinist. Technology has entailments and tendencies, but on the whole, history shows that it more generally reflects and mirrors the culture in which it evolves rather than guiding and directing it. We might want to recall, for example, that gunpowder democratized warfare in the West, but in China it reinforced the hold of hierarchical elites. We will note also that the internal combustion engine and electricity suburbanized America as a consequence of the political choice made after World War II in favor of private transportation (the interstate highway system) and the industries that supported it (rubber, cement, steel, oil, and automobile); yet at the very same historical moment, those technologies were put to the uses of a strong public transportation system in Europe. In other words, technologies tend not to be determinative but rather are conditioned by what is going on in the society in which they grow, which is why, when I talk about technology, I generally focus on the characteristics of the society beyond and why, I think, we really need to be focusing on those characteristics.

The second caveat I need do no more than mention, because Chris Harper makes the point in chapter 17 very eloquently. In that chapter, Harper reminds us that we can exaggerate the impact of new technology by overestimating how much of it is actually "new"; after all, 98 percent of the population still get their news and entertainment primarily from traditional media. We cannot allow ourselves to forget that despite the apostles of inevitable progress of technological convergence, our society at large has yet to arrive at the technological frontier. There is no convergence yet between computers, television, and telephones, and some argue it will never come. In the 1950s, engineers envisioned single, multiple-task gadgets in American kitchens, but it turned out that homemakers preferred dedicated machines that did one task—not a toast-oven-mix-master-blender-peeler, but separate toasters, mixers, ovens, can openers, blenders, and so forth. In any case, most people spend their time in the multiplex, or in front of the radio and the television, not on the Net, and when we make generalizations about democracy and media and gatekeepers and so on, we need to remember that the real action around censorship, news, entertainment, and "propaganda" is still provided by television, movies, radio, and newspapers.

Indeed, in what some people are now calling the "attention economy," the competition for attention is such that we don't necessarily want to conclude that the Net is automatically going to continue to increase its hold on an ever larger share of our time. Just because it is an efficient technology from the perspective of technicians does not mean it will be a successful technology from the perspective of consumers. Strikingly (though hardly unexpectedly from the point of view of this skeptical observer), a study in the *American Psychologist* (summer 1998) suggested that Internet use actually increases clinical depression in otherwise normal users. Ought the avoidance of depression to be a criterion for evaluating the Web?

The third caveat relates to the frequently debated question of spectrum abundance. We need to remind ourselves that spectrum abundance (the multiplication of conduits and outlets) is not the same thing as pluralism of content, programming, and software. When we distinguish content from the conduits that convey it, the consequences of monopolistic ownership patterns become much more obvious. For as the ownership of content programming, production, and software grows more centralized, the multiplication of outlets and conduits becomes less meaningful.

I know there is an element of subjective judgment here. When I turn on the television and surf the celebrated 50 or 100 (soon to be 500?) channels available to me, I am always astonished at how little real variety there seems to be. Other people say, "No, no, I can get sports, ethnic programs, history channels, nature programming, there's endless variety." Yet I fear we confound variety (different subject matter with genuinely distinctive perspectives) with segmentation (a narrowcasting niche-marketing approach to selling common products). I will return to this point later. But I will argue here that our celebrated "diversity" means little more than similar kinds and styles of material being directed toward different marketing niches. There is distinctive packaging, to be sure, but substantive differentiation is missing.

The final caveat I want to offer is what I want to call the generational fallacy, which is at play in the history of technology generally. Those who create and first use new technologies take for granted the values and frameworks of previous eras and previous technologies and assume that new generations will have those same values and frameworks. Wrapped in the cocoon of presentness, they forget that for a new generation introduced to the world only via the new technologies, the values and frameworks that conditioned and tempered those who invented the technologies will be absent. For the second generation of users, this can be corrupting in ways invisible to the pioneers and inventors.

To take a simple example—and I'll come back to this again later—the Net is primarily text-based. I cannot imagine it will stay that way. As soon as it becomes technologically feasible, it will become video- or picture-based. For the transitional generation, living in a word-oriented civilization (after all, in the beginning *was* the word!), the Net is simply another device for deploying words. Yet surely that is a primitive and unproductive use of a medium. Scrolling texts on the Net amount to little more than a souped-up telegraph, and we have had the telegraph for 150 years. What's new about the Net is the potential for graphics and moving pictures. Zines like *Slate* are at best a transition from text to something else, and the older generation knows that many of the data sets they access on the Net are just as easily consulted in reference books or libraries. But members of the generation that's introduced to the technology through television, computers, and the Web are anything but a word-cultured literati. And what the new generation eventually does with the technology may turn out to be quite different from what those of us who come from a word culture have in mind. Farewell text-based civilization!

I suspect that most of the people reading this chapter come from a context that is prejudiced in favor of text and that we simply assume words will continue to prevail, if with greater speed and with better graphics. As an educator, however, I suspect that people brought up in a world of fast-moving electronic images will lose touch with the significance and importance of words and cease to use the new technology as a word enhancer and instead focus on its more suitable use as an image enhancer. The effect of such a transition from word to image on democracy, in which constitutions and their tacit pledge to keep promises anchor our liberties, is scarcely calculable.

These several caveats, explored here only briefly, probably deserve a chapter in their own right; for they condition everything else I want to say specifically about the attributes and entailments of our new telecommunication technologies for democracy. To be sure, the terms we use are contested, and there will be many who dissent from my particular characterizations of digital media and of democracy. If you grant me some working definitions, however, you may find that my arguments suggest novel dangers for democracy from technology that is supposed to be democracy-friendly. They also suggest some remedies.

Democracy: What?

What then are we talking about when we refer to democracy? Without being pedantic, it is possible to elucidate and parse democracy in a number of different ways. In each case the requirements imposed on technology are different. In one case, we might say digital technology is well-suited to enhancing democracy understood in such and such a way; but with democracy understood in another way, we might regard the same technological features as hostile to it. I will differentiate here what I call "thin" or "representative democracy" from both "plebiscitary" and "strong democracy." For each, technology serves as a very different instrument.

In the case of thin democracy, representative institutions dominate and citizens are relatively passive. They are at best what Michael Schudson calls "monitors." They choose representatives but leave those representatives, who remain accountable to the voters in the abstract, to do most of the real governing. This is not so much self-government as (in Jefferson's term) elective aristocracy. Moreover, it creates an adversarial climate for democracy that pits people against one another and sharply distinguishes private and public, making liberty exclusively the product of the former (the Madisonian formula that sets interest against interest and faction against faction). Under thin democracy, experts and elites do the actual work of government, whereas citizens remain watchdogs and monitors, primarily engaged in private lives and private affairs.

A second version of democracy can be understood as primarily plebiscitary. This form of democracy is associated with mass culture and is sometimes even labeled totalitarian, since it is a form of democracy that eschews significant deliberation and debate and throws important decisions at an otherwise passive and propagandized public, who rubberstamp party choices by shouting out their prejudices. Critics of direct democracy and the referendum argue that this shortcut around representation too often approximates a manipulated plebiscite, in which private money and private prejudices almost always triumph, and few would argue that the plebiscitary model is anything other than a corruption of deliberative democracy. (Actually, there is ample evidence that the referendum as used in most American states is less vulnerable to money and special interests than critics claim, but that is another matter).

A third version of democracy can be understood (in the terms of my earlier book of the same name) as "strong" democracy: democracy that, though not necessarily always direct, incorporates strong participatory and deliberative elements. This is my preferred normative alternative, in which citizens are engaged at the local and national levels in a variety of political activities and regard discourse, debate, and deliberation as essential conditions for reaching common ground and arbitrating differences among people in a large, multicultural society. In strong democracy, citizens actually participate in governing themselves, if not in all matters all of the time, at least in some matters at least some of the time.

New Technologies: Which?

So far, we have complicated the question of whether the new media technologies serve democracy by problematizing the meaning of democracy. We can do the same with the overly simplistic construct "new media." For to graph the impact of media on democracy, we need several lines for different kinds of media—not just new and old, but traditional print, traditional broadcast, old cable, new cable (fiber optic), satellite broadcast, low-frequency, computer-mediated, Web-based (point-to-point), and so on. We will end up with a complex, multicelled graph that pairs each of the (at least) three kinds of democracy we have demarcated with each of four or five media genres, a graph that will immediately show that the media both are and are not supportive of this or that version of democracy. This reading is much less useful as a rhetorical argument but probably much more accurate as a portrait of possible outcomes of technological development.

Not that I think there are very many politicians or policymakers really concerned with accuracy in media, which turns out to be little more sought after in social science than in newscasting! For it draws us into a complicated exercise, far more demanding than Panglossian cyberenthusiasm or Pandorian cyberpessimism. Nonetheless, it is imperative that we problematize simplistic definitions; by doing so we can pose the generic question of how technology can affect democracy in specific terms that actually invite meaningful responses. And so, perhaps, it is an exercise that I can be permitted to pursue here.

I cannot fill in all the cells in a graph charting types of democracy and varieties of media technology in this brief exercise, but I would like to describe at least some of what is in a few cells, in order to give a feel for what this debate looks like. Readers need not agree with how I characterize the media, or even on how I interpret their interface with democracy in its several manifestations, to see that variations will multiply along with different approaches to and understandings of our two key terms.

I will focus on computer-based digitalized media, since they represent the newest forms of media. I want to remark on the consequences of some key attributes of new media, including their speed, their reductive simplicity and tendency to (digital) polarization, the solitariness of their user interface, their bias toward images over text, their point-to-point, lateral immediacy and consequent resistance to hierarchical mediation, their partiality to raw data rather than informed knowledge, and their inclination toward audience segmentation rather than toward a single, integrated community of users or viewers.

Speed, Reductive Simplicity, and Solitude

Let me start with what is perhaps the primary characteristic of digitalized media: speed. That is their greatest virtue and, for similar reasons, their greatest vice. Traditional media, whether print or broadcast, are not particularly in a hurry. Digital media are in a rush. The impact of "fast" varies, however, depending on the version of democracy we postulate. With representative democracy, for example, accelerated pace may make little difference or even look virtuous, at least for citizens. Where thought and deliberation are not essential, a speeded-up political process may simply appear as time saving, protective of private time, efficient.

With plebiscitary democracy, speed is a desiratum, for quickness means people cannot and will not stop and think about what they are doing or voting on. For a Mussolini or a big-money referendum sponsor in California, the faster the plebiscite comes and goes, the better. In a strong, deliberative democracy, however, this lickety-split virtue, the capacity to operate in a hurry, clearly becomes a defect. In a strong democracy, the primary civic injunction is "slow down!"

In *Strong Democracy,* I posited the virtues of a multireading referendum procedure that elongated the deliberation process over six months. In a completely contrary spirit, digital media have as their primary injunction "hurry up! and I will help you do it!" Now there is no reason why we cannot slow down digital media; but to do so would be contrary to the new technology's most attractive feature, like asking a hare to run a tortoise's race. In a culture in which fast film edits, fast music, and fast food replicate and reinforce the hustle of computers, we ought to be seeking the equivalent of civic governors for our political engines, devices that slow down and moderate the system's hyperkinetic obsessiveness.

Partly as a consequence of their addiction to speed, digital media are inclined to a certain reductive simplicity, the binary dualisms (on/off, zero/one) that define the world of the digital gainsay the nuanced, complexifying characteristics of political deliberation. Voting yes or no may ultimately be required by democratic decision making, but reducing participation to terminal choices between polarized alternatives is hardly a useful way to capture democracy's strengths. On the other hand, plebiscitary democracy is likely to be perfectly satisfied with bipolar alternatives, since it usually is aiming at a single outcome and does not wish to have its rational-choice grid problematized by nuance and complexity. Representative democracy prefers voting to deliberation (for citizens, if not for professional politicians) and may find digital simplicity reinforcing.

If the new media favor speed and simplicity, they also encourage a politics of solitude in which privatized individuals can sit at home in front of electronic screens and view the world and its political choices as so many consumer alternatives. In the nineteenth century, J. S. Mill and other critics of the secret ballot suggested that a vote not offered and defended in public is an irrational and biased vote, biased precisely because it is private. Democracy, Mill thought, requires giving public reasons for private choices; the public reasoning imparts to the choices their publicness. The privatized and privatizing nature of the new technology and its privileging of the home as a "political" venue take the idea of the secret ballot to its logical (illogical) extreme, leaving citizens as private choosers, exempted from the responsibility of explaining or defending their choices. That is presumably why champions of civic engagement, such as Harry Boyte, have nonetheless been critical of home voting by computer.

Some enthusiasts counter this criticism by alluding to "virtual communities," but for the most part, these turn out to be vicarious conglomerations lacking the empathy and need for common ground that define real-world communities. Lolling in your underwear in front of an electronic screen while accessing with dancing fingers the pixels generated by anonymous strangers across the world is not my idea of forging a community of concern or establishing common ground, let alone cementing a trusting friendship. If large-scale modern societies are already troubled by isolation, civic alienation, and a decline of trust, a cyberpolitics rooted in apartness hardly seems to offer appropriate remedies. The act of going online is, in its predominant form, always a privatizing act of simply solitude. This may serve the pacifying tendencies of representative democracy and the need of plebiscitary tyranny for isolated solitaries (the sociologists of totalitarianism have taught us that separating individuals from one another and stripping away their mediating associations is the first step toward pervasive control), but it undermines the needs of strong democracy for community and common ground. As noted earlier in the chapter, a controversial *American Psychologist* study suggests that time on the computer may be not only isolating, but depression-inducing as well. Little wonder.

Pictures, Not Words

In any case, at their most sophisticated, digital media are carriers of images and sounds, rather than words and thoughts, and whether we consult them in solitude or in some version of a virtual community, they are unlikely to do much for failing actual communities, say, in Kosovo or south central Los Angeles. To be sure, we have noted, the new media are currently text-based; but their promise lies in pictures. They, ultimately, are an efficient surrogate for television and film rather than for books and newspapers. (I have been astonished, but not surprised, to see how many computer addicts are now using their traveling laptops for private film screenings on their new DVD drives!) As they grow into their most promising potential, new media are then likely to acquire all of the political defects of a pictorially based, image-mongering, feeling-engendering, sentiment-arousing, one-on-one (one-screen-per-person) civic culture. A succession of fast-moving images is not conducive to thinking, but it does accommodate advertising, manipulation, and propaganda, and these are the hallmarks of modern consumer culture and its privatizing political ideology that displaces governments with markets.

The power of imagery cannot be overstated. A few years ago, Americans were treated to a horrific telepicture from the Horn of Africa: a television image of an American soldier's abused corpse being dragged across a square in which an American helicopter had crashed in flames. In a single instant, this image transformed American foreign policy and brought to an unceremonious and undeliberated end American strategic engagement in that part of the world. Democracy? I don't think so.

Words can, of course, also deceive, but the films of a Leni Riefenstahl are always likely to be more affecting than the texts of a Goebbels. Steven Spielberg's *Saving Private Ryan* can, for example (as Edward Rothstein argued in the *New York Times*), be understood to reinforce the political cynicism of our time; for although Spielberg celebrates quotidian courage on the part of stubborn, if inglorious, individuals, he simultaneously deconstructs World War II's global struggle and privatizes the aims and motives of its protagonists. In doing so, he seems to demean its higher ends and signs on to the privatization of all things public that is our epoch's signature.

Oliver Stone is an even more obvious case, his films filled with a dark and antidemocratic skepticism about government and public ideals. Whether he is deconstructing official explanations of the Kennedy assassination or of the war in Vietnam, he deploys pictures to distort history and give conspiracy the aspect of truth. Spielberg and Stone obviously have a right, even a duty, to make an argument about how to look at war or the Johnson administration, but their films are not really instructive provocations to thought (nor do they claim to be). Rather, they are entertaining prompts to parochialism whose messages are inadvertent and unargued because they come wrapped in a form of manipulation at which moving pictures excel. Arousing feelings only and avoiding argumentation based on reasons (how pedantic that would be!), they undergird unshakeable prejudice.

Digital technology enhances such manipulation. As it can morph forms and shapes to create a world of convincing illusion in studio films, it can morph feelings and sentiments to create a world of convincing prejudice on the Net. Our civilization has founded itself on the word, and founding documents, whether secular (the Constitution) or ecclesiastic (the Bible, the Torah, the Koran), have rooted us in reason, coherence, and promise keeping (the consistency of words trumping the mutability of personality).

We are anchored by what Aristotle called *logos,* the human facility (that facile humanity) that allows us to impose order and meaning on the world through language and signs and to provide ourselves with a common discourse through which we can mediate our essentially contestable interests and find a means to cooperate in spite of them. Democracy is, by this definition, the government of *logos,* and it is *logos* that legitimizes regimes rooted originally only in power and interest. In the beginning was the word, so if in the end there are only pictures, democracy can only be worse off.

As we allow symbols, slogans, and trademarks to displace ideas and words in defining our politics, we distort our politics. New media are not compelled toward such displacement, but they are disposed toward it by the traits we have portrayed. When Tony Blair affects to redefine his New Labor England not with words but by rebranding the nation and cleansing it of its historical association with red buses, bobbies' helmets, and high teas, he may be updating his nation's image, but he is not doing British democracy any favors (and British democracy needs all the favors it can get).

d Media? Information or Knowledge?

Speed and imagery reinforce the "point-to-point" character of the new media, and this turns out to be, depending on your perspective, both a virtue and a vice. Integrated systems of computers and the World Wide Web are point-to-point technologies that promise direct lateral communication among all participants and thus offer an unmediated horizontal access ("immediacy") and entail the elimination of overseers and middlemen, of facilitators and editors, and of hierarchical, busybody gatekeepers. The virtue of immediacy is that it facilitates equality and egalitarian forms of horizontal communication. Representative democracy favors vertical communication between elites and masses, but strong democracy (as I argued in my book of that name fifteen years ago) prefers lateral communication among citizens, who take precedence over leaders and representatives.

(The Net offers a useful alternative to elite mass communication in that it permits ordinary citizens to communicate directly around the world without the mediation of elites, whether they are editors filtering information or broadcasters shaping information or facilitators moderating conversation.) By challenging hierarchical discourse, the new media encourage direct democracy and so, as I suggested fifteen years ago, can be instruments of strong democracy.

At the same time, as an educator and editor, I know that there is no such thing as "raw information" pure and simple, that all of what passes as information either remains unusable in raw, meaningless clumps of data, or, becoming usable, gets filtered, selected, edited, imbued with coherence and meaning. This filtering always involves mediation in some form or other, either as a consequence of democratic (consensual) or authoritative (appropriately knowledgeable) criteria or via arbitrary criteria rooted in brute force (it is so because I say it is so, and I have the gun). The question is not whether or not to facilitate, mediate, and gate-keep. It is *which* form of facilitation, *which* mediation, and *which* gatekeeper? The pretense that there can be none at all, that discourse is possible on a wholly unmediated basis, breeds anarchy rather than liberty and data overload rather than knowledge.

As Jean-Jacques Rousseau once insisted that our only meaningful political choice is not between natural liberty and political authority, but only between legitimate authority and illegitimate authority, so our choice is not between unmediated information and manipulated information, but only between legitimate manipulated information and illegitimate manipulated information. The virtue of newspapers and magazines is that they offer authoritative interpretations of information that we select according to our own standards, interests, and norms. To put it bluntly, this is the difference between information and knowledge. *Slate* is a more democratic form of communication than randomly accessed data garnered from data banks, even though it purveys knowledge by claiming editorial authorship of its contents and thereby interferes with our personal selection process and interdicts the kinds of arbitrary access we achieve when we shop for data point to point and without guidance.

The new technologies are, however, information-based rather than knowledge-based and so may well obstruct the growth of knowledge. Defined as information organized according to values, theories, and paradigms, knowledge is the key to political competence as well as to culture and civilization. Unmediated, raw information lends itself to manipulators we do not choose; information organized as knowledge allows us to choose authoritative "manipulators." The good teacher, the good editor, and the good facilitator represent trustworthy intermediaries to whom we entrust the initial filtering of raw data to help educate and inform ourselves, keeping them accountable by retaining our right to choose them at will. To the degree that the Net dispenses with these intermediaries, even as it creates more egalitarian forms of interaction, it risks anarchy and/or unreflected (often random) biases in our knowledge.

Whether we understand these differences between information and knowledge may be a function of generational factors. For those familiar with library reference and hard data collections, technology can expedite research. We already know what we are looking for. But the mere presence of infinite reams of data means little for those without research experience, reference book literacy, and library knowledge. Such people may find themselves inundated and confused—or worse, lulled into thinking that research does itself while they sit and wait. They receive a flood of unfiltered information that puts them back into an infantile world where the senses are overwhelmed with chaotic and meaningless inputs: noise not sound, color but no patterns, images that never add up to pictures, all without significant meaning. The Net replicates this anarchic world, and only those with well-developed and literate minds are likely to be able to draw sense from it or impose sense upon it. Those less fortunate will be imprinted with its anarchy.

Mediators and gatekeepers, whether we call them editors, teachers, pastors, novelists, journalists, or philosophers, all help us make sense of the world: In a democracy, they are brought under democratic controls and are accountable to those they guide. Either we can select and replace them, or we can accept or reject their guidance at will: It is never compulsory. But to think democracy is better served by eliminating mediators is to opt not for liberty, but for anarchy and the fertile ground it proffers to the true manipulators.

For these reasons, I have some doubts about the desirability of government and civil-society efforts aimed at hard-wiring our schools. If the new "conducts" are dominated by data and commerce, then we are hard-wiring schools into data and commerce. If the real deficit in our schools is in *thinking* rather than in *information access,* then we are hard-wiring the children into an illusion that the computers will think for them. My students at Rutgers University have trouble making sense out of and integrating the six readings or so a semester I assign. Is having access to the Library of Congress and to raw data files from depositories around the world really going to make them smarter? more knowledgeable? wiser? or more likely to read? Perhaps, before going online, they should learn how to read a single essay; learn how to go looking for the datum they need, in a library or a laboratory, rather than gaining easy access to endless streams of data for which they have no need at all. In an age weak on synthesis, integration, and understanding, multiplying sources is unlikely to create a generation sufficiently educated to take advantage of the cornucopia of informational riches promised by universal access. Since democracy is the governance of knowledge learned and shared rather than of information stored and accessed, it is unlikely to prosper in any of its forms through a regimen of data.

Segmentation and the End of the Common Ground

There is a final characteristic of digitalization that is corrupting to democracy, one that hampers our capacity to harvest knowledge from the new technologies: the technology's tendency to segment and compartmentalize what we seek to know. Digitalization is, quite literally, a divisive, even polarizing epistemological strategy. It prefers bytes to whole knowledge and opts for spreadsheet presentation rather than integrated knowledge. It creates knowledge niches for niche markets and customizes data in ways that can be useful to individuals but does little for common ground. For plebiscitary democrats, it may help keep individuals apart from one another so that their commonalty can be monopolized by a populist tyrant, but for the same reasons, it obstructs the quest for common ground necessary to representative democracy and indispensable to strong democracy. Narrowcasting of the kind to which we have become accustomed on cable television and in a segmented magazine industry ("fly-fishing for Catholic accountants"!) undermines common ground and divides citizens into groups conducive to marketing but deadly to common deliberation. A culture of three television networks (or, in Europe, a couple of state networks) may have had limited variety, but it guaranteed common watching, common concerns, and common ground. It gave us a common vocabulary—at times, much too "common"—that permitted the forging of common values and common interests. Such community (let alone real communion) is harder to imagine in a world of 500 cable channels and infinitely variable raw information sources on a vast, segmented Internet. How much common experience is possible in a population divided into specialized, topic-specific, demographically segregated chat rooms of a dozen people each? The national hearthside that was once NBC is now a million little home fires with a couple of yous and mes huddled around narrowly conceived, but conflicting, interests (just tune into to MSNBC to be convinced!).

In moments of national gravity or national tragedy—the assassination of a president, a terrorist incident, the end of a war—we need common places to gather and common turf on which to grieve or celebrate. The segmented new media lack such public places, much as the suburbs lack sidewalks and public squares. When in my recent essay on civil society I call for "a place for us," I look specifically for civic space on the Internet—and I come up wanting.

The new media specialize and niche-market and individuate beautifully, and this may advantage the politics of special interests and nondeliberative polling; but it clearly disadvantages deliberation and the pursuit of common ground and undermines the politics of democratic participation. It cannot help in the pursuit of national, common, and civic identity, and without these forms of association, democracy itself becomes problematic.

Privatizing the Media: Destroying Democracy

This criticism returns us to the nub of my debate (in chapter 9) with Ira Magaziner. Absent the rhetoric, the argument turns on whether the new technologies, as envisioned by Magaziner and others who favor privatization (and its commercializing proclivities) to government direction (and its market-regulating interventions), can create a genuinely civic and public discourse. I argue that turning over these technologies to the market, and thus to the consequences of their privatizing, immediate, segmenting characteristics, could only imperil the conditions needed for public discourse and democracy. Now, perhaps, it is more apparent why I make this argument.

It is worth adding, however, that the universal reach of the new technologies can be useful in forging global institutional forms for civil society and democracy that would otherwise be difficult to achieve. International groups like CIVICUS and Civitas utilize the universal communication features of the technology to bring together local communities that would otherwise remain separate (just as Davos's World Economic Forum now offers its corporate members a global Web service tailored to their global ambitions).

A commercial Net creates global economic ties; a civic Net can create global civic ties—if given the chance. Here we again are witnesses to the dialectical tendencies of the Web. It can tie together communities across nations even as it divides two college roommates sitting side by side but communicating only via their screens! Young people are in touch with their cousins across the continent and the world but are losing touch with the communities they actually inhabit. Virtual community is undergirding a kind of virtual globalism without actually fomenting internationalism (I have seen no data suggesting that the Web's world-wide reach has actually drawn Americans out of their parochialism and isolationism). Indeed, virtual globalism seems to undermine real community.

There are nevertheless ways to mediate and direct the new technologies—to set their agenda—that enhance their civic and strong-democratic potential. But doing so requires precisely that we maintain their public character and prevent them from slipping into a domain of privatized choosing, unmediated communication, multiplying data, and commerce-driven solitude. The market may enhance private choices, but it does so at the expense of control over the public agenda. Without control of the public agenda, democracy is impossible. Or to put it more bluntly, democracy means control over the public agenda, and privatization condemns democracy to oblivion—ironically, in the name of liberty. The technology is not necessarily privatizing, but in a world of privatizing ideology, it is likely to become a crucial instrument of the triumph of privatization.

That is why I am so passionate in debating Magaziner about the question of whether to privatize the new technologies and indulge in what Senator Robert Dole called (with respect to the donation of digitalized spectra to those who already own the broadcast spectra) the "give-away of the century." I do not believe we can privatize what is essentially a public utility without grave consequences for democracy in general and strong democracy in particular. Not everything can pay its own way in the short term. Education, religion, culture, and democracy itself cannot. To insist they should is to condemn them. If profit becomes the driving incentive in shaping the development of the new technologies, we can be sure that democracy will be a casualty rather than a beneficiary.

If there is to be a place for us on the Net, if women and men wearing their civic clothes are to be able to benefit from the new technologies, the technical and digital agendas must be set publicly and democratically. Profit cannot be the standard. Technology cannot, in

Magaziner's phrase, be considered nothing more than the "engine of global commerce." It is or should be the engine of civilization and culture. It should serve democracy. And for that to happen, it must be democratic, and its agendas must be subject to democratic judgment. Political will and political presence must count as much as market profitability and commercial utility. The Net must offer a place for us, which means it must in a tangible sense "belong" to us. Anything else, at least with respect to democracy, is hypocrisy.

4 Click Here for Democracy: A History and Critique of an Information-Based Model of Citizenship

Michael Schudson

The 2000 California voter's information guide—or Oregon's, or that of any other state where electoral laws require distribution to the voting public of written arguments for and against ballot propositions as well as biographical information on candidates for state office—is the reductio ad absurdum of the ideal of the informed citizen in a mass democracy. This artifact of democracy is a material realization of a notion of democracy that the founding fathers would have found entirely foreign and that contemporary European democrats find bizarre. In what follows, I want to describe the historical context that gave rise to this peculiar artifact to understand why something that seems to many Americans to follow almost naturally from the basic notion of a self-governing people is so rare—and problematic—among the world's democracies.

My premise is that most popular accounts of how the digital media can enhance democracy are rooted in the same Progressive Era vision of citizenship that gave rise to the initiative and referendum, the direct election of senators, nonpartisan municipal elections, and the voter information guides that were first mandated in the 1910s and 1920s. The Progressive Era concept of democracy is centered on information. If information can be more complete, more widely disseminated, more easily tapped into by citizens at large, then democracy can flourish. This is all very well if information is at the heart of mass democracy. But it isn't. Whether digital media will make democracy easier or harder to practice will depend on what visions and versions of democracy we have in mind. My fear is that our use of digital media may be imprisoned by a concept of democracy that is a century old and, even at its inception, was a narrow and partial understanding.

If the new digital media are to be integrated into a new political democracy, they must be linked to a serious understanding of citizenship, and this cannot happen if we simply recycle the old notion of the informed citizen. There are three other concepts of democratic citizenship that have been influential in American political life, and a mature sense

of democracy must somehow incorporate all of them. We have had, in successive historical periods, a democracy of trust (though just barely a democracy), a democracy of par-
tisanship, a democracy of information, and a democracy of rights.

In everyday political practice, Americans do draw on these four distinct concepts of
citizenship, but our language of democracy and our vision of democratic ideals lag behind
our changing practices.[1]

"The Citizen" of the Founding Fathers

Only property-owning white males voted in colonial America and in the first generation
of the new nation. They voted without benefit of party primaries or formal nominating
procedures of any kind. The leading elites determined informally who should stand for
office. Even in New England town meetings, social hierarchy was so well established that
the acknowledged town leaders would be returned to office as selectmen over and over.
When elections were contested (and often they were not), voters were expected to vote
on the basis of character and reputation, not on the basis of stands on the issues. Ordi-
narily, there were no issues, no platforms, no public speeches. The voter's job was simply
to determine which candidate would be a man of sound judgment and make the best decisions in office.

If you were a voter in colonial Virginia, where George Washington, Patrick Henry, and
Thomas Jefferson learned their politics—if you were, that is, a white male owning at least
a modest amount of property—on election day you would travel to the one polling place
in the county where, at or outside the courthouse, you would see the sheriff, supervising
the election. Beside him stand two candidates for office, both of them members of prominent local families. You watch the most prominent members of the community, the leading landowner and the clergyman, approach the sheriff and announce their votes in loud,
clear voices. When your turn comes, you do the same. Then you step over to the candidate for whom you have voted, and he shakes your hand, heartily thanking you for your
vote.[2] Your vote has been an act of assent, restating and reaffirming the social hierarchy
of a community where no one but a local notable would think of standing for office,
where voting is conducted entirely in public view, and where voters are ritually rewarded
by the gentlemen they favor.

In such a world, what information did a voter require? Colonial education aimed to in-
still religious virtue, not to encourage competent citizenship. Schooling and reading were
understood to be instruments of inducting citizens more firmly into the established order. When people praised public enlightenment, this is what they usually had in mind.

Even the most broad-minded of the founders conceived plans for public education limited in objective (and, in any event, rarely enacted). Jefferson's "A Bill for the More General Diffusion of Knowledge" in Virginia aimed to provide for the liberal education of the state's leadership. The liberality of Jefferson's proposal consisted in its provision that elementary education be made generally available so that the net could be cast as widely as possible for leaders of "genius and virtue." But Jefferson did not doubt for a moment that governing should be undertaken by this "natural aristocracy" rather than ordinary citizens.[3]

As for the latter, the whole of their civic obligation was to recognize virtue well enough to be able to know and defeat its counterfeit. Citizens would turn back the ambitious and self-seeking at the polls. But they were not to evaluate public issues themselves. That was what representatives were for. Not parties, not interest groups, not newspapers, not citizens in the streets, but elected representatives alone would deliberate and decide.

When President George Washington looked at the "Democratic-Republican clubs," political discussion societies that sprang up in 1793 and 1794, he saw a genuine threat to civil order. The clubs were, to him, "self-created societies" that presumed, irresponsibly and dangerously, to make claims upon the government, to offer suggestions to the government about what it should decide—when they had not been elected by the people nor sat in the chambers of the Congress to hear the viewpoints of all. Washington spent much of his famous farewell address warning his countrymen against "all combinations and associations . . . with the real design to direct, control, counteract, or awe the regular deliberation and action of the constituted authorities."[4] The voluntary associations that de Tocqueville would one day praise, Washington excoriated.

The founders' faith in an informed citizenry was slight. They did not support broad publicity for governmental proceedings, they did not provide for general public education, and they discouraged informal public participation in governmental affairs. They viewed elections as affairs in which local citizens would vote for esteemed leaders of sound character and good family, deferring to a candidate's social pedigree more than siding with his policy preferences.

The Party Era and the Progressive Reformation

This model of politics faded in the early nineteenth century as a vigorous, much more democratically minded world emerged, one dominated by a new institution that made its first appearance in the world in the United States in the 1830s: the mass-based political party. Parties dominated nineteenth-century politics, even taking on the task of running elections themselves. Picture election day at any point between about 1830 and 1890. The area around the polling place is crowded with clumps of activists from rival parties. On election day, the parties hire tens of thousands of workers to get out the vote and to stand near the polling place to hand out the "tickets" they have printed. The voter approaches the polling place, takes a ticket from a "ticket peddler" of his own party, goes up to the voting station, and deposits his ticket in the ballot box. He need not look at it. He need not mark it in any way. Clearly, he need not be literate. He might cast his ballot free of charge, but it would not be surprising if he received payment for his effort. In New Jersey, as many as one third of the electorate in the 1880s expected payment for voting on election day, usually in an amount between one and three dollars.[5]

What did a vote express? Not a strong conviction that the party offered better public policies; parties tended to be more devoted to distributing offices than to advocating policies. Party was related more to comradeship than to policy: it was more an attachment than a choice, something like a contemporary loyalty to a high school or college and its teams. Voting was not a matter of assent but a statement of affiliation. Drink, dollars, and drama brought people to the polls, and more than that, social connection, rarely anything more elevated.

The historic process of including propertyless white men, and later immigrants and former slaves, among voters was driven—sometimes willingly and sometimes very reluctantly—by the mass-based political party, the chief agent of the new democracy. (Suffrage for women was another matter. Whereas Republicans championed votes for African Americans and Democrats sponsored immigrants, neither leading party reached out to women.) This was a democracy more wild and woolly than anything the founders had imagined, not least of all in its elevation of the election to an extraordinary carnivalesque ritual.

Gilded Age reformers were not keen on carnival, and the late nineteenth century saw a revolt against the party domination of politics. Reformers sponsored a "Protestant Reformation" in American politics, with a series of attacks on the emotional enthusiasm of political participation, attacks on corruption in campaign financing and campaign practices, attacks on the spoils system and advocacy of civil service reform, and rhetorical attacks on parties as usurpers of the direct connection between citizens and their governmental representatives. The shift away from the organizational and emotional centrality of the party was symbolized in the "Australian ballot." This was the state-printed rather than party-printed ballot that Americans still use today. It made voting secret for the first time in American history. It swept the country beginning in 1888, endorsed by the same genteel reformers who sponsored civil service reform and also by labor and other groups. By 1892, most states employed it. Until this time, a citizen in the act of voting reaffirmed his affiliation with the party that printed and then provided him with a ballot, rather than emphasizing, as the Australian ballot did, the voter's relationship to the state.[6]

The Australian ballot shifted the center of political gravity from party to voter. Voting changed from a social and public duty to a private right, from a social obligation to party, enforceable by social pressure, to a civic obligation or abstract loyalty, enforceable only by private conscience. The new ballot asked voters to make a choice among alternatives rather than to perform an act of affiliation with a group.

The Australian ballot did not by itself transform American politics, but it did exemplify a far-reaching political transformation. Where mugwump reformers began, the Progressives followed—and would soon face the curse of getting what they wished for: the elevation of the individual, educated, rational voter as the model citizen. Politics came to be organized and narrated in a way more accessible to rational reflection. Presidents made promises, crafted programs, offered comprehensive federal budgets, and championed policies. Newspapers claimed a new independence from parties and covered politics with a degree of detachment. Something we might term "rationality" became more possible, too, with the proliferation of private associations focused on lobbying the government. Women, long excluded from the franchise, had sought political ends through interest groups; with suffrage, they helped bring an issue-oriented and information-centered rather than party-oriented political style into the political mainstream. Citizens could express policy preferences much more exactly by supporting a national single-interest or single-issue lobbying organization than by supporting the broad, mixed efforts of a political party, by voting in a primary rather than a general election, by voting directly for senators (after 1913), and by voting on state initiatives and referenda. Beginning with Oregon and Montana in 1907, followed in the next decade by Oklahoma, California, Arizona, Nebraska, Ohio, Washington, Utah, Massachusetts, and North Dakota, state-prepared and -printed voter information guides were provided to all registered voters.[7]

Amid these developments and because of them, political participation drastically fell. The large voting public of the late nineteenth century, with voter turnout routinely at 75 to 80 percent, became the vanishing public of the 1920s, with turnout under 50 percent. For the voting public, the road to rational public participation was finally open, but the festive ritual of community and party affiliations and rivalries was now closed.

Rights-Conscious Citizenship

The replacement of the party-loyal citizen with the informed citizen as the ideal model of American citizenship was not the endpoint of evolving concepts of civic participation. A fourth model of citizenship emerged with the civil rights movement. The Supreme Court and American constitutionalism in general shifted from an emphasis in the nineteenth century on powers, concerned with the relative authority of the state and federal governments, to an emphasis on rights and the obligations of government and law to the claims of individuals.

Until the late 1930s at the earliest, the courts as makers of policy were not on the map of citizenship. The Supreme Court had little place in the public's heart and mind. The Supreme Court itself met, at first, in the basement of the Capitol and later in the old Senate chambers; the imposing Athenian structure that is its home today did not open until 1935. Only then was there an architectural representation in Washington of the concept that ours is a government of three branches. Before that time, the courts were important in everyday life but were not coequal to the executive and the Congress in the crafting of national public policy. Nor did the Supreme Court do much to define the individual's rights or responsibilities with respect to government. In 1935 the Court considered questions of civil liberties or civil rights in 2 of 160 opinions; in 1989 it was 66 of 132.[8] From the citizen's viewpoint, one went to court to resolve a dispute with a neighbor, not to challenge governmental authority. In the nineteenth century, the courtroom was rarely a focal point of popular protest, political theory, or social reform. Now a new avenue of national citizen power and a new model for political action emerged.

The new model citizenship added the courtroom to the voting booth as a locus of civic participation. Political movements and political organizations that, in the past, had only legislative points of access to political power found, from *Brown v. Board of Education* (1954) and the Montgomery bus boycott on, that the judicial system offered an alternative route to their goals.

The civil rights movement opened the door to a widening web of both constitutionally guaranteed citizen rights and statutory acts based on an expanded understanding of citizens' entitlements, state obligations, and the character of due process. This rights revolution affected not only the civil and political rights of African Americans but the rights of women and of the poor and, increasingly, of minority groups of all sorts. It came alive not only in the streets but in the Congress, making the 1960s the most energetic period of legislative activity since 1933–1935. The reach of federal regulatory powers grew, spurring a federalization of national consciousness and a striking expansion of the arenas that could be authentically understood as "political," that is, as having a relationship to things that government does or might be asked to do. In the decade 1964–1975, the federal government put more regulatory laws on the books than it had in the country's entire prior history.[9] In schools and in universities, in families, in the professions, in private places of employment, in human relations with the environment, and not least of all in political institutions themselves, including the political parties, the rights revolution brought federal power or national norms of equality to bear on local practices. In each of these domains, the outreach of the constitutional order spread ideals of equality, due process, and rights.

The civil-rights movement sprang the concept of "rights" from its confinement in dusty documents and in brave, but isolated, courtroom dramas. Individuals then carried the gospel of rights from one field of human endeavor to another, transporting rights across the cultural border of public and private.

Four Citizenships and One Internet

We have passed from a stage in which citizenship was manifested as an expression of trust in the solid (and wealthy) citizens of the community to a party-dominated era in which citizenship was expressed as a set of affiliations with political parties and interest groups. We moved on to an era that held up the informed citizen as the ideal and created a set of institutions to help make individual rationality in politics more possible. We have changed again to a form of citizenship nested in a strong, jealous rights-based political culture. Yet despite this rich and multifaceted legacy, most thinking about citizenship is confined to the model of the individual informed citizen and employs a rather rigid version of that model. This is the only model that springs readily to mind when people think about the connections between democracy and digital media. Everyone can know everything! Each citizen will have the voting record of every politician at his or her fingertips! A whole world of political knowledge is as close as one's computer and as fast as one's dial-up connection! Imagine a voter information guide not a mere hundred pages long, like California's in 2000, or 400 pages long, like Oregon's, but ten million pages long—and online! Oh, joy! Oh, rapture!

The Progressives ride again. True, the ways in which the Internet can be an informational resource are extraordinary. There is no denying that the World Wide Web is a wondrous development in human history—for science, for medicine, for commerce, for personal communications, and potentially for democratic self-governance. But it does not and cannot replace the necessary distribution across people and across issues of the cognitive demands of self-government. Consider an analogy: It is fun to go camping and to be able to take care of one's every need for a few days in the mountains. But in everyday life, most people are glad to turn on the stove rather than rub two sticks together and to buy a packaged chicken at the supermarket rather than trap a rabbit in the woods. We rely on the farms, milk processors, and government inspectors to see that milk is pasteurized, we do not do it ourselves; we trust in the metropolitan water supply to purify water, not our own chemicals. Why, then, in public life, do we expect people to be political backpackers? Why does political theory prepare us for camping trip politics rather than everyday politics? Why should we expect that when we are all wired, we will be closer to some kind of democracy?

Are citizens who have computer access but fail to consult each candidate's Web site during an election or the best of the Web sites that track candidate biographies, elected official voting records, and even keep tabs on campaign promises delinquent? Should they follow everything about everything? Or, in contrast, could they be judged exemplary if they know a lot about one thing and serve as sentries patrolling a segment (but not all) of the public interest's perimeter? Citizenship during a particular political season is for most people much less intense than in the nineteenth-century heyday of parties, but there are political dimensions to everyday life on a year-round and day-long basis as was only rarely true in the past. In this world, the gap between readily available political information and the individual's capacity to monitor it grows ever larger.

We cannot be political backpackers. Over the past century and a half, Americans have delegated firefighting in our cities to professionals rather than relying on volunteers, although it remains important that everyone understand basic fire safety, perhaps keep a fire extinguisher at home or in the car, maintain smoke detectors in the house, and know how to dial 9-1-1. We have subcontracted medical care to hospitals and physicians, on the one hand, and households, on the other, where shelves are stocked with diet books, women's magazines, Dr. Spock, and an array of over-the-counter medicines. We have arrived, in short, at a division of labor between expertise and self-help that gives credit to both. We do this in politics, too, but without having found a place in either popular rhetoric or democratic theory for the use of specialized knowledge. That is a task that merits renewed attention: the quest for a language of public life that reconciles democracy and expertise.

Most political commentary today operates within the culture of Progressivism and assumes the Progressivist fallacy: that being a good citizen means being well informed. This is only one view of the model citizen. Other views not only have been powerful in the past but persist today. The democracy of the trusted solid citizen, the democracy of party, and the democracy of rights all offer approaches to citizenship that are not information-centered. They should also be resources for reformulating what citizenship can be and what we would like it to be.

What does this mean, then, for the digital era? Only this: that to imagine that the potential of the computer age for democracy lies in the accessibility of information to individual citizens and voters who will be moved by the millions to petition and to vote more wisely than ever before is to imagine what will not be—and it is to exercise a very narrow democratic imagination in the first place. The Internet does not erase existing structures of politics. If it gives to ordinary citizens new tools for gathering information and expressing views, think of how much more it offers to political professionals who spend forty to eighty hours a week on politics, not forty to eighty minutes.

Consider the impact of computers on publishing. Book production has been transformed by computers. Book distribution, even more, has been revolutionized by computerized systems of inventory control that have been instrumental in making the chain bookstores and superstores a rousing success and a significant influence on publishers' decisions about what and how to publish. But the individual experience of reading a book is very much what it used to be. The e-book is a novelty, at best. The digital revolution, so far, has influenced the basic experience of reading a book far less than the paperback revolution of half a century ago.

To consider democracy in the digital era, first examine closely how political practices—the daily activities of politicians, candidates, government officials, pollsters, consultants, and political reporters—have been adapted to the new technologies. When we can more clearly see what is going on at the level of people who spend their full-time work on politics, we can better learn what digital democracy might bring to the ordinary citizen.

It does make good sense, of course, to ask how the Internet can enlarge the citizen's access to political information. This should be a key element in how the Internet is envisioned for democratic purposes, but it is also important to ask how digital media might contribute to the trust-based, party-based, or rights-based models of citizenship.

Computers might mean new opportunities for organizing and aggregating like-minded people or groups. Local list-servs are especially rich in this kind of possibility. Let me offer one small example that seems to offer a larger lesson. Early in 1999, Susan Myrland, a computer consultant in San Diego, organized a list-serv for a variety of community organizations in the region. I was on the list and noticed a great deal of traffic about "community technology centers" (CTCs), the libraries, public-housing projects, churches, boys and girls clubs, and other organizations that provide the general public, and especially the low-income public, with access to and sometimes instruction in computer use. I was involved in a campus initiative at the University of California, San Diego (UCSD), to encourage faculty and students to do research on civic and community life in our own region. The CTCs seemed like a set of institutions that UCSD could both help and learn from. So I contacted Myrland and asked whether the people at these different CTCs knew one another. She said it was very unlikely. I said UCSD could provide the coffee and bagels if Susan would organize a meeting.

Thirty-five people attended the first meeting, representing libraries, nonprofits, corporations, school districts, Internet service providers, city and county government, and other groups. The enthusiasm of participants was overwhelming. People were eager to share ideas, eager to meet again. Two years later, the San Diego Community Technology Group continues to be a catalyst for collaboration, helping groups help one another with community events, tracking and promoting new community technology initiatives, providing a central information source for fast distribution of recycled computers, stimulating donation of computers, and reducing duplication of efforts. Most important, it has reduced the sense of isolation people felt in their often underappreciated and underpaid efforts.

None of this would have happened without the original list-serv. Nor would very much of it have happened without the pleasures of face-to-face communication.

The Internet might mean new connections to political parties. I receive the e-mailed Democratic Party of San Diego County newsletter. Thanks to that newsletter, I joined the Democratic Party Club in my area of the county. I have not yet attended a meeting. Until I do, I am a member only by virtue of reading a newsletter. On the other hand, the newsletter is the only contact the Democratic Party has made with me in my twenty years here as a registered Democrat. I expect I will at some point go to a meeting. Only then will I become vulnerable to greater political involvement, turning the information of the newsletter into active participation. The newsletter informs me but has none of the persuasive power to be found in a smile, a handshake, or a kind word addressed to me, me personally.

I have no prescriptions for turning the Internet to democratic purposes. I urge only that the many good people who are trying to think their way toward a more democratic future through the Internet consider the various historic practices of American citizenship, see in them significant resources, and resist limiting their dream to a dream of information. Information is necessary for democracy, but information by itself is inert. It never was the be-all and end-all for the democratic citizen.

Notes

1. The argument of this chapter draws heavily on Michael Schudson, *The Good Citizen: A History of American Civic Life* (Cambridge: Harvard University Press, 1999).

2. See Charles Sydnor, *Gentlemen Freeholders* (Chapel Hill: University of North Carolina Press, 1952), 60, 68–70, 124.

3. "A Bill for the More General Diffusion of Knowledge" (1778) in *The Papers of Thomas Jefferson,* vol. 2, ed. Julian P. Boyd (Princeton: Princeton University Press, 1950), 526–527.

4. John Rhodehamel, ed., *George Washington: Writings* (New York: Library of America, 1997), 969. See Schudson, *The Good Citizen,* 55–64.

5. John F. Reynolds, *Testing Democracy: Electoral Behavior and Progressive Reform in New Jersey, 1880–1920* (Chapel Hill: University of North Carolina Press, 1988), 54.

6. See Schudson, *The Good Citizen,* 168–174.

7. Robert C. Brooks, *Political Parties and Electoral Problems* (New York: Harper, 1923), 473–476.

8. William E. Leuchtenburg, *The Supreme Court Reborn* (New York: Oxford University Press, 1995), 235.

9. R. Shep Melnick, *Regulation and the Courts: The Case of the Clean Air Act* (Washington, D.C.: Brookings, 1983), 5.

5 Growing a Democratic Culture: John Commons on the Wiring of Civil Society

Philip E. Agre

Is the Internet a friend of democracy? One prevailing discourse says no, that the Internet is actually the end of democracy, and that it deprives all governments, democratic or not, of the ability to enforce their laws. Whatever its utility as political prescription, this libertarian philosophy has usefully directed attention to the complex and variegated institutional field through which the great bulk of any society is actually organized.[1] Marx had no time for the institutions of civil society, which he regarded as epiphenomena of class relations.[2] But the concept of civil society is now popular throughout the world and across the political spectrum,[3] whether as a counterbalance to the overreaching of the state, as an integral constituent of democracy, or as the real and only substance of a free society.

Yet the libertarian commitment to civil society is unstable. Civil society consists largely of intermediaries: organizations that orchestrate and subserve a wide variety of social relationships. But as Dominique Colas has observed,[4] the concept of civil society did not enter European social thought as a liberal antidote to absolutism; its root meaning does not oppose it to the state. Rather, civil society was originally opposed to certain extreme forms of Protestantism that, in overthrowing the putative autocracy of the church, also sought to destroy all intermediaries and all representations—a mystical radicalism that sought to eliminate all obstacles to an unmediated communion with God. Political and technical ideas are routinely found to descend from secularized versions of medieval theology,[5] and thus here the radicalism of modern libertarians echoes in some detail the origins of the concept of civil society—not its supporters but its enemies: the smashers of idols, the extremist opponents of centralized authority, the militants seeking not to create their own intermediary institutions but to eliminate them altogether.

So it is, for example, that so many contemporary authors who seem to speak the libertarian language of Friedrich Hayek[6] in fact leave no room in their language for government at all, not even the minimal constitutional framework that Hayek regarded as necessary to administer the rule of law. These libertarian enthusiasts are anarchists, and they are more concerned about the exercise of government power than about money laundering, or pedophiles, or any of the genuine if overhyped evils of the age. What matters most to them is the power of the network to connect anyone to anyone, to circumvent anything, to short-circuit any intermediary, and therefore supposedly to destroy all hierarchies of whatever sort.[7] The state hierarchy, the monopoly—all will be smashed, all destroyed, all of their atoms scattered by the ecstasy of the bits. This technological teleology, this electronic eschatology, is, we are given to understand, the information revolution to end all revolutions.

But it is not so. Nothing like that is happening. Intermediaries are changing, to be sure, multiplying and dividing, their functions rebundling into different configurations, but they are as necessary as ever.[8] They are consolidating, indeed increasing their geographic scope.[9] States are not shrinking, and in fact they are compensating for the global reach of technology by creating a vast network of undemocratic and nontransparent global treaty organizations.[10] Mediation and representation, with all of the good and evil that they imply, are the very essence of the age. Once we see this, we can see at last the real upshot of the technology, the real action that it has already set in motion. It is not the elimination of civil society, any more than of the state. It is, however, in both realms, the renegotiation of the working rules of every institution of society.

This conception of social institutions as sets of working rules that govern the roles and relationships of their participants belongs to John Commons.[11] Commons was the mechanic philosopher of the New Deal. A printer, he eventually became a professor of economics at the University of Wisconsin, and in that position he trained many members of the generation that built the American welfare state. As the welfare state has come under assault, Commons has been nearly forgotten, mentioned only by a handful of legal theorists[12] and institutional economists.[13] Although theories of institutional change vary greatly, most contemporary theories of institutions themselves are largely compatible with Commons's early formulation; they seem different on the surface because they all overgeneralize from the particular case with which the author is most familiar. Commons's theory started from his experience of the negotiation of work rules in printing shops through collective bargaining, and that was the paradigm that he brought to every institution he considered.[14] He did not imagine that every set of rules arises through the same formal mechanism by which union contracts are negotiated. He did not presuppose that organized associations of buyers and sellers will necessarily delegate representatives to negotiate over a long table the form of contracts and other customary rules that govern a given industry at a given point in history. Nonetheless, Commons's project was to investigate the variety of mechanisms by which the stakeholder groups in a given institution do act collectively to carve out a space for their own customs and practices alongside and by compromise with those of everyone else.

Commons saw no better example of this process than the rise and evolution of the common law, in which successive social classes—merchants at one point, industrialists at another, and then industrial labor—wrote elements of their practices and values into the law as it emerged to govern the particular relationships of institutional life.[15] How this worked in practice was a matter for investigation. Normatively, the point was not for any one group to win out, but quite the contrary for every group to be able to hold its own, neither imposing its complete set of preferred rules on everyone else nor having anyone else's rules completely imposed on it.[16]

As increasingly complex social relationships are mediated by networked information technology, we are becoming accustomed to the idea that the protocols of these mediated interactions—the "code" in Lessig's terms[17]—constitutes a set of working rules in very much the sense that Commons suggests. Computers, like institutions generally, both enable and constrain, and both computers and institutions are, in one important aspect anyway, discourses made material—made, that is, into machinery that governs to some degree the lives of the people who use it.[18] Even when they are not formally part of the government, and even when they have no legal force, institutions and computers both govern, and it is this larger sense of governance that Commons views as the deep underlying unity of democratic government and democratic society. It is unlikely that one can exist without the other, and if the Internet encourages a democratic society, then it does so by promoting the diverse mechanisms of collective bargaining by which a democratic society orders its affairs.

The need for such mechanisms is clear. By providing a general mechanism for moving digital information and a general platform for constructing digital information utilities, the Internet provides new opportunities for the design of institutional mechanisms; it opens a vast new design space both for technology in the narrow sense and for the institutionalized social relationships within which the Internet is embedded. The Internet also necessitates a renegotiation of institutional rules in a more urgent way by destabilizing the balance of forces to which any successful negotiation gives form; by lending itself to the amplification of some forces and not others, the Internet undermines many of the institutionalized accommodations through which stakeholder groups with distinct interests and powers have gotten along.

It is not only the Internet that has such effects, of course; control over the legislature is a much more direct means of upsetting existing institutional arrangements, and more factors than information technology drive the disruptions of globalization. Nonetheless, the Internet, far from transporting its believers into the unmediated perfection of cyberspace, is unfreezing a multitude of thoroughly secular institutional arrangements right here on earth and is posing the challenge of how these arrangements might be remade, both efficiently and equitably, in a more digital world.

Fortunately, what the Internet makes necessary it also makes possible. If the working rules of universities will be remade through a negotiation between professors and students, among others; if the medical system will be remade through a negotiation between physicians, patients, and insurers, among others; if the political system will be remade through a negotiation among citizens and their representatives, among others, then the Internet has provided tools that allow each of these stakeholder groups to associate and, each in its own way, to press its interests. Once again the paradigm of collective bargaining can mislead if it is taken too literally. The point is not that every social group forms its own union, or even necessarily its own organization, and the point is not that the Internet necessarily facilitates any kind of formal bargaining process. Collective bargaining can be mediated by a great diversity of institutional forms, and it is the genius of the Internet to be indifferent to the details of such things.

The Internet makes visible a layer of social process that is more fundamental than organizations and just as fundamental as institutions, namely, the customs by which people who have something in common think together.[19] Before collective bargaining comes collective cognition, and collective cognition in its various modes is greatly facilitated by the community-building mechanisms of the Internet. Ideologies can form in the networked community of computer programmers, news can spread in the networked community of nurses, experiences can be shared in the networked community of cancer patients, patterns can be noticed by the networked community of pilots, agendas can be compared by the networked community of environmental activists, ideas can be exchanged in the networked community of entrepreneurs, stories can be told within the networked community of parents, and so on.

This sort of cognitive pooling is not an unambiguous good, of course; if taken too far, it can turn each particular community into a weakened intellectual monoculture. Nonetheless, in many cases the Internet is amplifying collective cognition in ways that equalize playing fields for all. Cancer patients no longer need to confront the medical and insurance systems as individuals. Parents can listen to other parents who have been in their shoes. Small players can learn what angles the big players are likely to work. Collective cognition is not the same as collective action, much less formally organized collective bargaining. But it is the soil from which these more complex phenomena of

solidarity grow. Without the habits of association, without the cultivated taste for sharing, without the concrete experience of helping others and being helped in turn, without
the very idea that others face the same situation as you, a democratic culture cannot grow.
Whatever its failings, the Internet fertilizes the soil of democratic culture.

The question, of course, is whether it does so enough: whether the Internet provides
the conditions for every social group, no matter how spread out, to take its rightful place
at the table, to play its own role in renegotiating all of the social institutions in which it
takes part. And the answer, just as clearly, is no. No technology is ever a suffcient condition for anything. It only facilitates. To truly build a democratic society, it will be necessary to build new social forms: new ideas, new movements, and new organizations that
are adequate the opportunities and challenges of a networked world.

The role of political organizations must change. An organization no longer needs to
carry the full burden of organizing the collective cognition of the social group that it
claims to represent. This is good when it frees resources for other purposes, and it is
bad when it reduces the binding force that makes membership in an organization attractive in the first place. It is good when it reduces the arbitrary power of the intermediaries through whom the information had flowed, and it is bad when it makes
consensus building and leadership impossible. What, then, is the role of an organization
in a networked world? An organization can place observers and advocates into complex
forums like legislatures and standards bodies, in which there is still no substitute for
being there. It can conduct the research that requires pulling together more information than any individual could manage. It can maintain the relationships that make negotiations possible. And it can build the legitimacy that is required to call for a solidary
action. These are all classical functions of an organization, and they will not go away.
But they will all happen in a more dynamic environment, and they will work only if they
draw upon and encourage the power of collective cognition, rather than trying to channel it. This is hard, because it is easier to deal with a centralized representative than a
sprawling associative community. But it is the democratic way, and it is the principal
hope today for a democratic society.

This perspective on democracy certainly has its limitations. Commons had a clear conception of institutions, but the language of collective bargaining was dangerously indeterminate in its prescriptions for the political system, as his misguided endorsement of
Mussolini's corporate state suggests.[20] But this is perhaps the central question of democracy in its newly wired manifestation: What is the proper relationship between collective
cognition among communities of shared interest and the actual formal mechanisms of
the state? Unequal access to the means of association is already a tremendous force for

inequality, especially in the United States, where professionalized lobbying on behalf of the powerful has been raised to a high art.

The answer cannot ride on the sort of bargaining that can be bought. Instead, it must ride on the massed creativity of a diverse people in diverse situations, all bringing their own experience to bear on the situations of others. If the Internet is a friend of democracy, then democracy will be won principally on the ground, and a central task for democratic theory right now is to understand this ground and to be useful to the innumerable people of goodwill who are out there trying to build on it.

Acknowledgments

I appreciate helpful comments by David Chess and Cosma Shalizi.

Notes

1. On the theory of institutions, see, among others, Jack Knight, *Institutions and Social Conflict* (Cambridge: Cambridge University Press, 1992); James G. March and Johan P. Olsen, *Rediscovering Institutions: The Organizational Basis of Politics* (New York: Free Press, 1989); Douglass C. North, *Institutions, Institutional Change, and Economic Performance* (Cambridge: Cambridge University Press, 1990); Walter W. Powell and Paul J. DiMaggio, eds., *The New Institutionalism in Organizational Analysis* (Chicago: University of Chicago Press, 1991); and James N. Rosenau, "Governance and Democracy in a Globalizing World," in *Re-imagining Political Community: Studies in Cosmopolitan Democracy,* ed. Daniele Archibugi, David Held, and Martin Kohler (Stanford: Stanford University Press, 1998), 28–57.

2. John Keane, *Democracy and Civil Society: On the Predicaments of European Socialism, the Prospects for Democracy, and the Problem of Controlling Social and Political Power* (London: Verso, 1998).

3. John Keane, *Civil Society: Old Images, New Visions* (Stanford: Stanford University Press, 1998).

4. Dominique Colas, *Civil Society and Fanaticism: Conjoined Histories,* trans. Amy Jacobs (Stanford: Stanford University Press, 1997).

5. Harold J. Berman, *Law and Revolution: The Formation of the Western Legal Tradition* (Cambridge: Harvard University Press, 1983); Karl Lowith, *Meaning in History* (Chicago: University of Chicago Press, 1949); David F. Noble, *The Religion of Technology: The Divinity of Man and the Spirit of Invention* (New York: Knopf, 1997); Carl Schmitt, *Political Theology: Four Chapters on the Concept of Sovereignty,* trans, George Schwab (Cambridge: MIT Press, 1985; originally published in German, 1922); and Lynn White Jr., *Medieval Religion and Technology: Collected Essays* (Berkeley and Los Angeles: University of California Press, 1978).

6. Friedrich A. Hayek, *The Constitution of Liberty* (Chicago: University of Chicago Press, 1960).

7. For example, George Gilder, *Life after Television* (New York: Norton, 1992).

8. Mitra Barun Sarkar, Brian Butler, and Charles Steinfield, "Intermediaries and Cyber-mediaries: A Continuing Role for Mediating Players in the Electronic Marketplace," *Journal of Computer-Mediated Communication* 1, no. 3 (1995); and Daniel F. Spulber, *Market Microstructure: Intermediaries and the Theory of the Firm* (Cambridge: Cambridge University Press, 1999).

9. Mark Casson, *Information and Organization: A New Perspective on the Theory of the Firm* (Oxford: Oxford University Press, 1997).

10. Daniel J. Elazar, *Constitutionalizing Globalization: The Postmodern Revival of Confederal Arrangements* (Lanham, Md.: Rowman and Littlefield, 1998).

11. John R. Commons, *Legal Foundations of Capitalism* (New York: Macmillan, 1924), *Institutional Economics: Its Place in Political Economy* (Madison: University of Wisconsin Press, 1934), and *The Economics of Collective Action* (Madison: University of Wisconsin Press, 1970; originally published 1950).

12. For example, Steven G. Medema, Nicholas Mercuro, and Warren J. Samuels, "Institutional Law and Economics," in *Encyclopedia of Law and Economics,* ed. Boudewijn Bouckaert and Gerrit de Geest (Cheltenham, England: Edward Elgar, 1999), 418–455.

13. For example, Geoffrey M. Hodgson, *Economics and Utopia: Why the Learning Economy Is Not the End of History* (London: Routledge, 1999).

14. Commons, *Economics of Collective Action,* 23–28.

15. Commons, *Legal Foundations of Capitalism.*

16. Commons, *Economics of Collective Action,* 30–31.

17. Lawrence Lessig, *Code and Other Laws of Cyberspace* (New York: Basic Books, 1999).

18. Madeline Akrich, "The De-scription of Technical Objects," in *Shaping Technology / Building Society: Studies in Sociotechnical Change,* ed. Wiebe E. Bikjern and John Law (Cambridge: MIT Press, 1992), 205–224; William Dutton, *Society on the Line: Information Politics in the Digital Age* (Oxford: Oxford University Press, 1999); Mark Poster, "Databases as Discourse, or, Electronic Interpellations," in *Computers, Surveillance, and Privacy,* ed. David Lyon and Elia Zureik (Minneapolis: University of Minnesota Press, 1996), 175–192; and Joel R. Reidenberg, "Lex Informatica: The Formulation of Information Policy Rules through Technology," *Texas Law Review* 76, no. 3 (1998): 553–593.

19. Philip E. Agre, "Designing Genres for New Media," in *Cybersociety 2.0: Revisiting CMC and Community,* ed. Steven G. Jones (Newbury Park, Calif.: Sage, 1998), 69–99.

20. Commons, *Economics of Collective Action,* 33.

6 Reports of the Close Relationship between Democracy and the Internet May Have Been Exaggerated

Douglas Schuler

A Platform for Change?

At a recent conference in Germany the question of the Internet as a "platform for change" received top billing. Although the rapidly expanding worldwide communication infrastructure may very well become a platform for change, it is far from obvious what the nature of the change will be. Different people have different things to say. If we listen to cyberpundits, the digerati, we will learn that in the future things will be really great, really exciting, really cool. We will also learn that the Net will be "immensely democratic" and, incidentally, there will be no need for government support, or, for that matter, government at all.

These views are dangerously simplistic. Certainly there is potential for wider democratic participation using the new medium. For the first time in human history, the possibility exists to establish a communication network that spans the globe, is affordable, and is open to all comers and points of view: in short, a democratic communication infrastructure. Unfortunately, the communication infrastructure of the future may turn out to be almost entirely broadcast, where the few (mostly governments and large corporations) will act as gatekeepers for the many, where elites can speak and the rest can only listen. (Even if the "Daily Me," the end-user-defined, totally individualized news services that Sunstein warns about in *Republic.com* become widely available, the services and information they provide are still likely to be owned and operated by big business.)[1] A decade ago commercial content was barred from the Internet; now an estimated 90 percent of all Web pages are for financial gain. In the mid-1990s the media were filled with talk about "electronic democracy," an idea that now seems quaint and antiquated in the e-commerce stampede. The future infrastructure will likely focus on entertainment and that which brings in the most revenue—sex, violence, special effects—and devote little attention to services that educate, inspire, or help bring communities together.

Responsive government, at least in theory, should be the best ally that citizens have in shaping an information and communication infrastructure that effectively meets human needs. This realization, however, may come too late for it to be of much use. Government has already ceded much of the leadership role it once had and does not seem overly interested in exploring new avenues for democratic participation. At a conference at the Massachusetts Institute of Technology, for example, devoted to democracy and the Internet, Ira Magaziner, the White House's head Internet advisor, extolled the virtues of e-commerce; not a single word was wasted on democracy. In the next few years the large telecommunications and media corporations are likely to gain control of nearly all aspects of the Internet and the technologies that arise from it. The strong, unified voice from citizens, activist organizations, nonprofits, libraries, and other groups that is required to promote a proactive government approach is unlikely to develop. Unfortunately the multitudes of smaller efforts are unlikely to coalesce with the necessary strength and speed to counter effectively the colonization of the Net by commercial forces.

Communication technology could undoubtedly play a major role in supporting the critical decisions related to the environment and social conflicts with which humankind will be faced in the years ahead. Because of the massive resources that corporations can bring to bear, new communication technology will probably reinforce and bolster existing patterns of ownership and control, reiterating the historical pattern that we have seen within (and outside of) the United States with other media.[2] On the other hand, the possibility, though remote, that new communication technology could be used to reorient the fulcrum of control by promoting a more democratic and inclusive dialogue does exist. New communication technology could provide forums for voices that have long been ignored: women's voices, voices of the poor, minorities, disabled people. And it could be used to enable communities to have a deeper involvement in their own health, education, and civic decisions. Moreover, the new communication technology could help relieve strains on government by unleashing the creativity and civic problem–solving capabilities of people and communities. To understand how we might begin actually to realize some of these possibilities, let us look more closely at what we mean by democracy.

Elements of Democracy

Democracy is not a commodity like shampoo or dog food. One doesn't buy it at a shopping mall or discover it nicely wrapped in pretty paper, a gift from the government or the technology gods. It is more like a philosophy, a way of life, and a lens for addressing social concerns. It is less like a noun and more like a verb, an active—not a passive—verb. Democracy is notoriously difficult to define; even among scholars there is no agreement on an exact definition. Nearly everybody, however, agrees on its basic attributes.[3] The first of these attributes is inclusivity. This means, that everybody can participate and, in theory, that those with more money than others should not be able to purchase more influence with their money, either directly or indirectly. It also means that society needs to examine closely the ways in which people participate in public decision making (at community meetings, for example) and help ensure that those ways don't favor the privileged. Second, there must be ways in which citizens can place their concerns on the public agenda. If the public agenda is monopolized and manipulated by corporations, politicians, or the media, for example, democracy is seriously imperiled. Third, democracy requires a deliberative public process. This statement involves three critical ideas: deliberative—adequate time must be allotted for hearing and considering multiple points of view; public—the discussion must take place in the daylight where it can be observed by all; and process—the procedures through which concerns are brought up, discussed and acted upon must be clear and widely known. Fourth, there needs to be equality at the decision stage. At some point in the process, the measure under consideration is accepted or rejected by a vote in which all those who are entitled to vote have equal influence. Finally, representation is usually part of a modern democracy, because of the impracticality of involving extremely large numbers of people in a legislative process. Incidentally, in a democracy, such a representative approach can be changed, by the will of the people, into a system that is more "direct" or, even, into one that is less direct. The existence of the Internet does little to obviate the need for representation. Imagine the complexity, confusion, and chaos if every citizen of a large country (or even a small city) were expected to propose, consider, discuss, and vote on legislation. We'd certainly get a lot more e-mail!

A system of government without active participation from the people is not a democracy, no matter how enlightened or benign the de facto guardians might be. If democracy is not championed and exercised by the people, it atrophies like a muscle that is never stressed. But what forces promote participation and which ones discourage it? Democratic participation in the United States, according to most indicators, has been steadily declining for several decades,[4] and many observers feel that this is at least partially due to the concentration of media ownership in private hands. Citizen participation must be encouraged, not merely tolerated, by the government. Without an active governmental role, it is likely that the decline in democratic participation will continue. But democracy can't be imposed from above. Democracy must be a partnership between the governed and the governing, a partnership with blurred and negotiated lines of responsibility, but a partnership nonetheless. Although many people within governments may never have given this matter much thought, all of these observations have important and immediate implications for proactive government involvement in the development and management of new democratic digital networked systems.

Democracy and the Internet

Technological utopians and cyberlibertarian pundits often ascribe near-magical qualities to the Internet. George Gilder, for example, said at the 1997 Camden Conference on Telecommunications that the Internet is "inherently" democratic (although, ironically, he believes that any government intervention would thwart this). On the other hand Gilder believes that television is inherently undemocratic and that there is nothing (especially government action!) that could possibly be done about that. Ideologically fogged fantasies aside, even a cursory glance reveals that the Internet is far from democratic, given the attributes of democracy discussed in the last section: Virtually none of democracy's basic attributes are present.

Unfortunately, the situation seems to be deteriorating. Although Internet usage is still wildly accelerating, much of its use is passive: Surfing the Web is often as idle and compulsive as surfing on television. Moreover, new users are drawn mostly from the upper economic brackets, resulting in a "digital divide" between those who effectively use electronic media and those who hardly know they exist.[5] The use of the Internet among those in the bottom economic fifth has hardly budged in the last decade. People in this quintile do not generally have computers at home, nor have they received the specialized training or free access that businesspeople and university attendees have historically enjoyed.

There are many demonstrations of the democratic impulse on the Internet, yet few demonstrations of democratic processes. Activists, for example, are forming transnational advocacy networks in record numbers.[6] The number of oppositional Web sites[7] and independent media using the Internet is also raising rapidly. At the same time fundamental misunderstanding is rampant: People typically equate and confuse open and undirected discussion with "democracy" (in, say, Usenet newsgroups). Democracy requires democratic processes, yet aside from electronic voting, there has been little research in the area of deliberation on the Internet. Henry Robert took nearly forty years to devise his rules of order, which enable people in face-to-face meetings to raise issues, discuss and debate alternatives, and make decisions collectively in an open, orderly manner.[8] His system, in everyday use by associative bodies both small and great all over the world, by no means guarantees that the decisions will be the best or that everybody will be happy with the outcome. The process guarantees only that there will be an opportunity for each person present to participate on an even footing.

It is important to realize that there is nothing inherently democratic about Internet technology; both radio or television could have been shaped into media systems that were more strongly democratic, yet this potential was largely ignored and swept aside as economic and legal policies that favored private use and control were enacted. The American taxpayer who paid for the initial Internet was never consulted on the possible directions it could take; all of the major decisions involving the development, deployment, or use of the Internet were made in a public-participation vacuum. In fact, it almost appears that many of these decisions were made with uncharacteristic speed so as to avoid public input, public input that might in fact raise uncomfortable questions about social uses or public ownership. Is it too late to think about shaping the Internet to make it support more humanistic ends?

Democratic Communication Technology

Currently all over the world there are an astonishing number of grassroots projects in the area of democratic communication technology. Not only are these projects evidence of an overdue renewal of interest in democracy, but they suggest that now is the time for a concerted effort to weave these projects, heretofore disconnected, into a tapestry of compelling strength and creativity.

Rainy City Projects

In this section, I focus on projects in a single city in order to show the richness and popularity of this new type of activism. Seattle may have more of these projects than many other cities,[9] but similar projects are being organized all over the world. (The recent Technology Opportunities Program [TOP] awards granted by the U.S. Commerce Department's National Telecommunications and Information Agency <http://www.ntia.doc.gov/otiahome/top/> showcase the diversity and creativity of these projects in the states. These projects can track their origins from many sources, including city government, grassroots activism, academia, and libraries, and many are the result of new collaborations and coalitions.) Although I have listed the projects below according to certain categories, this is not a rigid or exhaustive way to describe these projects, and many of the projects fall under two or more categories. Also please note that this list is far from exhaustive; ONE/NW, N*Power, and other important and innovative projects haven't been included.)

University Collaboration   There is apparently a renewed interest within academia in projects related to media and democracy. The Trust in Government project at the University of Washington was a good example. More recently, Andrew and Margaret Gordon led the Public Access Computing Project to evaluate the Bill and Melinda Gates Foundation's effort to bridge the digital divide. There are, of course, thousands of interesting possibilities in this area. I've described some of the many important opportunities that I see for increased academia-community collaboration elsewhere.[10]

Community Activism   There are a number of community activism projects in Seattle that use communication technology. Community activist Anthony Williams launched Project Compute to establish access to computer equipment, network services, and training programs in a low-income neighborhood community center. Several projects including Mary's Place at the First Methodist Church, Real Change's Empowerment Project, and Jubilee all have offered training and access specifically for homeless women. Other projects have also been started to work with Southeast Asians, East Africans, and other ethnic and migrant groups.

Free Public Networks   Loosely based on the FreeNet model, which was itself loosely based on the public-library model, the Seattle Community Network (SCN) <http://www.scn.org> is the best example of a free public computer network in Seattle. Offering free e-mail, mail lists, Web siting, and other Internet services to anybody (currently over 13,000 registered users) and computer training and support to community organizations, SCN, working in conjunction with the Seattle Public Library, is striving to remove barriers to access to communication technology. SCN, unlike most community networks, has developed a strong set of principles below that are intended to institutionalize the democratic objectives upon which it was founded.

Seattle Community Network Principles   The Seattle Community Network (SCN) is a free public-access computer network for exchanging and accessing information. Beyond that, however, it is a service conceived for community empowerment. Our principles are a series of commitments to help guide the ongoing development and management of the system for both the organizers and participating individuals and organizations.

Commitment to Access

Access to the SCN will be free to all.

We will provide access to all groups of people particularly those without ready access to information technology.

We will provide access to people with diverse needs. This may include special-purpose interfaces.

We will make the SCN accessible from public places.

Commitment to Service

The SCN will offer reliable and responsive service.

We will provide information that is timely and useful to the community.

We will provide access to databases and other services.

Commitment to Democracy

The SCN will promote participation in government and public dialogue.

The community will be actively involved in the ongoing development of the SCN.

We will place high value in freedom of speech and expression and in the free exchange of ideas.

We will make every effort to ensure privacy of the system users.

We will support democratic use of electronic technology.

Commitment to the World Community

In addition to serving the local community, we will become part of the regional, national and international community.

We will build a system that can serve as a model for other communities.

Commitment to the Future

We will continue to evolve and improve the SCN.

We will explore the use of innovative applications such as electronic town halls for community governance, or electronic encyclopedias for enhanced access to information.

We will work with information providers and with groups involved in similar projects using other media.

We will solicit feedback on the technology as it is used, and make it as accessible and humane as possible.

Community computer networks[11] represent an innovative democratic and community-oriented approach to communication. At a very general level, a community network is a big electronic bulletin board system that provides "one-stop shopping" for information and communication about community-related meetings, projects, events, issues, and organizations. SCN divides its Web site into thirteen basic categories ("Activism," "Arts," "Civil," "Earth," "Education," "Health," "Marketplace," "Neighborhoods," "News," "People," "Recreation," "Sci-Tech," and "Spiritual"), and there is a wide variety of diversity within each section. Community networks are free to use, and free public-access terminals are part of the community network vision. In addition to providing a convenient repository for information, these networks offer new participatory opportunities for community dialogue. Such dialogues can be used to explore community concerns, debate issues, build support networks, or discuss cats, dogs, children, parents, sports, computers, or any topic that people care to talk about. Although SCN has pledged, through its principles, to continue to evolve new technology and applications, it is, in fact, rarely able to do so. Keeping the system operational with an all-volunteer workforce and very little funding is very difficult, and many community networks and FreeNets have quietly stopped operations within the last few years.

More recently, the Seattle Wireless project <http://www.seattlewireless.net/> has been launched to provide another type of community network in Seattle. This project is using widely available, license-free technology based on the recently developed IEEE 802.11b standard (the standard wireless Ethernet networking protocol) to develop a free "metropolitan area network" in Seattle. Where this project will be in a year or so is anybody's guess, but it does help highlight the interest in bridging technological and social realms.

Government Programs Although the government needs to be more proactive in this area, it has not been totally inactive. The city government in Seattle, for example, is pushing in several directions. The Seattle Public Library provides public-access terminals in all its branch libraries. The city also runs the a Web site <http://www.pan.ci.seattle.wa.us/>, which provides extensive information on city agencies and city issues. People involved in the PAN project also work with community groups to help them develop in-house expertise and an electronic presence. The city also runs the Seattle Channel <http://www.seattlechannel.org/> (channels 21 and 28), which helps inform Seattle citizens about their government by developing its own content as well as broadcasting council and committee meetings over cable and via the Web. Ironically, whereas cities to the north and south are developing innovative services, Seattle's Department of Administration Services has ignored the city council's 1999 resolution to develop a feasibility study for a municipally owned communication infrastructure.

Community Research   One of the most intriguing possibilities that the Web medium offers is community research in which community members develop and implement research projects that they themselves have deemed relevant to their lives. The Sustainable Seattle project <http://www.sustainableseattle.org/> developed a set of indicators (including participation in the arts, wild salmon population, voting rates, and many others) that provide useful data regarding Seattle's "sustainability" over time. The project has launched electronic "forums" on SCN and has also put a great deal of available information on SCN to help Seattleites (as well as people in other locations: "Sustainable Penang" in Malaysia, for example) get involved with similar projects.

Independent Media   Students of U.S. history are aware of the importance of independent media for social change. There might not even be a United States without Tom Paine and his fellow pamphleteers. The Web currently is a natural haven for independent media, both as an adjunct to existing print media and as the sole publishing medium. *Real Change* <http://www.realchange.org>, *Washington Free Press* <http://www.speakeasy.org/wfp>, Eat the State <http://www.eatthestate.org>, and other Seattle-based periodicals are currently using the Web to complement their other work.

Public Advisory Boards   Seattle established a Citizen's Telecommunications and Technology Advisory Board (CTTAB) <http://www.pan.ci.seattle.wa.us/seattle/cttab> in 1995 to help advise the city on a wide range of communication technology issues, including public-access television, the city-government channel, citizen access to city government and to other electronic services, and citizen technology literacy in general. CTTAB has helped launch several innovative projects, including the Citizens Literacy and Access Fund, which provides matching funds to community technology projects and the Information Technology Indicators for a Healthy Community project,[12] which drew its inspiration from the Sustainable Seattle project mentioned above. The original idea was to learn what people in Seattle think about technology (including their apprehensions and fears) instead of just gathering basic facts (how many people access the Internet through work, etc.). Under pressure from the business community and areas within Seattle's government, the project may ultimately turn into a mere survey. In fact, there is increasing tension between some of the citizens on the CTTAB and the city, which believes that it should retain unwavering and final authority over the project.

Internet Cafes and Other Public Technology Centers   Until it burned down in May 2001, the Speakeasy Cafe <http://www.speakeasy.net/cafe> was the most successful Internet cafe in Seattle. Offering an informal atmosphere with food, drink, inexpensive Internet access, poetry readings, and art exhibits, the Speakeasy was an excellent example of how technology can be integrated with other community functions. There are other Internet cafes in Seattle and several projects in community centers. There are also several community computer centers set up in subsidized housing as part of the U.S. Department of Housing and Urban Development's Neighborhood Network program <http://www.hud.gov>.

Independent Media Centers   The Seattle Independent Media Center (IMC) <http://seattle.indymedia.org/> was established in the wake of the anti–World Trade Organization demonstrations of 1999. Since then it has served as a locus for a number of left or progressive media activities, including film screenings, discussions, and Webcast news from all over the world. The Seattle IMC currently serves as the backbone for a network of over eighty independent media centers worldwide. It was recently the center of an FBI raid in which the agents demanded all user connection logs (containing individual internet protocol [IP] addresses of over 1.25 million journalists, readers and technical volunteers) from IMC Web servers during the Free Trade Area of the Americas (FTAA) protests in Quebec City (April 20 and 21, 2001). The IMC refused to comply with the demand, and the FBI later dropped the case, but the lack of attention paid to the incident by the two Seattle daily newspapers, the *Seattle Times* and the *Seattle Post-Intelligencer,* was disheartening.

Conferences   Conferences and symposia are another type of "media" in which people can discuss common concerns. There have been several conferences in Seattle related to the democratization of information and communication technology. These include two Computer Professionals for Social Responsibility (CPSR) conferences: "Participatory Design" and "Shaping the Network Society," which were the seventh and eighth Directions and Implications of Advanced Computing (DIAC) symposia. At the 2000 DIAC symposium, the Seattle Statement <http://diac.cpsr.org/diac-00/seattle-statement.shtml> calling for a new public sphere was developed. CPSR's Public Sphere Project

(PSP) <http://www.scn.org/sphere>, devoted to extending the public sphere in cyberspace, was also a product of that symposium. The 2002 DIAC symposium was devoted to "Patterns for Participation, Action, and Change" <http://www.cpsr.org/conferences/diac02/>, and a participatory pattern language project that elicited 170 or so pattern proposals was further developed in concert with the symposium <http://www.cpsr.org/program/sphere/patterns/>.

Other Public Media   There are also other types of access programs, such as public-access television (channel 29). Radio station KSER in Lynnwood, north of Seattle, offers a wide range of community programming. Also, for a brief time, there was a lot of excitement over the prospects of noncommercial low-power (community) FM radio in the United States because of an FCC recommendation to allocate spectra for that purpose. Unfortunately, bowing to pressure from the National Association of Broadcasters (and, pathetically, the Public Broadcasting System), the Clinton administration overrode that recommendation. Both Free Seattle Radio and Black Ball Radio have been broadcasting over Seattle (illegally) and Webcasting all over the world (legally) sporadically over the last couple of years. And last but not least, realizing that the telephone may be the easiest and most commonly used two-way communication technology, the Community Voice Mail program <http://www.cvm.org/> has helped set up programs in thirty-five cities all over the United States to provide over 30,000 homeless and phoneless clients with free voice mail to help them to locate jobs, contact support services, and stay in touch with family and friends.

These projects, like democracy itself, are a complex social phenomenon and consequently promote democracy in a number of different ways:

1. raising issues about control of technology and access
2. supporting independent media
3. supporting civic associations
4. supporting civic assets (schools and nonprofit organizations, for example)
5. educating people about issues and about technology use
6. sponsoring public forums on civic and other issues
7. providing access to government, candidate, and referendum information and issues
8. providing communication channels to government workers

9. engaging in political work (organizing a rally in opposition to the U.S. Communications Decency Act, for example)

10. providing access to relevant data and other pertinent information and knowledge

11. promoting computer and network literacy through free-access systems

12. providing access to civic "stories"[13] analogous to "citizen schools" of the civil rights movement

In general, these projects provide important "existence proofs" that demonstrate that democracy in cyberspace is not an oxymoron and that it can be an important civic institution that deserves support.

Roles of Government and Community

It is the case, particularly as demonstrated in Scandinavia, that government can provide an effective vehicle for mitigating social hardships. Now there is increasing evidence that the conditions under which this is true (namely, competent and responsive government, adequate resources, and popular support) may not be holding: governments around the world are retreating from many of their previously shouldered social responsibilities. Although this trend may be not be as inexorable and inevitable as it is sometimes portrayed as being, it seems prudent to consider briefly the proper roles of government and the citizenry.

It is obvious that even under the benign eye of the hypothetically most concerned and custodial government, there are many tasks and enterprises that people and social groups will need to instigate and carry out on their own. The ability of the citizenry to address social challenges could be referred to as "community problem-solving competence" and community work the way to exercise it.

Community work is any activity that helps strengthen any of a community's six core values.[14] These core values (figure 6.1) are mutually interdependent; deficiencies in one area promote deficiencies in others; strengths, also, tend to build strengths in other areas. When U.S. Navy veteran and antiwar activist Country Joe McDonald (with the help of many others) made the names, ranks, and other information of all of Alameda County's (California) military casualties available electronically on Berkeley's "Community Memory"[15] community computer bulletin board system, he was doing community work. When people tutor neighborhood kids, testify to city council on the need for safe streets,

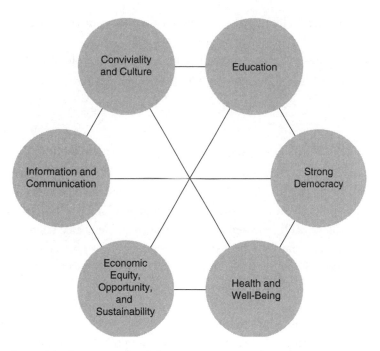

Figure 6.1. Community Core Values

publish an independent newspaper, help paint a day-care center, organize a rent strike, or start a farmer's market or neighborhood garden, they're all doing community work.

   With some provisos regarding specific principles and practices, it is clear that the stronger a community's problem-solving competence, the less need there would be for government intervention in that community. This does not imply that government competence and community competence sum to a constant, such that a decline in one means an increase in the other. On the contrary, some societies will be strong in both, whereas others, sadly, will be deficient in both. In fact, increasing the effectiveness of community work is important even if government competence is high. (And increasing community problem-solving competence may even lead to increased government competence.) In any case, strengthened community problem-solving competence is necessary, not just to compensate in cases of diminished government involvement, but to guide the future of government involvement even where government involvement is strong. In other words the community should play a substantial part in any change in the role of government in that community, even if this means flouting the conventional wisdom of the digerati. Finally, it is important to point out that increasing community problem-solving competence (through supporting community networks, for example) is a critical role of a democratic government, regardless of what that government is doing in other areas.

Actions for the Future

Clearly communication is at the heart of any democratic revitalization, and communication in the modern age necessarily implies communication *technology*. We therefore need to devise and implement projects that integrate democracy and communication technology. Projects that are not consciously and synergistically connected to other projects are unlikely to be influential, as they are likely to remain marginalized and unnoticed. An interwoven tapestry of democratic technology projects that is part of a broad social movement is required for any substantial and long-lived transformation to occur. Only if large numbers of people are involved in the movement is there any realistic hope for increased democratization. And only if there is a heightened awareness and a sense of necessity and opportunity can any major change and reorientation occur.

The key to the goal of democratizing cyberspace is not to cling blindly to simplistic technocratic or libertarian platitudes. Although the Internet as "platform for change" may ultimately be dominated by a handful of corporate interests (as are the rest of the media), there are scores of opportunities for communities that want to develop communication systems that are open, equitable, and useful. Communities need to develop such systems and at the same time fight for policies that strengthen public media.

The future begins today. We begin with a vision of the future—of democracy and of community and of increased human actualization—but also with the reality of the present, which includes people, programs, institutions, policies, and technology whose objectives and strategies are often at odds. Therefore, of necessity, our work involves new collaborations and coalitions. Community groups must find common cause with many groups including academia, labor, environmental groups, political parties, government, and, where appropriate, business, if there is to be any hope of developing genuinely democratic media. It will be helpful to look at what people are doing in Seattle and in other places, but these are only the first steps.

The future is not preordained, and we know that the shape that a technology ultimately assumes depends on many factors. For that reason, activists for democratic technology must work together if there is any hope of developing democratic space in cyberspace. It won't be easy. But as abolitionist Frederick Douglass reminds us, "Without struggle, there is no progress." I urge you all to enter the struggle for democratic media. The stakes are high: This may be our best and last chance.

Notes

1. C. Sunstein, *Republic.com* (Princeton: Princeton University Press, 2001).

2. B. Bagdikian, *The Media Monopoly* (Boston: Beacon, 1992).

3. See, for example, R. Dahl, *Democracy and Its Critics* (New Haven: Yale University Press, 1989).

4. M. Castells, *The Power of Identity* (Malden, Mass.: Blackwell, 1997).

5. T. Novak and D. Hoffman, "Bridging the Digital Divide: The Impact of Race on Computer Use and Internet Access" (1998), available online at <http://www.2000.ogsm.vanderbilt.edu/papers/race/science.html>; and U.S. Department of Commerce, "Falling through the Net: Defining the Digital Divide" (1999), available online at <http://www.ntia.doc.gov/ntiahome/fttn99/contents.html>.

6. M. Keck and K. Sikkink, *Activists beyond Borders: Advocacy Networks in International Politics* (Ithaca, N.Y.: Cornell University Press, 1998).

7. H. Cleaver, "The Zapatista Effect: The Internet and the Rise of an Alternative Political Effect" (1997), available online at http://www.eco.utexas.edu/faculty/Cleaver/zapeffect.html>.

8. H. Robert, *Robert's Rules of Order,* rev. ed. (New York: William Morrow, 1971).

9. See L. Servon, *Bridging the Digital Divide: Community, Technology, and Public Policy* (Malden, Mass.: Blackwell, 2002), for more in-depth reporting on this.

10. D. Schuler, *New Community Networks: Wired for Change* (Reading, Mass.: Addison-Wesley, 1996), "Community Computer Networks: An Opportunity for Collaboration among Democratic Technology Practitioners and Researchers," in *Proceedings of Technology and Democracy: Comparative Perspectives,* ed. D. Hakken and K. Maukelid (Oslo: Centre for Technology and Culture [TMV], 1997), 53–71, and "Computer Professionals and the Next Culture of Democracy," *Communications of the ACM* (January 2001): 52–57.

11. Schuler, *New Community Networks.*

12. City of Seattle, Department of Information Technology, "Information Technology Indicators for a Healthy Community" (2000), available online at <http://www.ci.seattle.us/tech/indicators.htm>.

13. C. Sirianni, L. Friedland and D. Schuler, "The New Citizenship and the Civic Practices Network (CPN)," ed. S. Cisler, *Ties That Bind: Converging Communities* (Cupertino: Apple Computer Corp. Library, 1995). See <http://www.cpn.org>, for example.

14. Schuler, *New Community Networks.*

15. C. Farrington and E. Pine, "Community Memory: A Case Study in Community Communication," in *Reinventing Technology, Rediscovering Community: Critical Explorations of Computing as a Social Practice,* ed. P. Agre and D. Schuler (Norwood, N.J.: Ablex, 1997), 219–227.

7 Are Virtual and Democratic Communities Feasible?

Amitai Etzioni

This chapter asks whether communities and democracy can thrive in the new world, in cyberspace. Answering this question requires a two-step examination. First, can there be virtual communities? Second, if so, can these—and other (including offline) communities—govern themselves in a democratic way by drawing on new developments in cyberspace?

Communities On and Off

Communities Defined

The very term "community" has often been criticized as denoting a concept that is vague and elusive, as a term that either has not been defined or cannot be defined, and as one that is used because of its political appeal rather than its scholarly merit.[1] In response one should note, first of all, that terms commonly used in social science often resist precise definition, as in the case of such widely used concepts as "rationality" and "class." And although "community" has often been used without an explicit definition, I have previously suggested the following definition. Communities are social entities that have two elements: one, a web of affect-laden relationships among a group of individuals, relationships that often criss-cross and reinforce one another (rather than merely one-on-one or chainlike individual relationships); the other, a measure of commitment to a set of shared values, norms, and meanings, and a shared history and identity—in short, to a particular culture.[2]

Among those who have responded to this definition of community, Benjamin Zablocki noted that although the definition is quite clear, few communities left in modern societies meet its requirements.[3] This is a common concern that has been with us since Emile Durkheim and Ferdinand Tönnies suggested that modern history is marked by a transition from Gemeinschaft to Gesselschaft. Others have viewed our society as a "mass" society composed of individuals without shared bonds or values. Actually, although there has been a decline in community, many social entities that fit the definition provided above abound even in large metropolitan areas. These communities are often ethnicity based, such as those found in Little Havana, Chinatowns, Koreatown, Spanish Harlem, on the south shore of Boston, and in Williamsburg, New York, among many others. Other communities are composed of people who share a sexual orientation (for instance, gay communities) or an occupation (for instance, the medical staff of some hospitals).

Important for the discussion that follows is that communities, as defined, need not be local or residential. The faculty members of some small colleges make a community even if they do not live next door to one another or on the campus. The same holds for the members of a labor-union local.

The definition excludes interest groups, however. Groups of people who merely share an interest in lower tariffs, in gaining a tax deduction, and so on, as a rule do not a community make. They share no affective bonds and no moral culture. (Of course, some social entities can both be a community and share some interests, but this does not negate the difference between these two concepts.) In short, communities can be defined and are far from defunct.

Are There Virtual Communities?

Many of those who argue that there can be no true communities in cyberspace implicitly follow a different notion as to what a community is than the one relied upon here (which, in my judgment, is quite close to what most people mean when they employ the term). These critics of virtual communities have in mind numerous accidental rather than essential features of offline communities, such as face-to-face meetings. One should grant that online communities do not have all the features of offline ones (nor do offline communities have all the features of online ones). But the question is, can cyberspace meet the basic prerequisites of communities?[4]

The answer is affirmative, although one must grant that the prerequisites are not often provided, at least not in full. Indeed, there is a distinct inclination by commercial sites to pretend that community exists (because such claims bring "eyeballs" to one's site) where there is none. To provide but one example, GeoCities purports to provide "neighborhoods" and "neighborhood clubs" within its "community," but these neighborhoods simply amount to collections of home pages and chat rooms that are about the same topic (for instance, "Sunset Strip" is a "neighborhood" of home pages and chat rooms devoted to the discussion of rock and punk rock).

More generally, a very large part of the communications and transactions on the Internet either are not interactive at all (e.g., placing an order for a consumer product) or are only point to point (e.g., exchange of e-mail messages), so that by themselves they do not make communities. In 1998, according to a survey conducted by the Pew Center for the People and the Press, the following percentages of online users engaged in the following activities at least once a week: 72 percent sent e-mail, 47 percent did research for work, and 38 percent got news on current events, public issues, and politics. Far fewer users participated in online group activities. Only 22 percent engaged in online forums or chat groups, and only 4 percent engaged in online political discussions.[5] A recent Gallup poll provided similar results, reporting that 95 percent of people online use the Internet to obtain information, 85 percent to send or receive e-mail, and 45 percent for shopping, whereas only 21 percent visit chat rooms.[6]

But all that these facts show is that, just as with offline interactions, the greater part of online interactions are not community focused. They do not indicate that communities cannot be formed over the Internet.

There are numerous informal accounts of strong affective bonds, the first element of communities, that have been formed via the Internet as people who did not previously know one another meet on the Internet and form intense relationships. There are a fair number of reports of people who abandon their spouses on the basis of liaisons they have formed online, and some of singles who met in cyberspace and married.

The second element, forming a shared moral culture, is much less often encountered. At first, it may seem that chat rooms could provide opportunities for developing such a culture (as well as affective bonds), because at first glance they bear some resemblance to communities: Groups of people meet and interact. The main reason, in my judgment, that the hundreds of thousands of chat rooms that exist do not, as a rule, provide for shared cultures (or affective bonds) has to do with the way they are set up. Typically, chat room participants use aliases and are keen to maintain their anonymity. Exchanges are very brief and intersected by other exchanges that occur in the same "space." Participants tend to engage in very limited exchanges and often engage in a false presentation of self.[7] As a result, piecing together a picture of the person with whom one deals, which may well be a prerequisite for forming shared values (as well as affective relationships), is hampered. The situation is akin to meeting someone for the first time on a bar stool or on an airplane flight. Conversation tends to be superficial, and no relationship develops.[8]

The conditions under which virtual communities would thrive are, in effect, the mirror opposite of chat rooms: Membership would be limited in number and relatively stable; members would have to disclose their true identities, which would be verified. In addition, the subjects explored would cover a broad range rather than be limited to a few such as stock tips or dating-related banter. The fact that so far these conditions are infrequently satisfied should not be viewed as suggesting that they cannot be met; it merely suggests that they do not readily lend themselves to profit making (and hence are of little interest to those who run chat rooms on the Internet) and that they conflict with the individualistic ideologies of those who originally shaped the Internet.

Although the stated conditions for successful community building are rarely satisfied in full by such chat rooms, some are met via thousands of so-called clubs run by Yahoo, Excite, and eCircles. Membership in these clubs is limited to a given number (say, 2,000). In some, one needs to apply to become a member. Although many of these clubs are listed in indexes maintained on the respective Web sites, one can refuse to list a club to protect it from open-ended participation.

At the same time, these clubs do not provide for disclosure of self or verified identity. In addition, the topics in which they specialize are often quite narrow and limited. Examples of Excite clubs include "Amateur Astronomers" (1,159 members), "Amateur Models of Virginia" (1,046 members), and "The Homebrewing Club" (340 members).

ECircles has a more personal focus than other online club sites. It provides families and friends with private areas within cyberspace in which to meet and exchange messages and is less interest- or issue-based. H-net runs some eighty "clubs" that fully meet the stated conditions for communities: Not only is participation in the clubs limited, but identities are disclosed. (Granted the subjects under discussion are rather specialized, such as French literature in one club and certain periods of German history in another.) So far there are no studies of the community-building effects of these clubs, although personal observation suggests that they are considerably stronger than those of the typical chat rooms.

MediaMOO has been occasionally referred to as a true online community, although the extent to which it lives up to this description is unclear.[9] Howard Rheingold's accounts of online communities are often cited as examples of the possibility of developing close relationships and a rich emotional life online. For instance, Rheingold describes an online funeral he attended as a "rite of passage for all of [the virtual community] CIX, a time when the original members of the group felt closest to each other."[10] According to Rheingold, there were strong affective bonds among group members, and there was a shared group history and culture (i.e, the group Rheingold describes qualifies as a real community according to the definition of community I proposed above).

Finally, one should also not overlook that some online communities work to complement and reinforce existing offline communities. (I refer to these as "hybrid communities.") There is something artificial about the very way the question is typically posed, comparing virtual to other communities. After all, nobody lives in cyberspace; even the avatars in Neal Stephenson's Snow Crash are put on by three-dimensional people. The more realistic questions that arise concern community (and democracy) in a new world in which there are both on- and offline group relationships. (Rheingold, who is a firm believer in the depth of online relationships and community, nevertheless describes how his online relationships often led to face-to-face meetings and friendships.)

Among the reports of neighborhood communities significantly reinforced by virtual links is the often-cited example of Blacksburg, Virginia. Around 87 percent of Blacksburg's residents are online,[11] and the town has an online community called Blacksburg Electronic Village <www.bev.net>. Both the town and the various groups and neighborhoods in it benefit from their ability to post meetings, share information, and interact via the shared site.

All said and done, there are very few reports of full-fledged purely online communities. It is rather difficult to establish whether the reason for this finding is that the Internet has not been set up to facilitate community building despite the fact that this could be quite readily done, or (as several have argued) that there is something in the structure of the Internet that inherently prevents true community formation. I personally hold that communities would thrive on the Internet if stable and disclosed membership were made relatively easy to attain, but this remains to be demonstrated. There is, though, little doubt that online communities can significantly reinforce offline ones.

Quantitative Data

The discussion so far has focused on so-called qualitative observations, one case at a time. There is, though, considerable quantitative data concerning the ability to form and to sustain social relations on the Internet. Because these data concern not merely friendships (which can be merely between two people, and are hence point to point) but also families (which contain community-like Web relationships), these data speak to the question of whether one of the key prerequisites of community building can be met online.

The question of whether cyberspace agitates against social bonds or enriches them has been recently examined by several studies. One study, by Norman H. Nie and Lutz Erbring, has claimed to find that the Internet is detrimental to social bonding.[12] According to them, "the more hours people use the Internet, the less time they spend in contact with real human beings."

Nie and Erbring say, "Internet time is coming out of time viewing television but also out at the expense of time people spend on the phone gabbing with family and friends or having a conversation with people in the room with them." They acknowledge that most Internet users use e-mail, which increases their "conversations" with family and friends via this medium, "but you can't share a coffee or a beer with somebody on e-mail or give them a hug." In short, according to a press release from the Stanford Institute for the Qualitative Study of Society, which sponsored Nie and Erbring's research, "the Internet could be the ultimate isolating technology that further reduces our participation in communities even more than did automobiles and television before it."[13] The findings of the study are summarized in table 7.1.

What do Nie and Erbring's figures actually show? In discussing the findings one must note that they concern two groups of people: Those who are not connected to the Internet ($N = 2,078$) and those who are connected ($N = 2,035$). The latter are further divided into light users (less than five hours per week; 64% of the "connected" sample) and heavy users (more than five hours per week; 36% of the "connected" sample). Of all users only 9 percent said that they spend less time with their family, and 9 percent said they spend less with their friends, whereas nearly ten times more people (86 and 87 percent, respectively) said that they spend the same amount of time with family and friends as before! Moreover, quite a few (6 and 4 percent, respectively) reported that they spend more time with family and friends. A more appropriate headline for the news story reporting on their study would have been "Internet Does Not Significantly Affect Social Life."

Table 7.1
Results of Nie and Erbring's study

Of those who use the Internet:

- 13% report that they spend less time with family and friends (than before they went online)
- 8% attend fewer social events
- 34% spend less time reading the newspaper
- 59% spend less time watching television
- 25% spend less time shopping in stores
- 25% are working more time at home (without any decline in work at the office)

Source: Stanford Institute for the Qualitative Study of Society. Results were published in *The New York Times,* February 16, 2000, p. A15.

The picture does not change much even if one focuses on the heavy users. Only 10 percent of those who spend five to ten hours online per week reported that they spend less time with family and friends than before, and only 15 percent of those who are online ten or more hours per week said that that was the case.

The finding that some Internet users spend more time with family and friends may at first seem unlikely, but it is hardly so. The study itself shows that by far the largest effect of Internet activity for all users is to reduce the amount of time spent watching television (46 percent of users) and shopping (19 percent). For heavy users, 59 percent spend less time watching television and 25 percent spend less time shopping. (Obviously it takes less time to order things from eToys or Amazon than to go to a mall or store.) The study did not inquire into how the time saved in these ways is used and whether or not some of it is allocated to increasing social life.

Along the same lines, the study found, as is widely known, that people's most common use of the Internet is communicating via e-mail. This, too, is a time-saving device compared to letter writing and even phone calls. Ergo the Internet readily allows people to spend both more time on the Internet and more time socializing. In effect, the fact that people use the Internet largely for communication (90 percent use e-mail) and not shopping (36 percent buy products online) or banking (12 percent) and that most of this communication is with people with whom they are familiar rather than with strangers strongly suggests that people relate to one another more rather than less because of the Internet.

A study on technology by the Kaiser Family Foundation, National Public Radio, and Harvard's Kennedy School of Government reported a number of interesting findings. Despite their overall positive attitudes, Americans do see some problems with computers and technology, according to the study. More than half say computers have led people to spend less time with their families and friends (58 percent). Furthermore, slightly fewer than half (46 percent) of Americans say that computers have given people less free time, although 24 percent say computers have given people more free time, and 28 percent say computers haven't made much of a difference in the amount of free time people have.[14]

Note, though, that in the Kaiser study, people were asked about computer use, not their Internet connections. The question the participants were asked was, "Do you think the use of computers has given people more free time, less free time, or hasn't it made much difference?" The wording of this question may have made people think about non-interactive uses of their computers, especially word processing, preparing documents, number crunching, and so on. Questions specifically about use of the Internet, which is merely one function of computers, are likely to be more revealing.

A study released in May 2000 by the Pew Internet and American Life Project found clear evidence that e-mail and the Web have enhanced users' relationships with their family and friends, a result that challenges the notion that the Internet contributes to isolation. Significant majorities of online Americans say their use of e-mail has increased the amount of contact they have with key family members and friends. Fifty-nine percent of those who exchange e-mail with a family member say they are in contact with that relative more often thanks to e-mail. Only 2 percent of those who exchange e-mail with a family member say they are in contact less often with this family member since they struck up their e-correspondence. E-mail users say virtually the same thing about the frequency of their contact with close friends via e-letters. Sixty percent of those who e-mail friends say they communicate more often with a key friend now that they use e-mail, and 2 percent say they do so less often.

Additional Pew findings make an even stronger case. As a group, Internet users are more likely than nonusers to have a robust social world. The use of e-mail seems to encourage deeper social connectedness. The longer users have been online, the more likely it is that they feel that e-mail has improved their ties to their families and friends. Forty percent of Internet veterans (those who have been online for at least three years) say there has been a great deal of improvement in their connections with family and friends because of e-mail, compared with just over a quarter of Internet newcomers (those online for six months or less) who report a high degree of improvement in that area.

Even more impressive are the Pew findings that more than those who have no Internet access, Internet users say they have a significant network of helpful relatives and friends. Some 48 percent of Internet users say they can turn to many people for support in a time of need, whereas just 38 percent of nonusers report they have a large social network. Furthermore, only 8 percent of Internet users indicate they are socially isolated; that is, they say they have no one or hardly anyone to whom they can turn for support. In contrast, 18 percent of nonusers say they have no one or hardly anyone to turn to.[15]

Finally, a Harris poll found that, because people are online, they tend to communicate more often with their friends and family. According to the poll, almost half (48 percent) of all adults who are online at home say they communicate more often with friends and family than they did before they could use e-mail. Only 3 percent say they communicate less. Perhaps the most interesting finding is that many more people say that they meet and socialize with friends and family more often because of the Internet than say they do so less often (27 percent vs. 9 percent). This debunks the theory that Internet users cut themselves off physically from social interaction.[16]

All said and done, meaningful and reinforcing interactions seem to be quite common in the online world. Under what conditions these suffice to satisfy the first prerequisite for community remains to be established. As I argued in the previous section, it is possible to create the conditions for forming shared cultures online, but such conditions are not often provided. Call me moderately optimistic on this account. As I see it, the evidence suggests that if the Internet were to be made more community friendly along the lines discussed in the first section, online communities might be much more common.

Communities' Cyberspace Democracy

The same question can be applied to online, offline, and hybrid communities: Can they be democratically governed by drawing on the Internet? For democracy to thrive, at least four prerequisites must be satisfied. Numerous studies show that two key prerequisites, sharing information and voting, are quite feasible on the Internet. The third prerequisite, deliberation, has been much less often explored, but I shall attempt to show below that it seems to pose no insurmountable difficulties, once Internet designers put their mind to fashioning the software needed for deliberation in cyberspace. The same holds for the fourth prerequisite, representation.

Sharing Information

Much has been made in several works on the subject, and even more in numerous projects dedicated to the subject, that information can be distributed, stored, retrieved, duplicated, and illustrated with much greater ease and at much lower costs on the Internet than in the offline world. This is undoubtably true. One should not, however, accord too much importance to information sharing as an element of democratic governance. True, providing voters with all the speeches made by all the candidates in a particular election, a full catalogue of all the positions they have taken in the past and every vote they have cast, is helpful. The same is true of having Web sites chock full of information about current issues.

Voters can cast only one vote per election, however. For instance, in a presidential election, they cannot vote for the environmental policies of a given candidate but against his foreign policy, for his position on reproductive choice but against his ideas about health insurance, and so on. Hence, detailed information about these issues and the positions of the candidates are not particularly useful for their decisions for whom to vote.

Those who suggest that people's decisions take the form of an index, in which they would inform themselves about numerous issues and then vote for the candidate who gets the highest score, do not take into account that, in actuality, decisions typically seem to be made in a lexographic form: Two or three considerations (for instance, the state of the economy and whether or not the country is involved in a war) make up most of the "index" for most voters.

More important, for numerous voters the process is much less information–driven than is quite often assumed. Values, party affiliations and loyalties, and community pressures play a very important role in determining the one choice they can make.

In short, the fabulous information features of the Internet are prodemocratic, but they surely add much less to existing democratic institutions than the more dedicated information enthusiasts presume.[17]

E-voting

Initially there was great concern that voting on the Internet would lead to large-scale ballot box stuffing, fraud, and other forms of electoral abuse. As new encryption techniques have developed, however, and procedures for recognizing e-signatures have been approved, these concerns have subsided. It seems that in the future, with proper procedures in place, e-voting could be made at least as secure as offline voting, which, after all, has never been perfectly authenticated.

The main difficulty in this area lies elsewhere, namely, in access. Democracy, of course, requires that all those who have reached a given age, are citizens of a given polity, and have not been convicted of a crime be allowed to vote. At the moment, significant parts of the population, especially the poorer and otherwise disadvantaged ones, do not have personal computers and hence cannot vote electronically. This obstacle is rapidly being removed, however, as the cost of computers and other devices that allow access to the Internet are plunging. Providing the rest of the population (those who do not own computers) with a device needed to vote could be easily contemplated.

France long ago provided all citizens with devices resembling personal computers to provide them access to Minitel, France's pre-Internet public electronic system. Although Minitel is not used for voting, the distribution of Minitel terminals to private citizens and their placement throughout France in public kiosks demonstrates that it is entirely possible to provide widespread access to an electronic network.

Deliberation and Community

Deliberation, an important prerequisite for sound democratic processes, is much less often discussed than information sharing or voting, because of a tendency to view democracy in a simple way, as one in which people vote and the majority rules. Ross Perot, for instance, proposed in the 1992 presidential campaign that leaders and experts could present Americans with a set of options, and then the people themselves could vote for their preferred one, skipping the deliberative step.[18]

It is, however, widely recognized that if a proposition is put before the voters, and they are allowed to immediately click their responses (say in some kind of electronic form of the kind many states offer their voters in initiatives), the result will reflect the worst impulses of the people, their raw emotions, readily wiped up by demagogues.

Democratic polities provide two antidotes to this danger: delay loops and opportunities for interaction among the voters. First, they allow time for voters to examine the issues and discuss them with other community members—in town meetings, over their fences, in bars, and so on—before votes are taken. For e-democracy not to turn demagogic, it will have to provide such delay loops (in other words, time for deliberation) and opportunities for interaction among the voters between the time a proposition or a slate of candidates is put before the voters and the time the votes are cast.

Delay per se provides no difficulties. There is no reason votes have to follow immediately, or even very closely, the presentation of a choice to an electorate.

The second antidotal element, interaction, provides more difficulties. As we have seen in the discussion of communities, chat rooms' composition and rules of access and anonymity do not provide sound conditions for meaningful interaction, let alone democratic deliberation. If democracy is to thrive on the Internet, the kinds of interaction deliberation requires will have to be provided for, indeed, fostered. Deliberation is most fruitful among people who know one another and in small-numbered groups with low turnover: the same conditions that nurture communities.

The difficulties here are not inherent in the technology; there seem to be no obvious reasons these conditions could not be readily met online, but so far they have not been, largely, it seems, because they may not be profitable and because of ideological objections to any setting aside of online anonymity.

Representation and Mandates

Democracy works best, as has been well and long established, when the voters do not decide directly which policies they favor (as they do in plebiscites and in initiatives), but instruct their elected representatives as to what their basic preferences are, and then allow them to work out the remaining differences. (The more limiting the mandate the voters provide their representatives, the stricter the instructions, the more difficulties representatives have in working out the inevitable compromises that democracy entails, as people of different values and interests must find a shared course.) This is, of course, the way parliaments work, as well as state assemblies and most city councils.

The Internet, which has not yet been groomed to serve democratic processes, has no established procedures for representation. There are on the face of it, however, no special difficulties in providing for representation on the Internet. Indeed, decades ago the author conducted an experiment on this matter, using a much more "primitive" technology than the Internet.

The experiment was conducted with the help of the League of Women Voters at a statewide level. The League's New Jersey chapter was attempting to decide, as it does once a year, which issues deserved priority. We organized the League's members into groups of ten, and they conducted "town meetings" by means of conference calls. Each group chose its own priorities and selected a representative to take these preferences to the next level for discussion. We then held conference calls with groups of ten *representatives,* who decided among themselves which views and preferences to carry to the third and final level, at which statewide policy decisions were made.

A survey established that the League's members, who participated in the decision and representation process, were highly satisfied with the results. The experiment allowed all the members of the League to participate in the decision-making process, and yet the elected representatives were free, within an area indicated by those who elected them, to work out a League-wide consensus.[19]

There is little reason to doubt that such a multilayered representative model can be applied to online communities, but can it serve nationwide democracy, in which many millions of individuals are involved? Can there be a representative nationwide democratic process that relies at least in part upon online devices?

I suggest that the answer is affirmative, drawing on the magical power of exponential curves: If representatives were layered in the suggested manner, millions of participants could quite readily be included. Suppose that various experts addressed the country on a Sunday from 10:00 to 11:00 A.M. about, say, whether the United States should cut back the military by 50 percent over the subsequent five years. The conference buzz would start with groups of fourteen citizens, each having an hour to discuss and vote. Each group would elect one representative to participate in conference call discussions with thirteen representatives of other groups. Each group of representatives would in turn elect an individual to speak for them, and so on in a rising pyramid. If this process occurred seven times, by six o'clock in the evening 105 million adults could be reached, which is more than the 91 million who voted in the 1988 presidential election.

The same basic approach could be readily applied to the Internet. Voters could convene in, say, twenty-five-person online town meetings. Their discussion would be much more productive than those of chat rooms, because the number of participants would be limited, they would already have some shared attributes (all from the same area?), and they would realize that at the end of a given time period they would have to provide a mandate to their elected representative on the next level of this town hall pyramid. Then the representatives of the separate twenty-five-member groups would be convened, and so on.

Participants would soon learn that the views of those groups that provide their representatives with very detailed instructions, and leaving them with little room to negotiate, as a rule would more than likely be left out of the final consensus-making process than the views of those that provide their representatives with relatively broad mandates. Moreover, members would realize that if many groups were to provide their representatives with narrow and strict instructions, national politics would tend to be confrontational and unproductive.

A major issue is left unaddressed here. Multilayered or representative democracy conducted via the Internet could vary a great deal in terms of two variables. One is the scope of issues submitted to a full-court, multilevel deliberative process of the kind depicted above. For instance, is the public at large going to be invited to deliberate and instruct its representatives only on a few issues every umpteen years, or much more often and on a greater number of issues? The other has to do with selection of representatives. Are the representatives chosen in the "lower" levels going to change with each issue, or will they serve set terms? And will any of the modifications suggested in the preceding discussion make virtual democracy more democratic or more populist?

In short, not only could the Internet fully duplicate offline democratic procedures and outcome, but it could improve upon them. It would be much easier online than offline for millions not merely to gain information and to vote, but also to participate in deliberations and in instructing their chosen representatives.

In Conclusion

This chapter argues that some qualitative accounts and quantitative data suggest that communities can be formed on the Internet. They are much more likely to thrive in clubs in which membership is relatively stable, participants disclose their identity, and the subjects under discussion are significant and encompassing rather than narrow and specialized. Furthermore, it is important to recognize that because people live both on- and offline, online communities can reinforce offline ones.

Regarding the use of the Internet for democratic processes for on- or offline communities—small or large ones—we agree with those who suggest that information sharing and voting can be quite readily accommodated. I stress the importance, however, of providing for deliberations and representation, the software for which is, as a rule, not available.

All that has been argued so far is that virtual democracy is quite feasible. It remains to be discussed whether or not greater reliance on virtual politics would make the joint on- and offline polity more or less democratic than it currently is.

Acknowledgments

I am indebted to my friend and colleague David Anderson for his comments and suggestions on this chapter. I am also indebted to Andrew Volmert for research assistance and valuable comments on previous drafts of the chapter.

Notes

1. See Elizabeth Frazer, *The Problems of Communitarian Politics: Unity and Conflict* (Oxford: Oxford University Press, 1999); and Robert Booth Fowler, *The Dance with Community: The Contemporary Debate in American Political Thought* (Lawrence: University Press of Kansas, 1991).

2. Amitai Etzioni, *The New Golden Rule* (New York: Basic Books, 1996), 127.

3. Benjamin D. Zablocki, "What Can the Study of Communities Teach Us About Community?" in *Autonomy and Order: A Communitarian Anthology*, ed. Edward W. Lehman (Lanham, Md.: Rowman and Littlefield, 2000), 72.

4. For more discussion, see Amitai Etzioni and Oren Etzioni, "Face-to-Face and Computer-Mediated Communities, A Comparative Analysis," *Information Society* 15, no. 4 (1999): 241–248. A revised version of the article is included in Amitai Etzioni's *The Monochrome Society* (Princeton: Princeton University Press, 2001).

5. Pew Center for the People and the Press, Technology and Online Use survey 1998 (November 1998), cited in Pippa Norris, "WhoSurfs?" in *Democracy.Com: Governance in a Networked World*, ed. Elaine Ciulla Kamarck and Joseph S. Nye (Hollis, N.H.: Hollis, 1999), 81.

6. Gallup Poll conducted February 20–21, 2000, reported in David W. Moore, "Americans Say Internet Makes Their Lives Better," Gallup News Service, February 23, 2000, available online at the Gallup Organization home page <http://www.gallup.com/index.html>.

7. Sherry Turkle, *Life on the Screen: Identity in the Age of the Internet* (New York: Touchstone, 1995).

8. For a contrary view, see Jerry Kang, "Cyber-Race," *Harvard Law Review* 113, no. 5 (2000): 1130–1208.

9. For a discussion of MediaMOO, see Amy Bruckman and Mitchel Resnick, "The MediaMOO Project: Constructionism and Professional Community," *Convergence* 1 (Spring 1995): 94–109. Available at <http://www.cc.gatech.edu/~asb/papers/convergence.html>.

10. Howard Rheingold, *The Virtual Community: Homesteading on the Electronic Frontier* (Reading, Mass.: HarperPerennial, 1993), 239. For information about the virtual community CIX Conferencing, see <http://web.conferencing.co.uk/default.aspx>.

11. Rob Kaiser, "Internet Has Neighborly Side as Users Build Virtual Communities," *Chicago Tribune,* December 20, 1999. For a discussion of the digital divide between Blacksburg and a neighboring town, see Marcia Stepanek, "A Small Town Reveals America's Digital Divide: Equality Has Yet to Reach the Net," *Business Week,* November 4, 1999, pp. 188ff.

12. Norman H. Nie and Lutz Erbring, "Internet and Society: A Preliminary Report," Stanford Institute for the Quantitative Study of Society, February 17, 2000, available online at <http://www.stanford.edu/group/siqss/>.

13. Press Release, Stanford Institute for the Qualitative Study of Society, February 16, 2000, available online at <http://www.stanford.edu/group/siqss>.

14. "Survey Shows Widespread Enthusiasm for High Technology," Report from the Kaiser Family Foundation, National Public Radio, and Harvard University's Kennedy School of Government, February 29, 2000, available online at <http://www.kff.org>.

15. Pew Internet and American Life Project, *Tracking Online Life: How Women Use the Internet to Cultivate Relationships with Family and Friends* (Washington, D.C.: Pew Internet and American Life Project, 2000), 21, available online at <http://www.pewinternet.org/reports/pdfs/Report1.pdf>.

16. Humphrey Taylor, "The Harris Poll #17: The Impact of Being Online at Home," Harris Interactive, New York, March 22, 2000.

17. See Bruce Bimber, "The Internet and Political Transformation: Populism, Community, and Accelerated Pluralism," *Polity* 31, no. 1 (1998): 133–160. Citing Walter Lippmann, Bimber argues that any problems with a democracy are not the result of a lack of information and that providing citizens with extensive information will not radically change their political

behavior. See also David M. Anderson, "The False Assumption about the Internet," *Computers and Society* (March 2000): 8–9. Anderson argues that the Internet can and does do much more than merely provide information.

18. See "Ross Perot, One-Way Wizard" (editorial), *New York Times,* April 24, 1992, p. A34.

19. For more about this experiment, see Amitai Etzioni, "Teledemocracy," Atlantic 270, no. 4 (1992): 36–39, and "Minerva: An Electronic Town Hall," Policy Sciences 3, no. 4 (1972): 457–474.

8 Who Needs Politics? Who Needs People? The Ironies of Democracy in Cyberspace

Roger Hurwitz

How will ubiquitous computer networks affect democratic politics? In the early 1990s, the spread of the Internet beyond the research (.edu) and United States military (.mil) domains raised hopes that it would revitalize Western democracies. Cyberspace was imagined alternatively as an "electronic frontier," where free thought and egalitarian associations would transcend political boundaries, and as an "electronic commons," where netizens would discuss issues and influence decision makers who are listening. The term "netizen," coined in 1994 from "Internet" and "citizen" to refer to an Internet user, suggested that as the Internet became a center of power, it would confer a new sociopolitical identity on its users, as the city did for citizens.

These libertarian and communitarian visions built on the Internet's technology, particularly its nonhierarchical structure, low transaction costs, global reach, scalability, rapid response time, and disruption-overcoming (and hence censorship-foiling) alternative routing.[1] Nevertheless, skeptics found reasons to doubt that either vision would be realized. First, given the individualistic ethos of "an electronic frontier" and the prevalent notion of paying for access, a democratic distribution of access seemed unlikely.[2] Second, without a tradition of online discourse, efforts to organize political actions online were likely to produce "flame wars" and fragmented constituencies rather than to consolidate public opinion.[3] Third, laws that hold service providers liable for material they carry could discourage the use of network architecture and encryption to evade censors or disguise transactions.[4] For others the problem was more than the visionaries having the sociology wrong; it was the technology itself. The Internet and computer networks in general are not dumb conduits for transactions and information seeking, but instruments that can report these activities and more generally enhance the state's surveillance capabilities.[5] The suspicion itself of such surveillance can decisively chill political activity.

This chapter first argues that the recent history of the Internet supports both sides of the debate. Cyberspace appears to be a contested area, with struggles of private versus public interests, along one dimension, and civil liberties/civil society versus state power, along another dimension. The tensions are indivisible from and even proceed from the formation of our civilian cyberspace from a military/statist core; they will not be quickly resolved at a political level, although they might be trivialized by the commercialization of the Internet. I therefore argue that it is more productive to assess the impact of computer networks by looking at implementations for network-based political activities. Do these support or undermine practices and models of democracy? With regard to practices, I conclude that Internet activists have succeeded remarkably in making government and political information available to netizens. They have done less well in creating significant, stable audiences for the information and commanding the attention of decision makers. "Models," here, refers to the patterns that people follow in coming together to steer their society. Cyberspace should prove most friendly for a monitorial model in which netizens, alerted to a crisis, join in a collective demand that officials take some action, then afterward return to their nonpolitical interests.

A Contested Area

The Internet has become a new tool and venue for political groups of all stripes. Advocacy and interest groups use it to organize their supporters for online lobbying of local, national, and foreign officials, who themselves need e-mail addresses to be credible in this information age. Ad hoc responses to major political events, like impeachment and massacres, can gain national attention in a few days, as network users redistribute petitions and sample letters to their personal distribution lists. Revolutionaries, like the Zapatistas in Chiapas, Mexico, and dissidents, like the Serbian radio group B92, can Webcast messages to audiences all over the globe and receive moral and financial support in return. Survivalist groups can network by exchanging pointers to respective Web sites and thereby increase the possibilities of so-called leaderless resistance. The chairman of the Democratic National Committee can interpret the adage that "all politics is local" to mean his party should use the Web to build narrowly focused, nationwide communities of interest that can involve people in policymaking on issues dear to them.

Participation in this embryonic political culture, however, is neither democratic nor secure. The demographic profile of users is skewed heavily toward the educated, affluent, and urban. Both in the United States and abroad, the differences in the percentage of users at the highest and lowest income and education levels have actually increased over time, because the wealthy and educated have come online more quickly than others. There is also apparent cultural bias in the propensity to use the Internet: In the United States, the gaps between white households, on one side, and black and Hispanic households, on the other, have similarly grown, even when income and education levels are the same.[6] In short, the Internet's diffusion has increased the opportunities for political action among those who are already the most politically active and informed. Yet even they cannot always act, for some governments, while sending their own political messages into cyberspace, do not easily concede that right to their netizens. The Serbian authorities eventually locked the B92 crew out of its studio and warned it not to return. China and Singapore have required users to register and make a pretense of logging their online activities. Even liberal regimes have sought powers to police cyberspace, as witnessed in struggles over the U.S. government's efforts to legislate Internet content (the Communications Decency Act) and mandate the use of an encryption algorithm that federal authorities can crack (the clipper chip).[7] These struggles uncannily recreate earlier tensions when the federal government owned ARPANET and researchers fretted that their using it for personal communications might run afoul of the overseers.[8]

Thus it is naïve to depict cyberspace as a frontier or commons where state power can be resisted[9] or, conversely, as a gigantic dragnet. Such framing is also increasingly quaint, given the rapid, thorough, and obvious commercialization of cyberspace. This transformation of cyberspace reduces its suitability for political actions but ironically requires strong security and privacy, so that consumers can shop online without anxiety. Instead of joining a virtual research community sharing a potlatch culture, typical users log on to a vast, numbing and bedazzling web of exchange relationships, which they navigate as individuals. Consumer sovereignty has replaced netizenship as the main political value in cyberspace, but as long as the economy remains strong and FedEx or UPS delivers the goods, who needs online political discourse, anyhow? Not surprisingly the use of the Web for shopping outstrips that for political and government information by at least a factor of ten, except perhaps at tax time and during elections.[10]

From what remains of a political perspective, one could more aptly characterize cyberspace as a contested area, beset by tensions between private and public interests, along one dimension, and between civil liberties and state power, along another. Accordingly, it is more reasonable to assess its benefits for democracy by looking at how network based political activities can support or undermine contemporary democratic practices, institutions and models. The Internet appears to be remarkably well used in making government and political information available to netizens. However there has been much less success in using it to create significant, stable audiences for the information and in commanding the attention of decision-makers. With regard to models, that is, patterns that draw people together to steer their society, cyberspace has proved most friendly for the monitorial model of democracy.

Those practices and institutions we could expect to have online manifestations include access to government information and officials, holding officials accountable for their actions, rights of association, political parties, campaigns for office, and elections, as well as unrestrained political speech and discussions of public policy. The models that might have online counterparts are not particular institutional arrangements, but designate the primary foci of political actions and the roles that are evoked in efforts to mobilize people for them, e.g., constituent, voter, party loyalist, concerned citizen.[11] The three models commonly found in the recent history of democracies and of the United States, in particular, can be suggestively termed "partisan," "deliberative," and "monitorial." In the partisan model, parties organize political activities primarily to get their candidates elected and then to have their plans adopted, if they have any. They appeal to citizens as party loyalists and voters. In the deliberative model, advocates organize around issues and call on people as concerned citizens to express their views to decision makers. In the monitorial model, politics comes to life when there is great dissatisfaction with a current state of affairs and finds expression in ad hoc protest movements often directed at elected officials. Traces of all three models are found in real-life democracies, but at various times and places, one or another model may be clearly dominant, for example, partisan democracy in the era of machine politics.

The Internet has been especially strong in facilitating quicker and more complete access than that of conventional media to political and government information at the local, national, and international levels. There is great democracy in what is available: If the documents (texts, audio clips, video) are machine readable and the government office or political group has the will to publish them and a server, the barriers to putting them online are low. Common knowledge of this state of affairs acts as an impetus for groups to make more information available, which the now low cost of storage enables. Consequently no time and space restrictions and few costs compel the material presented to the consumer to be edited, as occurs in broadcast and print media. Note, however, that government offices and political groups did not go online spontaneously. Network activists, an insider champion of the Internet, or the examples of high-profile organizations goaded them to it. The first wave of such activity, the FreeNet movement in the late 1980s and early 1990s, resulted in several municipalities' posting local information and hosting discussions of civic affairs on their mainframes.[12] In the mid-1990s, a fortuitous combination of inside champions, management of information systems (MIS) personnel, outside technologists, and a new technology (the World Wide Web) led the White House and then Congress to open Web sites, on which press releases, calendars, and organizational information were available.[13] Other federal government offices, foreign, state, and city governments, political parties, and other political organizations quickly followed.

Given the mass of available material, the user's problem often is finding precisely what she wants. At present search engines are blunt instruments that usually return more answers to a query than can be easily sifted by hand. Also they are continually falling behind in indexing new material. Still the online version of a source, once found, has the immense advantage of being able to be searched or data-mined. For example, Federal Election Commission <www.fec.gov> records of campaign contributions can be searched per candidate and per donor, allowing in this case nearly on-the-spot answers to the standard political question "Who gets what from whom?"

Most high elected officials at the municipal, state, and national levels in the United States and some elsewhere have e-mail addresses, and netizens have been quick to exploit that. Since sending e-mail to a local official, national representative, or foreign leader is equally easy, the netizen is not bound by geography or means in his efforts to influence decision makers. The real accessibility of such officials by e-mail is, however, another matter. In the United States, the electronic stream to officials has supplemented a message stream that had already become unmanageable by the early 1990s, due in part to more complex government operations and in part to the rise of interest and identity politics. By the mid-1990s, congressional staffs were devoting 50 percent of their time to mail and phone calls and desperately seeking software to handle or reduce the load. Their solutions include audio menu interfaces, automatic responders, routines to block e-mail from all but constituents, and content analysis programs that can identify the writer's issue, tally his opinion, and e-mail the appropriate form letter in return.

Deliberative Democracy

The availability of information and the occasional online accessibility of officials should encourage productive chat rooms, asynchronous forums, and other electronic formats appropriate for a deliberative democracy. Nevertheless, most online political discussions tend to lose focus quickly or break down in ugliness, often worse than that exhibited by the political pundits on television. The factors responsible for these failures include the absence of social and legal traditions that define acceptable online rhetoric and debate, the undermining of sincerity by cyberspace anonymity, and the high value placed there on rapid responses. Some software solutions to this situation have appeared in both political and nonpolitical discussion spaces, most notably:

- Human or intelligent software moderators that block hateful and obscene comments and any comments from persistent offenders.
- Rules of order that constrain the types of comments (or speech acts) that can be made at any point in the discussion and require participants to frame and label their comments accordingly.
- Annotation servers that present a text with sets of annotations by different individuals or small groups. Users retrieve the text with sets of their choice and can comment on any entry.

How effective and how democratic are these solutions? The use of moderators raises the transaction costs for the discussions and also raises the questions of who and what define acceptable comments and who owns the discussion space. A software moderator just moves the first questions one step back, since someone has programmed it either with rules to recognize unacceptable speech or with routines for learning to do that, possibly from examples or from observing the responses of listeners. The question of ownership has consequences, at least in the United States, where blocking someone's message to a publicly funded server site might violate his civil rights. On the other hand, if the discussion includes only those people who say mutually acceptable things, one might wonder to what degree it represents a wider population and how valid are any conclusions it reaches.

Of course, people who are seriously interested in a policy issue might accept some minimal rules of order for the sake of a discussion, that is, they might agree on procedure. Rules of order are composed of a small number of permitted comment types and constraints on how they can be strung together. The inclusion of more comment types than proposal, agreement, and disagreement (e.g., alternative proposal and example) can reduce confrontation in the process and expand exploration of the solution space for the issue. Online and absent a moderator, the rules of order can be weakly enforced with adaptive interfaces that limit a participant's choice of comment types to those that can be "legally" attached to the (previously typed) target of the comment. Having participants identify the type from this set encourages them to reflect on the intention of their comments while avoiding the hard problem of having a system infer it from their words.[14]

Annotation servers can present multiple perspectives of an issue in a nonconfrontational way. If a server's annotators have been chosen along an ideological spectrum, then an interested browser can select a subset that contrasts with or complements her own view. The effect is similar to reading accounts of the same event or issue in different newspapers, but at levels of granularity that the user can partly control and with the possibility of any annotation's being open to further comment.[15] The operator of an annotation server does not require the cooperation of the various annotators, who might be candidates for office, representatives of political parties and advocacy groups, newspapers columnists, or public intellectuals. If they have statements available on the Web that quote, paraphrase, or cite parts of a target document or comparable material, these can be collected passively and linked to the appropriate parts of the document. Indeed, if their material is accessible, an automatic search (Web walking) will probably prove faster than soliciting groups to provide it to a central compiler. Nevertheless, if the selected annotators knowingly cooperated in such a project, each might also extend and sharpen their own views by rebutting, questioning, or otherwise criticizing another's comment.

Partisan Democracy

By now, most candidates and parties at the national and regional levels in the United States and other developed countries have Web sites. A 1998 survey found that 63 percent of U.S. congressional and state-level campaigns did.[16] The candidate sites were primarily virtual campaign brochures: Of 270 sites included in the 1998 survey, 97 percent offered some sort of biographical information on the candidate and 90 percent included issue papers and policy statements. The existence of a home page is also part of the brochure: evidence that the candidate is at home in the Information Age. Thus Lamar Alexander in 1996 and Steve Forbes in 1999 officially announced their bids for a presidential nomination over the Internet, and Bob Dole lamely appealed for a youth vote during a 1996 presidential debate by inviting the young to visit his Web site.[17] The sites were secondarily means for testing messages and soliciting contributions: 52 percent of the sites in the survey included some type of interactive communications, feedback (typically mail) or polling mechanism; 38 percent had electronic volunteer recruitment or fundraising forms. They were not places that invite people to discuss the issues of the day and the positions they would like the candidate to take: Only 4 percent provided chat rooms.

Some campaign sites have offered wider opportunities for participation. Exploiting the idea that the home page extends one's persona into cyberspace, many encourage visitors to download a logo or banner and paste it onto their own home pages, like sporting a campaign button. The Gore2000 site, eager to demonstrate candidate Al Gore's technological savvy, invites programmers to examine the Web site code and improve it or to write their own extensions for it. Because such code would be a campaign contribution, participants must agree that they are writing the code on their own time and relinquish any claim to copyright. The campaigning in cyberspace has also spawned unsolicited fan sites, attack sites, and spoof pages. The Federal Election Commission has advised that to the extent a fan site urges a viewer to vote for the candidate, it constitutes a contribution and is subject to limits on individual contributions to a candidate and to reporting requirements (See Federal Election Commission Advisory Opinion Number 1998–22, available online at <http://herndon2.sdrdc.com/ao/ao/980022.html>). Some campaigns, most notably George W. Bush's for president in 2000, have tried to preempt spoofs by registering domain names resembling their own or suppress already existing spoofs by claiming, so far unsuccessfully, trademark violations. The attack and spoof sites are still less nasty than a hack of a candidate's site or a denial-of-service attack on it, though these can almost certainly be expected in future campaigns.

The candidates' and parties' presence in cyberspace fits the model of American democracy as a ubiquitous and permanent campaign in which carefully packaged candidates are sold to the voter, an ideologically demobilized, passive consumer of information. The model can be extended by using customer relations management solutions to simulate a personalized relationship between the candidate and the site visitor, with the aim of increasing the visitor's positive feeling about the site, the number of her return visits, and the likelihood of her voting for the candidate. These solutions could, for example, (a) ask or infer the visitor's issue interests and inform her by e-mail when additional information on them appears on site; (b) manage online focus groups or sessions in which the visitor participates; and (c) list contributors and other supporters in the visitor's neighborhood or organization. These personal touches will be needed, because supersites that offer exhaustive feature-by-feature comparisons of the candidates (and their parties) will inevitably supersede the brochure-ware.

Monitorial Democracy

In the monitorial model, the citizen is called to action by volunteers who foresee some national or local crisis (e.g., a presidential impeachment, a neighborhood-destroying highway plan) and believe that some action must be taken in response. The aroused citizens join in lobbying, petition drives, protest meetings, and efforts to widen support by addressing others who may have the same concern. The organizations for such actions are typically ephemeral and initially rely on word of mouth to publicize their cause. The Internet is an obvious and powerful tool for such democratic action, because it can help create communities of interest that transcend space, time, and the need for formal introductions. Alerts can be quickly spread through supporters' preexisting mail and distribution lists. Web sites set up to coordinate actions can include small programs that route messages from the aroused citizens to their respective representatives. Indeed the online protest resembles a contagion like the chain letter.

One notable such protest was organized in 1999 by two software developers in response to the impeachment of President Bill Clinton. Working initially through e-mail and later adding a Web site <www.MoveOn.org>, they collected the names and e-mail addresses of over 450,000 netizens who supported a call on Congress to drop impeachment, censure Clinton instead, and then resume important legislative work. After impeachment was voted, the organizers initiated a campaign to collect pledges of money and volunteer hours for candidates in 2000 running against congresspeople who had supported impeachment. Within several weeks, the pledges totaled more than 700,000 hours and $13 million, a remarkable sum of money when compared to the $65 million contributed to congressional campaigns in all of 1997, the previous election off year. This success and the media attention it garnered left the organizers and supporters reluctant to demobilize once the impeachment crisis ended with Clinton's acquittal. The Littleton, Colorado, Columbine School massacre in 1999 prompted them to launch another online drive for gun control and against the Republican congresspeople who opposed it.

Successful actions in the online monitorial model are triggered by high-profile situations that can motivate citizens to take positions without much information and deliberation. The process could be highly automated with a system resembling a clipping service. It would have a newsreader that recognizes alerting events, a database of people that indicates the event types for which they want to be alerted, and a mailer that sends the alerts when a particular condition is recognized. The mailer could also send protest letters to relevant officials in the names of those alerted. The costs of the system could be defrayed through subscriptions or through e-mail appeals to the database whenever the bank balance drops too low. Any similarity of this system to current practices of lobbying and advocacy groups may indicate the extent to which the monitorial model has been institutionalized in contemporary democracies.

Conclusion

The heroic landscape of cyberspace as an electronic frontier or commons should be repainted as an area contested by state and society or perhaps as a shopping mall where politics does not matter until one's credit card is rejected. Cyberspace does, however, resemble a frontier in one important respect: It lacks a tradition of governance that can be generalized to the world beyond it. The various deliberative bodies and consultative committees that set standards for it have fairly narrow technological outlooks that ignore the social and power relations of people and entities in it. Consequently, online political behavior has followed models developed in other spheres and boosted them with information technology. Ironically, like overdoses of steroids, these boosts threaten the health of the models themselves. The deliberative model must contend with scalability: If everyone from everywhere can join the conversation, how can it be orderly, coherent, or decisive? The partisan model seems doomed by its own success in marketing; it can be superseded by the online ease in comparison shopping for candidates and in changing affiliations. The monitorial model, on the other hand, may succeed too well by transforming politics into consultations among computer systems. The prospect can remind us that political society, as Hobbes knew, is the creation of an artificial being.[18]

Notes

1. Recall that the Internet and its characteristic packet switching were developed as a solution to the potential disruption and damage of other U.S. military communications, especially telephony, in the event of nuclear war.

2. J. Lockard, "Progressive Politics, Electronic Individualism and the Myth of Virtual Community," in *Internet Culture,* ed. D. Porter (New York: Routledge, 1997), 219–232. "Access" as used in this chapter includes both access to material in cyberspace and access to an audience in cyberspace. The latter is even more constrained by money: Search engines have not kept up with the number of sites coming online and often do not return a usable list of responses to a user's query. Hence sites must advertise to attract audiences. For that reason, the assignment or appropriation of magnet/intuitive addresses (e.g., drugs.com, arts.com) has become increasingly determined by money. Who should decide who owns/represents arts.com? The Internet Corporation for Assigned Names and Numbers (ICANN)? Finally, as the Internet has become multimedia, its production values have risen, with the consequent rise in the cost of a credible, audience-capturing presentation.

3. J. Tabbi, "Reading, Writing, Hypertext: Democratic Politics in the Virtual Classroom," in *Internet Culture,* ed. D. Porter (New York: Routledge, 1997), 233–252.

4. J. Boyle, "Foucault in Cyberspace: Surveillance, Sovereignty, and Hard-Wired Censors" (1997), available online at <http://www.wcl.american.edu/pub/faculty/boyle/foucault.htm>.

5. See G. Marx, *Undercover: Police Surveillance in America* (Berkeley and Los Angeles: University of California Press, 1988); and D. Lyon, *The Electronic Eye: The Rise of Surveillance Society* (Minneapolis: University of Minnesota Press, 1994), for the standard alarms over this potential. D. Brin, *The Transparent Society: Will Technology Force Us to Choose between Privacy and Freedom?* (New York: Wiley, 1998), offers a technologically savvy, more sanguine discussion. Note that we need not frame this development in the traditional struggle between distributed civil society and centralizing state authority, because there is no need for a central monitoring agency (Foucault's state qua Panopticon), database, or regimentation of the people to facilitate monitoring. The system can be distributed, with local nodes activated only when some questionable action is logged, and data on suspicious activities can be shared automatically and laterally among different authorities.

6. National Telecommunications and Information Administration (NTIA), "Americans in the Information Age: Falling through the Cracks" (1999), available online at <http://www.ntia.doc.gov/ntiahome/digitaldivide>.

7. At first blush civil libertarians and technologists who oppose such laws and policies seem to acknowledge that the government could eventually detect proscribed contents or encryption, with or without the legislation/technology in question. Most activists, however, would rather have the laws and policies invalidated by courts and public opinion than have to break laws to prove that they cannot be enforced.

8. In one incident in the 1970s, a senior ARPANET funder remarked that he had heard that a few researchers had a mailing list to buy imported wine collectively. The researchers immediately closed down the list, only to learn later that the offcial had mentioned the list because he wanted to join it. In the 1980s, some researchers more boldly used ARPANET to mobilize academic opposition to the Strategic Computing Initiative twin of Star Wars, but this was within the parameters of genuine computer science research.

9. Hackers who individually or in teams break into government or large corporate networks have often claimed that they are demonstrating the vulnerability of these systems and so the possibility of resisting their parent organizations. Such claims confuse the information with the organizational capacity to produce the information, a mistake characteristic of "primitive rebels," as discussed in E. Hobbsbawn, *Primitive Rebels: Studies in Archaic Forms of Social Movement in the 19th and 20th Centuries* (New York: Norton, 1965).

10. The comparison is based on MediaMetrix <www.mediametrix.com> data for unique visitors to shopping sites, among the 50 sites with the most unique visitors, and to the U.S. Treasury site, during March and April 1999, the only times a government site appears in the top 50. It is also based on privately communicated data on visitors to major election information sites in November 1998.

11. M. Schudson, "Click Here for Democracy," in this volume.

12. The Santa Monica (California) Public Electronic Network (PEN), which went online in February 1989, is a frequently discussed early municipal network (e.g., S. Doctor and W. Dutton, "The First Amendment Online: Santa Monica's Public Electronic Network," in *Cyberdemocracy: Technology, Cities and Civic Networks,* ed. R. Tsagarousianou et al. [London: Routledge, 1998], 125–151).

13. The White House Web site <www.whitehouse.gov>, which opened in the summer of 1994, expanded the e-mail-based White House Electronic Publications Service, started by the Clinton administration, under the auspices of a special assistant for electronic media. This was itself based on a nonpartisan campaign server at the Massachusetts Institute of Technology's Artificial Intelligence Laboratory in 1992 that distributed by Internet position papers of the national presidential candidates and cleared electronic volunteer signups for the candidates. The House of Representatives Web site had been developed by its MIS staff in mid-1994 but was not opened, mainly because of a squabble over which House committee would have oversight of it. Upon his election as speaker in late 1994, Newt Gingrich demanded its immediate opening.

14. For a technical description of such a system and a report on its performance in a large-scale online meeting, see R. Hurwitz and J. Mallery, "The Open Meeting: A Web-Based System for Conferencing and Collaboration," *World Wide Web Journal: The Fourth International WWW Conference Proceedings* 1, no. 1 (Winter 1996): 19–46, available online at <http://www.ai.mit.edu/projects/iiip/doc/open-meeting/abstract.html>, and R. Hurwitz and J. Mallery, "Managing Large Scale Online Discussions: Secrets of the Open Meeting," in *Community Computing and Support Systems: Social Interaction in Networked Communities,* ed. T. Ishida (Berlin: Springer, 1999), 55–69.

15. See Third Voice <www.thirdvoice.com> and CritLink <www.crit.org> for implementations of annotation servers.

16. The survey was available online at <http://www.policy.com> on Oct. 10, 1998. Unfortunately, the Web site no longer exists.

17. It did not help that he misquoted the URL.

18. G. Dyson, *Darwin among the Machines: The Evolution of Global Intelligence* (New York: Helix, 1998), provides an illuminating, albeit quirky, history of speculation on collective machine intelligence commencing with Hobbes.

9 *Democracy and Cyberspace: First Principles*

Ira Magaziner

Editors' note: *The following is an edited transcript of a talk given from notes on May 8, 1998, by Ira Magaziner, then Senior Advisor for Policy Development to President Bill Clinton. His report to the president in that year defined U.S. government strategy for promoting global commerce on the Internet and confirmed his role as the chief architect of digital policy in the Clinton White House.*

Let me start by noting a couple of things that I believe readers of this volume probably already know. We are quite convinced that we really are in a period of fundamental economic transformation, and the Commerce Department recently released a study saying this. To get the Commerce Department to agree that this is so means it must be so. Even though we're given to hyperbole in the Washington area, we don't think it's hyperbole to say that this economic transformation is on the order of what occurred in the Industrial Revolution. Our reason for making such a claim is that the information technology industries have gone from constituting 4 percent to 6 percent to over 8 percent of the economy over the past decade. Directly, they account for over one third of the real growth in the economy over the past three years.

What has caused this to occur has been the building out of the Internet and the networking of computers. The Internet has gone from having 4 million to about 100 million users. One may argue about exactly what year it will take place—I think Nicholas Negroponte is a little more optimistic than some—but I think there's no doubt that we're going to reach a billion Internet users by the year 2005 at the latest. That building out from 100 million to a billion is only going to accelerate the importance of the information technology industries in the growth of the economy. There are some other indicators of this. We had a 2.1 percent inflation rate this past year, which, given the growth that we had in the economy, is quite good. It would have been a 3.2 percent inflation rate, were it not for the decline in prices in computers alone.

So the declining prices that occurred in one small sector of the economy took more than a third off the inflation rate in the economy as a whole while still contributing a third of the real growth to the economy in broader information technology. It's a remarkable occurrence that we now have over seven million people employed in information technology occupations. The average wage in those occupations is over $46,000 a year, compared to $28,000 for the rest of the private economy. Thus the information technology industry is creating high-paying jobs, contributing to real growth, and holding down inflation.

The information technology industry is only a small piece of what is going to occur in the coming years. On top of that, we have the phenomenon of electronic commerce. When we speak of "electronic commerce," we are talking about a couple of different things. The first is the fact that businesses are now putting up their purchasing, their supply-chain management, their inventory management, their customer relations logistics, and their business-to-business transactions on the Internet. They are realizing very significant cost savings and productivity improvements. Virtually every sector of the economy is affected.

Last year about $6 billion in commerce was transacted electronically. With investments now being made (so this is not speculative), that total will exceed $300 billion of business-to-business electronic commerce in the United States alone by the year 2002. Driving the growth in electronic commerce are companies engaging in a wide range of economic activities—from the General Electrics and Boeings to the Federal Expresses, to the Ciscos, to the Grangers of wholesaling, to the Wal-Marts in retailing—that have made these investments. They have realized such substantial savings, productivity improvements, and cycle time improvements through electronic commerce that it is driving them to spread their investments in this area throughout their companies, and it is driving other companies to try to emulate them. So General Electric, which transacted $1 billion in business-to-business commerce on the Internet in 1998, projects that it will be transacting $6 billion by 2000. That's the kind of growth that we are seeing taking place.

We can then look to one final statistic, which is that 45 percent of all investment in business equipment is now in information technology equipment. That means businesses are essentially creating the environment for business-to-business electronic commerce. In addition to that, we're seeing the beginnings of the digital sale-on-delivery of products and services across the Internet. This is very much in its infancy, although it will eventually be bigger than the business-to-business transactions. It ranges from people purchasing and having delivered to them games and music to online delivery of movies and software of various sorts. About 10 million people are now doing their banking, or some piece of their banking, on the Internet. Seven percent of all travel tickets for airlines purchased in the United States next year will be purchased and delivered electronically on the Internet.

We're also beginning to see professional consulting services, educational services, medical diagnostic services, news services, and a range of other activities being sold and delivered over the Internet. The selling or retailing of physical goods—books, flowers, automobiles, clothing—over the Internet, followed obviously by physical delivery of the products purchased, is also growing in a dramatic fashion. The final type of business activity that I want to mention in this context is essentially a new type of business that involves direct marketing and advertising to affinity groups; companies initially collect discussion groups of people with common interests and essentially develop businesses in which people advertise to those groups or do direct marketing to them or sell merchandise to them, and so on.

The point of the foregoing economic discussion is that increasingly, economies are going to be dependent upon the Internet for their economic growth over the next couple of decades—and I think governments all around the world are realizing this now. Five years down the road, we will add the effects of the Human Genome Project to the information technology industries, and those two areas will drive our economies for the next quarter century and will affect broad swaths of the economy.

This means that the Internet, which started as a research tool, developed a bit as an educational tool, and had a very libertarian culture grow up around it, is now confronting a commercial culture in the form of those who are now betting their company on the Internet. Governments are also becoming much more interested in the Internet as an economic force, because the success of their economic policies, in some way, is related to what occurs now in the development of information technology and the Internet. The clash of cultures that occurs among the commercial, the governmental, and what you might call the traditional Internet community is something that I observe in my office every day in one way or another, and it's quite remarkable. It's something that one wishes one could have a movie of, because it's quite interesting.

The issue of how to develop governance for the technical management of the Internet—the domain name system, the numbering system, and so on—has presented significant challenges. In December 1997 and January 1998, a number of the key players interested in the issue of technical management of the Internet came to have lunch with me at the White House. The clash of cultures noted above was very evident in these meetings, and I'll discuss this further below, because it involves questions of governance in this new digital age. I think we are going to have to make some fundamental changes in our commercial, legal, and economic paradigms, and also in the way in which we interrelate politically, to resolve these technical management issues successfully. Like the economic transformation we are undergoing, those changes will also be on the order of magnitude of what occurred during the Industrial Revolution.

This project of coordinating our work in the Internet and electronic commerce grew out of a request a number of years ago from President Bill Clinton that I try to identify a couple of major initiatives he could undertake, if he got a second term, that would extend the strong economy of his first term into the next century. The "bridge to the next century" that voters heard about during the 1996 campaign is something we in the Clinton administration took seriously. The country had a good economy since 1992, and depending upon your political persuasion you may or may not give this administration credit for it. At least you have to say we didn't screw it up. It's been a pretty good economy, and we think that the good economy will continue for a few more years. So his question was, "What can we do that will ensure its longer-term continuation?" The digital economy was something that wasn't even on the original list. But as I went around talking to people, it became clear that it would be, perhaps, the fundamental driver. And so we elevated it to great importance in the White House, and made it one of our strategic objectives.

One of the first things I did when I started working on this issue was to read some histories of the Industrial Revolution. It was interesting, because there were fundamental changes that took place because of this revolution. Some countries embraced them and, inevitably, were the ones who succeeded. Those that did not and tried to hold on to their old ways of doing things were the ones who fell backward. We are in a similar period right now. And the questions are, "What are those new paradigms, who will embrace them, and who won't?"

The subject is "first principles" of democracy and cyberspace, so let me make a couple of suggestions about what I think some of those principles are. Let me say up front that I suspect I am probably wrong about some of what I have to say here, and I won't know for a couple of years. But what I will set forth here represents our best thinking, at least, among those of us in the Clinton administration that dealt with the issue, about what some of those principles were and are.

The first principle is that the digital economy will be an environment or a world in which private actors lead, not governments. The reason for that is not ideological, from our point of view. We are Democrats; we don't dislike government. We think government has legitimate roles to play in society. For example, consider the issue of health care. I think the government should guarantee everybody adequate access to health care. I have a very different view about the role of government in the digital economy, however, because the digital economy moves too quickly and requires too much flexibility for the processes of government to be, in most cases, successful in relating to it.

Having worked in the private sector for twenty years in my career and in government for five, I can say with some certainty that although the private sector has its bureaucracies—and those are sometimes forgotten—government bureaucracies really are much more burdensome. It's very difficult to work at a high productivity level in government; it's very difficult to work flexibly; it's very difficult to move quickly; and the Internet requires all of those things. It also is often true in government that irrationality, fueled by some particular event that occurs in the public dialogue, can take hold and sweep bad ideas into actions without enough forethought. That can happen anywhere in society, but I think governments can be particularly susceptible to it. And so for those reasons, we believed that even where collective action with respect to digital commerce is necessary as a first instance—and it won't work in all cases, but as a first instance—we ought to look to private collective action in one way or another to handle questions or issues that need to be dealt with. (And I'll give some examples below.)

The second principle is that there are two different ways in which one can envision the Internet and the Internet economy growing up. One model is the traditional telecommunications and broadcast model, in which governments all around the world for various reasons either own it or regulate the Internet, as we do the telecommunications and broadcast industries here in the United States through the Federal Communications Commission. The other model is that the Internet ought to be market driven, that is, that private buyers and sellers should be able to come together to do business and communicate with each other over the Internet free of government regulation and that, with respect to the economic activity involved, governments should provide a uniform commercial environment for the conduct of contracts. If a buyer and seller or two people coming together wish to have the protection of a legal regime of contracts, they can do so. They don't have to, but it's there if they want to choose to operate within it. The history of free enterprise teaches us that, in most cases, buyers and sellers will wish to have that protection. The role of governments is to help codify contracts rather than regulation.

Now we believe that the second of these paradigms, the market-driven environment, ought to be the one that governs in this Internet economy. Again, this is not ideological; it's practical. We think that competition and consumer choice should be the driving forces in this new world. We don't think that the reasons why telecommunications and broadcast were regulated held anymore. For example, with broadcast, there was a limited amount of spectrum to be allocated, so the government, in the 1920s, began doing the allocation. It was because the government was conferring commercial value on certain groups that it decided to regulate them. With the telephone system, when the infrastructure was being built, the size of the investment necessary to build that infrastructure relative to the size of the companies was huge. So governments licensed monopolies and then regulated them to build the infrastructure. The Internet, in contrast, offers almost unlimited bandwidth, and spectrum allocation is thus not required.

In my view, the competition to build the infrastructure of the Internet will be the greatest that we've ever seen in free-market economies. Computer companies, software companies, telecommunications companies, broadcast companies, consumer electronics companies, wireless companies, even electric utilities, publishers—all are vying to build the infrastructure for the Internet. The best thing we can do is to let competition between them take place, with consumer choice driving. What makes this significant is that telecommunications, broadcast, and the Internet are all going to converge [as most readers of this volume are already aware], although most people in the United States haven't come to that realization yet. The Internet will be on television. Broadcast television will be on personal computers. Telephone calls will be able to be made from both of them. The Internet will be delivered to the home by satellite, wireless, television cable or telephone line. What I am saying is that the "conversion" environment in which these technologies converge should be a market-driven environment, which means considerable deregulation will be necessary. Now that doesn't mean there aren't certain public purposes that need to be considered and ensured, but it means that the basic structure should be market driven.

The third principle is that when government does need to act in this arena, as it will to help codify uniform commercial code for dealing with issues of taxation, intellectual property protection, and the like, its actions ought to be precise, uniform, and transparent. So rather than passing omnibus legislation of some sort, government should act only in precise ways and only when it is necessary to act.

The fourth principle—and this is one that's probably the hardest thing for people to understand, at least in Washington—is that whatever is done needs to take cognizance of the nature of the medium. For example, technology changes very rapidly with this medium, so any policy formulated needs to be technology neutral. This is because if a policy is tied to a given technology, it will be outmoded before it can even be enacted.

Similarly, the Internet is a decentralized medium. Therefore, attempts to centrally control it or censor it are destined to fail, even if they were desirable (which I would argue they're not). Life is too short to spend too much time trying to do things that are impossible, so the nature of the medium needs to be respected in the approach to dealing with policy issues related to it. Finally, this is the first medium and the first marketplace that is global from the very beginning. Therefore, the traditional model in which industries or mediums grow up within countries, and countries negotiate how they work together, doesn't apply here. From the beginning, a global framework is required, which is why strategy has involved pursuing a global set of agreements.

Now, added to these basic principles, let me throw out a couple more, and then I'll give some examples of what I mean by these and how we are working with them. There are a series of areas in which we are trying to gain international agreement, and also agreement among the states in the United States, to create the kind of framework that can allow this medium to grow in a free way. These include things like dealing with tariff and tax issues: the Internet to become a duty-free environment, and we are hoping to get an agreement to that effect through the World Trade Organization. We oppose any discriminatory taxation of the Internet: no bit taxes or Internet-access taxes or intertelephony taxes.

We also work to form agreements on uniform commercial code, on intellectual property protection, on ensuring that standards will be set and electronic payments developed in a market-driven way, without government regulation. We are trying to get systems put in place that will allow privacy to be protected, and so on. But we have gone about these things in a way to respect the principles that I mentioned earlier. Let me offer a couple of examples.

On the question of content of Internet materials, we started down a path that was not the correct one, but eventually we got to a better place. We have arrived at the realization that governments should not attempt to censor the Internet. As I said earlier, even if they wanted to, they couldn't, but, in my view, they shouldn't want to anyway. What should be put in place is a model of empowering people to make their own decisions in an individual way; this should be a question of consumer or individual choice. If a parent is afraid of the Internet—because her children understand it better than she does, and she's afraid of what they might be getting into—when she signs up with her Internet service provider, she should have the ability to regulate certain settings according to her own value system. This would offer her a choice in a simple way that would result in access of a type that conformed to her needs and values.

Software packages for regulating Internet access should be available that might be identified with or perhaps endorsed by organizations with which parents feel comfortable. For example, the Christian Coalition might have a particular package it endorses, or the Children's Television Network, or whatever organization. Parents can then say, "Well, that's OK—if they have a filtering package, I'll go with that and feel comfortable." The important thing is that there's choice for the consumer or the parent to do what he wishes, not the government making the decisions as to what that should be. On the other hand, parents who mistakenly believe they understand the Internet better than their children can make the decision to let everything through with no filtering. In the browser or search-engine software chosen, the consumer should be able to do the filtering she wants—or no filtering at all. Someone who loves violence and hates sex can filter out the sex and let the violence through. Of course, the methods for doing this are not going to be foolproof or anywhere near it, when I was growing up, there were parents who didn't want their kids to see *Playboy* magazine . . . and their methods weren't foolproof either. I think the important paradigm here is one of empowering people to make their own choices, and the Internet uniquely offers the ability to do that.

Similarly, with respect to privacy protection, it is very important that people be able to protect their privacy on the Internet. This is probably the most difficult issue we're facing right now. It's a fundamental value that we thought should be respected. It is also important, we feel, just an economic matter. The biggest concern people have about doing business on the Internet is the fear of losing their privacy. The fact that we feel strongly about the issue, however, does not lead us to propose a thousand pages of regulations to protect privacy, because if we were to pass those regulations, we'd be lying to the American people. We would be saying to them, "Don't worry—we're protecting your privacy," when we couldn't enforce the laws and cannot, in fact, deliver on that promise. Now what do I mean by that?

On the order of 10,000 new Web pages can be formed every week, and there's no way that any government agency could possibly monitor them all to determine whether they are conforming with whatever laws or regulations might be passed to ensure and protect the privacy of those who use the sites. Not too far down the road, the vast majority of those 10,000 Web pages will be somewhere else in the world besides the United States. They might be on servers almost anywhere, so that even if the government did find some place that it thought was violating users' privacy, tracking it down to enforce the laws or regulations would be a hard thing to do. By the time such tracking could be completed, then prosecuting the offenders would be very hard. So the notion that government can somehow protect these things in a central way is false. Instead, what we were looking for was something that would empower people to protect themselves, if they chose to do so.

The way we envision this working is based on getting some private-sector industry and consumer groups to come up with codes of conduct on privacy based on the widely accepted privacy principles of the Organisation for Economic Cooperation and Development. That is, a seller or somebody running a Web site should notify a consumer or somebody who visits that Web site that information is being collected or that it wants to collect it, and there should be an option for the consumer to say, "No, I don't want that." Users would have the ability to control their own data. Thanks to pioneering work at the Massachusetts Institute of Technology that will give consumers the technical ability to do this, a user might say, "Yeah, it's OK with me if you collect this information, but only if you use it in this way, and not that way." The consumer should then have the ability to update the information, check it for accuracy, and so on.

Effectively, there's a contract being formed here between the seller and the buyer, and the buyer has control of what is done with her information. The code-of-conduct organization would specify the terms of this contract, and there would be a series of enforcement organizations that would enforce the code of conduct. So if a Web site joined the code-of-conduct organization and was conforming with its standards, the site would be able to display a privacy seal. The code-of-conduct organization would hire personnel to surf the Web to make sure all sites displaying the seal were conforming to the organization's standards, and the organization would also be able to process consumer complaints and would be able to refer cases of fraudulent behavior to the Federal Trade Commission under the existing antifraud laws.

Such a system would allow the government and the private sector (both consumer groups and industry) to go to Net users and say, "Look, this is a free medium; you can go wherever you want, but be careful if you go some place that doesn't have one or another of these seals, because your privacy may not be protected." It would be up to each individual user to protect himself (or not). The medium would remain free, but as a matter of information and education, where a consumer saw a seal, she would know that she was protected; where she didn't, she might or might not be. The businesses with which consumers wanted to do business would presumably be those that had a seal, but it would be up to each individual consumer with what businesses he interacted. This would create a market incentive for Web sites to get such a seal because, otherwise, they would be limiting the potential number of people who came and visited them and presumably did business with them. Some sites would choose to get the seal; others wouldn't. But most who were serious about wanting to do business, I think, would. Now, again, the paradigm here is to understand up front that in this new world, no government in a central way can guarantee its citizens that it can fully protect Net transactions. But what it can do is provide tools for such protection and give the ability to the citizens to protect themselves; I think that is a more likely outcome in this new world.

Let me now turn to a couple of other issues that represent fundamental values, and these will get more to the question of the media and the question of the political realities. The new digital economy is scrambling some traditional political alliances and identifications in ways that are not predictable. It has been a shock to some in Washington that I, being identified along with the First Lady as among the big liberals in the Clinton administration, nevertheless have been advocating what would be regarded as a more libertarian or a more market-oriented or a more government-backing-off approach with respect to Internet policy. To me, it's not surprising. My background is as a business strategy consultant, and, basically, you look to solve problems; you don't start with ideologies. You start with what you need to do to solve problems. And the advent of the new medium is causing changes in the alliances that one sees formed. For nearly everything that we are trying to do in this whole area of Internet commerce and, also, the Internet in general—about 80 percent of it—we have bipartisan support. It is a bipartisan effort, and we therefore are able to move ahead on the issues, but the coalitions are very different than those one sees almost anywhere else.

There are a couple of areas in which, I think, we don't yet have it right, and these represent very fundamental challenges. First, in this whole question of how to create the right kind of environment in terms of the government-business relationship, I think we are moving in the right direction in almost all areas and were also having success. But I am very concerned about what effect the new digital economy will have on income distribution and on the relationships of rich and poor, both in this country and in the rest of the world, because these are tremendously empowering technologies. It is important to ensure that it's not just the wealthier in our society or in the world who have access to these technologies, because if that's the case, it will widen the existing gaps between rich and poor enormously. And so for those reasons, when I said earlier that the Internet should not be a regulated environment, I did not mean that the government has no role to play in it. The government does have roles to play.

For example, my colleagues and I have advocated wiring all the schools and libraries, engaging in significant funding of training programs for teachers, and working with private-sector people to bring these technologies to the inner city, to rural areas, and so on. We think it is crucial that this happen. If it does happen in a serious way, then the new technologies, we think, can narrow income gaps, because the problem that you see in so many inner-city schools of kids working with twenty-year-old textbooks, even in science and math, can be overcome with the Internet if it's done right. And a variety of other disadvantages that now exist in the society can also be, if not overcome, at least lessened, through the Internet and related technologies. But the fundamental question is, will we make sure that this resource is fully distributed in the society or not—though it is essential that this happen.

We feel the same way in the international arena. More than half the world's people don't have access to a telephone now; but as the lower earth-orbital satellites are put into orbit, the most remote villages in Africa will be able to have access to the Internet. It will be cheaper for them to have that access that way than to build the telephone system to accommodate the Internet. All that will be needed is a local area network with a power source in a village and somebody able to train and educate a couple of people to operate it. In fact, it will be easier to maintain than the telephone system. Now I don't mean to minimize the difficulties involved in making this a reality, we needed to put on a major effort to ensure that it occurred. So we undertook a major initiative with respect to the World Bank and some of the aid organizations elsewhere to try to make it happen.

A second issue, which is probably an even greater concern to me, is that as the new digital economy comes, much as with the industrial economy when it came, tens of millions of jobs will be lost, and tens of millions of jobs created. There'll be losses in areas like retailing, middlemen-type functions, insurance agents, travel agents, and so on. There will be gains in information technology–related industries—design industries, media industries. The good news is that the jobs created will, on average, be higher-skilled, higher-paying jobs than the ones lost. The bad news is that, if our citizens aren't educated enough and if we don't have a sufficient retraining program in this society, they won't be able to take those new jobs. Right now, our educational systems and training systems are woefully inadequate to accomplish the necessary training and retraining, and I think that of the issues we are now facing, this one is my greatest concern.

Let me address one more central issue: the effect of digital media on the political process. When I first came to Washington, I remember there was a profile written of me—I think it was in the *Washington Post Magazine*—and there were one or two critical comments in it. Objectively, by and large, it was probably a very positive article. I think it said I was humorless or I didn't have much of a personality, at which I took great umbrage. If that was now said about me in a newspaper article, I'd bring it up as the best article that was ever written. At that time, it probably was the best profile ever written about me, but I nevertheless took great umbrage.

One of the things I've learned, and I think it's something that we all are going to have to learn in the digital age, is that we're going to have to have thicker skins. Things that would have previously gone on as gossip behind one's back will now be publicly available to everybody. Actually, I think it's probably better to know what people are saying directly than to have it happen behind your back. Personally, I welcome this. I don't think it's a bad thing that there are going to be thousands and thousands of information sources. Anything that someone tries to do, particularly in a public arena, is going to be commented upon in chat rooms, posted about in discussion groups, and so on. I also don't think it's a bad thing that there will be all kinds of rumor mills and things posing as news activities that are based purely on rumor, as well as some intending to be outright slanderous. Having observed close up how the media are working now, including reputable newspapers and other sources on which we all rely, I don't think that's a bad thing either.

In many respects, I was one of the more—I was going to say "most"—naive people coming to Washington with the Clinton administration. I had been in the private sector all my life, and it was my first job in Washington. And one of the ways in which I was very naive was that when I was living in Rhode Island and I picked up some of our more credible newspapers and read them, I just assumed what I read was accurate; I just assumed it was accurate if it was in the *New York Times* or *Washington Post*. One of the things I learned in Washington is that that's not true at all.

The pressures under which reporters operate in terms of deadlines, the way in which the spin game works, and the way in which the leak game works means that reporting is quite often inaccurate. When it's inaccurate, it's not necessarily maliciously so. Most reporters are trying to do the best they can. Some of them are more successful at it than others, just as in any field of endeavor. I think most sincerely want to try to do it right and report objectively, but the nature of the way the process works means that they are often not successful. Given that, to my way of thinking, it's better to have more and more sources out there and let people judge for themselves what they find credible and what they don't. If that means that as a public official one gets whacked more often, so what? That's just part of the game, and public officials need to accept it, understand it, and just move on. I don't find that offensive anymore; I find it just part of what one signs up for when one goes into public life.

What will be interesting is that some news organizations, if they're going to continue to command the revenue streams and the audiences that they have been used to traditionally, are going to have to find ways to brand credibility. That will be an interesting challenge for some of them. In my twenty years as a business strategist, I'd often talk to a business in an industry in which a fundamental change was occurring and the business was being threatened, and the business would say, "but we have this great value, and the consumer will see that." I remember sitting with minicomputer companies whose executives said, "The personal computer, yeah, OK, but my minicomputer can do things that personal computer can never do." They just didn't want to admit that they had to change fundamentally. That's a common phenomenon in business. A lot of news organizations and reporters in Washington say about the Internet press, which they look down on, "Sure people will pay to read my stories, because I give more in-depth analysis, or I give my judgment." It doesn't ring too true to me in many cases. The public is not necessarily going to accept that.

So I think there are going to have to be fundamental changes, and I don't think having more sources is a bad thing. I also think there will be more openness, and I think that's a good thing. One of the things we did regarding our electronic-commerce strategy, which broke new ground in the White House, was to post the first draft of our paper outlining the strategy on the Internet for comment. It took about a month or two of argument for me to get agreement to do that, but I finally did. We went through eighteen drafts and treated it as a virtual document, we received comments, we made revisions, and so on. We heard from hundreds of people we would never have heard from normally in a White House/*Federal Register* comment process, and we got fifty or sixty suggestions from the Internet traffic that were very good, good enough that we incorporated them in the paper. We got some of the comments you'd expect, like "The best thing you could do is die." But a lot of what we got was very useful and constructive. We subsequently followed that procedure with everything: All our papers were posted; they all went through revisions; it was all open. And guess what? The people who said, "Life as we know it will come to an end if you open up the decision-making processes," were wrong. It was very effective, and it didn't hamper anything. I think the openness that the Internet is going to usher in is a positive thing. Obviously, there are certain national security areas and matters in which people's lives can be in jeopardy and so on in which you have to keep a process that's not open. But I think that for most policymaking, an open process is entirely possible.

Let me conclude by saying what I started by saying, which is that I don't think any of us really understands where all of this is headed. It is part of what led us in the Clinton administration to take a cautious approach. We have been very successful in concluding agreements to enact a moratorium on taxation on the Internet and electronic commerce, and we have avoided the kind of restrictions on databases that some had proposed, so I think we have achieved a balanced intellectual-property protection. I hope and think we're going to get a duty-free zone on the Internet. We're moving to privatize the technical management of the Internet. We are also moving toward a paradigm in which we essentially have said we will not have intergovernmental organizations like the International Telecommunications Union governing the Internet. Instead decentralized, private, nonprofit bodies—stakeholder based—like the Internet Engineering Task Force or the Internet Architecture Board or the new nonprofit organization set up for the domain-name system, not some centralized governing body. I will share responsibilities for Internet governance, we are going to succeed in getting private-sector-led privacy protection regimes in place.

So we're succeeding in a great number of the areas in which we have had concerns. Despite all that, however, we have to be very humble about our accomplishments, because we don't really understand it.

DEMOCRACY AND CYBERSPACE: RESPONSE TO IRA MAGAZINER

Benjamin Barber

I certainly welcome the opportunity to respond to Ira Magaziner's talk about the marketplace and its virtues in the context of electronic commerce. I have a fairly good idea of what the Clinton administration has been doing with respect to these issues, and Magaziner didn't disappoint me in his discussion. Moreover, just as during the Industrial Revolution in the nineteenth century to which he drew some comparisons, those who made that revolution spoke the powerful language of laissez-faire and said that government should keep its hands off and not mess up the wonderful new cartel-economy being developed, it does not surprise me to find that he has made exactly the same arguments about the current technologies.

The one word largely absent from his discussion—and I expected it to be absent—is the word "democracy." Among Republicans like him, the word "democracy" is never used when there's a discussion of government. One talks about "bureaucracy," "government," "them," "it," as if we lived in the Soviet Union under a Marxist regime or in fascist Germany. One wouldn't know from his speech that the inefficient, inflexible institutions to which he was referring that we had to get rid of in dealing with this wonderful new age were our democratic institutions, our elected representatives, the only institutions we have by which we can deliberate and think about how this new technology might be used as a public utility.

Every confusion about the marketplace and its supposed virtues is discussed by Magaziner in his presentation. It's no wonder that the health policy battle was lost in the first Clinton administration because it, too, had little to do with democracy or a discussion with the American people. It was a technocratic appeal to a complicated plan that few Americans understood that was done in their name, but not with their participation or any understanding of the nature of American democracy.

I find the notion that, in an era in which—and this is the one thing on which I agree with Ira—caution is needed and in which none of us knows exactly what's going to happen, we should turn the development of new technologies about which we know so little and whose impact is so uncertain over to a marketplace whose effects we do know and whose aims and objectives we understand well enough. The motivation of the marketplace is, by the way, appropriate—I have no problem with it; I'm a capitalist. I have no problem with the fact that the motivation of the marketplace is profit, that its stakeholders are its shareholders, its stockholders, not anybody else, however. That's as it should be. And there are many important ways in which the marketplace has made America one of the most productive and successful countries in the world. But the notion that we should turn over so precious a commodity as knowledge and information and the media and the communications that go with them to that private marketplace and let profit, greed, and private shareholders arbitrate what will happen to it, and think that in doing that, we are somehow being cautious, that we are somehow looking out for the difficulties that might come is, to me, a kind of lunacy.

We can't have this discussion without talking a little bit about democracy. The discussion, particularly as Magaziner frames it, is part of an extraordinary belief that democracy is no more than bureaucracy and that our representative institutions don't belong to us but do belong to pig-headed technocrats. I do understand why people tend to think that, given what somehow happens in Washington, as it did in the health care debate. But nonetheless, it is deeply antidemocratic to think that our democratic institutions don't belong to us and that our power to deliberate publicly over how we use and deploy communication, which is the essence of our civilization, our culture, our arts, our education, and our democracy, should be taken away. Is it not clear that communication is what democracy is about? Is it not clear that our capacity to talk to one another and inform one another is the essence of Western civilization? The essence of what it means to be free men and women?

It doesn't have anything to do with spectrum scarcity; that's not why communication is important. That's not why it's a public utility. It's because it's the essence of how we share a culture, share our values; it's how we arbitrate conflict; it's how we learn to live together, despite our differences. How has it come to pass even in traditional broadcast media that these public utilities that we owned and that our government licensed to the private sector have to be bought back by us during elections for billions of dollars, bankrupting us, forcing our politicians to cut all sorts of nasty deals to raise the money for it? It's exactly the same logic. There is no more spectrum scarcity. There is enough for everybody, so let these private-license holders now bill us and use the proceeds to pay for the public use of our utilities that we, I thought, had leased to them, and then give away the digital spectra, for nothing. Even Bob Dole—it's hard to tell who's a Republican and who's a Democrat nowadays—even Bob Dole called it "the giveaway of the century." But that didn't bother the Clinton administration and its technology representatives, because the marketplace was going to solve all the problems.

I wonder, Ira, if you look at the Net often. I do. Let me read you something that I just came across in one of the chat rooms through a project at my Whitman Center; we're looking for civic spaces on the Internet where serious political dialogue takes place. I went into a political chat room, and I'll share just a little bit of what I found, just so we have some reality here about what this Net is, what this new communication mode is that's being hard-wired into the schools. (You know, when you hard-wire the Net into the schools, everything on the Net goes into the schools.)

Frankly, I think poverty is going to protect some of our schools (and maybe the Third World as well) from the worst of what's on the Internet. Poverty may turn out to be an insulation from the worst of our commercial culture. But here's one of the things that will now be in our schools and libraries (the bracketed material is my commentary):

> On-line host: You're in Town Square. Deep Phase/Faze [These are handles the kids use themselves]: What guy wants to eat me out? Junior Tweety: What's everyone talking about? Iceburn 911: Me, Lodino. I don't no [spelled "no"]. Deep Phase: [Sorry for this, folks] Fuck me. DWHKW: No problem. Lodino: OK. Iceburn: Deep is gay. Biania: It's no way, pal. DWJO: I'm a girl. Hulk Dog: Hi. JW101: I'm a new aol-user from Long Island. Where are any of you from? Jan Yeets: Big fat Harry Deal. Lean 77: Dork. Iceburn 911: Let's have cybersex. Otter Hawk: Get a clue. Jan Yeets: What's clue?

Then the conversation is concluded by the posting of an ingenious digital image provided by one Ku-Yung Pro, apparently an image of Hulk Dog being fellated by his "little sister."

That's not rare. That's typical. Go on the Net. Go into the chat rooms and look. It makes what happens on talk radio in the daytime look relatively placid and uninteresting.

If you're interested in a more serious study of this, the Whitman Center has done a study of the fifty top Internet chat-room sites that claim to be, in some meaningful sense, political. Few of them are interactive. The decent ones provide one-way, passive information. None of them are among the top fifty sites in terms of hits, all of which are entertainment, porn-based, or commercially involved. And nothing more than that.

In fact, technology is always a mirror. This is something I want to say in general to those who think that technology and changed technologies are going to change our society, because there are still those in the Electronic Frontier Foundation and others who believe that somehow the new technology is going to be more democratic than the old technologies. One of the first things I learned back in the late 1970s was the acronym GIGO: "Garbage in, garbage out." Well, you can say it in a lot of ways: PIPO: "Pornography in, pornography out." CICO: "Commerce in, commerce out." And that's what Ira Magaziner is talking about. Of course, the fastest growing part of the Net is the commercial part. Obviously, if we live in a society colonized by commerce—day and night, malled and theme-parked to death, with advertisements everywhere, on the telephone, stores open twenty-four hours a day—it's hardly a surprise that this brave new democratic technology should become one more tool of commerce and that our government should see fit to say, "What a wonderful new tool in the spread of enterprise."

We can be sure that it will do that. But for those of us who believed that it also had some pedagogical, some cultural, some educational, some civic, and even some democratic promise, we need to ask ourselves why on earth we would think that this new technology born of a commercial culture would be anything other than as basely commercial as the rest of the culture. Why would we think it would look different?

The Net today has ceased to be much of anything other than a technology that reproduces, once again, the major and dominant characteristics of the larger society. Of course, it looks like that society. Of course, it's dominated by pornography, by polarizing, flaming-style talk radio, by mindless debate and, of course, increasingly by commerce, which is the growing phase. I knew that two years ago when *U.S. News and World Report* had a cover entitled "Gold Rush in Cyberspace." That was the beginning of the end. Once the big boys figured out that they could make big bucks over the Internet, you knew the little folks who thought that maybe it would be an instrument of democracy, an electronic frontier, were going to lose out, just as when the frontier thesis was first developed by a group of late-nineteenth-century historians, that frontier was already being closed down by the industrial cartels of the nineteenth century—even as the language of the frontier was being developed. So, too, we develop here in our hermeneutic little cells, where we still think the Net holds out democratic promises and we talk about the frontier, while the big boys are taking it over and putting it to their uses, and our government is putting out the welcome mat for them and saying they'll do a much better job than the American people could possibly do.

When Ira Magaziner says government can't do the job, it's inflexible, it's bureaucratic, we have to put a translation in there. What he's saying is: "The American people, our democratic institutions, and our public will are inflexible, inefficient, can't get the job done. We can't make thoughtful, deliberative decisions about how we want to use our communication media, whether we want to use them on behalf of education or commerce; whether we want to use them on behalf of culture or crassness; whether we want to use them on behalf of democratic deliberation and elections that don't depend on raising billions of dollars or use them for the push technologies that sell our children things they don't even know are being sold."

You know that these new technologies being turned over to the Internet are being used to exploit and abuse our children, and I'm waiting for a presidential administration to do something about the push technologies that ask four-year-olds to give reports on their parents and their parents' likes when they go on the Toys"R"Us Web site. I'm waiting for a presidential administration to take an interest in the missing buffers that, on broadcast television, say, "You can't run ads together with shows," but on the Internet simply don't exist. Right now, our children can be watching something that, for a minute, they think is an ad and the next minute, it's a show, and the next minute it's somebody selling something to them. Apparently, to the Clinton administration these issues are better arbitrated by Toys"R"Us than parents, the PTA, and the American people themselves.

Let me conclude, then, by saying that this is a confusion that runs deep in our society, and it's not just about the Internet. It's a confusion about public and private. We talk about privatization, and all laissez-faire, marketplace Republicans talk about the power of choice in the consumer marketplace, but there's a fundamental difference between democratic choice and consumer choice. Consumers make private choices about their private needs and wants. Citizens make choices about the public needs and the public goods of the nation.

There is no way, as private consumers, we can do that. We all know that. I love driving a fast car, and I bought myself a fast car. As a consumer, I love it, but as a citizen, I helped to make laws that limit the size and speed of cars because I know having a lot of large, gas-guzzling, fast-moving cars is dangerous for the health of me, my children, and every citizen of the United States. I know the difference between those two things. I can distinguish the citizen in me and the consumer in me. You can't turn over civic public choices to private consumers. We cannot, one by one, as private persons deal with the social consequences of those private choices. That's why we have public institutions. That's why we have government: precisely to make the tough choices about and deal with the social consequences of private choices.

Private choice, consumer choice is choice without power. Ira talks about empowerment, and we agree that we need empowerment. One's right in Los Angeles to choose a Chevrolet or a Dodge or a Mercedes, although they're all roughly the same thing now after the recent mergers, is not the same thing as one's right to choose between private and public transportation—a choice that people who live in Los Angeles don't have, as there is no public transportation there. But the illusion is there of a lot of choice. One has the choice between eighty-nine kinds of toothpaste, but, as Ira will be the first to agree, one apparently cannot make the choice to have public health service in America for every American. But we have this notion that because we can choose the medicaments that we buy, we have meaningful choices. There's no way that when one goes into the drugstore and makes consumer choices, one can choose a meaningful public health system in America. That can be done only by our democratic institutions. There is no way we can make choices about how the Net will be used for cultural and educational and civic and democratic uses unless we make those choices in public as citizens. And what we do as consumers on the Net and with the media is utterly irrelevant to the fundamental questions of what the role of communications in the new media will be in our larger society. To think anything else is to misunderstand fundamentally the nature of democracy and the distinction between private and public.

I think that the most dangerous thing in our society today is the ideology of privatization: the notion that by privatizing, by yielding public to private choice, we are somehow improving not just the efficiency and flexibility but, more importantly, the liberty of our system, that there's more freedom when we privatize. There's not more freedom when we privatize. There is less freedom, because our political liberty, our real civic liberty, consists in our capacity together to make tough choices about the kind of world we want to live in, the kinds of public utilities we want, and the ways in which we use all of the instrumentalities of our society. The liberty we have in private to make consumer choices is always choice without power.

It's time for Ira Magaziner to take a course in democracy and the meaning of democracy. Once he does that, he'll be in a position to talk about the future of the new media.

10 Digital Democracy and the New Age of Reason

David Winston

Editors' note: Like Ira Magaziner in the preceding chapter, David Winston speaks as a policymaker whose experience included an extended term as a chief technology adviser to the Republican National Committee. The following is an edited transcript of his remarks at the MIT conference on democracy and new media, May 8–9, 1998. At the time of his talk, Winston was Director of Planning for the Office of Newt Gingrich, who was Speaker of the House.

I think I should let the reader know up front that I am an unabashed optimist. Not everyone would agree that this is necessarily a good thing. Somebody once said that if one sees good in everything, one may be an optimist or one may just be nuts. Readers will have to make up their own minds when I've finished as to which category I belong to, but I appreciate the opportunity to discuss the most important issue facing us as a civilization: the future of democracy in the information age.

But before we head into the future, I think it's important to reflect upon where we've been. In 1517, a young priest tacked ninety-five theses to the door of the Castle Church in Wittenberg, Germany, and created a cultural upheaval now known as the Reformation that sent shock waves across the Old World. His ideas, put to paper with pen and ink, divided families and brought down kings. The world would never be the same, all because a single man posted a powerful idea in a public place.

In Martin Luther's time, however, communicating an idea was much more difficult—in fact, nearly impossible—and so political conversations were, for the most part, the purview of the elite. Luther's ideas were powerful, but political conversation was almost entirely dependent on oral communications that only time could facilitate.

Now let's fast forward two centuries to 1776. This time a fiery young printer wrote a pamphlet that called for revolution and freedom from an oppressive king. One hundred thousand copies of *Common Sense* were printed on a cumbersome hand press—still a very slow way to disseminate information, but light years faster than the pen and ink of

Luther's time. Political conversation now reached a mass audience despite obstacles of illiteracy, geography, and government opposition. Out of that political conversation and the power of ideas, democracy was born.

Now, let's fast forward again . . . this time to the present. Today, we have the most fantastic means of communication in the history of the world literally at our fingertips, and more people are literate than ever before. Yet we have a system of democracy in which political conversation has become ten-second sound bites, in which we hear media monologues instead of political dialogue, and in which politics has become the cult of personality instead of the power of ideas. The end result? People are rejecting current political conversation by simply saying, "This is not an important part of my world," returning politics more and more to the elite, and that is dangerous to the future of democracy.

But as I said earlier, I am an optimist, and I believe the era of digital communications is, in fact, the prescription for what ails our current political system. Digital technology is the best way to communicate ideas, and democracy is the best means of realizing those ideas. I believe this to be the most powerful combination available for improving civilization in the future.

Let me explain why. To me democracy is based on individualism, which is reflected in our ideas, in freedom in all its forms, and in the effective balance of government and its people. Digital communications will change the political landscape in an extremely profound way. But it's also important to understand that the political terrain has undergone a dramatic transformation itself over the past decade or so. Previously, we fought the war of ideas upon an ideological battlefield. Every issue or value had a conservative viewpoint and a liberal viewpoint. The philosophical battle lines were clearly drawn, having evolved since the beginning of the New Deal. In recent years, however, culture—in a broad sense—has replaced ideology as the battlefield for the war of ideas.

The focus in an ideological world is on individual values viewed by groups. In a cultural world, although values or issues may still have conservative or liberal viewpoints, it's the mix of values viewed by individuals that matters, and the relative importance of any one value is seen through a prism of other values. This creates our changing fabric of culture. So, for example, in an ideological world, the Communications Decency Act is a discussion about pornography with social conservatives favoring the legislation whereas libertarians oppose it. In a cultural world, it is a debate about pornography, international commerce, freedom of speech, family responsibility, and our right to define values for the world and government regulation. Individuals weigh all or some of these competing values in deciding how they stand on the issue.

Another way to see the change in the political terrain is to look at the evolution of technology magazines over the past twenty years. In the 1980s, the content of these magazines consisted of a litany of new products coming to market—how to use them, their cost, and their quality. There were several prominent magazines—*PC Week, PC World, BYTE*—all very good, but focused on the "how to" of technology. This is now shifting. *Wired* isn't really about technology as much as it is about the vast behavioral change technology is bringing to our culture and just in time.

Over the past fifty years, we have strayed from our democratic roots. Robert Hutchins said, "The death of democracy is not likely to be an assassination from ambush. It will be a slow extinction from apathy, indifference and undernourishment." Digital technology gives us a second chance to revive political conversation in this country and bring democracy to the world, to go beyond the information age to a new Age of Reason.

We began to see the change in the country's political landscape in the early 1990s, when we, as a culture, crossed a digital Rubicon, moving beyond mere computing to what I call the "four Cs" of the digital world—communications, content, collaboration, and community—and no area of our lives will be more affected by this change than our political conversation.

With the advent of the Internet, digital technology changed fundamentally from computing to communications. This transformation reached critical mass in the early 1990s when the Internet became a reliable means of communication between individuals. This gave people the ability to create better and richer content by combining the written word with voice and video. Additionally, content became data and could be searched for important bits of information. Suddenly, millions of documents were searchable instead of having to look up indexes in books or review video or audiotapes. The ease with which content could be developed was combined with a tremendous increase in speed and in a convenient asynchronous communications paradigm that led to more effective collaboration than in the past. Finally, the ability to communicate more easily, the ability to develop better and more usable content, and the ability to collaborate more effectively led to new communities that allowed people, in a new way, to share interests and discuss them. So I'd like to talk next about how these four elements are changing this new world.

First, in this new Age of Reason, digital communications will deliver content and meaning in a way that empowers individuals at the expense of the elite. It will be individual based. By that I don't mean extreme niche marketing down to a market of one. In the niche-marketing paradigm, all relevant information that can be obtained about a particular person is gathered, and then the message most likely to succeed with that person is delivered to him. In this way, several sets of characteristics are used to target the message (e.g., young, eastern, white, wealthy, educated, liberal). In the new digital communications model, creation of a relationship is undertaken to develop knowledge of what interests the individual and the best way to address her concerns, awareness of the degree of success at this is instantaneous. This is a model that requires efforts to be focused beyond simply communicating an idea to creating a relationship to ensure that the ideas being communicated have meaning for the individual to whom they are communicated.

Second, this new communications medium will move at a pace that is barely comprehensible today. There will be fallout. Most organizations are incapable of operating at this pace, and failures will occur. Speed brings with it immense pressures as well. Whether you are CNN or network television or MSNBC or Al's *News on the Web,* deadlines become irrelevant or in reality, nonexistent. With the pressure to disseminate news in real time increasing dramatically, political conversation will become constant.

Third, digital communications are also asynchronous. Both the political world and the media world will find it extremely difficult to make the changes this will require. With increasing speed of communications, we will see the electorate demanding political information on their terms and in their time. Individual convenience will be an integral part of political conversation in the future.

Fourth, the American people will become increasingly more difficult to reach as information options explode. Today, we have several hundred channels of satellite television, remote controls to bounce from one information source to another, and videotapes, computer games, and chat rooms, as well as traditional outlets like radio and newspapers. This fracturing of the information market has serious implications for those whose function in life is political conversation, namely, the media and campaign professionals. In the 1980s, a 400 gross-rating-point buy was considered an effective level of advertising. In theory a single gross rating point means that an advertisement has been seen by one percent of the media market in which it was shown. A 400-point buy would mean that on average each person in the media market was exposed to an advertisement four times. In reality, some would see it six times, and others would see it only twice. If the buy were very targeted, some would see it eight times, others not at all. Now, it can take 1,000 points a week or more to create a memorable impression with an audience, and this fracturing is likely to continue.

Fewer and fewer people are reading newspapers. In fact, according to James Adams, the CEO of United Press International (UPI), the number of newspaper readers has declined by 600,000 a year for each of the last ten years. Moreover, younger adults are abandoning the newspaper en masse. Whereas adult readership has dipped from 81 percent to 64 percent over the past thirty years, the majority of young people ages eighteen through twenty-four don't read a newspaper at all.

Television isn't doing much better. A Veronis Suhler survey predicts that we would see a 20 percent decline between 1990 and 2000 in the number of hours of television watched per person per year. Another survey, by ActivMedia Incorporated found that Internet users spend less time reading books, and 70 percent said they watched less television. Reaching people with a political message is becoming problematic and will only get more difficult.

Fifth, in the past, even bad programs could get an audience. Now content is king, and without it the audience evaporates. Message must be clear, pertinent, persuasive, and personalized, and people are demanding more and more interactivity in their communications. Political conversation must function within the same parameters.

Finally, the delivery of message—the cost of political conversation—will become much cheaper. The expense will be in creating the message and identifying the participants.

Communications, content, collaboration, and community, then, will clearly be the new arbiters of political conversation in the new Age of Reason. Readers should keep one thing in the back of their minds, however: There is a real conflict going on in the communications world that is not party based or ideologically based and is not limited to the political arena. It's a paradigm shift from those who are analog based in the way they think and communicate to those who are digital based in their approach. This transition is difficult for any entity, whether it is a Fortune 500 company or an elementary school or the U.S. Congress, because it requires a fundamental shift in behavior—never an easy task even for the most flexible among us.

I believe, inevitably, digital will succeed. Our culture will dramatically transform itself. It's already happening, and nowhere is the pressure more evident than in the three areas that most affect democracy: the media, the Congress, and political campaigns.

I'd like to talk now about these key elements of democracy and how their role is changing in a digital environment. Let me start with what I know best: the Congress. There are two major relational shifts occurring in the congressional world. First, members are beginning to build relationships with their constituents in different ways that provide a richer experience for both; and second, average citizens are gaining access to the kind of information that only highly paid Washington lobbyists had previously available to them.

This second shift was a particular priority of House Speaker Newt Gingrich and was an important construct of his clear vision for an information age Congress.

The Congress has begun to move to a more information friendly environment. Votes, texts of bill, schedules, and floor statements are now available online as well as information on members through their individual Web sites. Most congressional committees have made the same material available. All are realizing that they have a unique opportunity to talk directly to the public. Moreover, they can communicate without the filters of the news media, an important political consideration.

We do see a certain unevenness in the implementation of digital technology, member by member having more to do with age and attitude than party affiliation or ideology. Congress is still struggling with the concept of relationship building with constituents in place of traditional one-way communication.

The fear of constituent e-mail is a major hurdle. Many offices refuse to change how they do business to accommodate e-mail traffic. They view several hundred daily additional requests for information as a problem that will overwhelm their operations. Since most are still analog in behavior, they're probably right. Culturally, they must begin to view these new requests for information as an opportunity to convey their views to more citizens and from a mechanical standpoint must redesign their internal processes to achieve this goal.

A great deal of progress has been made, but major changes in organizational behavior are still necessary. In most offices, there is a "geek" who puts up the Web page. It's updated maybe once a week if at all. Many Web pages are put up by a central technology support unit for the House, never to be changed again. There are some offices that make regular updates. Speaker Gingrich's Web site was kept current, as were other members' sites, like that of Rick White of Washington, but too many waste their Web sites through lack of content and timeliness.

As a body, the Congress needs to understand the four Cs and the fact that the Web is not primarily a technical environment, but a communications environment. In most Capitol Hill offices today, a techie operates the Web site and begs the press person for something to put up on the Web site to keep it fresh. It is usually not a part of the overall communications plan but simply a device that lets the communications director present the member as technically savvy. As the Congress becomes younger, however, the number of members who understand the value of the Web is increasing.

Eventually, offices will learn that it is much easier, faster, and cheaper to respond to e-mail than other forms of communication. Additionally, once a constituent's e-mail address has been captured, a member can begin to develop a relationship with that person. This shift alone makes me optimistic about the interaction of the Internet and democracy. Technology will make it easier and easier for Congress to talk to the public and vice versa, and it is that political conversation that will generate the ideas needed to sustain democracy. When members change their focus, and they will, and begin building e-mail list-servs of 15,000–20,000 people, they will be able to generate levels of contact with constituents unheard of before. As a result, they will be more effective in understanding and representing their constituents' views, and in a democracy, that's the name of the game.

Campaign politics is no different. Building a relationship with voters in a campaign is just as important as congressional constituent service. Digital communications, I believe, will radically change the way we conduct campaigns in this new Age of Reason.

Campaigns have been using the Internet for the last three cycles, but it is still a secondary consideration particularly in contrast to television advertising. Many campaigns have had Web sites, but, like congressional office sites, these sites have not been a part of the communications plan here either. In reality, campaign sites have amounted to little more than digital direct mail or an easy outlet for media contacts. Once the content has been put up, it changes little as the campaign progresses.

The Dole '96 Web site is a perfect example. It was a sophisticated site put together by techies, but in a campaign full of people looking at the world through analog-colored glasses, no one saw the value in providing content that could have helped build relationships with potential voters.

Even though e-mail is free, in contrast to snail mail, it also has not yet been effectively used to contact and deliver message in campaigns. A mechanism for creating good e-mail lists has not been developed, either in the political arena or in the marketplace. Most campaigns, however, are mass-media oriented. It is much easier for campaigns to purchase advertising than to build a knowledge base of their relationships and then sustain those relationships through communication, content, collaboration, and a sense of community.

But as we move into a digital world, as the market fractures and people demand convenient and personally meaningful information, the mass-media paradigm that has been the staple of political campaigns and the bread and butter of consultants for years will become obsolete. This shift is not only a fundamental change. It will be a major battle as well. Many political consultants ridicule the concepts of the digital communications world or try to interpret them in an analog context to sustain mass media or keep the gravy train running.

The idea of not using mass media to win a campaign is outside most political operatives' sphere of comprehension or, given the lucrative nature of mass media, is beyond their willingness to accept as reality. Certainly, for the foreseeable future, mass media will continue to be more important than digital media in the success of political campaigns, but as the audience continues to fracture, the effectiveness of mass media will only decline. Eventually, even their staunchest defenders will have to admit defeat and move toward a digital campaign environment or go the way of the dinosaurs of another age.

Speaking of dinosaurs, the last area I want to discuss in terms of the impact of a digital world is the traditional mainstream media. Here again, the four Cs—communications, content, collaboration, and community—will shape the future of the media and their role in encouraging and sustaining democracy.

We know that voter participation has declined steadily over the past thirty years, with just over 50 percent of eligible voters casting a ballot in the last presidential election. We don't know all the reasons why, but what we do know is that people have tuned out the political conversation, and that occurred long before the latest Washington scandal. The traditional media must accept some of the blame for this apathy and television the lion's share. In fact, Paddy Chayevsky once called television "democracy at its ugliest."

Can you imagine ABC News covering the Boston Tea Party? "This is Peter Jennings. Extremists polluted Boston Harbor today claiming to be fighting for lower taxes. Environmentalists called them tools of the landed gentry." George the Third calling George Washington "out of control," I suspect, would earn more air time on CBS than a content-driven explanation of the key message points of Tom Paine's *Common Sense.* And *Dateline, 20/20, 60 Minutes,* and *Prime Time Live* can all be counted on to compete for the first exclusive interview with Benjamin Franklin's landlady on the good doctor's latest dalliance.

It's no wonder that today's political conversation means so little to most people, and why many now seek alternative sources—digital sources—of information. That search for unfiltered (or at least self-filtered) news is what's got the media elite up in arms.

Mainstream journalists will say they're fighting to maintain ethics and credibility in news dissemination, but they're actually fighting for their very existence. They understand that to lose control of the content and timing of news is to lose their power base. Online reporters are generally given the same status in the mainstream-reporting world that Ken Starr would get lunching at the White House mess these days. A digital-based reporter is considered credible only when he or she is published or appears in the mainstream media.

We see more and more analog stories on the dangers of the Internet: the threat of spreading wild rumors, the pressure of producing news in real time leading to bad reporting, the risk of having so-called nonprofessionals allowed to report news, the ability of any and every kind of group to push propaganda, the dangers of the Internet to our children. It's a Chicken Little approach to change that has little merit, more self-protective coloration than legitimate complaint.

James Adams, UPI's chief, of whom I spoke earlier, has had a lot to say on the subject of the traditional media's ostrich-like rejection of online information as potential competition. He told a story of appearing on a panel of media representatives in Washington when the topic of the Web and the future of the media was raised. "Among my colleagues on the panel," he said, "the word Internet was received like a bad smell, a passing inconvenience that no members of polite society would wish to discuss in public. It is that attitude that has contributed to the current sorry state of the traditional media." Those are the words of the leader of one of the world's oldest news organizations.

Clearly, the demise of traditional media, if it comes, will be the result of the media's failure to acknowledge the four Cs of the digital age. They refuse to acknowledge the value of digital communication. They fail to understand that the increasingly filtered content of their news and, in the case of television, its thirty-second sound-bite paradigm no longer provide what people want. They seem unable to adapt to the notion that new collaborations are necessary in the new digital community in which we seek information and ideas.

News in the digital age, the new Age of Reason, will be increasingly individual based. Someone who wants to watch hype will still be able to watch analog media, but those who want to understand the substance of issues will have many locations to walk them through even the most complicated of proposals. That doesn't mean these sources are any less biased than traditional news organizations, but the filter will be out front, and the focus will be on content, on ideas—which in anybody's framework is a better result.

America will be better off because political discussion will be driven more by the electorate; and when the electorate is engaged, it becomes more participatory. That's good for democracy. I think all of us understand that not all ideas are equal nor is every idea a good one. Winston Churchill put it this way, "When there is a great deal of free speech, there is always a certain amount of foolish speech."

The digital world doesn't prejudge ideas. It simply makes them more accessible— good and bad. But it isn't a substitute for the human mind. The individual must make the distinction between ideas of merit and madness. We didn't ban books because *Mein Kampf* was written. There will always be evil in the world, but censorship is never an acceptable substitute for diligence. Consequently, culture, values, and education become more important in a digital democracy because the individual will be vested once again with real power: the power of ideas.

I began the chapter by revealing that I am an optimist. Digital technology, I believe, has the potential to change the world order radically, much as Martin Luther's rough parchment and Thomas Paine's ink-stained pamphlets did in their time. I believe it can change the world for the better, bringing education and enlightenment to corners of the world held too long in dark tyranny.

We've already seen the beginnings. Under siege in the Russian White House, Boris Yeltsin sent a fax to let the world know freedom was still alive. As academics connected online to reach across the Iron Curtain, the undeniable power of democratic ideals brought down the Berlin Wall. Today, over 600,000 people in China have access to the Net, and that number is expected to reach seven million in the unbelievably short span of the next three years. Can democracy long be denied a people once they have tasted freedom? I believe the answer is no.

Franklin Roosevelt said, "Democracy is not a static thing." He was right. It is constantly changing, reinventing itself, expanding and retracting as the political environment warms and cools to its precepts. Digital democracy will be no different at its core, but it has an opportunity unlike any in the history of the world to bring people and ideas together. If we embrace this exciting digital world, our own democracy will be strengthened, and civilization will surely embark on a new Age of Reason and a new era of individual freedom.

11 Voting, Campaigns, and Elections in the Future: Looking Back from 2008

Nolan A. Bowie

Editors' note: *In this chapter Nolan A. Bowie uses the tradition of speculative history to imagine the consequences of current trends in new media and political culture. In his scenario, the election of 2004 becomes a crisis point for democracy, resulting in fundamental shifts in public opinion and dramatic calls for reforming the system. Bowie wrote this essay some four years prior to the presidential election of 2000, which the U.S. Supreme Court was forced to resolve following voting irregularities in Florida. Although Bowie's time frame is mistaken—the crisis occurred earlier than predicted—the reality of the contested election gives new urgency to his analysis and his speculations about possible solutions to the problems confronting American democracy. We are, therefore, running the chapter without altering his original dates.*

When the director of The Aspen Institute's Communications and Society Program, Charles Firestone, first asked me to consider writing a scenario on the future of political campaign elections in the United States, he concluded our conversation by cheerfully commenting, "Just use the best of your pessimistic views when you explore the possibilities. We're looking for a paper that will stimulate discussion."

"Great," I thought, "this should I easy assignment."

I expect continuing, rapidly changing information technology and large doses of uncertainty concerning the emerging, evolving, knowledge-based, global economy. In the long term, I expect that these changes ultimately threaten not only the United States as an independent sovereign, but the very concept of the nation-state and democracy.[1] In the following view of science fiction, I am guided by current significant trends regarding campaigns, elections, and voting patterns in the United States.[2]

I begin my scenario in the year 2008 and look back, describe some of the significant pessimistic circumstances surrounding general elections of the years 2000 and 2004 that got us to that glorious point in time, 2008, when the demand for democracy reform was manifest—a time in forehistory when all good citizens took to the public sphere[3] and knowingly reclaimed their government and its infrastructure (commonwealth) for themselves and their common interests (also known as "the public interest"), as they believed they were mandated to do under the Declaration of Independence. In other words, in the year 2008, a nation of viewers and consumers finally took the step to act as *citizens*.

What moved the people toward dramatic political reform was the intervening presidential elections of four and eight years earlier. Those were the years of "bad campaigns" for citizens—that is to say, campaigns that did not inform or motivate them to action. Conversely, those were the years of "good campaigns" for the candidates, candidates' spin doctors and consultants, political pundits, pollsters, and the owners of television stations that reaped between 70 and 80 percent of candidates' campaign expenditures in exchange for a little access to the public's airwaves.

I create a "worst world" scenario (in the best of my pessimistic nature) to conclude with the optimistic hope of saving democracy. The common denominator of both worlds is ubiquitous information technology. The difference is information and choice—information that is relevant and accessible to citizens. In the best world, citizens are informed and empowered to make political choices about issues affecting the daily lives of all the people. In the worst world, wealth and power are synonymous, and "corporate citizens" determine the public agenda as they determine markets. If our experiment with democracy evolves into a plutocracy or *corporatocracy*—my worst world scenario—we will have only ourselves, not technology, to blame.

From the Future, Looking Back

Today is October 1, 2008. In a little over thirty days from now will begin the first month-long voting period for a general election in the United States. The turnout is expected to top 98 percent of those citizens eligible to vote. This relatively high number of persons expected to cast votes is due to a number of significant reforms enacted by Congress following the "boycotted" election of 2004, when voter turnout reached an embarrassing low, representing a mere 22 percent of the electorate. The old saw "What if we gave an election and no one came?" was too close for comfort in 2004. But it served as a wake-up call to all the people of the United States, including the almost 80 percent of nonvoters. In the next presidential election, they could either re-create civil society, and exercise their potential power, or simply amuse themselves to death with the large variety of electronic soma available to those connected to the wired nation.

The reasons for the especially low turnout, according to a number of respected polls (e.g., those conducted by The Disney/New York Times Company, Time-Warner-Westinghouse, Inc., and AT&TMCI/Microsoft/Sony Ltd.) was that American voters had somehow become disillusioned, disaffected, alienated, or just plain ambivalent about a political process and system that did not speak to them and their real needs and did not represent their true interests. According to a front-page article appearing in the *Boston Globe* in mid-March of 2004, a Berlin, New Hampshire, man summed up the feelings of Americans when he said: "There is no choice. Politicians are all alike. They tell me what I want to hear, go across the street and tell you what you want to hear."[4]

The voter turnout for the election of 2004 was historically low, so low in fact that the election was referred to as "the boycotted election of 2004." It was used by several newly wealthy but authoritarian nations of Asia, the Middle East, and South America to ridicule U.S. delegates at international conferences and negotiations throughout the world. These nations claimed to have cultures and political systems superior to that of the United States because their citizens participated in far greater numbers in their elections. Citing the fact that elections in Taiwan in 1996 had a voter turnout of 78 percent and that turnout in the presidential election in South Africa was slightly more than 90 percent in April 1994, one foreign leader said to the U.S. secretary of state, "You Americans stay home amusing yourselves, having virtual experiences, and watching high-definition television."

Moreover, since the United States still had the world's highest murder rate—some 40,000 per year since the repeal of all regulations governing fully automatic weapons— even iron-fisted foreign leaders would joke that the United States had the lowest voter turnout of any other democracy because "your people are simply afraid to go to the polls to vote for fear of being mugged or murdered." Ironically, at that time, the U.S. Department of State was still funding and otherwise supporting emerging democracies throughout the world. Apparently, American democracy was better exported than at home.

U.S. delegates and international representatives could not provide any reliable excuse to lessen their shame, because the people of the nation with the longest-standing democratic form of government had lost the confidence in the procedures and substance of democracy required to actively practice it. The term "democracy" had come to mean little more than a slogan, like "Drink Coke!" or "Just do it!" It had come to be, for too many once hopeful people, an empty promise, just as "the American dream" had come to be during the mid- to late-twentieth century.

During the ten-year period from 1994 to 2003, the effects of globalism, privatization, deregulation, liberalization, and market reliance as the dominant arbiters of consumer welfare, coupled with the maturation of the new economy of knowledge and information, began to take their toll on traditional concepts of democracy and its institutions: "the public sphere," "civic society," and "the public interest."[5] These terms and their meanings became distorted and twisted beyond recognition. As a matter of fact, the conservative slogan that best defined this rather mean-spirited era—going back to a mid-1980s origin—was a ditty first articulated by Ronald Reagan's chairman of the Federal Communications Commission (FCC), Mark Fowler, who had said, laughingly, that "the public interest is what the public is interested in."

The FCC, under Fowler's direction and leadership, proceeded rapidly to deregulate radio and television's public trustee requirements, including their obligations to present news and informational programs, to keep and maintain programming records, and to place limits on advertising. Also, the FCC canceled broadcast stations' affirmative burden formally to ascertain the needs and interests of the communities in which they were located. Those rules had required station officials to sample public opinion from members of the general population, and, specifically, to survey community leaders. This ascertainment process provided radio and television officials with knowledge of what was important in their local communities. But because of the belief that the market would satisfy consumer welfare, deregulation drove broadcast stations in the 1980s to become pure entertainment machines in which even the news lost its edge because news, too, had to produce a profit cut. To meet its new demand, news evolved *infotainment*. More and more, political campaigns were covered superficially as horse races or as personality contests, rather than as debates over clearly defined issues and values that represented choice to the viewing electorate.

Unfortunately, because of the competitive pressure of bottom-line journalism, the electorate became less and less informed. By 1987, the so-called fairness doctrine was eliminated from the requirements imposed on public broadcast stations. Thus, in addition to having no mandate to present any news or informational programs, radio and television stations had no obligation nor to present any controversial issues of public importance, nor did they explore the nuances in contrasting views on these subjects. It was no wonder that by the 1990s the public was primarily interested in diversions and amusements rather than real politics. Citizens were effectively offered no relevant choice, while ironically, the number of channels multiplied and grew.

Freedom of choice was the American illusion; freedom *from* choice was the reality. Had real or meaningful choice been available, the general public would not have allowed its government to deteriorate as it did. By the late 1990s, it was becoming clear that there were too few alternative choices of candidates or policies competing for public acceptance. One of the chief reasons was the high cost of running for office. The barrier of money filtered out all but candidates who were clones of one another, representing very similar viewpoints on issues, with only slight variations. As a consequence, good people began to lose their desire to serve or participate as citizens.

Another key reason for citizen turnoff was the widely hold perception by ordinary Americans that their participation in the political process did not matter. The primary function of government appeared to be promoting the narrow interests of nonelected, nonhuman, noncitizen multinational corporations that too often bullied government officials at all levels by threatening that they would cut off political contributions and jobs if government attempted to burden them with the imposition of excessive taxes or regulations.[6] By the year 1999, almost any regulation or tax, no matter how small or necessary, began to fit the large corporations' definition of excessive. What was once understood as protecting the public interest was excoriated as heavy-handed regulatory browbeating that discouraged competition and efficiency.

As time moved on, corporations began to define not only what was or wasn't the appropriate role of government, but most of society's core values. Corporate culture became American culture and vice versa. This transformation was not difficult to understand, since corporations owned the mass media, corporations controlled all channels of communicating values, and corporations were setting agendas both private and public. Their core value was simple and straight to the point: freedom to compete in local and global markets, efficiently and effectively. Democracy and free-market capitalism were the same thing to the multinational corporations. To them, consumers were paramount; citizens were merely potential customers.

In the mature era of globalization, communications satellites, and the *superinformationentertainment highway*—as the privately owned, interconnected digital networks came to be called by 2001—the giant corporations were, in effect, governments unto themselves that virtually orchestrated public opinion, public discussion, and the public agenda. Political campaigning became a mere ritual of changing personalities for an audience. Citizens were no longer invited to take a hard look at their situations. It began to seem pointless to hold government and government officials accountable for their performance in office. The people simply did not get enough relevant information to make rational choices among candidates.

Because the mass media were becoming more and more concentrated, fewer and fewer viewpoints were made available. Marginal views and dissenting opinions were dismissed from the remaining mainstream. Popular audio and video information was purposely sanitized in order not to offend potential consumers or to get them really thinking about mobilizing around political issues. Public issues that appeared on broadcast radio and television were presented in a sensational manner but that fact that they were controversial did not guarantee they were of public importance. This was particularly the case on talk radio and daytime television infotainment programs. Thus, the political discussion that appeared on broadcast programs was nonthreatening to the status quo, although it was always commercial, entertaining, violent (not withstanding the V-chip), superficial and most of all, irrelevant to the needs of a society in transition.

Political information in which serious discussion or fact, appeared was almost exclusively in text format on the pages of the few remaining newspapers that survived the bankruptcy and takeovers of the years 1999–2003. The Internet also developed as a reliable and valuable source of political information. But by the year 2000, only 50 percent of U.S. households had access to it. "Onliners," those who could afford to connect to the *superinfomationentertainment highway* and to subscribe to several of the commercial services selling information, were rich with information. They were almost too rich, to the point of glut. Many onliners tended to rely on digital proxies to make up their minds for them. Too little time, too much information to surf.

This, of course, created the need for the virtual political party that collected, synthesized, filtered, and transmitted politically appropriate information to Internet users who were predetermined to support certain issues and candidates of the virtual political party or digital lobbyist. These political information providers would scan the Net to pick up pieces of useful information based on how or what information an individual or member of a household consumed. They would then develop an electronic profile based on scientific probability analysis procedures that were created to identify attitudes and predict behavior. These virtual political watchdogs then fed political information to potential voters much the way smart agents (discussed below) filtered and distributed information to busy executives. Attitudes and information consumption behavior of online users not adequately encrypted left a trail of digital "crumbs" that could be detected by digital accountants or detectives using tracer software called "cookies." Moreover, the user's trail of information consumption was in the public domain, since the network was in plain view and public.

As a result of the new technology, issues and information concerning campaigns, politicians, and election results were readily available, at least to those Americans who were part of the information-rich class. These Americans had upscale incomes of more than $50,000 per year, and they had higher levels of education. Their ranks included a disproportionate number of college graduates and professionals. This demographic group had access to an abundance of digital information. They provided the revenue that enabled the information publishers and distributors to work the magic of the market, selling for profit information that once was freely given away as public goods. Thus, they were not only the best-informed members of society, they were also the most well-to-do. Of course, they were also politically powerful, using their access to information to reaffirm the status quo that allowed them to enjoy their current privilege.

Onliners had ready access to a multitude of opinions and editorial views, but in this case many views did not mean many viewpoints. Consumer/citizen choices of entertainment and political information merely reaffirmed their preexisting prejudices, or their "sophisticated tastes," as they were conditioned to call their predilections. As a matter of fact, many onliners actually subscribed to "smart agents" that had become popular during the late 1990s. Smart agents were essentially electronic versions of clipping services that individually provided a set of information tailored to meet predetermined needs and/or desires. Also available to the information-rich were data, news, chat, or whatever they wanted from a variety of free and commercial electronic newspapers, bulletin boards, Web sites, and online chat stations, including those that provided points of view from the middle to the extremes. For those with access, the Internet had become the closest thing to the public sphere.

The Internet, however, was utilized by less than half of the American population. As a consequence, much information of critical importance never reached the plain of public debate or entered into the conversation of the masses that depended primarily on television for their information. This "information gap" caused citizens to arrive at different decisions on candidates or issues depending on whether they did or did not have access to information over the Internet. And the problem got worse in 2001, when the FCC ruled that the more than fifty-year-old National Television Standards Committee (NTSC) broadcast television standard would be finally phased out as obsolete and replaced by the new high-definition television (HDTV) standard.

Because of the relatively expensive cost of a new high-definition television receiver (between $1,000 and $4,000 a set), not everyone could afford one, especially not those in low-income households disproportionately made up of African Americans, Hispanic Americans, and single-parent families (generally unmarried women and their children). So universal access to broadcast television was lost. It became even more difficult for the common person to access current information, infotainment, or cheap entertainment. Therefore, poor people began to depend on radio as their prime source of information. They continued to use their now obsolete television sets and VCRs to watch old television programs and movies, while the information-rich watched slick pay-per-view state-of-the-art movies and sporting events, or played online computer games, or took virtual trips in high definition on huge, vivid screens. And since HDTV was essentially a big-screen computer monitor, the Internet could be accessed remotely and viewed clearly from anywhere in a room. As a matter of fact, "television programs" were now transmitted via the expanded broadband, fiber-optic-based Internet, as well as directly by communication satellites—all in the new high-definition, digital format. The most popular advertiser-supported programs were sitcoms, drama series, movies, and sports.

The general election of 2000 was significant because of sameness. The election of 2000 was essentially the same as the general election of 1996, only more so: excesses of money spent, lobbying, and negative advertising, and the lack of genuine serious discussion on issues, controversies, or possible solutions offered by the candidates themselves. In four years, the political sound bite had shrunk from seven seconds to five seconds of babble. And with the funding for public radio having been removed earlier in that year, there was practically no meaningful public political information except to those citizens who read the *New York Times* or the *Washington Post* or those who were logged onto the Internet, where rich and full conversations, dialogue, discussion, and political information services were to be found in abundance—for those who had access, knew how to search, and were interested.

The only problem was that not everyone had such rich access. Only about 27 percent of U.S. households were actually using political information provided online, although some 50 percent actually had access to the emerging superinforinationentertainment wire or wireless network of networks. Most Americans then, even when given the choice, selected among the 10,000 or more channels of entertainment or infotainment—from virtual experiences with dream dates to virtual competition in make-believe sporting events or astral traveling toward pseudoknowledge; few had time to explore real politics. "It is the job of professionals to keep up with politics," said Joe Average. "I want my HDTV-MTV-Pay-Per-View-movie. And I want it now!"

But for concerned citizens, the Net provided a wealth of political information. For the political information junkie, there was lots of political information. But there was also much political infojunk. The really good material included online voter guides, modeled after projects initiated in the spring of 1996 by the California Voter Foundation,[7] and online disclosures of all campaign finance and lobbying expenditure information, modeled from legislation introduced by California State Assemblywoman Jackie Speier, that required all state-level candidates and lobbying entities to file electronically all campaign information with the secretary of state. The secretary of state then made the filings immediately available on the Internet, enabling government watchdog organizations and members of the public to review current disclosures, as well as services such as PoliticsUSA On-Line, the daily feed of political gossip and facts.

The problem with the availability of rich, textual information for some (elites) while the great majority of citizens relied on broadcast information is that the national plebiscite was ill-educated, thus favoring the elites. Research has shown that those whose primary source of news is print are able to articulate arguments for their positions on issues and choices of candidates, whereas those whose primary source of news is radio and television may have positions and candidates they favor but are not able to articulate their reasoning. Perhaps this is so because those who rely on broadcasting are primarily fed empty but momentarily satisfying emotional appeals rather than substance. In any event, in the year 2000, the Fox Television Network was still the only television network to provide free air time to leading presidential candidates, including an hour on the evening before the election. In addition to the provision of that one hour, provided a second hour of live, in-person coverage in minute segments during prime time, beginning thirty-one days prior election. But of Fox's more than 1,400 affiliates, more than 75 percent refused to run the segments or the one-hour election eve access program.[8]

Because so many Americans had long before discovered how to program their V-chips to filter out "undesirable" programs containing excessive violence and sex, early in 2002, a group of hackers discovered how to reengineer the V-chip devices to take out television commercials. By 2004, many television viewers were filtering out political ads as well. Although illegal since the advertising industry successfully lobbied Congress to ban the super V-chips that eliminated ads on the argument that they would undermine the financial base of advertiser supported television, many citizens continued to use them, especially to filter out negative political campaign ads and the mudslinging that become a norm of the "good campaign." "The super V-chip does no less than the remote control device," claimed Congressman Ralph Nader of the Green Party.

The only information about the election came from campaign commercials; very few Americans watched commercial television. Those who could afford to watch could also afford the super V-chip. They did hold an election in 2004, but no one came.

Upon analyzing the demographic makeup of those who actually voted, through exit polling techniques and electronic means, it became apparent to all that the 22 percent of the electorate who actually voted were primarily information rich elites, who represented a primary stakeholder class in support of the status quo. The election of 2004 was the first to use home-based personal computers and the superinformationentertainment highway both to register and to vote.

Relatively satisfied citizens wanting to ratify and confirm that "I'm all right, Jack!" and "I've got mine, now you earn yours" comprised the group that was most likely to vote in the general election of 2004. This group tended to be made up primarily of young, white, highly educated citizens with above average incomes who resided in a variety of places, including wilderness areas and beach homes. Telecommuters, programmers, writers, smart agents, instructors, teachers, and "problem-solvers" were the job descriptions of the largest segment of voters in the election of 2004. But their skills and facility with computers and in the digital information environment did not protect them from participating in an election that later turned out to be tainted with fraud and misconduct: The incumbent tried to steal the election by changing votes by manipulating the bits.

Several months after the incumbent administration had been sworn in and the president had given his State of the Union address, evidence began appearing that computer security had been inadequate to protect the integrity of the ballots. Rogue security agents within government had tampered with the national vote-counter computer system by placing a stealth virus into the tabulation software to change every hundredth vote for the opposition candidate into a vote for the incumbent in those states where the race was close.

Moreover, it is now believed that the incumbent administration may have used new second-generation "clipper chip" technology to identify individual voter ballots and to create huge enemies lists, next to which the attempt to identify political opponents during the Nixon administration pales. The case is still under investigation by the Office of the Special Prosecutor.

It now appears certain that electronic ballots were not secret ballots at all. Anyone who voted with a personal computer did so openly. It was subsequently pointed out that any technology that can continuously verify the identity of computer users inherently can also violate voter privacy and security. "But without such verification technology," the incumbent administration argued, "ineligible persons such as noncitizens, children, felons, and the insane would vote illegally."

"Security is an illusion!" shouted Opra D. Gates, an official with the National Information Infrastructure (NII) Liberation Front, a hacker group that in 2002 penetrated secure commercial systems and even the U.S. Department of Defense firewall-protected systems, using "snifter" software to gain illegal access. "No computer network is absolutely secure from us. We can break into any data bank in the world if given enough time."

Civil rights groups made another set of arguments about computer voting that merited consideration on equity grounds: They said that since only 60 percent of U.S. households had access to either a personal computer or a network computer, the concept of one-person, one-vote had been undermined. Poor people generally, racial minorities, and even the elderly were disproportionately without access to the means of voting electronically if they stayed home, particularly during the record-setting weather in the Northeast and Midwestern parts of the nation during the month of November. And because of the relatively high cost of going online, the new computer balloting was tantamount to a new form of poll tax. In addition, because of the broader, deeper levels of literacy required to use complex computer software, electronic voting represented a literacy test that kept almost one third of the adult population at home on election day.

When the numbers came in reporting on the unprecedented low voter turnout, not only were the candidates dumbfounded, even citizens who failed to exercise their franchise by their failure to vote "because it wouldn't make a difference anyway" realized that something had radically and profoundly changed our political culture. Everyone was frightened that the government elected into power had very little legitimacy and practically no mandate to represent the collective will of the people.

The president was elected by only 14.5 percent of all eligible voters. Up to this point, no one really took the responsibility of civil society seriously, nor was there any meaningful attempt toward significant political reform. Ironically, anyone who even suggested dramatic but necessary reform previously was labeled with such divisive terms as "anti-democratic," "left-wing," and "radical rabble rouser." Incumbent politicians and lobbyists, as well as the eight colossal, conglomerate media and communications firms that dominated access and the flow of culture, were quite satisfied with the status quo until the surprising election of 2004. To them, prior to the election of 2004, America had the best political system in the world. The old system of politics had been theirs for the buying.

As a result of the disastrous presidential election of 2004, people's viewing and information consumption habits began to change. The burning issues following the election of 2004 were American democracy and its possible demise, or as some cynics said, its evolution into "corporate plutocracy." Ironically, radical solutions offered by marginalized groups ultimately provided the ideas essential to save the Republic.

"Democracy Now" movements sprang up spontaneously across the United States and began to sweep the nation. Chants from the 1960s were heard from city to city: "Power to the people! More power to the people!"

Citizens began to demonstrate at public places, claiming them as "demospheres"—places where citizens addressed government openly in rational and public deliberations about what kind of society they wanted and what actions of government would be necessary to promote the common good. These public rallies were not dissimilar to those that occurred at Tienanmen Square in China during the early 1990s, but without, of course, the state or corporate security forces using tanks or authoritarian suppression techniques against the citizens (probably because the public and private police were, in the final analysis, also angry citizens). The American people just could not take being treated as mere consumers any longer. They demanded to be treated with the respect accorded citizens.

By the year 2005, the people demanded full citizenship and assumed their responsibility to act accordingly, toward building a better civic society. No more could the American people stand by or sit idly watching HDTV while their democracy was being advertised, sold, lobbied, and traded away like pork bellies, electronic digits, or widgets in the marketplace. The poor showing of American democracy in the boycotted election of 2004 was a wake-up call for the average citizen to create a true government by the people, for the people, and of the people.

No one seemed to be paying attention to the electorate. The voter turnout for the previous presidential election in 2000 had been down to only 33 percent of those eligible to vote, continuing a decades-long slide, but no one worried at the time, except a few scholars and marginalized groups who didn't own or watch HDTV. Politicians, candidates, spin doctors, and television executives all had been taking citizens and the interests of citizens for granted and, as a consequence, they were all blindsided by the results of the boycotted election of 2004—and by what it represented: a vote of no confidence in what then remained of American democratic institutions, a national mirage with little substance. "What Kind of Society Have We Become?" "Where Do We Go from Here?" "Don't We Care Anymore about Our National Interests?" "It's Wake Up Time—Democracy on the Brink"—these were the headlines on the day after the 2004 election in the remaining hard-text national newspapers.

Now, almost four years later, just a month prior to the general election, knowledgeable sources are predicting a historically high voter turnout. Almost 99 percent of those citizens eligible to vote are expected actually to turn out and vote in this year's election. During the month-long period[9] in which some 180 million registered adult citizens will go into a voting booth or mail in their ballots, there will be public ceremonies, teach-ins, and affirmative participation by people at public places in their communities. These efforts are aimed at building democratic bridges and including all the people not just politically, but civically and socially in American society and culture.

The primary reason for such jubilant celebration concerning the upcoming election is perhaps provided in large measure by a market incentive to vote—the lottery—that is being called the "great American dream ballot box" that lubricates democracy in the United States. But, first, more context.

In 2005, Congress enacted the Compulsory Voter Registration Act, which requires the fifty states as well as the District of Columbia and U.S. territories to register to vote all U.S. citizens who are or will be 18 years old prior to midnight on the last day of the month-long voting period for any presidential election. Because the federal government under the new law has the authority to withhold a percentage of money from federal block grants to the states equal to twice the percentage of unregistered eligible voters in a state, states have ample incentive to enforce the voter registration. Consequently, the various states have enacted local mandatory registration laws and a system of monetary fines that start at ten dollars during the first three-month period after a minor turns 18. Thereafter, the state may fine an individual for failing to register to vote in amounts that increase by ten dollars per month for each month he is not registered, until the total of the fine reaches $250. Although all citizens have an affirmative duty to register to vote under the act, there is no legal requirement that they actually vote. Instead, affirmative incentives are provided for that.

Registration is now very easy. A person eligible to vote may register by mail, at public schools, at post offices, on their jobs, at their cable/telephone/television utility company when paying their monthly information bill, or at any government agency. The information utility companies automatically provide reminder registration notices to people within sixty days prior to their eighteenth birthday, as a public service.

State governments have been delighted with the imposition of mandatory voter registration because of the benefits they receive, including full payment of their block grant allocation, a substantial increase in the diversity of jury pools, and more accurate census counts that yield a fairer distribution of public benefits.

Privacy violation has not been a serious concern; no one worries about privacy issues, since they are now protected by a recently ratified constitutional amendment guaranteeing to individuals the right to a reasonable expectation of privacy.[10] As a consequence of the new privacy amendment, Congress also enacted the Privacy Act of 2005, which established a Federal Privacy Commission, modeled after a similar agency in Canada. The Privacy Act requires that any nonprofit or commercial entity that uses an individual's name and/or personal identifying information for any fund-raising or commercial purpose on a mailing list, print or electronic, must notify that individual, in writing, by April 15 of each year. Also, if commercial gain or profit results from the sale, lease, or rental of any such mailing list, then the business enterprise must, under the provisions of the act, pay a user fee to each individual whose name or personal identifying information is used in an amount totaling one-tenth of one cent per use of the name. This legislation establishes a property ownership right in an individual's name, rewards the person for any appropriation of his name and identifying information, and guarantees notification to the individual each year so that the person whose name is being used has adequate notice of who is using his name and for what purpose (e.g., to solicit contributions, to recruit to a cause, or to profit on the sale of behavioral profiles).

Responding to the wake-up call of the 2004 election, Congress realized that the federal government was democratic in form but not in substance. Drastic measures were deemed necessary to restore the substance of American democracy. Therefore, both the campaign finance system and the winner-take-all plurality system needed to be changed radically. Money and the unfairness of the "first past the post" plurality system, which encourages a two-party monopoly (because votes for third parties are wasted) and rewards the gerrymandering of single-member districts to give parties or particular racial groups built-in advantages, had to be taken out of politics.[11]

First, regarding the undue influence of money, the solution offered by Congressional sBut because more and more viewers of television were filtering out political ads with their super V-chips, fewer potential voters were watching political advertisements anyway. Moreover, by this time, most political campaign money was being spent on reaching smaller, discrete, targeted audiences through the new technologies, primarily the Internet, which now transmitted television programs, movies on demand, and cable fare.[12] Therefore, something more radical was required to minimize the influence of money in political campaigns. The solution ultimately arrived at by Congress was to ban all political advertising and to require both print and electronic media to provide free public-service notices concerning elections.[13]

Next, Congress showed even more leadership and courage by eliminating the plurality system and replacing it with a "party system" of proportional representation.[14] Now the states are divided into multimember districts in which several political parties present lists of candidates. The voter selects one party and its slate of candidates to represent her. Party slates can be either "closed," requiring the voter to select the entire slate, or "open," allowing the voter to indicate a preference for individual candidates on the slate. The available seats in the election are then divided proportionally among the parties according to the vote tally. If, for example, a party receives 30 percent of the votes, then that party gets 30 percent of the seats up for grabs in the legislature; 10 percent of the vote entitles the party to receive 10 percent of the seats, and so on, with the exception of parties receiving less than 5 percent of the vote, which are awarded no seats.

This new proportional representation system encourages multiparty democracy because it permits even small parties to elect representatives. Environmentalists, labor, and consumer parties are now among the interests being represented in the new Congress. To qualify as a viable political party under this new system, parties must pass a minimum threshold of the total vote; the 5 percent threshold mentioned above has checked extremist parties. One of the key benefits of the proportional representation system is that it has reduced the incentives to engage in partisan or racial gerrymandering because every significant party or voting bloc in the multimember districts is represented more or less in proportion to its strength in the entire electorate, regardless of how the district lines have been drawn. Moreover, the new system is encouraging greater citizen participation in government because everyone now feels that his interests are being represented and his vote now makes a difference.

Other significant political reforms that promote the "new democracy movement" include provisions of the Universal Service and Access to Information and Technology Act of 2005.[15] This law defines "universal service and access" as requiring "for all the people of the United States, access to (1) essential information, (2) appropriate information technology, (3) audiences, both small (one-to-one) and mass (broadcasting), (4) the means (funding) for producing information in digital formats and distributing them, and (5) a reasonable right of privacy."[16]

The privacy provisions of the Act became law prior to the ratification of the constitutional amendment guaranteeing citizens' right to privacy but were necessary at the time because too many users of online communications services were reluctant to provide personal or financial data. Users' concerns stemmed from the high possibility of fraud or privacy abuse, notwithstanding the pleas of digital entrepreneurs who said, "It's safe. Trust me."

"Essential information" has been interpreted to mean, among other things, public information that government keeps, maintains, processes, and uses in the course of doing government work: that information which taxpayers have paid for, with the exception of government information that is subject to exceptions under the Freedom of Information Act. Thus, information concerning criminal investigations, personnel records, national defense and security, etc., are still not available to the general public. Moreover, the Internet and e-mail[17] have now been deemed essential information services, as well as public education—from cradle to grave, if an individual wants to take advantage of this public utility. Public broadcasting and video are also essential under the Act.

"Appropriate information technology" has been defined to mean a wide range of digital technology, delivered via radio and by wire, as well as the hardware for receiving digital signals from wireless and wired services. This provision was found to be necessary to create a national information infrastructure that is truly national. The hands-off approach of market reliance had led to a form of digital feudalism.

Although the mega-telecommunications companies at one time competed vigorously with one another, by 2001 it was obvious that "market competition" was a concept from a different age, as reflected by the lack of any significant antitrust enforcement in decades, even when the "baby Bells," cable companies, and former long distance service providers (AT&T, MCI, and Sprint) merged with one another or entered into some form of strategic alliance to compete globally.

The threat of global competition seemed to have made competition in the domestic market unnecessary, and "bigness" was now thought to be necessary to give "American champions" playing in the global arena a competitive edge against foreign-based multinational corporations. It was a sort of economic nationalism that seemed to regard corporations as supercitizens. But these giant media-information-entertainment-communications corporations did not necessarily promote the interests of Americans, at least not those who were not stockholders. Because large segments of society simply could not afford access to the conglomerates' services, they were passed over as "undeserving poor." Thus, the gap between the rich and poor grew wider—that is, until Congress passed the historic Information Access Act of 2005, "to unite the peoples of America within a common public information infrastructure and to promote national defense." Accordingly, access to both the common carrier Public Broadcast Network and access to the National Public Telecommunication Network was mandated. With these new network services, government has again become the service provider of last resort by developing and making available appropriate information technology and software, enabling all the people of the United States to be productive, creative, and self-realized members of a national community.

Funding for the development of the public infrastructure and public information products and services (on both the public wire[18] and public air) is obtained by charging all commercial users of public airwaves reasonable user fees. This continuous revenue source would not have been available had Congress allowed the sale of broadcast frequencies during the late 1990s, as certain special interests had lobbied for.[19] This arrangement was thought to be only fair, since the $100 billion investment that the public had made in the old, now obsolete NTSC television technology was lost. There is also a 10 percent surcharge on the purchase of new digital TV sets. Since over-the-air television reception is now restricted to sets equipped to handle transmissions in accordance with the new HDTV or Digital Advanced TV standards, which are incompatible with the now obsolete NTSC standard, enough surplus revenue has been collected to build an endowment for a public-information trust that distributes funding grants and subsidies to independent makers of public information products, goods, and services in various formats.

Wire-delivered services on the new public broadband fiber-optic network, include e-mail service (which has greatly relieved the old U.S. Postal Service). The broadband fiber-optic network provides all the people of the United States with efficient access to essential public information, including public education, civic information, medical and health care information, and information regarding any government function or service. As a matter of fact, all government records and public information that were not otherwise legally classified under exceptions to the Freedom of Information Act are now available on public networks.

Creation of this public information utility was justified on the basis of enhancing America's national defense, in accord with the long-standing mandate of Title 1, Section 1 of the Communications Act of 1934, as amended. The underlying rationale is that what is needed to safeguard our defense in the long run is a strong and viable workforce—one that is intelligent and educated—and an inclusive, cohesive society capable of winning global competition in knowledge markets. The national defense rationale, after all, provided government incentives in education and training after the Soviet Union successfully launched the world's first man-made communications satellite, Sputnik. Our response was to invest in educating our children and adult populations. Education and information was then deemed to be a strategic resource and a weapon against ignorance and tyranny. In response to Sputnik, the Eisenhower administration launched the National Defense Education Act. Now, in our present global crisis following the near collapse of American democracy, a similarly appropriate response is called for and has been adopted.

On the broadcast end, because of the recognition that digital compression technology could multiply the number of television channels fourfold or tenfold, scarcity was no long a restraining barrier to keep the airwaves out of the hands of the people. Therefore, Congress enacted laws that set aside, in each market, six terrestrial broadcast channels and six satellite broadcast channels as dedicated public-network common-carrier channels. The satellite broadcast channels provide nationwide and regional programming services that include independent nonprofit television programming; a C-SPAN service with regional, statewide, and national government programming; a public education/literacy network; a children's television network, and a first amendment–free speech–demosphere channel, on which political issues are debated and discussed and to which candidates for national, statewide, and local office have free limited access. The same types of services are available for ea based television channels set aside for these purposes. Also, no radio or television station, or any media entity, may sell time for political advertisements. Such advertisements are banned, although broadcast radio or television stations may offer any amount of time to any candidate for public office, so long as all other legally qualified candidates for the same office are offered an equal opportunity of access.

Public schools are now required to teach a new media literacy curriculum consisting of a range of courses that attempt to empower individuals with critical-thinking and communication skills, as well as a core body of information concerning democracy, civil culture, and civics. The intent of these courses is to teach all U.S. citizens how to survive and succeed in the information-knowledge-global economy. For example, beginning as early as kindergarten, children must be taught not only traditional literacy skills, but also how to listen critically and how to communicate effectively; how to recognize propaganda and to deconstruct messages of all sorts, including messages of the media; how to analyze cartoons, commercials, movies, books, and newspapers; and, as they advance in age, how to use effectively information technologies such as computers, digital recording, and display devices and how to create their own messages, writings, graphics, videos, art, music, etc. Online and broadcast education is also available twenty-four hours a day to supplement in-class teaching. Equal educational opportunities are provided to all of the people of the United States, from cradle to grave. Lifelong learning is no longer the exception, but the norm. The national objective of public education, besides skills acquisition, is to develop an objectively informed and intellectually vigorous citizenry—an informed and active public.

Conclusion

In conclusion, a few words on the prime reason for the expected record-high voter turnout for the election of 2008. It is indeed the lottery, touted as "the great American dream ballot box." In each state or territory during a presidential election, the federal government contributes 25 cents per voter into a state voter lottery. A single voter in each state wins the lottery, notwithstanding for whom they voted, so long as she has voted during the month-long period that the polls remain open. A lottery of this sort gets almost everyone eligible to the voting booth for the chance of realizing two American dreams: the chance of becoming instantly wealthy and the opportunity to exercise a meaningful vote.

When I explained this lottery scheme to one of my colleagues at Harvard, as a means of maximizing voter turnout, I was presented with the following reply: "But who would want all those people to vote anyway?"

I thought about that response a lot since then: "Who would want all those people to vote anyway?" The response reveals that the real problem with contemporary elections, campaigning, and voting in the United States is not technology, per se. It is power, per se. Comfortable elites simply don't want others included in the equation of American democracy, regardless of what technology is available or utilized. Until we rethink that equation, democracy in the United States will be an illusion. In the present equation, elections are won by minimizing choice and the opportunity for people to make real decisions. Yet elections should be, and in the year 2008, they may finally be, about maximizing real choice and the opportunity for ordinary citizens to participate in making those choices—by whatever technology necessary.

Notes

A version of this chapter previously appeared in Anthony Corrado and Charles Firestone, eds., *Elections in Cyberspace: Toward a New Era in American Politics,* a Report of the Aspen Institute Communications and Society Program and the American Bar Association Standing Committee on Election Law (Washington, D.C.: The Aspen Institute, 1996).

1. "[T]he transformation of the information infrastructure and emergence of the "net"—the telecommunications network—as the dominant medium has led to a wide variety of frustrations for nation-states as they exercise traditional modes of power, such as control over either financial or information flows across their borders . . . transnational corporations have come to rival and sometimes outweigh nation-states in the exercise of a variety of forms of power."

William Berry et al., in *Last Rights: Revisiting Four Theories- of the Press,* ed. John C. Nerone (Urbana: University of Illinois Press, 1995), 160.

2. Here, I assume that the more things change, the more they will stay the same, or as Dwight D. Eisenhower is quoted as having said: "Things are more like they are today than they have ever been before." Jack Dann an Dozois, ed. *Future Power: A Science Fiction Anthology* (New York: Random House, 1976).

3. More appropriately called the "demosphere," according to Ronnie Dugger, publisher of *The Texas Observer* and fellow of the Shorenstein Center on Press, Politics, and Public Policy, Kennedy School of Government, Harvard University, spring term, 1996.

4. Actual quotation of Lion Caron of Berlin, New Hampshire, in the *Boston Globe,* March 22, 1996.

5. "McWorld" [globalism and universal markets] makes "national borders porous from without." Like the Jihad, "McWorld . . . make[s] war on the nation-state and thus undermine(s) the nation-state's democratic institutions . . . [t] eschews civil society and belittles democratic citizenship, . . . indifferent to civil liberty. Jihad forges communities of blood rooted in exclusion and hatred, communities that slight democracy in favor of tyrannical paternalism or consensual tribalism. McWorld forges global markets rooted in consumption and profit, leaving to an untrustworthy, if not altogether fictitious, invisible hand issues of public interest and common good that once might have been nurtured, by democratic citizenries and their watchful governments." Benjamin R. Barber, *Jihad vs. McWorld* (New York: Times/ Random House, 1995), 6–7.

6. Pollster Daniel Yankelovich rebuts the conventional wisdom that the decline in participation by Americans in presidential and congressional elections is due to voter apathy: the view that Americans do not get involved because they do not care. Instead, he claims that "[t]he chief reason so many Americans do not vote is because they do not think their votes will make a difference." He goes on to say that "[b]eneath the surface of formal arrangements to ensure citizen participation, the political reality is that an intangible something [a barrier] separates the general public from the thin layer of elites—officials, experts, and leaders who hold the real power and make the important decisions." That barrier that exists between America's elites and its average citizens is, according to Yankelovich, intellectual snobbery. Whereupon he offers the following observation:

> An adversarial struggle exists between experts and the public on who will govern America. On one side are the experts—smaller in number and weaker than the public in formal power but holding an indispensable piece of the solution. As a group, these experts respect the institution of democracy and would be chagrined if their good faith were challenged. At the same time, however, their view of the general public is that it is ill-informed and ill-equipped to deal with the problems to which they, the experts, have devoted their lives. . . .

Unfortunately . . . most average citizens are ill-prepared to exercise their responsibilities for self-governance, even though they have a deep-seated desire to have more of a say in decisions. People want their opinions heeded—not every whim and impulse that may be registered in an opinion poll, but their thoughtful, considered judgments. But in present-day America, few institutions are devoted to helping the public to form considered judgments, and the public is discouraged from doing the necessary hard work because there is little incentive to do so. In principle, the people are sovereign. In practice, the experts and technocrats have spilled over their legitimate boundaries and are encroaching on the public's territory. (From Daniel Yankelovich, *Coming to Public Judgment, Making Democracy Work in a Complex World* [Syracuse: Syracuse University Press, 1991], 3–4).

7. The California Voter Foundation (CVF) <http://www.wcbconi.coitx/cvf/> is a nonpartisan, nonprofit organization based in Sacramento. The 19 percent voter guide was produced in partnership with California Secretary of State Bill Jones, who also unveiled two new Web sites: the 1996 California primary election server, which features live returns on election night <http://www.primary96.ca.gov>, and the California Secretary of State home page <http://www.primary96.ss.cagov>. Voters can use the California Online Voter Guide to find information about statewide measures as well as presidential, congressional, legislative, and candidates running for office in California. In 1994, CVF produced its first online guide, which was accessed times and registered over 36,000 file retrievals. In 1995, CVF produced the San Francisco Online Voter Guide, which featured the first Internet da of campaign contributions and expenditures. The San Francisco registered over 23,000 file retrievals prior to the election and was rated by *PC* as one of the top 100 Web sites of 1995.

8. By 1997, the Federal Communications Commission had established a HDTV standard, but instead of making the standard mandatory, it allowed broadcasters the discretion to adopt HDTV or split their 6 MHz frequency into four, six, eight or even sixteen Digital Advanced TV channels, which the industry did in order to increase its revenue streams. The irony of this abundance of television channels was that programming was just as bad and noninnovative as it had been; and, moreover, only a handful of TV licensees saw themselves as public trustees, except in name only. Neither the *HDTV nor the Advanced TV* standards were compatible with NTSC, however.

9. According to John Deardourff of The Media Company, one of the country's leading political strategists and a pioneer of political advertising in a statement made during a brown bag lunch at the Shorenstein Center on the Press Politics and Public Policy, Kennedy School of Government, Harvard University, on April 15, 1996, the citizens of Texas may already vote up to 20 days, leading up to the close of certain state and local elections.

10. Such an amendment could be modeled after the provision in the Constitution of the Republic of South Africa, ACT No. 20, 1993, under Chapter 3, 13, which states: "Every person shall have the right to his or her personal privacy which shall include the right not to be the subject to searches of his or her person, home, or property, the seizure of private possessions

or the violation of private communications" (emphasis added). California also has an amendment in its constitution guaranteeing a right to privacy.

11. Michael Lind, "Prescription for a New National Democracy," *Political Science Quarterly* 110, no. 4 (1995–1996): 563–586.

12. "[D]espite their limitations, new media are replacing the press as conduits for information flows from governments to people and from people to governments. In similar fashion, the press is losing its privileged role as a definer of facticity." Nerone, Id., *Last Rights,* 174. Also, trends in media technology are toward replacing broad audiences with increasingly narrow ones.

13. "Candidates without enormous amounts of money, either from their fortunes or from rich individuals and special interest groups, cannot hope to win party primaries, much less general elections. Indeed, the Buckley decision is one reason why more than half of the members of the Senate today are millionaires [citation omitted]. The bias toward the rich embodied in American campaign finance practices makes a mockery of America's democratic ideals. Genuine democracy requires not only juridical equality among races when it comes to individual rights, but also political equality among the different socioeconomic classes of citizens.

> It is time to build a wall of separation between check and state. Curing the disease of plutocratic politics requires a correct diagnosis of its cause: the costs of political advertising. The basic problem is that special interests buy access and favors by donating the money needed for expensive political advertising in the media. Elaborate schemes governing the flow of money do nothing to address the central problem: paid political advertising. Instead of devising unworkable limits on campaign financing that leave the basic system intact, we should cut the Gordian knot of campaign corruption by simply outlawing paid political advertising on behalf of any candidate for public office. The replacement of political advertising by free informational public service notices in the electronic and print media would level the playing field of politics and kill off an entire parasitic industry of media consultants and spin doctors.

> "An outright ban on paid political advertising and the imposition of free time requirements on the media are radical measures, but nothing less is necessary if we are to prevent our government from continuing to be sold to the highest bidders. The argument against strict public regulation of money in politics is based on a false analogy between free spending and free speech protected under the First Amendment. The analogy is false, because limits on campaign finance do not address the content of speech—only its volume, as it were. It is not an infringement on free speech to say that, in a large public auditorium, Douglas will not be allowed to use a microphone unless Lincoln can as well." Lind, "Prescriptions for a New National Democracy," *Political Science Quarterly* 110, no. 4 (1995–1996): 570.

14. There are many different types of proportional representation (PR). PR is the voting system used by most of the world's major democracies, because it is a flexible system that may be adapted to the situation of any city, state, or nation. Besides the list system, discussed below, the three additional types most commonly used are

   1. Mixed-member system. This PR hybrid elects half the legislature from single-seat, winner-take-all districts and the other half by the list system. The mixed-member system smoothly combines geographic, ideological, and proportional representation.

   2. Preference voting (PV). In PV, the voter simply ranks candidates in an order of preference (1, 2, 3, 4, etc.). Once a voter's first choice is elected or eliminated, excess votes are "transferred" to subsequent preferences until all positions are filled. Voters can vote for their favorite candidate(s), knowing that if that candidate doesn't receive enough votes, their vote will "transfer" to their next preference. With PV, every vote counts, and very few votes are wasted. PV is ideal for nonpartisan elections like city councils.

   3. Majority preference voting (MPV). Related to PV, MPV is ideal when selecting a single candidate such as president, mayor, or governor who must win a majority. As in PV, the voter simply ranks candidates in an order of preference (e.g., 1. Clinton, 2. Dole, 3. Perot). The candidate with the least number of first-place votes is eliminated, and his or her votes are "transferred" to each voter's second choice, etc., until a candidate has a majority.

   "Proportional Representation; W About?" Center for Voting and Democracy, Washington, D.C. (2002), available online at <http://www.fairvote.org/pr/index.html>.

15. "Federal support for a national information infrastructure—a postal service is generally justified by the need to ensure that representatives of it can communicate with their constituents in a two-way process." Nerone, Id., 171. See also Robert H. Anderson, Tora K. Bikson, Sally Ann Law and Bridger M. Mitchell, *Universal Access to Email: Feasibility and Societal Implications* (Santa Monica, Calif.: RAND, 1995). The United States is by no means the only nation that guarantees the freedoms of speech or the press in its constitution. As a matter of fact, some nations go further by providing the guarantees to freedoms of expression and even information. For example, Article 21 of the Japanese constitution, written by American officials over a four-day time span, reads as follows: "Freedom of assembly and association as well as speech, press and all, other forms of expression are guaranteed. No censorship shall be maintained, nor shall the secrecy of any means of communications be violated."

   Moreover, the constitution of the Republic of South Africa provides even broader freedoms. The following articles under the heading "Fundamental Rights" in chapter 3 are examples:

   Religion, belief and opinion: 14.(1) Every person shall have the rights to freedom of conscience, religion, thought, belief, and opinion, which shall include academic freedom in institutions of higher learning . . .

Freedom of expression: 15.(1) Every person shall have the freedom of speech and expression, which shall include freedom of the press and other media, and the freedom of artistic creativity and scientific research. (2) All media financed by or under the control of the state shall be regulated in a manner which ensures impartiality and the expression of a diversity of opinion. . . .

Political rights: 21.(1) Every person shall have the right—(a) to form, to participate in the activities of and to recruit members for a political party; (b) to campaign for a political party or cause; and (c) to make political choices. (2) Every citizen shall have the right to vote, to do so in se to stand for election to public office. . . .

Access to information: 23. Every person shall have the right of access to all information held by the state or any of its organs at any level of government in so far as such information is required for the exercise or protection of any of his or her rights. . . .

Language and culture: 31. Every person shall have the right to use the language and to participate in the cultural life of his or her choice.

Education: 32. Every person shall have the right—(a) to basic education and to equal access to educational institutions; (b) to instruction in the language of his or her choice where this is reasonably practicable; and (c) to establish, where practicable, educational institutions based on a common culture, language or religion, provided that there shall be no discrimination on the ground of race.

16. See, generally, Nolan Bowie, "Equity and Access to Information Technology," in *Annual Review,* ed. (Institute for Information Studies, 1990), Jorge Reina Schement and Terry Curtis, "Distributional Justice," in *Tendencies and Tensions of the Information Age,* ed. (New Brunswick, N.J.: Transaction, 1995), Francis Dummer Fisher, "Open Sesame! How to Get to the Treasure of Electronic Information," in U.S. Department of Commerce, *20/20 Vision: The Development of a National Information Infrastructure* (Washington, D.C., 1994), and Susan G. Hadden, "Universal Service: Policy Options for the Future," Policy working paper, Benton Foundation, Washington, D.C. 1994.

17. "We find that use of electronic mail is valuable for individuals and communities, for the practice and spread of democracy, and for the general development of a viable National Information Infrastructure (NII). Consequently, the nation should support universal access to e-mail through appropriate public and private policies. . . .

"Individuals' accessibility to e-mail is hampered by increasing income, education, and racial gaps in the availability of computers and access to network services. Some policy remedies appear to be required. . . .

It is critical that electronic mail be a basic service in a National Information Infrastructure. . . .

It is important to reduce the increasing gaps in access to basic electronic information system services, specifically, access to electronic mail services. (Anderson et al., *Universal Access to Email: Feasibility and Societal Implications,* xiv–xv)

18. The public wire had its origins in the now obsolete, twisted-pair telephone system used by the federal government as the emergency backup communications service FTS-2000. This system was upgraded into a national grid, based on broadband, interactive, fiber-optic technology. It now provides information services to people who cannot afford commercial online information services as a matter of right, including the provision of e-mail and other essential information and services that the unregulated market had denied the former "information have-nots."

19. Because spectrum user fees could be collected only if the public still owned the airwaves, Congress had decided, after much debate, that it was in the public's long-term interest not to sell, via auction or otherwise, any additional radiomagnetic spectrum other than the limited amounts of microwave frequencies that had been sold during the mid-1990s for the development of personal digital services and cellular services.

II *Global Developments*

12 Democracy and New Media in Developing Nations: Opportunities and Challenges

Adam Clayton Powell III

In January 2000, journalists from around Europe gathered in London to discuss the role of online journalism in their countries. Late in the session, editors began to volunteer their favorite Internet-based sources of research and information. Most were predictable: the Web sites of the BBC, the *Guardian* and the *New York Times.* A few mentioned cnn.com. No one mentioned the Voice of America site. But one group of editors had a different choice: The Croatians said their favorite source was the online edition of the *Washington Post.* They found washingtonpost.com had better coverage of the Balkans than other Web sites, and they were checking the *Post* site every day.[1]

Consider the implications: Only six years after the start of popular adoption of the World Wide Web, editors in Zagreb and Dubrovnik were not listening to Voice of America or CNN but reading the *Washington Post,* a local newspaper with insignificant distribution outside of the Washington, D.C., metropolitan area. It is also a newspaper whose lead story that month was American football, but no matter: Editors in Croatia, or anywhere else in the world, could bookmark the washingtonpost.com international news section and go straight to the coverage they wanted. And as they decide which stories to play and how to play them, these editors view the *Washington Post* as the voice of America. (At washingtonpost.com, readership data are proprietary, but Mark Stencel, washingtonpost.com political editor, confirmed that a substantial portion of the site's traffic is from outside the United States).

This means that people living in the Balkans must now assume that the faraway *Post* has an influence on the news background that was unthinkable even a decade ago. And it means that U.S. diplomats and others traveling to that part of the world should be prepared to react to stories in the *Post* filed by the newspaper's reporters in the Balkans, at NATO headquarters, at the United Nations, and in Washington.

This is just an anecdote that tells a larger story. From on-the-ground experience on five continents over the past five years, it is clear that what editors are doing in Zagreb is also happening in newsrooms from Delhi to Bangkok, Dakar to Nairobi, Lima to Santiago.

And this has clear implications for censorship, content controls, and the democratic dialogue in countries around the world.

Following international news by going directly to the Internet editions of the *New York Times* is now routine. Going directly to the Web sites of the *Washington Post, Los Angeles Times,* or *Miami Herald* is not unusual. For regional coverage, journalists in Mexico have discovered that the *Dallas Morning News* devotes a great deal of effort and space to coverage of their country. And editors in Moscow found insights into U.S. views in the surprisingly extensive coverage of Chechnya in, of all places, the *Des Moines Register,* which was also a prime source of information about U.S. wheat exports to Russia. And everyone seemed to know, or at least know of, Matt Drudge's drudgereport.com.

With the large caveat that behaviors can always change, it seems clear that the Internet is enabling journalists—and, more important, everyone else—to bypass traditional gatekeepers of all kinds. Today, it means financial journalists, financiers, and anyone else interested in news of U.S. agriculture can access it directly from Iowa and the *Des Moines Register.* Tomorrow, they will be able to bypass the *Register* and cultivate their own sources, filing by e-mail.

Consider the coverage of *Al Ahram* in Egypt, an influential voice in the Arab world, where in the fall of 1998 stringer coverage of the U.S. was being phased in. Gamal Nkrumah, international affairs editor, described the e-mail stringer network his newspaper was assembling, covering the United States through the eyes of reporters in Brooklyn, Detroit, and other cities with large Arab American populations.[2] Nkrumah said he even had a stringer filing by e-mail from inside a federal prison in the United States, an inmate who was writing essays on Islam and U.S. politics.

"We could never do this even by fax," Nkrumah said. "But by e-mail, we can cover America."

And needless to say, *Al Ahram*'s stringer network provided a very different picture of the United States from the news budgets of CNN or the *New York Times.* That, in turn, means Egyptians and Americans must take account the daily news budget *Al Ahram*'s readers were starting to see—in 1998.

This far more complex, far more transparent view of the United States is also becoming the standard for most of the world. Almost every country in the world is now connected to the rest of the world by the Internet, so anyone on line anywhere can delve into another country and find information, sources, and people of interest.

At the very least, this means global professionals must also be schooled in these new tools, so that they can remain current with events and trends in their regions. But international relations and democracy must also be reimagined in a more public context: Anyone at a public computer kiosk or an Internet cafe has access to information resources of unprecedented breadth and depth.

And those kiosks and cafes are an important trend. Many argue that in much of the world, the Internet reaches only elites: government officials and business leaders, university professors and students, the wealthy and the influential. But through Net-connected elites, information from the Internet reaches radio listeners and newspaper readers around the world, so the Internet has an important secondary readership, those who hear or are influenced by online information via its shaping of more widely distributed media, outside of traditional, controlled media lanes of the past.

But remember those kiosks: In the past few years, it is clear that Internet use has spread beyond elites. Consider the case of Peru: The Internet is just for Peru's elite, according to the official figures, which showed that only 1 percent of the population had Internet access at home in 1999.[3] But drive down any street in Lima and you can see another story. In block after block, rich neighborhood and less affluent, there were signs for "Internet cabinas" everywhere. And some cabinas were "unofficial": families renting their PCs and Net connections by the hour, in their homes.

The reason for the spread of these homegrown kiosks was cost: The price of using a cabina for a quarter hour of e-mail was about the same as the price of a stamp for a postcard to the United States. At prime tourist locations, cabinas sprouted almost next to each other, even in remote corners of Peru. In the old Inca capital of Cusco, population 300,000 and over 11,000 feet up in the Andes, there are at least five Internet cabinas on the town square. Walk a block or two from the square and you can find others tucked into alleys, behind small, almost invisible signs.

But in Lima, the engine of Internet growth was more visible: It was not tourists, but residents, who were fueling the growth of the Net. And the killer application was not checking your office e-mail or surfing the Web, but chatting with relatives on other continents. And much of that chat had started to shift from text to voice: Internet telephony.

Lima's Miraflores neighborhood is one of forty-two official districts in the city, each with its own mayor and town hall. Just across from Miraflores's town hall, beyond the main church and John F. Kennedy Park, is a collection of small restaurants and local businesses where commuter buses converge from around the city. Look up to the second floor, where hand-painted red letters across eight windows spell "Internet." Welcome to Macrostudio, a neighborhood Internet center open twenty-four hours a day. Up from the street via a flight of spiral stairs, Macrostudio boasts two dozen PCs with Internet connections, with another computer by the stairs, just for play.

Over the cashier's window at the top of the stairs, prices were posted: one hour online for 4 soles (just over a dollar), 3 soles for a half hour and 2 soles for fifteen minutes. But wait: There was also peak pricing. At 12:30 P.M., the price for an hour increased from 4 to 6 soles (not quite two dollars). The truly cheap prices started at 11 P.M., when access prices dropped to 3.50 soles an hour (almost exactly a dollar). If you could produce a student I.D. you could get the overnight rate around the clock. And if you brought two or more friends, the group rates were even lower.

Then there were frequent surfer bonuses: For every hour you were online, you received one entry for a lottery for fifty free hours. A photo of the winner of the most recent drawing was next to the cashier.

By comparison, the price of a stamp for a postcard to the United States was 3 soles, and to see a movie at the twelve-screen multiplex down the street from Macrostudio cost 15 soles.

And this was not a cyber cafe. Instead of espresso, Macromedia featured techie cuisine: A vending machine sold Coke and Diet Coke, and in a country that grows 150 varieties of potatoes, the food choices were dominated by three varieties of Pringles. At midday on a Friday, just before peak pricing started, there were nine cabinas in use, most by men. Walter Merino Stapleton, the manager of Macrostudio, told me the cabinas drew equally from tourists and from local residents. Most, he said, come for e-mail, to surf the Web, and to chat with people "all over the world."

And there was that other price list over the cashier's window: Internet telephone to the United States: 1 sole for one minute, 10 soles for fifteen minutes. For the price of three postcard stamps, you get fifteen minutes on the Internet "phone" with a relative. A fifteen-minute call to the United States from one of the many telephone booths on the street nearby cost many times Macrostudio's three-dollar charge.

If you own your own PC, in Peru or anywhere else in the world, you can use Internet telephony almost free. The quality has become much better, and instead of computer-to-computer "chat," the software now supports computer-to-telephone conversations. Just enter the telephone area code and phone number, and you can talk across the street or across the ocean. But few in Peru can afford to buy a PC, so the cabinas were doing a thriving business.

Macrostudio used two different software packages, according to Merino, to link PC users in Lima to people all over the world in real-time voice contact: For calls to the United States, he said, www.dialpad.com seemed best. To other continents, *Net2Phone* was his preferred package. The tourists, most calling Europe, used *Net2Phone,* which had prices including 1.50 soles per minute to London, and 2 soles per minute to Argentina (no one ever said the Net respected geography).

Merino looked toward the back of the room, where there were two fully enclosed rooms (*Net2Phone* booths, as it were) for those who wanted to use Internet telephony. The tourists came to call Europe, he said, but neighborhood residents came to call North America. And where were they calling? In March 2000, there were over a million Peruvians living in the United States, estimated John Hamilton, the American ambassador to Peru. Many of Lima's eight million residents have relatives in America, said Hamilton, and they want to talk to them.

Voice telephony "is driving (Internet) use," Krishna Urs, the economic counselor at the U.S. embassy in Lima, told the author in an interview. "It's a way of leapfrogging." And until very recently, Internet use was limited to Peru's "A demographic," the highest of five income levels in the country, according to Urs. "People in the B demographic are now using it, at Internet cabinas," Urs said.

But in 1999 and 2000, the cabina business exploded: Entrepreneurs created a new industry in under two years, with Internet cabinas "one of the fastest-growing businesses in Peru," according to Rosental Calmon Alves, a professor at the University of Texas in Austin who studies Latin American media. A family might rent out its PC by the hour, according to Calmon Alves. When there was more demand, they could buy a second or third PC, still running the cabinas from their homes. And indeed a drive around Lima found "Internet cabina" signs in some unlikely places, definitely outside of the leafy residential neighborhoods of Lima's "A demographic." Prices were lower than in Miraflores:—5 soles for two hours online, lower even than Macrostudio's overnight rate—but the policy was cash only, no credit cards.

Which brings us back to Macrostudio. Merino said his business, then just one year old, already faced fierce competition from a rapidly growing number of new neighborhood cabinas. Merino was correct: One of his many competitors showed us a copy purportedly of one page of the survey done by Lima authorities: the page on the Miraflores district. In a neat computer printout, it listed thirty-seven new Internet cabinas in that district. A check on five of the thirty-seven at random showed that the list was accurate: Internet cabinas were at those locations.

One of the newest, open just three months, was around the corner on Avenida Pardo, next to a new McDonald's advertising a cone for 0.90 soles and a Mac Fiesta (looking very much like a Big Mac) for 2.50 soles. It was the high-end glitzy Studio 2K Cybercafe, whose slogan, in English, was "your interactive home." Decorated in postmodern high-tech but painted purple (think Soho meets Barney), Studio 2K was right on the street, all hard surfaces, mirrors, and a ceiling-mounted projector to show Web sites on a large screen over the bar. Upstairs was a second floor just now being expanded, with twenty-one new PCs (some still in boxes) and more on the way. Clearly not competing on price, Studio 2K quoted an hourly price of 7.50 soles. But Studio 2K competed on high-end service.

On Friday afternoon, young women in uniforms were showing a stream of visitors to their PCs. And as soon as a computer was free, an attendant would reset its PC to Studio 2K's slick home page (purple, of course).

The cuisine was a big step up from Diet Coke and Pringles—and a big step up in prices. Sandwiches ranged from ham and cheese (5 soles, or about $1.50) to "American roast beef" (11.25 soles). There were also salads; the most expensive was "American chef salad" at 10.50 soles. The coffee menu topped off at 7 soles for an amaretto cappuccino.

But it was Macrostudio and its low-rent competitors that were driving Internet penetration into something close to a mass medium. And the impact on the information environment was already obvious: To take just one example, if the many Peruvians living in the Washington, D.C., area saw stories of special interest about Peru in the *Washington Post* (and there have been many), word of those stories spread quickly via the Internet to relatives living in Lima. So in Lima, where the government controlled almost all broadcasting and newspapers, people could still find more independent voices and information, either e-mailed from relatives abroad or by surfing on their own.

Canada and Greece were among the early adopters of another Internet technology that many now view as routine: Webcasting. In an early demonstration of radio over the Internet at a Freedom Forum program for media managers in 1995 in New York City, Andrew Patrick of Canada's Communications Research Centre demonstrated online transmission of CBC radio news broadcasts.

"We are a small country," he said, and this has allowed Canadian embassies around the world to hear newscasts from home. Transmitting CBC newscasts over the Internet, said Patrick, cost a tiny fraction of the cost of maintaining radio transmitters powerful enough to reach Canadians around the world. But these transmissions were not restricted or encrypted: Anyone in the world could now listen to CBC domestic newscasts.

In the years since those early experiments, government and private broadcasters around the world have begun to transmit their signals over the Internet, creating another layer of independent information flow outside of government control. In Ghana alone, every major radio station in the capital is now available worldwide on the Internet. Whatever Ghana's government is telling its citizens can be heard by anyone, anywhere, who wants to tune in from his or her PC.

And this means the rest of the world can hear U.S. local radio and watch U.S. local television. In Africa, Asia, South America or Europe, if you want to hear the voices of America, you can hear Washington, D.C., local all-news WTOP radio <http://www.wtop.com/index.jhtml> or Rush Limbaugh's national program <www.rushlimbaugh.com> just as easily as the Voice of America <http://www.voa.gov/>. This may seem a recipe for cacophony. It certainly is a reality of decentralization and pluralism. And it may be an opportunity for democracy.

In the 1950s, when Greece was on the edge of Communist control and crowds gathered to stone the American embassy, the U.S. fought back not only with a diplomatic offensive but also with Dizzy Gillespie. A State Department-sponsored tour sent the Gillespie band (and a young manager-orchestrator named Quincy Jones) to the hot spots of the Mediterranean, and in country after country angry crowds, mostly young people, turned into crowds of young fans. Jazz trumped politics.

Later it was rock music and blue jeans that became worldwide synonyms for freedom and democracy. Millions around the world, especially young people, who had never heard of Adam Smith knew Paul Simon.

Today millions around the world have embraced the Internet and new media, especially young people. There is a case to be made that information technology is the new jazz, capturing the imagination of people on every continent. In an attempt to create a communications network that would survive a nuclear attack, the United States also has created a technology that is dissolving censorship and totalitarian control more effectively than could have been imagined a generation ago.

Notes

1. The source for this information was a discussion the author had at the Freedom Forum European Center, London, January 25, 2000.

2. From remarks made by Nkrumah at a Freedom Forum program at *Al Ahram*, Cairo, September 13, 1998.

3. Information about Peru was gathered during the author's March 2000 visit to that country. See "Internet Use Up Sharply in Peru," (March 13, 2000), available online at <http://www.freedomforum.org/templates/document.asp?documentID=11876>

13 *Will the Internet Spoil Fidel Castro's Cuba?*

Cristina Venegas

On a trip to Havana in the summer of 1996, just prior to Cuba's official linkage to the Internet, I was having a late-night snack at the ostentatious Cohiba Hotel, aptly named after the cigar brand that Fidel Castro once smoked, and still considered to be the finest cigar in the world. The hotel had opened the previous year and as the new addition to the Havana skyline it signaled the coming wave of post-Soviet era investments in tourism. This glass, monolithic oceanfront hotel became part of Havana's architectural "style without a style," as Alejo Carpentier once called it, and is part of the Melia Spanish hotel chain, home to an international flock of businesspeople and tourists. A hotel room can cost US$200 a night, and a cup of ice cream goes for US$6 dollars, clearly the terrain of the international visitor. A computer placed discreetly in the lobby with a touch-screen interface gave one access to the virtual hotel via a hypertext document: we could find out about services, shows, locations, restaurants, and spa hours.

The virtual Cohiba was entertaining at best, but ultimately useless since the information found in the menu was fixed, static, whereas the actual information in real time and space was fluid and unpredictable. Although I could find out through the computer that there was an international newsstand, I had no way of knowing that the newspapers were a week old. The presence of the computer, with its virtual, graphic-rich information, in this spacious lobby, is an index of the importance of high-end technologies for Cuba's accelerated entry into the global marketplace. In one instant, the new hotels and their postmodern architecture were linked to emerging trends in technology and the illusion that inside these structures one could be connected to the world of up-to-the-minute information. The lack of newspapers was a reminder of the ongoing U.S. embargo and the complex reality that would evolve.

What becomes clear from this anecdote is that the relationship between high-end technologies and the particular social landscape of a Cuba in its deepest economic and political crisis is mired in contradictions. The contradictions do not disappear as the island pushes toward technological development in a restricted political space, and it is precisely the nature of this clash that interests me. By the end of the twentieth century, the Melia Habana, the newest hotel in the Melia Spanish chain, was wired from inception to provide Internet connections to its guests. The fee of US$5 per hour (which has gone down since it first offered the service to guests) allows you to check e-mail without ever leaving the hotel. Given the slow connection rates and low salaries of Cuban workers, these fees prove prohibitive to locals.

Cubans do have access to the Internet, but on a restricted basis. Out of eleven million Cubans, there are approximately 40,000 researchers and professionals with e-mail accounts. Browsing on the Web is also limited and requires separate clearance. But the government has promised to expand access and liberalize controls once the proper mechanisms are set in place for national security and the telephone system is upgraded to digital lines.

The double edge of the embargo and the Internet are plainly evident in Cuba. Although the embargo has blocked Cuba's economic trade and development, it has not ignored communications issues. The Helms-Burton law of 1992 calls for the improvement of U.S. telecommunications connections and information exchanges with Cuba, in order to increase the potential for change there. The Cuban government is using the Internet to bolster its tourism industry and break through economic challenges. Tourists may plan their trip to Cuba, rent a car and a cell phone, and reserve a hotel room through the official cubaweb.cu site.

After the collapse of the Soviet Union, there was a tightening of the U.S. economic embargo of Cuba through new legislation, which included a revision of policies toward communications. Previously, communications had been signaled as viable means for bringing about the end to the Castro regime. In 1983, the Radio Broadcasting to Cuba Act (P.L. 98–111) established Radio Marti, followed by Public Law 101–246 in 1990, which created TV Marti. Both Radio and TV Marti, ironically named after José Martí, Cuba's greatest hero of independence, broadcasts anti-Castro propaganda funded by the U.S. government interspersed in programming that was meant to offer listeners comprehensive news reports deemed to be missing from Cuban media, and thus an alternative ideology. After the fall of the Soviet Union, Senator Robert G. Torricelli, from New Jersey, authored the Cuban Democracy Act (1992), which, in addition to tightening the embargo, called for improving telecommunications connections with Cuba in order to force change. The Cuban Liberty and Democratic Solidarity Act of 1996 amended the Cuban Democracy Act in restricting investment in Cuba's domestic communications infrastructure.[1]

Despite continued funding for Radio Marti, and a continued commitment to this strategy of U.S. Cuba policy, there is evidence from professional survey research contracted by the Broadcasting Board of Governors (BBG) that audience share has dramatically reduced (5 percent in 2001, down from 9 percent in 2000 and 71 percent 1992).[2] Between 1997 and 1998 the BBG and the Office of the Inspector General mandated an independent panel of experts to conduct a review of Radio Marti journalistic practices, program content, and the adherence to Voice of America standards. The review was a response to mounting allegations of problems at Radio Marti culled from numerous reports, audits, and evaluations by various U.S. governmental agencies. The final report in 1999 called for, among other things, a revision of oversight policies, a charge implicating top management. The International Media Center at Florida International University, which oversaw the programming reviews for the panel of experts, was also contacted to carry out training needs in an effort to improve the quality of reporting.

Opinions vary about the potential of the Internet to democratize society because there is no easy way to link access to the Internet with the potential for democracy to develop. This teleology proves as naïve as the assumption that the functioning of the electoral process guarantees democracy.[3] History has proven this assumption not to be true in many countries in Latin America. Although some argue that this new medium will amplify previous patterns of economic inequality, others are hopeful that proper guidance will allow users to benefit from the information bounty. Carlos Lage Davila, the Cuban vice president of the State Council, observes that one fundamental advantage of this technology for Cuba is that it can level the playing field of mass media, so that Cuba can represent itself to world.[4] If we check the official site of the Cuban Republic <cubagov.cu>, we can see the emphasis on basic information regarding the workings of the government, special ministries, the communist party, central agencies, and political figures, as well as the sites that document the ongoing fight in the Cuban courts against the United States. The difficulty is that at this point the state and the economic conditions limit broader access. The restrictions are justified as part of national security (not a surprising response to the type of aggression that continues against the Cuban state), limited infrastructure, and a chaotic economic scenario.

In the debate outside Cuba, restriction of access to the Internet in Cuba is in part viewed as restraints on democratic participation and freedom of expression. Within Cuba, this sentiment is expressed in subtler ways (borrowing access codes, sharing accounts, etc). A medium that, on the one hand, is promoted for its potential to improve education, research, and self-expression is also perceived as a danger in light of the constant threat to the Cuban government by outside forces. Cubans share with the rest of the world concerns about pornography (there are also Web sites that traffic in black Cuban women) and the implications for children. In Cuba, however, it becomes difficult to separate the emphasis on national security from censorship, when official government discourses highlight these dangers and the extreme right-wing exile community (aided by the U.S. government) continues to flood Cuban networks with counterrevolutionary e-mails. Cuban computer experts are constantly blocking these activities, but the very existence of this aggression jeopardizes the potential for the opening of the Internet as a space for more democratic participation.

The limitations on Internet access also drive the expansion of a thriving black market on which it is rumored anyone can buy Internet provider numbers and the proper tools for navigation. It is not enough then to point to the limits on access without looking at the context in which they occur, as well as the other ways in which the Cuban government has been providing some smart Internet solutions to serious problems in health care, economic development, professional publishing, and cultural promotion. It is ultimately one more place where the Cuban state can legitimize itself. At stake, however, are the fragile conditions that the restrictions create, so that nongovernmental groups within Cuba are limited in their Net visibility, and the official government site reveals the dearth of political plurality.

Cuba is thus a rich case study of how global media penetrate one particular culture and politic, because of the way discourses about democratization and empowerment around new technologies are provocatively tested. There is in Cuba an intellectual and political legacy of decolonization discourses before (1890s) and after the revolution of 1959, a socialist experiment that breaks with Stalinist Marxist doctrine and refigures the paradigm in the Caribbean, and a notion of democracy that, albeit problematic for the West and limited in facilitating direct public advocacy, has contributed to achieving greater levels of equality in Latin America than any other system. Cuba has existed for the last four decades under the same charismatic leadership of Fidel Castro, endured the longest-lasting economic embargo against any nation in history, and weathered a climate of constant aggression. There must be space for thoughtful consideration of the implications of technological advancements for underdeveloped nations. It is not enough to listen to the prophecies of Nicholas Negroponte in *Being Digital* that postulate a peaceful and prosperous world brought about by technology-driven development. Utopian visions of technology come under scrutiny when one notices the widening gap between poverty and wealth in the world today. Nonetheless, prophetic visions have tremendous driving power for the commercial interests of the Internet, which since 1996, when commercialization began, has grown by an astounding 47 percent. Even if the beginning of a new millennium did not find the entire planet connected, we could still observe the force with which, in developing nations, telecommunications companies rush to find new and innovative ways of providing computers, connectivity, and even telephone lines to those who don't have them.

These utopian visions are nonetheless diversions, and they also represent the biased discourse about digital media that is carried on in elite circles in the developed world.[5]

Even in well-intentioned analyses of the growth, development, and uses of the Internet, there is a tendency to equate what occurs in the United States with what happens, or will happen, in the world as a whole. Even the European Union has a variety of disagreements within its own membership on policies toward developments in the new economy of the Internet. The analytical gap posed by U.S.-centric debates around technology for example, positions the development of the Internet in Latin America merely as a question of free commerce, but clearly there has to be a consideration of how differing political paradigms might bring about a different development for technology. In the case of Cuba, the question remains to what extent state-centered control can help or hinder the kind of transition that is taking place.

While the U.S. embargo remains in force, and administrations in the United States appear disinterested in revisiting the absurdity of this policy, Cubans work on ways to use the Internet to circumvent some of obstacles of the embargo. Through its national Web site (<www.cubaweb.cu>), individuals can send cash from the United States to anyone in Cuba and charge it to a major credit card. The transaction is negotiated through a bank in Canada, which guarantees that the funds are received in Cuba. The ability to remit cash to island-based Cubans is not entirely new. In fact, President Bill Clinton, under Track II provision of the Cuban Democracy Act of 1992, allowed Cuban Americans to send money to their relatives. Given the success of this plan, Western Union was also approved in July 1999 to provide the service through the commercial Cuban Corporation CIMEX, S.A. The possibility of this virtual transaction is now several years old, but at the beginning it was perceived with great hyperbole by the Webmaster at cubaweb.cu as a way to break through the blockade. Obviously, this is an exaggerated response, since a third party has to effect the transaction. The Webmaster's hubris is more telling of the political value of participating in a global communications revolution than of really overthrowing the U.S. embargo. The steps are particularly significant since they have made possible an increase in remittances to Cuba (anywhere from US$375 million to US$1 billion). Nonetheless, overcoming the limitations of the embargo is an official priority.

Of Cold Wars and New World Orders

Early computing in Cuba coincides with computer developments in the United States at the time, albeit from a different position of power. According to Armand Mattelart, data-processing systems were installed in Latin America at almost the same time as in the producing countries,[6] an occurrence that derives from the internal logic of the capitalist system. In other words, contiguous development was key to achieving a planetary expansion of the system. The main conduits of this technological transfer were the large transnational enterprises that had interests in the vast productive resources of Latin America.

In the late 1950s, by the time integrated circuits had been manufactured out of silicon (1954) and the prices of semiconductors had dropped significantly (1959–1962),[7] two first-generation U.S. computers were installed in Cuba, the presence of which reveals a curious antecedent. These electronic machines were used to control processes and computations, and the first experiments with the computers were conducted by Americans at the Esso refinery, a division of Exxon. Cuban communications scholar Enrique Gonzalez-Manet chronicles how the operating costs of such experiments were charged to the Cuban affiliate in Havana and were carried out under strict secrecy. After the nationalization of petroleum and other industries in 1960, the only remnant of the electronic calculators was the complex web of cabling that had made communication possible. Up until that point most people believed that the only electronic calculator in the country was a UNIVAC 120 that had been obtained through the interests of Americans to compute gambling payouts in horse racing. The Mafia in Cuba used this system to have automatic control over "premiums" and for the stability of its profit margins.[8] Likewise, the first computer in greater Latin America was installed in the Venezuelan offices of the Creole Petroleum Corporation, which, according to Mattelart, "became a launching pad for computer development" in that nation. In Peru, Occidental Petroleum "installed the most advanced system of communication, so as to be linked to the world network of information."[9]

In Cuba, the emergence of computers is the story of how Cold War adversaries (Russia and the United States) played an influential role in the technological development of the island throughout the twentieth century and how Cuba, in turn, appropriated the technology for its own historical needs and reinvented itself in the second half of the century. This also meant a shift in the relations of technology to society from a strictly commercial and profit-driven model, to centralized, state interests. In other words, technological development acquired a new ideological role in the development of society. One practical example of this Cold War legacy was the renovation of the electrical infrastructure carried out during the revolution (after 1959), when 94.5 percent of homes were connected to the electric grid. The project was completed, as were many others, through credits and materials acquired from the Eastern bloc. The communications infrastructure, however, had been in the hands of American companies, and its development was thus guided by different historical conditions.[10]

In 1921, AT&T laid down the underwater cable between the United States and Cuba, replaced it in 1950, and in 1966 was exempted from the 1962 trade embargo for humanitarian reasons. But ongoing political conflicts between the two nations have affected the way in which AT&T is able to carry out operations, and Cuba's own retaliatory measures have at times curtailed the number of lines available for telephone service to the United States.[11] The nature of telephone service between Cuba and the United States continues to be highly ironic. While e-mail communication between the two nations flows regularly, telephone communication can always be interrupted by the Cuban government, which uses this as a retaliatory measure against the United States' unfavorable policies toward Cuba. Perhaps this instance underscores the fragile boundaries erected by transnational communications corporations.

The suspension of trade between the United States and Cuba subsequent to the revolution meant that machines of all types were purchased from France and more permanently from the Soviet Union and other eastern European nations. The Cuban telephone system for example, was constructed by acquiring the necessary equipment from available sources that often meant from different places. Arnaldo Coro, a telecommunications expert and a professor at the University of Havana, confirms that this is one of the biggest obstacles to a better operation of the telephone system since the admixture of equipment from a variety of countries and systems, i.e., France, the United States, Canada, Scandinavia, East Germany, and Hungary, makes interoperability and maintenance difficult.[12] The current digitization of the telephone system, which will modernize telecommunications operations, must contend with the difficult reality of Cuba's complex political history.

In 1964 the relationship with eastern Europe was further solidified through the purchase of equipment from Poland and the training of specialists in East Germany and the Soviet Union. According to analyst Larry Press, during the 1970s "Cuba embarked on a program to develop its own second generation minicomputers at the Central Institute for Digital Research,"[13] and this began the use of computers in planning and more efficient use of resources. The Cubans set out to produce microcomputers, which would help them in the areas of transport, agricultural machinery, labor efficiency, design of equipment, and buildings and communications. For its part the state employed hollowed slogans to underscore these goals: "The development of a productive force will make socialism triumph!"[14] Bilateral agreements with the Soviet Union supported the nascent industry, and the first computers were assembled in 1978. Mainframes, minicomputers, and microcomputers were produced.[15]

In 1969 Gonzalez-Manet wrote a three-part feature series in *Granma,* the Communist Party's official daily newspaper, on the development of cybernetics and what these technological advances meant for Cuba. He suggested then that "given the things that Cuba was doing, it could situate itself as an example of the enormous endeavors in the area of productivity."[16] It was necessary, he wrote, to incorporate "cybernetic technology both in directing the economy and in production, at its various levels, and in helping the development of scientific and technological research."[17] Cybernetics was perceived as a "science of salvation," a way to build communism,[18] and today Cuba is using the same advancements in cybernetic technology and similar slogans to salvage its forty-year-old socialist trajectory.

Technological development was thus linked to the process of building a communist nation, and in this way it became a discourse about progress. The reality of the revolution would position Cuba in a favorable status for incorporating technology, not, the new leadership thought, in the dependent model that was perpetuated in the Third World, but rather as a force to escape underdevelopment. Ironically Cuba's development became intertwined with the financial support and preferential trade status from the Soviet Union, a situation that, although different from the neocolonial relationship it had had with the United States, was still less than ideal. The Soviets traded economic support for a foothold on the "island of freedom" ninety miles off the coast of their Cold War enemy; they could also thereby position Soviet listening posts on the north coast of Cuba at the Lourdes base, which remained until 2001. The relationship with the Soviets was duly tested during the 1962 missile crisis, when Cuba came close to becoming the launching pad for nuclear weapons. It was at the high point of the negotiations between Soviet Premier Nikita Khrushchev and U.S. President John F. Kennedy, that the Soviets' salient strategy was revealed: Castro was not only not consulted in the agreement, but he found out only after the agreements were signed. In return for the Soviets' removing the nuclear missiles from Cuba, the United States agreed not to invade the island.

Having overthrown the pre-1959 power structure, and the privileged position the United States held, Cuba set out on a course on which the new nation, what the new government considered a legitimate republic, could chart its own development strategies in a society no longer tied to neocolonial structures and poverty. Gonzalez-Manet affirms that, "to apply science and technology at the highest levels you have to overcome underdevelopment . . . and for this task one must first have a revolution."[19] In the early years of utopic and revolutionary enthusiasm the Cuban government and indeed the people of Cuba believed they were well underway to defeating underdevelopment. The rupture in the historical process of the island transformed, almost overnight, its social, political, economic, and cultural relations. The new process had to be constructed, and the new attitudes toward development included gaining the necessary tools to jump-start the new nation.

Viewing technology as a force that shapes the modern nation is not particular to Cuba and is echoed in all discourses of modernization. It is also a view that is, in another instance, tied to theories of development that emerge in the post–World War II period, when the concept of underdevelopment itself was designated to account for the differences in industrial development worldwide. Cuba's historical situation, however, does not assume that technology itself will lead the island out of underdevelopment, since national discourses—those that propose the creation of a new society—point to the necessity of first altering the society in which the technology is introduced. Gonzalez-Manet's reading of Cuba's potential to use technology as a way out of colonization, given the already successful revolution, positions this discourse within the movements and rhythms of the process of building communism in the Caribbean.

Gonzalez-Manet's enthusiasm, in 1969, coincided with the patriotic fervor of the era. A ten-ton sugar harvest had been set as the goal for 1970, the largest projection ever, and it acted in the social consciousness, placed there through the media, as a great force to achieve the impossible. It also had the effect of providing an image of a population working side by side toward common goals. In fact, the notion of beating the odds has always been a rallying cry for Castro and for the Communist Party, as is still evident in the speeches of the late 1990s, when the Cuban government positioned itself as the survivor of aggressions from the United States and the inhumanity of the embargo. In the context of 1969, technological advances were absorbed into the planning processes and the industrial machinery to achieve the impossible as a representation of the will and spirit of the new nation.

By 1978 the Centro Nacional de Superación y Adiestramiento en Informaticas (CEN-SAI, the National Center for Teaching and Self-Advancement in Informatics) began training what would in two decades of its existence become over 60,000 specialists. CENSAI's first decade was devoted to training experts who could make efficient use of the national computers, revealing a commitment to achieving some form of future self-sufficiency and the possibility of establishing a domestic computer industry. It was with the use of these first-generation Cuban computers that CENSAI began to prioritize information in health, business, and defense sectors, areas that influenced the introduction of new technologies and defined the relationship between technology and the state.[20] CENSAI also invested in technical support for the nascent Joven Club de Computación (Computing Youth Clubs) as well as in vocational work with children from the Palacio Central de Pioneros (Central Palace for Pioneers) and in the creation of a methodology for curriculum planning from the earliest possible ages. The Computing Youth Clubs have received support since their inception in 1987 and have been the means through which youths received instruction in basic computing. Clubs, institutions, and individuals in the social sciences, culture, health, education and other fields were all connected through a network called TINORED, which operated as a nonprofit, nongovernmental association. The network connection was at first established through Canada's Web networks, which covered the cost of the telephone connection. As of early 1997, TINORED was no longer operating, since the Canadian partnership could no longer carry the cost of connecting and Cuba had already established its own network connection in 1996.[21] TINORED and other networks were caught in the shift and have been offline for quite sometime but are still planning to reestablish a network connection through another Cuban organization. Despite Cuba's closer ties to the Soviet Union during the 1970s, which signaled a period of Marxism by the book and the political ramifications this change in the relationship between the two countries implied, investment in computer technology, at this time, was timely, given the innovations in the field of microelectronics elsewhere, even though the decade would also seal the leadership of American computer entrepreneurship. It was in fact in the 1970s that new information technologies were diffused widely, despite the fact that many of the important discoveries in the field had been made in prior decades. In 1964 IBM, despite its early reservations about entering the personal computer business, came to dominate the computer industry (and still does in Latin America), and the invention of the microprocessor in 1971, which allowed a computer to be placed on a chip, revolutionized the computer industry.[22]

During the 1970s and 1980s, Cuba created a small computer hardware industry. But the domestic economy was not large or sophisticated enough to drive higher levels of consumption, which may account for how Cuba became "an outlier of the partially integrated CMEA [computer] industries, building subsystems from imported components and with guaranteed exports to the CMEA countries.[23] The collapse of communism in Europe affected the manufacturing sector particularly severely, and the process of rebuilding to begin to operate at previous levels has been a slow one. The accelerated pace of developments in new information technologies in the years that Cuba has been hardest hit economically indicates that Cuba's competitive edge might just as well be found in marketing its highly trained labor force and in pursuing small inroads into software production.

Cuba's changing relationship with the centers of technology—that between Cuba, the United States, and the former Soviet Union—supported, in a variety of ways, revolutionary change in Cuba. It is possible to speculate that early Cuban contact with U.S. industrialists, although limited, and the technological advancements brought about by that relationship helped the revolutionary government to perceive technological development as an effective means for consolidating the revolution. The technological traces that remain of this contact, although they do not have immediate results in the economy or the production system, do show up in the importance technological training in microelectronics was given in the 1970s, as well as in the emphasis on education in this field in Cuba, and the move to invest in a national microcomputer industry. In other words, although there was practically an exodus of the Cuban entrepreneurial class after the revolution, a class that had driven the development of technological transfers and experiments, there remained a memory or an experience of what could be achieved if technology had a different social and economic function. Cuba's closer relationship with the Soviets during the 1970s led it to make technology the engine for realizing the triumph of socialism. Nonetheless, Cuba's political and physical proximity to the centers of innovation, although through an undesirable neocolonial situation with the United States, fueled the transformation of Cuban society from plantation economy to consumerism and from socialism to what some jokingly call "market Leninism."

The revolution's endeavors in education, biomedical engineering, and scientific development have been fostered by a need for the Cuban state to become more economically independent and flexible and could lay the foundation for future economic growth to revolve around the use of a highly trained workforce. It is imperative, however, for Cuba to take measures to prevent the brain drain generated by the severe economic cutbacks that have taken place or because citizens can no longer find it possible to make the daily sacrifices that the government asks of them.[24] One method the Cuban state is using to prevent this flow of trained people is through a slight liberalization of the private sector—mixed ownership of enterprises between the State and foreign investors—and a less intrusive presence in the commercial firms the government has created to streamline services. Of course this tactic is no guarantee that brain drain will not continue. There are serious consequences for the future of Cuba whose young population is coming of age in a world of limited economic and professional opportunities and who, having repeatedly made many sacrifices in their formative years, find themselves in less than satisfactory jobs in the tourist sector.

Confronting a global economy, and considering the inevitable steps that Cuba took in the late 1990s to enter into the challenges, that such an economy presents, Gonzalez-Manet regards the emergence of the Internet as a revolution that cannot be stopped. Granting its merits as a source and access to information, Gonzalez-Manet also warns that views of this technology as a great equalizer and democratizer are misleading, since we must take into consideration that in the Third World, "75% of the population barely has access to 10% of communications media, 6% of the telephones, 5% of the computers, and 2% of the satellites."[25] His position is grounded within current debates on globalization and of development organizations like the United Nations Educational, Scientific, and Cultural Organisation (UNESCO). From this point of view, then, there is a need at the level of government to put in place coherent policies that take into consideration the vast cultural changes that occur as new economic structures coincide with a global information network. Gonzalez-Manet worries about the vast inequality of access, both to resources and financing, that will accelerate and broaden the inequalities of the past. Despite the fact that for many years Cuba had taken a leadership role in the Movement of Non-Aligned Nations and the fight for a new information and communication order, it was also caught off guard in formulating a coherent position toward Internet technology. According to Gonzalez-Manet, "There are isolated gains . . . technocratic and sectarian perspectives, stand in the way of real advancement, but there are strategic achievements, which position Cuba favorably, if and when, these other internal dilemmas are reconciled."[26]

Gonzalez-Manet's position, which is undoubtedly shared by other cultural critics, reveals certain theoretical limitations, if we wish to examine the broader implications of the function of the Internet in Cuba. If the focus of the inquiry is restricted to views of dependency, we run the risk of omitting the unpredictable aspects of culture and appropriations, as well a rigorous internal critique. Such a focus fails to examine the way in which the official Web sites position a version of Cuba that is perhaps the ideal goal of the revolution: a classless and equal society, reimagined for the tourist and investor, effacing the turbulence that lies beneath as a result of both internal and external contradictions. Although there exists a very real and unequal relationship between North and South, one that has a long historic lineage, there is also a need to look at the other aspect of this relationship, the unofficial, marginal responses to policies and governments, the disruptive potential of Caribbean rhythms.

Cuba's social and economic crisis is a key element in interpreting the needs that arise for new uses of the Internet in the nation. The dwindling salaries of the highest-level professionals make it almost prohibitive for them to buy personal computers, making these available largely through donations or gifts from friends. Traditionally in Latin America, the high cost of peripherals, software, hardware, etc., determines an elite user profile. Cuban computer specialists, who have suffered an editorial crisis because of the scarcity of paper in the country and reduced access to other information mechanisms, are designated, according to state planners, as the principal users of the Internet. In other words, we have to look to how Cubans resolve the limitations imposed by economics beyond the mandates of the state.

The information blockade is one of Cuba's motivations to embrace the use of the Internet, and yet the government's current push to decentralize production while maintaining a centralized political system suggests the potential difficulties that lie ahead. The government's strategy appears contradictory to the nature of a network that is meant to be decentralized and open, but Cuba's connection to the Internet is recent, and we might remember that during the early years of its development, ARPANET (eventually the Internet) was limited to a privileged community of scientific and academic users and was basically research oriented. It wasn't until the Internet became a proven commercial outlet that access to it became more widespread. Cuba's experience can thus be helpful in exploring the limits of centralized planning, the nature of democracy in communication, and the need to construct viable social demands for new technological developments.

Virtual Centralization

The current structure of connectivity in Cuba is the result of a reorganization of the informatics communication sector in 1993, and it is a centralized structure. The restructuring pooled scarce resources to maximize access and controls access to the Internet by private individuals. The Center for Automated Interchange of Information (CENIAI) of the Academy of Sciences became the hub for organization, and in 1996, the official connection to the Internet for Cuba.[27] The Network Information Center (NIC) manages the .cu domain, under which most accounts in Cuba are registered.[28] CITMATEL is the government firm that commercializes both the service and native products. Prior to this reorganization, however, there was already a considerable computer user community (in the various scientific and academic institutions), which operated various networks that connected with networks in the former Soviet Union and in eastern Europe.

Electronic-mail connection with the Soviet Union had been established in 1981, but information technologies had not been prioritized as part of a central mechanism for economic development until the dissolution of the Soviet bloc a decade later. Even in the United States, the commercial possibilities of the Internet were not salient until the mid-1990s, and thus there was a convergence of necessity and technological innovation that allowed Cuba to apply this technology to deal with some of its short-term and long-term problems. The notion of prioritizing within the central command economy must be understood as the means through which the government, adhering to a central plan, directs its investments and therefore its support. Priorities do not hide interests per se, but rather they are the way in which the scarcity of economic resources focuses development strategies. In the late 1980s and 1990s, amid the government's worst crisis in its history, a connection to the Internet posed a threat and required a substantial technological investment, but it also offered ways of moving out of isolation and the information embargo. Indeed, it was and is the dictator's digital dilemma.[29]

In 1989, as the situation in the Soviet Union disintegrated, Cuba made its first e-mail contact with Peacenet in Canada. According to Press, "twice a week WEB/NIRV, an Association for Progressive Computing (APC) affiliate in Toronto, Canada, called CENIAI and exchanged international traffic."[30] This first connection, although inefficient, was the best way to communicate with people on the island. By 1990 the United Nations, through its development program (UNDP), began fomenting connectivity throughout the Third World and funded the start-up costs for various networks like CENIAI and InfoMed.

The role of the United Nations through UNESCO (United Nations Education, Science and Cultural Organization) and UNDP in promoting connectivity in the developing world is significant and has in part guided Cuba's Internet policy. Given Cuba's political isolation, the United Nations has served as a supportive forum for voting against the restrictions of the embargo and as a platform for Cuba to air its complaints. In 1997 UNESCO's executive council drafted a platform regarding the problems that face developing nations with respect to information technologies. The platform approves funding initiatives and supports policies that help provide access, resources, and training of personnel who will explore and maintain new economic markets made viable through information technologies. The magnitude of the investment in developing nations and the task of carrying out such a plan (particularly in Africa, which is the least-connected continent), if one considers just the laying of telephonic cable, influences UNESCO's policy to "focus on community programs and the strengthening of development sectors like education, prior to wiring each individual home."[31] Cuba's focus on access to the Internet through institutions in the sciences, tourism, and education is in line with this proposal.

Cuba's connectivity is also orchestrated in line with the strategies of other Latin American countries, in an effort to share insights on successes and to establish common bonds for future networking. Early on, prior to having full Internet connectivity, Cuba maintained generic country information in a Gopher server in Uruguay, and in 1991 a Cuban representative attended the international forum on the Internet in Brazil, where plans were discussed to create a Latin American high-speed backbone to facilitate connectivity in the region. CENIAI's director also established personal links with network leaders in Peru and Venezuela, and indeed pan-American cooperation will be key in fortifying commercial domestic markets as well as in expanding trade possibilities. For example, Cuba maintains distributors in Mexico for the biomedical products it advertises on the CIGB-net Web site, since the restrictions of the embargo prevent it from shipping or selling to many of its customers.

By 1992 Cuba had established e-mail networks connecting medical, scientific, and cultural institutions within the country, and by the end of 1993 the number of Unix-to-Unix Copy Program (UUCP) nodes had increased in the previous year from three to twenty. There were at that time four networks with dial-up international Internet connections: CENIAI, TINORED, CIGBnet, and InfoMed. (All of the networks now connect to the Internet through CENIAI.) The reorganization presented a challenging economic situation for CENIAI/CITMATEL, since it had to prove to be an efficient and profitable service provider or be closed down. The inability of the government to fund fully the needed technology translates to CENIAI's operating in a dollar global economy, and this influences the focus of its services.[32] The reorganization, which sought to give a structure to Cuba's unorganized e-mail networks, established service contracts with other institutions, rates for connecting, and technical support, training, Web design, and other types of assistance for its customers. In addition to its mandate to be an efficient and profitable enterprise, CENIAI/CITMATEL also has a mandate to benefit the sciences in Cuba.

In 1994, after receiving government approval, CENIAI took the first steps to secure a license for connecting to the Internet, and held a working conference in 1995 to continue discussions about the viable means and strategies available to them. On June 14, 1996, the Executive Committee of the Council of Ministers (made up of Ministries of Science, Technology and the Environment, Communications, Justice, and the Interior) agreed on the legal and constitutional ramifications under which Cuba would make the Internet available to Cubans and issued Decree 209. The ministerial committee will continue to oversee development and policy implementation. Decree 209, does not establish a new information policy, but rather it sets forth the laws governing all connectivity in Cuba and the role of each Ministry in this process. The ruling expresses "the need for the country to establish laws for connecting, and regulations that guarantee a harmonious development as well as the interests of national security and defense."[33] In 1997, Cuba connected directly to the Internet via CENIAI. This institution is thus the official link, which is handled through international communications channels under a contract with Sprint and Telecom Italy. There are plans to lay fiber-optic cable and to digitize all telephone service. Full Internet connectivity foments research, business, and tourism and improves communications. According to Cuba's daily *Granma,* Cuba's Internet connection must "focus on national priorities."[34]

One of the state's priorities is to make Cuba a software development site, and various steps have been taken toward this end. I've already mentioned the commitment to educating engineers and computer experts (and younger generations with the creation of the Youth Computing Clubs). The *Informatica* conferences, held biannually since 1988, are also part of this commitment and are a way to converge the interests of international academics, engineers, developers, and distributors. They also give the government the opportunity to show off its support for the Cuban informatics and computing sector. To create a national software industry Cuba must find areas in which its software products can compete without the interference of software giants. It believes that its own domestic market is one place where it may find some maneuvering room through the development of native software for specific national uses, not programs that re-create leading commercial software applications. The obvious areas that can capitalize on this are tourism and science, in which new systems can help solve problems generic to Cuba's situation. In the late 1990s, the different software applications that were developed were geared toward making systems more efficient, thereby saving money and time, and toward educational-assistance applications for all ages.

In 1993, Cuba was designated by UNESCO's Intergovernmental Program on Informatics as a regional coordinating center in the fight against computer viruses. The Latin American Laboratory for the Protection against Information Viruses was established with the mandate of detecting new viruses in member countries and putting at those countries' disposal the appropriate information to counteract the damages done by the viruses.[35] It is in the area of antivirus software development that Cuba has been most successful in exporting its products. This means that any violations of copyright laws that may have existed must be attended to if Cuba wants to be taken seriously as a software-developing nation. The production of software is also facilitated by the exchange between domestic users.

There are various motives that lead to the centralized infrastructure of the Internet, beyond the fact that the state continues to adhere to this logic. One of the stated arguments in support of centralization of the infrastructure is financial, the other structural. Connectivity is still very expensive and must be paid for in dollars, and use of the Internet for generating hard currency is immature, in large measure due to the embargo and to the centralized banking system. Domestic telephone infrastructure is still a problem, even though the telephone company was one of the first to be privatized and it is making progress in digitizing lines. The projected investments to digitize all telephone lines and replace outdated systems should alleviate this problem, but it will take some time for this to happen. In the meantime, people figure out ways of dealing with uncertainty, like having several e-mail accounts—in case one isn't connecting—if that is an option, borrowing access numbers, among others. These difficulties have in fact fostered an informal (without official access) use of the Internet that is resourceful and quite inventive.

Centralization is also a way of directing the uses of the Internet. In a country where there has been limited freedom of the press and information has been controlled by the state, we can expect the policy toward the Internet to impose some form of constraint. There will be a limit to the restrictions imposed as the user community becomes more adept and the Internet more pervasive. At the moment, online access is available through work sites, although this often means a single computer with access, and a designated person that handles the access for the user. E-mail is available through several Internet service providers (ISPs), but fees for access are high in comparison with the average Cuban salary, and again, accounts are paid for in dollars. Oftentimes there are structural installations that have to be made to provide Internet access that are handled by different agencies, and thus the whole project of setting up access can become ensnared in a bureaucratic tangle. But there is an exception to every situation, and there are those who have Internet access through pirated connections from home.

Despite the fact that Cuba has made significant changes in the past few years with regard to economic policy, tax laws, employment, and the like, the Communist Party reiterates that these changes are in line with a socialist agenda. Cuba rejects wholeheartedly, under the rubric of anti-imperialism, the potential of neoliberal reforms taking place in the rest of Latin America, emphasizing that these have only exacerbated the already devastating disparity between wealth and poverty in the countries that have undertaken them. The Internet and any other communication medium that is adopted in Cuba is welcomed (at least for the moment) within the parameters of the socialist agenda. This agenda, however, is not monolithic, even though in moments of crisis orthodox views still possess a great deal of power. The opening to alternative political positions, religious practice, and global markets redefined the cultural landscape of Cuba at the end of the 1990s. This doesn't mean that Cuba's current centralized Internet structure and the information the state provides on Web sites question the socialist agenda in significant ways, as is evident by the lack of plurality in political parties and limited participation by nongovernmental organizations. The latter have access to e-mail networks but lack a power base from which to operate. Nonetheless, there is an increasing number of institutional Web sites in Cuba, a sign that the Internet is becoming more accepted there, even if access to it is still limited.

The question of Internet-infused democracy in Cuba sounds too much like a determinist dream. It is evident that the not-so-distant debates about independence and the resulting anticolonial discourses create a social landscape weary of outside forces, of neocolonial relations, of technologies that must be imported at high costs, of invaders that come from the north. At the same time the Cuban government has defined democracy not as something achieved strictly through an electoral process, but rather, something in which the state provides for its citizens and creates the conditions necessary for a participatory process. This notion has been more successful in theory than in practice, and it has been further complicated by the very nature of an underdeveloped economic structure. The assumption that access to a worldwide network of information, action, and participation helps deter some of the very basic historical problems of any poor nation is simply an illusion. But this does not mean that by its very questioning of the notion of democracy, the Cuban state (or perhaps credit should be given to the young, forward-thinking new generation of digital players), with its very specific problems, has found interesting ways to construct a community of informed researchers, doctors, scientists, and even entrepreneurs.

When I began to research the workings of the Internet in Cuba in 1995, I understood that the Cuban government had exerted certain restrictions to access and that outside the authorized institutions, foreign businesses, and foreigners, the average Cuban citizen still thought that navigating was something you did in the Florida Straits or through the Cuban bureaucracy. It would be all too simple to chalk this up to a repressive, undemocratic regime, as the U.S. government and the exile community would have us do. The fact is that as information flows become more complex and hackers more skilled and daring, governments all over the globe are trying to determine ways to monitor Internet use and establish controls to prevent crime. The irony of course is that we end up in the same place, establishing Big Brother controls. Cuba's political and cultural reality has, for the last century, been shaped by its love-hate relationship with the United States, and by the political, cultural, and personal events that transpire between them. And so, the emergence of the Internet, which as one interviewee who wanted to remain anonymous jokingly put it, "was designed by the enemy, but we have to take advantage of it," is also defined by this flow of politics and history.

Cuban reality has undergone considerable changes in the past decade, particularly in international relations. During the 1980s, when the economic recession in Cuba began to manifest itself, Cuba's foreign relations with the West were almost nonexistent. In a matter of ten years, Cuba made an about turn in foreign policy (except for that with respect to the United States, and now entertains business accords with European, Asian, and Latin American nations and may entertain future ones with the United States. It has reformed its banking structure, creating four banks serving the needs of this international business, which also includes an eye to the future of electronic commerce. The economy is beginning to grow, and in 1999 economists projected a growth rate of 3–4 percent.[36] Nonetheless, the sugar cane harvest in 1998 was the lowest ever, and nickel production was also down. Despite the fact that tourism is now driving the Cuban economic engine, its cost is still high at 67 cents on the dollar. The internationalization of the Cuban economic sector has been key in developing uses for the Internet. The marriage of business cultures created by the aforementioned partnerships with foreign business concerns has also put Cuban software and hardware specialists to work on solving problems engendered by these new relations. That is, when a Spanish or Canadian company is interested in doing business in Cuba, it has to deal with the technological and infrastructural demands of Cuba, like its outdated telephone structure, energy production problems, and a different work culture. ETECSA, the telephone company co-owned with an Italian enterprise, has to acclimate itself to working with Cuban ministries to overhaul the country's system of communications and to deal with the complex web of telephone equipment from varying countries that exist in Cuba. It must also deal with the restrictions imposed by the Helms-Burton law. As mentioned earlier in the chapter, the United States has lifted restrictions on sending money to relatives in Cuba, and the remittances in one year alone (1998) reached $800 million. The circulation of extra dollars is evident in the increase in the number of stores for Cubans, who are buying everything from shoes to televisions. All of these changes obviously imply a dramatic shift in the country's economic policy.

The consolidation of democracy has become a foreign policy tool for the United States, defining democracy on its own terms and for the acquiescence of "violating" nations. But for Cuba, democracy and democratic institutions have a complex historical legacy that must be the starting point for an analysis of how to improve a democratic process. The deployment of the Internet through official institutions is defined as a way in which to build a working civil society. Is the Internet a threat to Cuba's own democratic aspirations? It is surely perceived as such. Nonetheless, it is difficult both to transform a culture of information control and to control the use of a medium that appeals to a younger generation impatient for reforms. The negotiation of these factors will be key in the transformation of Cuban culture in the current millennium.

Notes

1. Larry Press, "Cuban Telecommunications Infrastructure and Investment," paper presented at conference of the Association for the Study of the Cuban Economy (Miami, August 1996), available online at <http://som.csudh.edu/fac/lpress/devnat/nations/cuba/asce.htm>.

2. Philip Peters, "Radio Marti's Shrinking Audience and What to Do About It," testimony before the subcommittee on International Operations and Human Rights, Committee on International Relations, Lexington Institute, June 6, 2002, available online at <http://www.lexintoninstitute.org/cuba/radiomarti.htm>.

3. In order to begin to normalize relations with Cuba, the U.S. goverment requires that Cuba hold free elections. "Support for a Democratic Transition in Cuba," January 1997, USAID. See online <http://www.usaid.gov/regions/lac/cu/english.htm>.

4. Carlos Lage Davila, "Seminario Nacional Internet" (National Internet Seminar), opening plenary, Havana, Cuba, June 17, 1996. Speech by the vice president of the Cuban State Coun-

cil: "One of the essential advantages of this new technology is that it is the proper means through which we can reveal to the world, on a more even field of struggle than that of other mass media, the realities of our country and of the revolution. Therefore, in addition to it being a strategic necessity for the country, it is also an important challenge not only technologically, but also economically and politically" (author translation).

5. Enrique Gonzalez-Manet, "Internet: espejismos y promesas de la cultura electronica" (Internet: Promises and Mirages of Electronic Culture), unpublished essay, 1998.

6. Armand Mattelart and Hector Schmucler, *Communication and Information Technologies: Freedom or Choice for Latin America?* trans. David Buxton (Norwood, N.J.: Ablex, 1985), 46.

7. Manuel Castells, *The Information Age: Economy, Society and Culture,* 3 vols. (Cambridge, Mass.: Blackwell, 1996), vol. 1, 43–44. Castells retells, with clarity and detail, the convergence of the technological axes that made the information age possible.

8. Enrique Gonzalez-Manet, "La cibernética en Cuba" (Cybernetics in Cuba), *Granma,* November 6, 1969.

9. Mattelart and Schmucler, *Communication and Information Technologies,* 71.

10. Arnaldo Coro, interview, August 1998. Coro is a telecommunications expert and a professor at the University of Havana.

11. Press, "Cuban Telecommunications Infrastructure and Investment."

12. Ibid., 3.

13. Larry Press, "Cuba, Communism, and Computing," *Communications of the ACM* 35, no. 11 (November 1992): 27–29, 112. The second-generation computers were based on Digital's PDP-11.

14. Jose Luis Acanda, quoted in Manual Vázquez Montalbán, *Y Dios entro en la Habana* (And God Entered Havana) (Madrid: Aguilar, 1998), 382.

15. Alfredo Luis del Valle, "Cuba, Internet and U.S. Foreign Policy," unpublished paper presented at XII Conference of the Mexican International Studies Association, Oaxaca, Mexico, October 17, 1998.

16. Enrique Gonzalez-Manet, "Cibernética, política y desarrollo" (Cybernetics, Politics and Development), *Granma,* November 3, 1969 (author translation).

17. Ibid.

18. Enrique Gonzalez-Manet, "Qué es la cibernética?" (What Is Cybernetics?), *Granma,* November 1, 1969.

19. Gonzalez-Manet, "Cybernetics, Politics and Development."

20. O.P., "Dos decadas de capacitación en las técnicas de computación," (Two Decades of Training in Computer Technology) *Granma,* December 5, 1997.

21. Nelson P. Valdés, "Cuba, The Internet, and U.S. Policy," Cuba Briefing Paper Series, no. 13 (March 1997), available online at <http://www.georgetown.edu/sfs/programs/clas/Caribe/bp13.htm>.

22. Castells, *The Information Age,* vol. 1, 44.

23. Press, "Cuba, Communism, and Computing," 27.

24. Ibid., 29. Press addresses the significant problem of the failure to create a software industry in Cuba and argues that one of the main obstacles Cuba has in developing a significant software export industry is in its not recognizing software copyrights. He claims that Cuba maintains a National Software Interchange Center in which copies of all kinds of foreign software are made available to any Cuban citizen free of charge. Aside from this, under the Cuban policy of not recognizing software copyrights, if someone were to come up with a successful piece of software, it would have no direct benefits for that person, severely reducing the incentives to develop software.

25. Gonzalez-Manet, "Internet: Espejismos y promesas de la cultura electronica."

26. Julio García Luis, *Cuba en la era de Internet y las autopistas electronicas: An interview with Enrique Gonzalez-Manet (Cuba in the Era of the Internet and the Electronic Highways: An Interview with Enrique Gonzalez-Manet)* (Havana: Pablo de la Torriente Editorial, 1997), 6.

27. Cuba has a class B license, which means that CENIAI can distribute 256 Internet Protocol real numbers to a subnetwork, and in turn the subnetwork can create another 256 class C providers. See Naghim Vázquez, "Cuba in the Internet Window," master's thesis, University of Havana, 1998.

28. There are several .com domain names registered to companies that are the most likely to engage in effective e-commerce once this becomes a viable business option. This is further evidence of the way in which Cuba is preparing a more secure business environment for Cuban firms. Some of the current registered domains are for companies doing business in the following areas: music <discuba.caribbeansources.com>, cash remittances <Quickcash: careebecons.com>, mobile phone provision <cubacel.com>, export promotion <infomaster.com>, medical and sugar industry supply <cambiomed.com>, and genetic engineering <cigb.edu.cu>.

29. Larry Press, "Cuban Computer Networks and Their Impact" (1996), 344, available online at <http://www.lanic.utexas.edu/la/cb/cuba/asce/cuba6/43press2.fm.pdf>.

30. Larry Press, "Cuban Networking Update," *OnTheInternet,* The Internet Society, Reston, Va., (January/February 1996): 46–49, available online at <http://som.csudh.edu/fac/lpress/devnat/nations/cuba/update.htm>.

31. UNESCO, Executive Board, 151st session, 151EX/16Add, Paris, May 20, 1997, 4 (author translation).

32. For a detailed description of all the services provided by CITMATEL see <http://www.citmatel.com>.

33. Susana Lee, "Aprueban decreto sobre acceso a redes informaticas de alcance global" (Decree Granting Access to Global Information Networks is Approved), *Granma,* June 20, 1996 (author translation).

34. Ibid.

35. Garcia Luis, *Cuba en la era de Internet y las autopistas electronicas.*

36. Jorge Hernández Martinez, "Cuba y las relaciones interamericanas: Revolución y politica exterior" (Cuba and Inter-American Relations: Revolution and Foreign Policy), paper presented at the Fourth Annual International Conference of the Americas (Puebla, Mexico, October 1999).

14

Ethnic Diversity, "Race," and the Cultural Political Economy of Cyberspace

Andrew Jakubowicz

Introduction

Although cyberspace is a virtual space, its cultural politics are no less real than those in other more traditionally comprehended locales. As with cultural analysis of any mediascape, cyberspace needs to be understood as a realm within which political economy, textual analyses, and audience analyses all need to be integrated. This chapter addresses the particular issue of cultural diversity and race relations within cyberia. Cyberia should be understood as worldwide phenomena exuded from within processes of globalization that involve regimes of power seeking to expand and impose themselves on previously uncolonized social and cultural spaces. It is a realm within which cultures and communities are formed, deformed, and transformed in these emerging fields of power.

'Race' is one critical parameter in these processes, where "race" is understood as the social manifestation of cultural differences based on broadly ascribed characteristics. 'Race' is often placed within single quotation marks to indicate that it is a term of social usage but without scientific specificity—that is, that it is a political, not a biosocial, concept. In this discussion, the use of the term reflects its different meanings in different cultural environments: It can allude to apparent physical characteristics (skin color, eye shape, hair forms, physical size), to cultural elements (belief systems, social mores, values), and to social practices (family marriage patterns, gender hierarchies).

Although race has entered the lexicon of cyberanalysts,[1] much of the focus has been on the domestic politics of race within North America, the creation of virtual identity communities,[2] or the activities of racist organizations on the Internet.[3] Although these analyses offer valuable counterpoints to the dominance of white masculinity as the lingua franca of cyberdiscourse, they fall short of an analysis that links race practices in cyberspace to the wider race issues of globalization. This chapter then seeks to locate race in cyberspace within a global political economy of new media, teasing out the numerous dimensions of conflict, superordination, and subordination that this economy allows and enshrines.

If we think of cyberspace as a zone in which competing cyberia (the plural of cyberium and a neologism based on the concept of the imperium) are extending their Webby fingers, then we have the metaphor for approaching what happens when cyberialism (imperialism in cyberspace) reaches the takeoff point. In many ways the contemporary moment is an electronic re-creation of the globe in the sixteenth century, the early phase of European expansionism into the rest of the world. Large dot.com corporations mirror the marauding and self-justifying chauvinism of the early trading companies that sought to carve up the physical planet among themselves,[4] employing or allowing privateers to raid the competitors for the spoils to be taken on the high seas. As imperialism brought about the creation of 'race' as a social category and racial hierarchies as a then-global ideology of imperialism, so cyberialism creates its own racially marked categories, which reflect racial hierarchies and power struggles within the globalizing electronic world. Cyberia present themselves as the terrain in which a globalizing inevitability marks new media as the apex of cultural and economic development.

To grasp the ramifications of the processes involved in the constitution of race in cyberspace, we need to move systematically through a number of spheres of analysis, examining the internal dynamics in each case, and then exploring the linkages among the spheres (rather like the string-of-pearls metaphor used in multimedia design). The broadest picture is presented by the political economy of cyberspace, which encompasses the overarching globalization of communication and locational consequences of these processes. We then must move to an examination of the cultures and cultural hierarchies in cyberspace and the value of the concept of 'multiculturalism.' Globalization is tested by the role of nation-states, and cyberspace has been seen to leap-frog national governments and their desires for control of intranational dialogue; for instance, protection of national cultures (and national power hierarchies) has merged as a critical issue in cyberia. Texts produced in cyberia take various notice of cultural difference, ranging from denial to celebration and commodification. Cyberaudiences, meanwhile, are fashioned by the power of the media to which they are exposed, yet at the same time develop local responses that appropriate and refashion the global into locally meaningful experiences. Ranging across this extraordinarily complex scene are the raptors of racialized cyberia: the racist organizations that have found a new avenue for reaching those whom globalization terrifies and for whom simplistic racial hierarchies of power offer succor.

Approaching the Cultural Political Economy of Cyberia

Political economy as an approach in media studies tends to identify two related elements: the economic interests of the main participants and their expression in political practice, and the attempts by states to regulate both the economic and political operations. In areas of cultural production, the cultural political economy requires an understanding both of these economic interests and of the cultural power embedded in and promulgated through the media environment within and between nation-states (and now apart from or beyond nation-states). In terms of cyberia, culture is produced through the relations of production and is conveyed, contested, and transformed in myriads of interchanges and "glocalizations."[5] Thus the economic factors are revealed in questions of commodification of culture and its processing to extract commercial value from its exchange and use, and in contradistinction, attempts to create a culture that transgresses and subverts the economic rationale. This political economy also has consequences for the nature of civil society, particularly in complex societies in which it may contribute to the deconstitution of social relations of community and their replacement by atomized and despatialized market relations.[6]

The early period of cyberia was characterized by the appearance of innovatory enterprises and innovations in government agencies (e.g., the concept of the Internet as an indestructible defense resource in the United States, the interuniversity links designed to facilitate government-sponsored research, and the development of the idea of the World Wide Web in labs supported by European governments). The U.S. National Science Foundation took over the running of the U.S. side of the Internet, from where it was passed to major private telecommunications carriers, such as Sprint and Pacific Bell.[7] The mass development of cyberia as zones of economic exploitation awaited the emergence of the supercorporations with their capacity to imagine what cyberia might become and the resources to push them in those directions. Most of these corporations were based in the United States (most famously the software—i.e., "language"—giant Microsoft, with its motto of "Where do you want to go today?") and assumed American English as their primary communication milieu.

As with previous periods of explosive capitalism on a global scale, entrepreneurs sought out new markets, developed new products, and sought to capture market segments through innovation and strategies of exclusion focused on competitors (most obviously with Microsoft and the legal battles over the Web software *Explorer*). At the same time, the focus was placed on sectors that could maximize profit and minimize costs. While the design teams for the system were concentrated in First World brain sinks such as Palo Alto, California, and Seattle, Washington, most production of the hardware was moved to lower-cost locations in the Third World (Taiwan, Thailand, Malaysia, etc.). Thus the classic pyramid of power in production was reinforced by cultural hierarchy, mainly white, English-speaking men determining the priorities and directions of an industry that employed vast numbers of low-paid Third World workers, usually women. Even when non-Anglo innovators wanted to enter the industry, they were drawn into the same sort of cultural relations of production, a situation that really began to change only three decades into the cyberian adventure, at the end of the twentieth century.

One country that sought to move past this nexus, Malaysia, developed a strategy for 2020, in the expectation that it could seduce the creative and innovative corporations to its cybercity outside Kuala Lumpur. It found, however, that most of the innovation remained "at home," whereas assembly and low-wage production came to the archipelago in pursuit of the low-tax and high-incentive environment the government had engineered.

Cyberspace has been described as the "darker side of the West," where "the hunger for new conquests stems from the insatiable desire to acquire new wealth and riches which in turn provides impetus for the development of new 'technologies of subjugation.'" In this Manichaeistic imaginary, cyberspace, "with its techno-Utopian ideology, is an instrument for distracting Western society from its increasing spiritual poverty, utter meaninglessness, and grinding misery and inhumanity of everyday lives."[8] Although such a view dredges the colonial metaphor for all it is worth, it does show up the lines of power that are embedded in cyberia and that have reverberations throughout the multidimensional universe.

To take this line of argument a step further, Jay Kinney quotes a Global Business Network cofounder in support of the end-of-nationalism argument: "Just as during the Enlightenment the 'nation-state' took over from 'the church' to become the dominant seat of action, so the nation-state is now receding, yielding centre stage to the 'marketplace'; the action in the marketplace is interestingly everywhere; local, global, wherever."[9] Cyberia become increasingly global, ingesting smaller corporations and zones of cultural development, to exude huge conglomerates that have no particular national base but reflect their history in the West and North.

Multiculturalism in Cyberia

How might we use the ideas generated by the concept of "multiculturalism" to provide an analytical take on cyberia? It is important to note that "multiculturalism" is a highly politicized term in every context in which it is used. Given that, we should also note that its North American meanings (including the divergence between Canada and the United States) are rather different from the way the term is used in the United Kingdom and Europe, or again in Australia or New Zealand.

"Multicultural" can be taken to refer to a statement about demographic differences among groups, based on some idea of culture distinctiveness (national history, country or region of origin, shared family history, language, religion, cultural practices, etc.). Yet to speak of a multicultural world is to take a further step, to require an equivalence of the respect for different cultures as a political ideal. This may entail an implicit challenge to hierarchies based on "the discursive residue or precipitate of colonialism . . . and its imperative mode, its attempted submission of the world to a single 'universal' regime of truth and power."[10] In this sense multiculturalism can offer a radical critique of Eurocentric hierarchies and stands in opposition to other possible multiculturalisms, such as those distinguished as "conservative"/corporate, liberal, and left/"liberal."[11] Critical multiculturalism questions essentialist conceptualizations of culture and instead posits culture as a process of struggles over signs and meanings in a constantly changing "ethnoscape." Culture and meaning are constituted as relationships within and between groups, so that cyberspace has become a field in which those relationships are negotiated and re-created.

Cyberia already inhabit a multicultural landscape, one that reflects the relative power of cultural economies across the globe. Thus the majority of the exchanges currently in cyberspace use English as the assumed language (often in its cybervariations), while at the same time reflecting the economic and cultural assumptions of the major transnational corporations that control the Internet and generate its 'production' resources (software, etc.) (In September 2000, BBC World reported that whereas half the number of Internet users at that time were from non-English-speaking countries, something like 80 percent of interactions over the Internet were in English). Although these global corporations might appear to have no need to be culturally specific, their growth out of North American culture is reflected in the style, language, and habitus[12] of their products and the processes they engender. Perhaps this is best exemplified by the world impact of CNN, the

Time Warner company that publishes on the Internet, on cable and by satellite, interchangeably between broadcast television and cyberspace. Although it is available almost everywhere that there is a satellite dish to receive it, what it makes available speaks to those who view Los Angeles, Seattle, and New York as the legs of the cybertripod on which their reality rests. Although CNN provides some portals for non-U.S.-generated local news, the structure of news values and the style of presentation has an anodyne Eurocentric and North American quality.

The policy discourses of multiculturalism and cyberspace reflect the different cultural politics referred to by McLaren.[13] In general a corporate form of multiculturalism retains the overarching control of cultural diversity. It assumes the dominance of Western/Northern cultural forms, language, and modes of being and mobilizes images and meanings associated with modernity and ever-expanding capitalism. It seeks to commodify all relationships and transform them from associations based on traditional forms of interaction into relationships mediated in all ways by the market. A self-consciously elaborate version of this approach can be found in the Internet marketing and related strategies of the Italian-based lifestyle corporation Benetton.

Benetton is renowned for its innovative marketing programs and its hard-copy magazine *Colors,* with its emphasis on the erotic aesthetics of skin and physical features and the "universal" attraction of youth and vitality irrespective of cultural origin. In the presentation of the "Benetton lifestyle," consumers are interwoven with a world of racing cars (Benetton sponsors a Formula One team), high-cheeked, gaunt models, often black African, and smiling Asian children. In mid-2000, Benetton published a Web version of the Milan Colors exhibition, with a virtual-reality display and access to "color" commodities, from black African–faced playing cards to chocolate-colored "flesh tone" Band-Aids. Associated with the site is a museum of culture, established in southern Chile, exploring the relationship between indigenous Americans and the waves of invaders and immigrants who first stole, then settled on their land. The site has a curious quality, as it both mourns the past and celebrates its incorporation into a "multicultural" future—one built, however, on the assumptions and worldviews of the descendants of the invaders. Difference becomes a commodity to be consumed by the more powerful, especially those located in the "north."[14]

Liberal discourses of multiculturalism posit an egalitarian ethos, yet still within a hierarchical model of cultural practices derived from Western "market" models of individual consumer preference. Thus different ethnic groups or cultures are validated as having equally "worthwhile" cultures, but the hierarchy of social values against which this is placed remains implacably Western/Northern. For instance, rights to individual social mobility and choice are placed above communal rights to set constraints for social behavior. Thus arranged marriages are seen as culturally located and respected but have to play a subordinate role if a young person whose marriage has been arranged decides not to follow her parents' wishes and instead to make a choice based on personal desire. Multicultural policy discourses here seek to ensure "equal access" and find their clearest expression in projects such as those concerned with "the digital divide." A study by Novak et al.[15] concentrated on issues of race and access to and usage of the Internet, operationalizing race under the headings of Native American, African American, Hispanic, Asian, and white. These categories are socially derived but are based on very different attributes: region of origin, culture and language, and skin color. In fact they represent hierarchies of social power, and Internet usage may reflect not cultural attributes of the groups, but their access to social power and their representation in various media. I will return to the findings of this study later in this chapter.

Left/liberal perspectives on multiculturalism move into a different space again, working from more "essentialist" positions that seek to sanctify subordinated groups' cultures separate from the value set of the West/North. From this perspective, individuals are seen as carriers of their group's culture, a biological vector for cultural performance. Cultures are presented not as relationships, but rather as fixed entities bumping into each other. From this perspective the highest value is authenticity, as though there exist cultural cores that can be discerned as yet untainted by other "cultures." This reification of culture has implications for analyses of Internet cultural politics, in which politically subordinated groups are defended irrespective of their internal cultural practices (for instance, the right of groups to project their prejudices without reference to the impact of their values on other groups offended by them).

Given the specific limitations of each of the foregoing approaches to multiculturalism, the value of the critical multiculturalist approach lies in its capacity to explain social phenomena as at all times the momentary outcome of the relationships between groups and their unequal power relations, resting in this case in the political economy of culture. To understand multiculturalism as a terrain of interaction, conflict, struggle, and transformation allows us to examine the local and relate it to global processes of change. Nation-states seem to be potentially vulnerable entities when confronted with transborder cultural flows through global communication channels. We can move then to an examination of how the conflicts between national and international cultural forms may be conceived and experienced in cyberspace.

States and Cyberpluralism

Challenges to the cultural and economic domination of transnational corporations have emerged rapidly, not only through the numbers of antihegemonic groups that litter cyberspace, but also in the explosion of key non-English networks, including Hispanic, Arabic, Hindu, and most importantly, Chinese. Yet each of these are occurring within their own micropolitical economies, in which tensions rub at the boundaries between language and nation, between individual, civil society, and the state.

One example of this can be found in the People's Republic of China. The Chinese government has made a major commitment to getting its population "online," though with constraints that reflect central-government fears of "anarchic" communication. An example of this relationship, which also demonstrates the role of English language as the lingua franca of cyberia, can be found in a hotel in SuZhou outside Shanghai. The hotel offers Internet services to guests; they are warned, however, in a leaflet left in their rooms that "[Y]ou must keep the law, the rules and the executive by law and institution of the PRC about it . . . [It is] forbidden being engaged in endangering the security of the PRC, disclosing our country secret and other criminal act . . . [Y]ou should obey international rules of Internet. Forbidden sending spiteful and provocative files . . . and forbidden sending business advertisement to the unknown's mail box at will [i.e., spamming]."

The link between cultural and social diversity and cyberspace can be seen in the major cyberwar being waged by the Chinese government against the Falun Gong movement. The movement was banned in China in July 1999 and has been castigated by the government as a dangerous cult and a destabilizing political formation. The Falun Gong (or Falun Dafa) challenges the dominant role of the Communist Party in Chinese society through its active recruitment of members into the practices of the movement based on principles of "truth, compassion, forbearance." The Falun Gong movement claims it has been attacked because it has recruited far more members than the Communist Party and was threatening to become the single largest civil-society institution inside the country. Whatever the truth of these claims, the organization has been hunted down and its cyberspace existence harassed as systematically as its human membership. Sophisticated hacking and wrecking strategies have been used to knock out the electronic networks the movement has established internationally, a much more elaborate and well-resourced exercise than the low-intensity cyberengagements between the democracy movement and the regime in a country like Myanmar.

This sort of contradiction, between the urge to use the Net and the urge to control populations, does not overcome the necessity felt by governments in countries such as China to ensure that their populations are readied for the wider struggles of economic and cultural survival that will eventuate in cyberspace in coming decades. With a major program of introducing computers and the Internet into schools, the recognition has emerged that older citizens may need to know about the technology, if not become expert in its use. Thus CCTV (the main national government channel in China) has developed a weekly broadcast that explains computers and the Internet to its viewers. In order to "sell" the program, there are two presenters—both men, one of them a Mandarin-speaking Caucasian. It is as though the importance of understanding the technology requires a "Westerner" to legitimate the exercise, even though the Westerner in question was already a well-known television personality.

Meanwhile Chinese authorities were also pushing at the global level for the recognition of Chinese ideograms as address labels for Internet traffic. In November 2000, the international regulatory body for Internet standards agreed that e-mail addresses that carried Chinese characters to the left and right of the @ sign could be used, though the category characters (.com, etc.) would remain in English for the moment.[16] This would still restrict Web site categories to roman characters, however and require user facility in reading Roman characters in general. While the romanization of Mandarin has progressed with the use of PinYin transliteration (and is widely understood by young Chinese who have been exposed to standard Chinese—Mandarin), PinYin represents only the vocalization of characters in the Mandarin language of Beijing and does not adequately deal with the many varied pronunciations of the characters in other regional languages (e.g., Shanghaiese or Cantonese). To open up the Internet to widespread use (possibly to many hundreds of millions of users), Chinese authorities pressed for the international community to accept full Chinese character sets for Web and e-mail addresses, a goal they realized in 2001. In one step, of course, this would create a huge internal market in the Chinese diaspora, while locking out Internet users unable to understand or use Chinese characters.

The design that created cyberia as part of an anarchic web with no center and enormous multidirectional flows of information, although originally conceived to protect the state (the U.S. government in the event of attack), has confronted states with major issues of control and regulation. The most publicly debated of these have to do with sex, especially violent or exploitative sex, in which vulnerable innocents might be captured and abused by electronic predators. The sharper edges of cyberspace, however, tend to cut at cultural conflicts of a different kind, in which national governments built on ethnic hierarchies of power seek to maintain their dominance over ethnic minorities in their own societies and see the dissident voice in the cyberwilderness as dangerous. Groups that have found themselves constrained by controls on hate speech or demands for ethnic or racial independence/purity in the past, however these are conceptualized, have found in cyberspace as well pathways through which they may evade governmental surveillance.

Cybertexts of Difference

Cybertexts can be subjected to the same type of analysis offered for hard-copy materials, though ideas of audience need to be extended and loosened for the former. Texts are themselves locales for the working through of relationships between authors and audiences. These power relations are given form through the production of texts that encapsulate the intent of the producers as either proponents and reproducers of dominant discourses or as antagonists to the realms of control they are seeking to challenge or evade. If we selectively examine some of these texts (Web sites, list-servs, CD-ROMs, computer games, DVDs, etc.), it is possible to discern within them the dynamics of cultural creation, control, appropriation and resistance. Although feminist scholars have examined cyberia for evidence of such works as gendered artifacts,[17] far less attention had been paid to the subtleties of race and ethnicity.

In his discussion of the "locations" of arguments about the virtual worlds created by new technology, Harris Breslow has suggested that the Internet (which is only one arena of new media communication) has generated three intellectual/political spaces.[18] These can be summarized as the "anarchist" space of unmediated communication, the postmodernist space of multiple subjectivities, and the moral space of state control of both of these components.[19]

Many commentators have seen in cyberspace the chance for a new form of relationship in which when people can become whatever they wish and in which race may become a "skin" to be slipped into or shed as desired.[20] An example of this perception can be found in Peder Norlund's 2000 short Norwegian film *Sorthvit* (*Black and White*). In contemporary Oslo a neo-Nazi skinhead pecks away at his keyboard, seeking a partner for chat. He is repulsed by offers of kiddie porn and the other rubbish dumped by his network of contacts. One night, as he chain-drinks Coca Cola (the symbol of globalization sine qua non), a woman comes on and asks him to join her in a multiuser domain (MUD), where he can choose his avatar. By mistake he chooses Othello (he had wanted to be Romeo), and his correspondent takes on the role of Desdemona. Neither can see the bodies that appear on screen of themselves, only that of the other. The woman, who is a black separatist activist feminist, sees this black man (Othello); he sees a beautiful white woman. And so the comedy of errors develops with the real-world Catherine-wheeling into conflict and violence, while in the cyberforest there is love and passion. The two agree to meet in person, then fail to do so, but each realizes s/he has in fact seen the other and that s/he is their most potent hate. They put this to one side, however, and marry in a cyber-chapel, falling passionately into each other's animated arms. The End. We never discover whether their cyberromance cools out the real-world conflict; the suggestion is that the cathode ray tube is now the place where reality exists and that broken heads and racist hatred will dissipate as though the power had been turned off at the powerpoint of the corporeal world.

Most metropolitan First World societies face considerable difficulties in coming to terms with their own histories, in ways that both reinforce social values of cooperation and cultural pride and recognize and deal with pasts (and presents) that are intolerant, racist, and violent. In a world where "ethnic cleansing" has become a crude neologism for extermination and where "new racism" has emerged as a serious ideology justifying cultural and material genocide, issues of cultural respect and mutual cooperation between ethnically diverse populations confront governments as possibly the most challenging issue for the third millennium.

If we bring together cyberspace and cultural conflict, we can begin to see a space where communities can take greater control of the representation of their own histories, and in so doing, move toward a future that is infused with a greater awareness of the necessity, but also the fragility, of cultural collaboration. In some circles, such collaboration has been identified with the emergence of hybrid cultures through a postmodernist fusion in which the edges of cultures (which ethnic purists have sought to freeze and sharpen) are instead softened, melded, and dissolved into something new and inclusive. There is pain in such dissolution, and the fear of loss marks the politics of ethnic conflict with a particular anger and viciousness.

Yet if we start to spell out the elements that may be necessary to move through this pain, we can see that the new media can provide an avenue for building multifocal narratives. Such approaches can, if used creatively and in ways that recognize the power relations embedded in new media practices, empower audiences to build their own stories of the past and their own analyses of the present, by offering them a range of materials and competing interpretations.

Evidence from the United States suggests that new media associated with education are in fact coming under tighter corporate control, with the strategies of major textbook and information software suppliers geared toward market dominance.[21] Commenting on the U.S. scene, Sewall and Emberling have noted that "[e]ducational publishing is a business, and it is a business increasingly linked to global communications corporations. These media giants see school textbooks as one product among many other media that must make money or else." They go on to note that "[t]he mass-market textbooks that succeed in the market beyond the next few years will have vast influence on social studies. . . . [T]hey will reveal the kinds of civic knowledge and the literacy skills that educators expect of younger citizens. They will reflect how the nation intends to represent itself and its ideals to the youth of the twenty-first century. They will be important indicators of 'who we are' and 'what we are' as a nation and a people after a decade of exposure to multiculturalism."[22]

Although Sewall and Emberling refer primarily to textbooks, their commentary is clearly relevant to new media in education. In addition it is important to recognize that they are hostile to what they see as a dangerous California-ization of curriculum (spreading to other states, and they refer in particular to Texas) with its associated multiculturalism and orientation to world cultures. They are also hostile to new media, which they claim "dumb down" the quality of education, and are unaware of the development of cyberliteracy and its associated multimedia skills.

The most significant U.S. creation in relation to cultural diversity has been the proliferation of various anthropological encyclopedias on CD-ROM, in which again large corporations have sought to provide authoritative accounts of ethnicities and their content. Jasco's review of three of these (by the Gale Corporation, Macmillan, and Microsoft in conjunction with Brigham Young University's Culturgram project) indicates that they offer little if any scope to interrogate or question the interpretations offered and provide no sense that culture is a contested space in which conflict and change is characteristic rather than deviant.[23]

Within the United States there are now multitudes of CD-ROMs that attempt to address the national history of invasion and occupation, two of which give a sense of how the position of indigenous people and other minorities have been addressed. In Microsoft's *500 Nations: Stories of the North American Indian Experience,* produced in 1995, Kevin Costner hosts a CD-ROM version of a book and film of the same name. The project offers the authoritative narrator introducing a variety of locales, from Mexico to Canada, and offers both a celebration of precontact societies and a memorial to the history of the

Indian peoples after European contact. It pays little attention to the contemporary situation and the processes of de- and retribalization.

As well as the database and encyclopedic approaches, there are many simulation games, the most heralded of which have been the succeeding versions of *The Oregon Trail*. In his review of these CDs, Bigelow undertakes a detailed deconstruction of the content, examining the highly individualized subjectivities the simulation requires of its participants.[24] He concludes by asking, "Which social groups are students not invited to identify with in the simulation? For example, Native Americans, African Americans, women and Latinos are superficially represented in The Oregon Trail, but the 'stuff' of their lives is missing."

The new media, with CD-ROMs linking through the Internet to World Wide Web sites and other online databases and update sources, are becoming a central element in educational strategies in advanced capitalist societies. Holzberg notes, in her brief discussion of historical narratives on CD-ROM, the increasingly important role they were playing even in 1995.[25] In the United States nearly all schools have multimedia-capable machines and access to the Internet (and are gearing up for the broadband revolution associated with Internet 2), whereas in other technologically sophisticated societies such as Singapore, all schools and most residential locations will have direct access to high-speed Internet connections within two to three years. In New South Wales, Australia, the state government has committed to every school's having multiple computers and Internet access by 2002 and has demanded that all teachers, irrespective of discipline, be computer literate.

In new media projects about national histories, we have already seen how little room is given to controversy and how much energy is spent on producing anodyne and non-confrontational material. Perlmutter concludes that "the visual depiction of history and society . . . is a construction derived from industrial, commercial, and social influences . . . [and] undermines the assumption that visual or verbal educational messages are neutral transmissions of self-evident, naturally arising, unstructured or objective content."[26]

Thus we need to be aware of the processes through which new media national imaginings are produced (such as *Vital Links*, produced by Davidson and Associates and published by Addison Wesley, to support the U.S. history curriculum *Vital Issues: Reshaping and Industrializing the Nation*).[27] These products provide very carefully programmed learning environments that help students build cyberliteracy skills but may not facilitate alternative interpretations of events and skills in critical thinking.

When the new technologies are used specifically with the aim of empowering the traditionally "silenced" elements of society, however, voices emerge that have a resonance and authority that might otherwise not be available. Although most histories are written by the victors and tell the stories of the powerful and victorious, popular history can move beyond these versions to more subtle, multilayered, and complex pictures of the past and the present. This is Thomson's conclusion in his discussion of oral history practices, in which he sees in new media "the potential to expand such possibilities. Multimedia formats can include a massive amount of textual, oral, visual, and video material. They facilitate the simultaneous juxtaposition of diverse forms of evidence, including both complementary and contradictory accounts."[28]

The Washington-based Smithsonian Institution offers an African culture and history exhibition online. This exhibition seems to have been designed for two audiences, both North American. The first are those non–African Americans with an interest in African history as it affected the conditions under which black slaves were transported to the Americas. That is, it offers a cultural archeology of contemporary America by opening up sites of African experience and suggesting trajectories of cultural continuities. The second audience directly addressed is African Americans, for whom African heritage is validated and African culture celebrated. Such cultural anthropological theorizing of the African experiences underplays, however, the impact of colonialism on African society (though not that of the slave traders, who were directly relevant to the United States). Thus many of the contemporary problems of Africa that permeate the global media do not receive any sustained consideration in the exhibition, and yet the ambiguities of African American experience resonate with the conflicts and traumas of postcolonial Africa. The potential for a critical multiculturalism has not been realized, with a liberal and sociocentric view—an essentially anthropological account from outside Africa—having to suffice.

One attempt to develop a cyberian history from within a multicultural society occurred with the CD-ROM project *Making Multicultural Australia* (MMA)[29] and its development as a Web site through "Remarking Multicultural Australia" in 2001.[30] Ethnic and racial conflict have played a critical part in the development of Australian society, from the suppression and attempted extermination of the indigenous peoples by the invading colonists through to the exclusion of Asian and other immigrants of color as part of the establishment of the nation in 1901. It was not until the mid-1970s that 'multiculturalism' was adopted as national policy in relation to settlement of immigrants, race was removed as a criterion for their selection, and indigenous rights were asserted. Yet as these changes worked their way through the body politic, they were also resisted, with race issues (in relation to Asian immigration and indigenous land and political rights) re-emerging as points of great political division from 1996. The MMA project sought to narrate a nation.[31] from the perspective of those subordinated communities that had experienced exclusion. It was also designed to fit closely with the emerging revisionist curricula in schools, which recognizes the multiplicity of histories in the society and addresses the progressive agenda of reconciliation between indigenous and settler communities. The project adopted the metaphor of an earlier technology, the filmed documentary, but positioned the audience as active participants in the construction of the narrative, offering additional research materials, alternative voices, and critical commentaries on the "mainstream" versions of the histories.

Cybertexts of difference are given meaning by the audiences who use them and who invest their experience in the negotiation of useful meanings. Audiences are called into existence through joining the virtual community formed by those who use the particular text. Access, then, is a critical issue in joining such communities.

Cyberaudiences and Cultural Diversity

Access to cyberia requires permission: knowledge about how to gain access, a point through which the neural web can be opened, and resources to pay for the process. The potential pattern of audiences does not match the actual avenues of access, for many of those least equipped to walk in the new world are cultural minorities. These dimensions of inequality can be understood on a global scale—North/South—and inside nations, where gender, disability status, ethnicity, race, class, age, education, and language skills affect the power to generate or even consume new media discourses.

Some of the consequences of this pattern were made evident in a number of U.S. studies carried out from the mid-1990s. The Clinton administration, especially under the U.S. economy to take advantage of new computer-based technologies. As part of this process, the federal Department of Commerce became involved in a series of studies around the concept of the digital divide. Although a variety of dimensions were given consideration—regional variations, gender, education, income, age, disability, family status—the characteristic most resistant to government policy initiatives remained that associated with race and poverty combined.

Novak, Hoffmann, and Venkatesh, in their 1997 study (based on the first U.S. national survey of Internet usage that recorded race) found that race (meaning African American) combined with poverty provided the best predictor of low Internet access and usage.[32] A key finding of the report was that black Americans wanted to use the Net and intended to, but the Internet industry had abandoned them because it felt that they were unlikely to use the Net and would therefore not be a commercial proposition.[33]

The U.S. Department of Commerce, in the first "Falling through the Net" digital divide report[34] (see <http://digitaldivide.gov>), found that wealthy Asian American households had thirty-four times the access to new technology available to poorer African Americans. In the debate around this work, and in the wake of the Novak/Hoffmann studies, *Business Week* in 1999 noted that "[b]lack children living with one parent are less than one-fourth as likely to have Net access as those in two-parent households."[35]

When the Commerce Department reported its findings in terms of Internet take-up as of August 2000, it was claiming a "tremendous growth rate" for Hispanic Americans over twenty months, from a household access rate of 12.6 percent in December 1998 to 23.6 percent. Similarly, black households had risen from 11.2 percent to 23.5 percent. Overall, though, for all households, the rate had risen from 26.2 percent to reach 41.5 percent, with a projected access of over 50 percent by July 2001. The "gap" between black and all and Hispanic and all had become wider—by 3 percent for blacks and 4.3 percent for Hispanics. On the other hand, Asian Americans and Pacific Islanders had the highest rate of access of any ethnic groups: 56.8 percent.[36]

A February 2002 report by the National Telecommunications and Information Administration, called "A Nation Online" (available online at <http://www.ntia.doc.gov/ntiahome/dn/>), found that White and Asian American access to the Internet had risen to 60 percent, while Black access was 39.8 percent and Hispanic 31.6 percent, while in Spanish-language only households access rates were 14 percent. While the publicity from the Bush administration celebrated progress, in key areas the racial divide continued.

One of the underlying questions about "racial differences" and access and usage of the Net remains what the meaning of the differences might be. There clearly are differences that correlate with race, yet in what sense does race explain the differences? Are we seeing race here as a shorthand for cultural practices/cultural capital and therefore characteristics of the groups, or as a shorthand for race relations, that is, relative social power? The detailed data do indicate that cultural orientations toward Internet use may be a function of racialized power structures and the individual's place within them. Thus middle-class blacks are only marginally distinguishable from middle-class whites in relation to access and use: Black women use the Internet at work in exactly the same ratio as white women. But black youth use the Internet less in homes in which there is no computer than do white youth without a home computer. This suggests patterns of access to public places in which Internet computers are available that restrict black youth more than white, perhaps coupled with lack of meaningful sites on the Net to attract black youth at the same intensity as sites that are available and attract white youths.

The various U.S. studies demonstrate that the racialization of cyberspace is occurring among audiences not simply in terms of virtual ethnic communities (of which there are many), but also in terms of access and potential to become part of such a community and thus play a role in constructing the discursive zones that make up cyberia. Evidence exists of similar issues (though not necessarily the same patterns) in other countries such as Australia. A study of some 54,000 media consumers in that country over a year, from September 1998 to September 1999, indicated that Internet access figures (34 percent of sample in the last month) could be usefully differentiated along ethnic grounds, with highest usage among groups born in the United States (185) and Canada (184) and lowest among those born in Italy (70) and Greece (71) (where 100 is average).[37]

Cyberaudiences enter a terrain that is politically loaded, and they are often seen as targets by racial marauders, eager to advance a racial agenda unrestrained by national legal systems or truncated by limited means of distributing propaganda or organizing linkages.

Cyberracism

The widespread diffusion of the Internet has meant that many organizations devoted to the promotion of racist views have found it invaluable for their work. Addressing a United Nations seminar, "Racism and Racial Discrimination on Internet," in 1997, Debra Guzman, executive director of the Human Rights Information Network, asked whether if "racism is this fearsome instrument, and we agree the Internet is a powerful instrument for global communication, then is not the combination of the two something to be concerned with?"[38] The UN seminar marked a formalization at the international level of a debate running widely within the Internet community. As early as 1995 there were calls for some sort of regulation of hate sites, with a variety of strategies being proposed.

Hatewatch, the U.S.-based body that documents the emergence of organized hate actions around the world, has concluded that there are five broad types of hate sites that mobilize concepts of race (or racially marked religion): white power sites (with neo-Nazi ideological orientations), Holocaust denial sites (which are primarily anti-Semitic), anti-Arab and anti-Moslem sites, black power sites, and white Christian sites. Probably the best known of the white power sites, Stormfront, was established in 1995 by a former leader of the Knights of the Ku Klux Klan. It has now grown to be a center for links throughout the white power world, mirrored widely, and offering everything from rally dates to t-shirts.

The 1997 UN seminar documented the growth of the issues associated with cyber-hate, but with the failure before the U.S. Supreme Court of the Communications Decency Act in 1995, government control of hate sites based in the United States came to an effective halt. Indeed the capacity of any authority to censor the Internet seems very limited, primarily as the ability to move locations and servers is so simple. This has resulted in a situation that Michael Whine has characterized as being akin to terrorism, quoting a writer in the white supremacist U.K. National Front journal *The Nationalist:* "The Internet will be the main political campaigning tool of the next decade and beyond."[39]

Commenting on the expansion of hate groups in cyberspace, Kim has reported that in the United States alone in 1998, there were some 537 active hate groups, with over half sponsoring Web sites.[40] For three obvious reasons—the global reach of the Net, its comparative cheapness as a means of distributing information, and its untrammeled capacity to operate outside the control of states (especially in relation to the United States), Web sites have become the new version of the agitator's printing press, but with potentially far greater impact (at least among those who want to access the material or fall across it while surfing). Kim comments that this rise in race hate sites on the Internet seems to run against the assumption that rising educational levels in the West should be correlated with a decline in irrational sentiments and a reduction in the acceptability of racist speech.

There is broad evidence, however, of the role of racial hate in the ideological armory of right-wing and nationalist groups concerned to defend an ethnocentric space against the forces of globalization, however defined. This model of racialized prejudice fits closely with the orientation of alienated and economically marginalized groups seeking scapegoats for their perceived problems. Thus it is to be expected that hate groups will expand to fill the vacuum left by declining capacities of national states to manage the local impacts of globalization and offer psychologically meaningful strategies of valorization of the marginalized and damaged sectors of a society. As the Internet becomes an increasingly prevalent element in the lives of populations in industrialized countries, so the number and reach of hate sites will increase.

There are a number of options that have been advanced by groups seeking to stem the impact of hate propaganda, on the one hand, and undermine the organizing capacity the Internet provides for racist groups, on the other. The Anti-Defamation League (ADL) of the B'nai Brith, a Jewish antihate group in this case based in the United States, has developed a range of proposals to confront the impact of and expansion of hate groups.[41] Its primary strategy is educational: providing materials to teachers and parents about the dangers of hate sites. It also provides a free downloadable HateFilter that contains lists of hate site URLs and automatically redirects attempts to access those sites to the ADL itself. The ADL has noted, however, that whereas private institutions in the United States can mandate the use of such filters in any Internet access they provide, public institutions probably cannot act to limit the access of adults to the Internet in any way.

Cyberia have therefore become an arena for constant political struggles over racialized hate speech, with antihate groups engaging in hacking, blocking, filtering, and varieties of legal action (only the United States has freedom-of-speech parameters that prevent government controls). In France, Yahoo.fr banned the use of its auction site for the sale of Nazi memorabilia (as a preemptive move to avoid triggering government action that might regulate Internet service providers more widely), and in Australia the Human Rights Commission sought to have the Adelaide Institute's Holocaust denial site taken down under racial vilification laws (a tortuous process requiring many rounds of court action with no certainty of final effective success: the site could always move to the United States).

Conclusion

Cyberia are very much phenomena of globalization, which is itself about the accelerated movement and interaction of capital, culture, and populations. Cultural pluralism in new media is both an expression of and a fundamental contribution to how globalization operates. The category of 'race' remains highly problematic, carrying connotations of cultural difference, enforced cultural hierarchies, and racialized political economies of information. Governments have sought to develop strategies to regulate activities in cyberspace, yet across racial boundaries and in ethnic diasporic communities, nation-states seem often to have even less purchase than they do in the physical world.

Cyberspace provides many dimensions in which cultural alternatives can be explored, evoked, and manipulated, so that hybridity and coalescence and refashioning of meanings can occur almost instantaneously. In cyberia, freedom takes on new possibilities, both in terms of creativity and in terms of malicious and destructive intent. Often it depends on from where you view the multidimensional space as to what "take" you see and how you make sense of it. The potential exists for a deepening and solidifying of divisions on the one hand, and/or a dissolving of historic conflicts on another.

In October 1999 a group of survivors of the ethnic cleansing of Yugoslavia set up a new site, Cyber Yugoslavia. It had no place, no space, but soon thousands of citizens. Its goal was to reach five million members; then it would petition the United Nations to become a nation and would scan the earth for twenty square meters of land for itself. On that land it would place its server. And thus it might seek to end the madness that had plagued the physical country that had torn itself apart for the previous decade. In August 2001, it had reached 15,000 members; and as of October 2002, it counted 16,000 members.

Notes

1. B. Kolko, L. Nakamura and G. Rodman, eds., *Race in Cyberspace* (New York: Routledge, 2000).

2. S. Zickmund, "Approaching the Radical Other: The Discursive Culture of Cyberhate," in *Virtual Culture: Identity and Communication in Cybersociety,* ed. S. Jones (London: Sage, 1997), 185–205.

3. D. Guzman, "Racism and Racial Discrimination on Internet," Office for the High Commissioner for Human Rights, Geneva, (Nov. 10, 1997), available online at <http://www.unhchr.ch/html/menu2/10/c/racism/guzman.htm>.

4. For example, M. Hall, "Virtual Colonization," *Journal of Material Culture* 4, no. 1 (1999): 39–55.

5. R. Robertson, "Mapping the Global Condition: Globalization as the Central Concept," in *Global Culture: Nationalism, Globalization and Modernity,* ed. M. Featherstone (London: Sage, 1990), 15–30; and L. N.-h. Fang and S.-w. Sun, "Globalization and Identity Politics: Reflections on Globalization Theories from the Taiwanese Experience," *Asian Journal of Communication* 9, no. 2 (1999): 79–98.

6. H. Brealow, "Civil Society, Political Economy and the Internet," in *Virtual Culture: Identity and Communication in Cybersociety,* ed. S. Jones (London: Sage, 1997), 236–257.

7. Z. Sardar, "alt.civilizations.faq: Cyberspace as the Darker Side of the West," in *Cyberfutures: Culture and Politics on the Information Superhighway,* ed. Z. Sardar and J. Ravetz (London: Pluto, 1996), 14–41, at 21.

8. Sardar, "alt.civilizations.faq," 15, 39.

9. J. Kinney, "Is There a New Political Paradigm Lurking in Cyberspace?" in *Cyberfutures: Culture and Politics on the Information Superhighway,* ed. Z. Sardar and J. Ravetz (London: Pluto, 1996), 138–153, at 146.

10. R. Stam and E. Shohat, "Contested Histories: Eurocentrism, Multiculturalism and the Media," in *Multiculturalism: A Critical Reader,* ed. D. Goldberg (Cambridge, Mass.: Blackwell, 1994), 296–324, at 297.

11. P. McLaren, "White Terror and Oppositional Agency: Towards a Critical Multiculturalism," in *Multiculturalism: A Critical Reader,* ed. D. Goldberg (Cambridge, Mass.: Blackwell, 1994), 45–74, at 47.

12. P. Sulkunen, "Society Made Visible—On the Cultural Sociology of Pierre Bourdieu," *Acta Sociologica* 25, no. 2 (1982): 103–115.

13. McLaren, "White Terror and Oppositional Agency."

14. L. Back and V. Quaade, "Dream Utopias, Nightmare Realities: Imaging Race and Culture within the World of Benetton Advertising," *Third Text* 22 (Spring 1993): 65–80.

15. T. P. Novak, D. Hoffman, and A. Venkatesh, "Diversity on the Internet: The Relationship of Race to Access and Usage," paper presented at the Aspen Institute's Forum on Diversity and the Media (Queenstown, Md., November 5–7, 1997).

16. H. Jia, "Chinese Language Reaches New Domain," *China Daily* 2 (Nov. 8, 2000).

17. For example, L. Cherny and E. Weise, eds., *Wired_Women: Gender and New Realities in Cyberspace* (Seattle: Seal, 1996).

18. Breslow, "Civil Society, Political Economy and the Internet."

19. A. Jakubowicz, "Human Rights and the Public Sphere: An Exploration of Communications and Democracy at the 'fin-de-siecle' in Australia, Indonesia and Malaysia," *Journal of International Communication* 5, nos. 1–2 (1998): 165–180.

20. Kolko et al., *Race in Cyberspace.*

21. D. Perlmutter, "Manufacturing Visions of Society and History in Textbooks," *Journal of Communication* 47, no. 3 (1997): 68–81.

22. G. Sewall and S. Emberling, "A New Generation of History Textbooks," *Society* (November/December 1998): 78–82.

23. P. Jasco, "State-of-the-Art Multimedia in 1996: The 'Big Four' General Encyclopedias on CD-ROM," *Computers in Libraries* 16, no. 4 (1996): 26–32.

24. B. Bigelow, "On the Road to Cultural Bias: A Critique of The Oregon Trail CD-ROM," *Language Arts* 74, no. 2 (1997): 84–93, at 92.

25. C. Holzberg, "Through Changing Rivers of Time," *Electronic Learning* 15, no. 3 (1995): 40–41.

26. Perlmutter, "Manufacturing Visions of Society and History in Textbooks."

27. Holzberg, "Through Changing Rivers of Time."

28. A. Thomson, "Fifty Years On: An International Perspective on Oral History," *Journal of American History* 85, no. 2 (1998): 581–595, at 595.

29. A. Jakubowicz, *Making Multicultural Australia: A Multimedia Documentary* [CD-ROM] (Sydney: Office of the Board of Studies New South Wales, 1999).

30. New South Wales Board of Studies and A. Jakubowicz, "Remaking Multicultural Australia" [Web site], Office of the Board of Studies New South Wales, 2001), <http://www.multiculturalaustralia.edu.au>.

31. H. Bhabha, *Nation and Narration* (London: Routledge, 1990).

32. Novak et al., "Diversity on the Internet."

33. J. Raloff, "Internet Access: A Black-and-White Issue," *Science News* 153, no. 16 (1998): 247.

34. National Telecommunications and Information Administration, *Falling through the Net: Defining the Digital Divide* (Washington, D.C.: U.S. Department of Commerce, 1999).

35. R. S. Dunham, "Across America, a Troubling 'Digital Divide,'" *Business Week*, August 2, 1999, 40.

36. "A Nation Online," National Telecommunications and Information Administration, February 2002, available online at <http://www.ntia.doc.gov/ntiahome/dn/>.

37. A. Jakubowicz, "Australian Dreamings—Cultural Diversity and Audience Desire in a Multinational and Polyethnic State," in *Black Marks: Research Studies with Minority Ethnic Audiences*, ed. K. Ross (London: Ashgate, 2001), summary.

38. D. Guzman, "Racism and Racial Discrimination on Internet" online at <http://www.unhchr.ch/html/menu2/10/c/racism/guzman.htm>.

39. M. Whine, "Cyberspace: A New Medium for Communication, Command and Control by Extremists," The International Policy Institute for Counter-Terrorism, Herzliya, Israel (May 5, 1999), available online at <http://www.ict.org.il/articles/articledet.cfm?articleid=76>.

40. Y. M. Kim, "Hate Propaganda in Cyberspace: Censorship, Freedom of Speech, and Critical Surfing," *CSS Journal* 10, no. 4 (2002) available online at <http://www.cssjournal.com/y_m_kim.html>.

41. Anti-Defamation League, *Hate on the World Wide Web: A Brief Guide to Cyberspace Bigotry* (New York, 1998).

15 Documenting Democratization: New Media Practices in Post-Apartheid South Africa

Ashley Dawson

Freedom of expression has always been one of the hallmarks of democracy. South Africans only recently tasted this liberty. Until the creation and ratification of the country's new constitution in the mid-1990s, the South African government was empowered to curtail free speech as it saw fit. During the final years of apartheid, it often exercised this prerogative. Newspapers were frequently shut down, novels banned, and films censored. Yet the ruling regime did not wield power in a purely negative manner. It also attempted to impose its dogma through the creation of a system of radio and television broadcasting authorities that faithfully replicated the central credo of the ruling party. The South African Broadcasting Corporation (SABC) gave the regime a powerful tool for articulating apartheid ideology and for controlling access to representations from outside the borders of the apartheid state. During the transition to democracy after 1990, South Africa faced the pressing question of how to transform this strategic organ of racist ideology into a forum for the advancement of national unity and equality.

The abiding urgency of this task has been made clear by the recent controversy surrounding the Human Rights Commission's inquiry into racism in the post-apartheid media.[1] By ordering thirty-six editors of the country's main newspapers, radio, and television stations to testify at the inquiry, the commission set off a firestorm of controversy concerning the ruling African National Congress (ANC) regime's attempts to muzzle criticism. Substantial debate has taken place concerning the autonomy of the commission from a ruling party that appears increasingly skittish about charges of corruption coming from the press. Particularly noteworthy in this controversy is the dissension among the editors themselves. Breaking ranks with white editors who refused to appear before the commission in response to a subpoena, five black editors agreed to cooperate with the inquiry. The commission's pointed argument that little institutional change has taken place within the media, 76 percent of whose top managers are white, appears to be gaining increasing traction as the hard realities of post-apartheid economic and social inequality hit home.[2]

The task of democratizing South Africa's media is complicated by the broader changes that accompanied the demise of apartheid. Public-service broadcasting is in retreat around the world. In an era of information capitalism, the clarion call to build the nation through the creation of public authorities has grown increasingly faint. Moreover, the rise of transnational technologies such as satellite broadcasting has undermined both the regulatory power and the ideological presumptions of many national broadcasters to a significant extent. After being denied access to the national broadcaster by the apartheid regime for decades, democratic forces are now confronted with a similar problem as a result of globalizing currents. Yet such trends are by no means inexorable. As Neil Lazarus has stressed, neoliberal ideology that represents globalization as uncontrollable effectively obscures the specific social and economic policies that canalize the transnational flows of capital and culture.[3] Indeed, one of the many galvanizing dramas during South Africa's transition period has been the struggle to establish a national public sphere using the media. From the organization of the Campaign for Independent Broadcasting in opposition to the National Party's plans to privatize the SABC to the contemporary struggles over racism in the media that I described above, democratizing the media has been a central issue in post-apartheid South Africa.[4]

The new nation's ability to foster popular access to the airwaves is, admittedly, limited in a variety of ways. In the years since the unbanning of resistance organizations such as the ANC, South African society has been transformed to an extent few could have predicted. The transition to democracy offers a beacon of hope in a world where almost all forms of collective belonging and belief seem to be suspect. Yet the sweeping changes of the last decade have also shifted the terms that animated the national liberation struggle. Despite the ANC's electoral victories, South Africa remains one of the most materially unequal societies on earth. The issue of democratizing the media may seem relatively unimportant in a nation faced with spiraling crime, urban and rural immiseration, and a collapsing health care system. Yet as Benedict Anderson has argued, forms such as the newspaper, and now film and television, are integral to a nation's consolidation of its identity as an imagined community.[5] If any of the country's material problems are to be addressed on a national level, the primary media site on which the imagined community is conjured up will have to become vehicles through which demands for change can be phrased. Recognition of the crises that vex the nation may not in and of itself be adequate, however, serving in many cases simply to divert attention from the sources of such problems. To what extent, then, does popular culture reflect both the promises and the pitfalls of current initiatives to establish democracy in post-apartheid South Africa?[6] What kind of national subject was being constructed by indigenous television broadcasts during the transition period of the mid-1990s?

I intend to explore these questions through discussion of a specific television series that punctuated the transition to democracy in South Africa in a particularly dramatic manner. *Ordinary People* was the first independently produced current-affairs program to be aired by the SABC. Broadcast for three seasons, from 1993 to 1996, the series was conceived as a concrete embodiment of the ANC's call for a multicultural, nonracial South Africa. Episodes of *Ordinary People* were aired during prime viewing time on channel 1 of SABC-TV, which also commissioned the program, on Thursday evenings. This prime slot suggests that both the producers and the channel strove to garner the broadest possible national audience for the series.

Obviously, many South Africans living in rural areas may not have had access to television, lacking either the material or linguistic resources necessary for such access. However, given the fact that *Ordinary People* was broadcast on the channel associated with the nation's new lingua franca, English, it seems logical to assume that the series' producers imagined themselves as broadcasting to and, to a certain extent, constituting the nation. Production and transmission of the series would have been unthinkable without the signal institutional transformations that took place at the SABC in response to popular mobilizations for equitable access to the media. Consequently, this milestone documentary program offers a particularly significant case study of the struggle to forge a new South African national identity during the transition to democracy.

The Campaign for Independent Broadcasting

Despite the qualms that retarded the introduction of television until 1976 in South Africa, the apartheid regime quickly found the means to use the medium to further its separatist ideology.[7] While adopting the model of public broadcasting embodied in agencies such as the British Broadcasting Corporation, however, South Africa departed radically from other nations in which broadcasting played a historic role as the primary public sphere of the nation during the postwar period. Seeking to allay the concerns of ideologues who argued against the potential for cultural fusion implicit in the model of a unitary public sphere, SABC-TV began broadcasting exclusively in Afrikaans and English, the two languages of the hegemonic white minority in South Africa. After four years, this policy was supplemented through the addition of two channels, TV2 and TV3, which broadcast in the major African languages. Programming for whites and blacks was thus rigidly segregated according to the spuriously multicultural, essentialist logic that characterized apartheid ideology following the introduction of the Bantustans, or "native homelands," in 1971. This arrangement banished fears that television could act as an agent of cultural miscegenation.[8] The SABC's instrumental use by the apartheid regime has given the question of equality of access to the public sphere a far higher profile than in other nations during our current era of globalization. Consequently, although the move away from state regulation is being felt in South Africa as it is in other nations, this move is not taking place in the typical ideological environment in which the public good and decentralization are disaggregated from one another and wholly subject to a market logic.

Despite the fact that the SABC is no longer the only broadcaster in South Africa, its transformation during the years following 1990 suggests that noncommercial, democratic media systems remain a crucial resource in that country. Changes at the SABC were initially catalyzed by a group of anti-apartheid film and media organizations and unions that publicly claimed the right of access to the national broadcaster.[9] Such claims were particularly important given the ruling National Party's move to privatize the SABC before losing power. The importance of these claims to democratic access was further underlined by the need to ensure the SABC's independence before the first democratic elections. A coalition of labor and progressive political groups coalesced in the early 1990s as the Campaign for Independent Broadcasting. This coalition managed to pressure the government into electing a new board for the SABC prior to the 1994 elections and helped establish an Independent Broadcasting Authority (IBA) to diminish state power over broadcasting. The act that established the IBA emphasizes the responsibility of broadcasters to advance the right to representation of historically disadvantaged groups in the nation.[10] These goals have been cemented through the promulgation of broadcasting regulations stipulating linguistic equality for South Africa's eleven major languages and through content quotas that aim to increase the representation of local issues in programming. Despite the limitations imposed on such laudable objectives by lack of funding and worries over continued state intervention, the establishment of the IBA and its subsequent democratic initiatives clearly represent an important foundation for future extensions of equal access to the media in South Africa.

Concurrent with these institutional forms of democratization has been an emphasis on documenting the popular history suppressed during the apartheid era. Many of the approaches employed in programming such as *Ordinary People* were pioneered by anti-apartheid media activists during the 1980s. Radical collectives such as Video News Services (VNS) made documentary programming for local branches of the United Democratic Front, a broad anti-apartheid alliance of workers, community organizations, and youth groups founded in 1983. Following the unbanning of anti-apartheid organizations in 1990, VNS members and other anti-apartheid activists began to produce documentary material for the SABC. By stressing popular identity and power in their work, these documentarians moved beyond the white-dominated view of South African history disseminated by previous media.

Recuperating Popular History

Ordinary People is one of the landmark broadcasts that embodies this strategy of recuperating popular history. Produced by Free Filmmakers, a collective composed of former members of one of the apartheid era's underground video groups, the series was conceived as a video journal of changes in South Africa during the transition to democracy. The first season of episodes was aired on SABC-TV's channel 1 during the powder keg year of 1993, shortly before the first democratic elections confirmed South Africa's transition from apartheid. Each episode of *Ordinary People* frames the radical changes and social disruptions of this period from multiple points of view. Cameras follow three or four "ordinary" people as they experience some of the events that define the new nation. Through this populist strategy, the series sets out to chronicle a significant set of events from a series of different perspectives, producing a complex weave of voices that reflects the variety of contemporary South Africa. In addition, however, the disparities that are revealed as different individuals and groups of people experience identical events offer a powerful implicit comment on the social polarization that is apartheid's primary legacy. Indeed, by opening up the lives of South Africans to one another, *Ordinary People* bears witness to the dramatic inequalities that have to be overcome in the process of nation building. Yet in doing so, the series allows the viewer to engage in the process of identification and understanding that structures other aspects of the nation's negotiated transition. Perhaps the most internationally well-known embodiment of this process of transformation has been the Truth and Reconciliation Commission. Yet *Ordinary People* suggests that the commission is but one element in a much broader culture of confession and conciliation, as well as, on occasion, aggression and dissent, that characterized South Africa during these years.

Ordinary People includes episodes that focus on extremely public moments in the nation's history. They include one that depicts a day in the life of President Nelson Mandela, which was, according to the group's promotional material, the most watched documentary in the history of South African television. In addition, the filmmakers also focus on the moments of spectacular antagonism that occurred during the transition. Perhaps the most well-known episode along these lines is the collective's account of an extreme right-wing Afrikaner party's storming of the conference hall where multiparty negotiations were being carried on. Certainly, such accounts are an important document of their time. By recording the reactions of workers inside the conference hall as swastika-wearing Afrikaners smashed through the hall's glass doors, the filmmakers provided a galvanizing portrait of the menacing violence that pervaded everyday life in South Africa during the period. Given the reconfiguration of the nation's political terrain since the mid-1990s, however, these episodes now seem dated. Although many of the underlying cultural and racial attitudes documented in these episodes persist, the specific political forms through which they are organized have changed markedly and, in some cases, completely disappeared from the scene.

However, the series also includes portraits of more mundane, if no less grave, events in the lives of South Africans. These episodes, though perhaps less spectacular or sensational than those previously described, nonetheless more aptly embody the series' brief to elevate the everyday life of the average South African citizen to historic significance. I will be concentrating my discussion on two such episodes. The first of these is entitled "The Tooth of the Times." As the voice-over introduction explains, this episode focuses on the impact of an Afrikaner's loss of his family farm. According to this introduction, the government's reversal of its policy of "buying" white votes by subsidizing farmers has, in conjunction with years of drought, forced many farmers to default on their substantial loans. *Ordinary People* documents the impact of this situation not simply on the Afrikaner family who own the farm, but also on the black laborers who have lived for generations alongside the white landowners.

Shortly after providing us with this information, the film cuts to the series' introductory sequence, a medley of images that captures the essence of the program. In ravishing black-and-white photography, we are treated to a sweeping tour of contemporary South Africa. The camera zooms down rural roads and over urban highways, stressing the dynamic and varied character of the new nation. The camera's focus on black and white faces, on women and men, children and grandparents invokes the celebratory multiculturalism that has become a part of mainstream discourse in the United States since the civil rights movement, a discourse that leaders in post-apartheid South Africa have appropriated to great effect. Yet we are also shown signs of the tensions that simmer in the country today. A young white man scuffles with a black man in a street. The swastika of the neo-Nazi Afrikaner People's Party is etched on a wall next to which a white woman stands passively. Squatting like an ominous metallic beetle, an armored troop carrier parks itself on a plain outside a township that is engulfed in acrid smoke. A couple of black men argue over a fence with a film crew, seemingly intent on rejecting the version of reality members of the media are constructing. If the series is devoted to documenting the common experiences of South Africans, this introductory sequence also insistently draws our attention to the grim realities that trouble the utopian hopes of the transition.

The primary narrative threads from the body of "The Tooth of the Times" enlarge on this interweaving of identity and difference. Eddie Jacobs, the patriarch of the Afrikaner family depicted in the episode, has left his farm while the implements, livestock, and land that have given him and his family a sense of meaning for five generations are auctioned off. His son watches, anger at the humiliation of having to buy back the tractor he grew up with clouding his face. Yet the scene set up by the filmmakers to follow this account of the auction jars the sense of identification we feel with the Jacobs family. The camera cuts to Fanie Letsimo, perched on his crutches in the middle of a desolate plain, within which are buried generations of his ancestors. His prayer to them suggests the absolute sense of loss he will experience when the Jacobs farm passes into new hands. Not only will his connection with the land he has worked on but never owned be ruptured, but he will also be deprived of the link with generations of his ancestors who are buried on the farm. While the Jacobs family confronts a tragic loss of vocation that might be seen as analogous in many ways, Fanie Letsimo and his family are faced not simply with emotional and spiritual loss, but also with total destitution. Without the *baas* upon whom he depends as a result of the enduringly feudal system of labor relations in rural South Africa, Fanie is helpless.

I have not yet touched on one of *Ordinary People*'s most significant features: language. Both Fanie and the Jacobs family speak in their respective languages in the episode, with English subtitles illuminating the meaning of their words. This strategy allows each to speak using the resonant linguistic forms employed by their diverse communities. Moreover, the Jacobs family often slips in and out of English, dramatizing the importance of Afrikaans as a badge of cultural identity as well as a form through which the deepest feelings of grief are articulated. The filmmakers' strategy is particularly significant in this regard. Although they use English, the lingua franca of the new nation, they also allow individuals to speak in their mother tongues. Given the history of linguistic, cultural, and racial segregation that, as I argued previously, has characterized SABC-TV services, this constitutes a signal recognition of difference. *Ordinary People*'s use of subtitling is a subtle but crucial part of a nationalist pedagogy, one that emphasizes forms of common experience that link South Africa's diverse cultures.

The central element in this strategy of interpellating national subjectivity comes through the different narrators employed by the episode. As I mentioned earlier, the series typically employs three or four narrators within each episode. So far, however, I have discussed only two such narrators: Fanie Letsimo and Eddie Jacobs. Although they experience a similar set of events, the binary arrangement of these two narrators would seem to reinscribe problematic racial oppositions. The third narrator, however, whom I have not yet mentioned, disrupts this binary, helping to create a sense of unity among the two primary narrators. The filmmakers choose the visiting auctioneer to be their third narrator. We see him arriving at the farm, telling the film crew in the car with him that the boers don't feel animosity toward him but rather see him as simply doing his job. As we find out in the bitter auction scenes that follow, however, both the Jacobs and the Letsimo families see themselves as the victims of the bank for whom the auctioneer works. A human community with long traditions of mutual conciliation is conjured up in contrast to the largely faceless and rapacious force of capital. Through the common feelings of despair articulated by Eddie—he returns to his farm after everything has been sold and says, "Now I'm under the mud"—and Fanie, a structure of collective feeling is created by the filmmakers. Linked in a grieving community, Eddie and Fanie offer a microcosm of national identity. Although viewers are certainly offered the materials with which to produce an oppositional reading that focuses on the material disparities differentiating the subjects of this community, this episode of *Ordinary People* strongly evokes the project of nation building by asking us to identify with the common sufferings of all the inhabitants of the Jacobs farm.[11]

The Transition and Land Reform

"The Tooth of the Times" demonstrates the complex bonds that link blacks and whites and thereby gives the viewer an important opportunity to perceive the complex, wounded humanity of both groups in South Africa. Yet the episode also suggests that the political transformation that has galvanized the world's attention following 1990 is a necessary but not sufficient condition for meaningful democratization. Without genuine agrarian reforms that benefit the rural African population, South Africa's fledgling democracy will be built on shaky foundations. The ANC's legitimacy as the hegemonic party of national liberation during the apartheid era rested to a significant extent on its promises to redistribute the ill-gotten gains of colonialism and apartheid, both through the return of land to African farmers and through broader forms of economic and social leveling. Restitution of at least a portion of the lands of which Africans have been dispossessed during the four-hundred-year-long European domination of South Africa was an important element in the process of multiparty negotiations that produced the country's new constitution during the mid-1990s. These negotiations achieved many dramatic successes: South Africa's new constitution has some of the most progressive human rights clauses of any nation's in the world. The issue of land reform and restitution has, however, proven an intractable problem. Currently, a small portion of the nation's white minority owns 86 percent of South Africa's land.

One of the chief catalysts behind the formation of the ANC early in the twentieth century was the upcoming passage of the Natives Land Act of 1913 by the newly formed South African legislature. The Land Act constituted a precedent for much of the legal framework established during the era of formal apartheid after 1948. In response to the growing wealth of African farmers during the late nineteenth and early twentieth centuries, the act introduced the division of land in the nation between firmly mapped out areas of white and black settlement. The minority white population was given control of over 92 percent of South Africa's territory; Africans were limited to reserves covering less than 8 percent of the nation's land. The act also contained provisions intended to limit the numbers of Africans settled on white farms, where they had been carrying out highly competitive agricultural production. The long-term effect of the act was to reduce African agriculture to purely subsistence conditions, ensuring that sharecropping and other rent operations would be transformed into labor tenancy, which would in turn become (unfree) wage labor as part of a cycle of increasingly capitalized white agriculture.[12] This move placated the white owners of large farms, who had been meeting increasingly stiff competition from African family farms. In addition, the act helped push African labor into the gaping maws of the gold and diamond industries. The "reserves," which eventually mutated into the nominally independent Bantustans after the creation of formal apartheid, became overpopulated, economically and environmentally devastated holding pens for the black industrial reserve army needed by South Africa's mining industries. By allowing these industries to shift the cost of reproduction to Africans themselves and by permitting industry owners to pay exorbitantly low wages to migrant laborers who were seen as "supplementing" income earned through farming by working in the mines, rural segregation became an integral element in the massive accumulation of profits that gave

South Africa's white population one of the highest living standards in the world through-out most of the past century.

In the course of the twentieth century, the newly organized South African state built a virtually impregnable position by consolidating a two-nations hegemony.[13] The state, in other words, garnered support from the white working class and from industrial and agri-cultural capital by passing on the benefits of the extreme exploitation of the black major-ity to the white minority. Hein Marais calls the situation instituted by apartheid in which high standards of living for whites were fostered through superexploitation of blacks "racial Fordism."[14] Although the impact of this strategy may be most visible in the creation of a middle-class Afrikaner bureaucracy during the apartheid years, it is also evident in terms of the agricultural policies pursued by the regime. In addition to the racial legisla-tion described above, substantial subsidies were allocated to white farmers, keeping fam-ilies like the Jacobses afloat. Moreover, the postapartheid state continues to support white farmers by sanctifying private property, which translates into routine police intervention on the side of landowners in disputes over land claims. Afrikaner farmers essentially operate as a rentier class, extracting rent in the form of labor from African tenant farm-ers, whose land had been seized during early colonial period.[15] The establishment of the Bantustans coincided with yet another attack on the tenure labor system. The illegality of tenure labor proved highly convenient to white farmers, who, as a result of the mech-anization of agricultural production that characterized the "green revolution" of the 1960s, had less and less call for the large numbers of Africans whose labor they once exploited. Indeed, migrant farm labor is a far more effective solution in this case, since it means that the white farmer does not have to pay the costs associated with the reproduction of his labor force. The "homelands" were thus also a convenient solution for changes prompted by the increasing industrialization of large-scale South African farming.

Despite the central role that land dispossession has played in South African colonial-ism and apartheid and its own origins as a movement of protest against the Land Act, the ANC has paid scant attention to land issues since its founding.[16] Rural issues have been displaced in the organization's thought by the task of mobilizing the urban black working class. It might be argued that the ANC has so steadfastly refused to focus on rural issues to deny the apartheid regime any legitimation for its Bantustan policy, which was predi-cated on representations of Africans as inherently rural people. Given the constitutive re-lation between land dispossession and labor migration discussed above, however, this lack of attention to rural issues represents a key theoretical and strategic elision. The organi-zation's failure to capitalize upon and augment rural uprisings during the period before its banning in 1960 has, for example, been seen as a crucial missed opportunity to expand the ANC's support beyond an urban base. This elision seems particularly grave given that some of the central pillars of apartheid, the "efflux and influx controls" embodied in the notorious pass laws, were based on nakedly economic considerations related to the regulated distribution of black labor between agricultural, mining, and urban sectors. Approximately three and a half million Africans were affected by the accelerated rate of forced removals between 1960 and 1983 that accompanied the increasingly capital-intensive character of South African agriculture and industry during this period.[17]

The ANC's historical inattention to agrarian issues has also created key dilemmas during the transition period. While in exile, the ANC concentrated on mobilizing its urban constituency for a frontal assault on the state. Significant forms of grassroots organization took place, however, outside the ambit of ANC power. The United Democratic Front (UDF), formed in 1983 in opposition to the regime's attempts to create a tricameral parliament that would include representation for "coloreds" and South Asians, was instrumental in creating a structure of civic organizations in urban and rural areas.[18] After its unbanning, however, the ANC attempted to absorb these local initiatives and to refocus them on building regional and national structures.[19] Local activists and protesters found that the local issues that had helped mobilize a popular constituency for the UDF were now being given short shrift. Despite establishing a National Land Commission and affiliated regional land commissions in short order following the organization's unbanning, the ANC failed to connect these organizations to grassroots groups adequately.[20] As a result, the rhetoric of "nation building" often actively militated against local organizations' attempts to foster social and economic justice.

One of the key initiatives taken by the ANC during its first term of office was to endorse the Reconstruction and Development Program (RDP) developed by a Congress of South African Trade Unions (COSATU) affiliated group shortly prior to the 1994 elections. The RDP's ambitious plans included a targeted redistribution of 30 percent of South Africa's land to poor, black, rural households during the party's first five-year term. According to a report published by the National Land Committee (NLC) in 1998, however, less than 1 percent of the country's total farmlands area had been reallocated by the government by that time.[21] The NLC report found fault with, among other things, the government's market-based policy of redistribution. Faced with the fear of capital flight should it follow through on any of the hopes raised by the socialist language of the Freedom Charter of 1955, the ANC foregrounded the sacrosanct status of private property during constitutional negotiations. As Levin and Weiner argue, the prominent place accorded to private property rights in the new constitution was ample evidence of the ANC's decision to subordinate the interests of the nation's rural dispossessed to other considerations.[22] Rather than expropriating land from the politically powerful white farming sector or turning over vacant state lands to the dispossessed, the architects of land reform proposed to subsidize the petitions of black farmers for land, allowing them to buy such land back from willing white farmers. Not entirely surprisingly, this strategy not only failed to convince many white farmers to sell their land, but also helped to drive up the price of land, making it impossible for individual rural households to gain access to land with their relatively meager government grants. To buy land, people were forced to band together into communities whose lack of common interests sometimes produced very uneven results following successful purchase of land. In addition, money was allocated exclusively to male heads of households, revealing a disturbing gender inequity in the ANC's thinking about rural communities. The fundamental unworkability of this market-based approach, however, results from the enormous historical imbalances in terms of access to rural land resources produced by colonialism and apartheid, not to mention the income inequalities that persist in post-apartheid South Africa. The two other initiatives taken by the Department of Land Affairs during this period, the Restitution of Land Rights Act of 1994 and the Land Reform (Labor Tenants) Act of 1995, had a similarly insignificant impact on rural poverty and homelessness. As the editors of a volume produced during the initial debates over the government's plans put it, "the countervailing tendency to push people off the land . . . is likely to override state supported efforts to buy into the land market."[23]

The ANC has been given the unenviable task of forging a historical class compromise.[24] Accordingly, during the period of transition, the party valiantly embraced the language of nation building. Yet, as Marais has argued, this rhetoric obscures the fundamental class character of the nation.[25] Although it has made genuine and impressive changes in the political character of the nation, it has been far less effective in challenging the economic inequalities produced by apartheid. The transition should be seen, then, less as a total rupture, as the term "post-apartheid" suggests, than as a reconfiguration of existing class-, race- and gender-based inequalities.[26] In other words, although the ANC employs a rhetoric that implies the fostering of consensus and has made genuine and original efforts to make such consensus possible, the economic policies that the party administers often militate against the livelihood and rights of its major constituency. The party is caught between two tendencies, between the alliances forged in the name of "nation building" and the aspirations and demands of its own support base. Without substantial economic changes that entitle the economically disenfranchised African majority, the project of national unity implies the legitimation of social inequalities. Denied such substantial reforms, the ANC's mass constituency is likely to challenge the party's commitment to "national reconciliation," seeing that this rhetoric increasingly serves the class interests of dominant sectors of both industrial and agricultural capital in the country.[27]

These questions are not significant simply in South Africa's rural areas. Pushed off the land by a vicious combination of forces, South Africa's immiserated rural population winds up as slum dwellers in rural towns as well as in increasingly violent and dysfunctional urban conglomerations such as Gauteng. The inequalities that deprive African communities of basic services, job prospects, and educational opportunities have been coming home to roost in the cities—where the majority of the white population lives—since the National Party's abandonment of the pass laws in the mid-1980s. In 1986, the National Party's "White Paper on Urbanization" sketched out a new policy of what it called "orderly urbanization." Abandoning its earlier role as direct provider of housing for urban blacks, the state sought to reap the benefits of the accelerated urbanization of the period without absorbing any of the costs.[28] The outcome was the spread of squatter camps, accommodating an estimated seven million people or one quarter of the nation's black population shortly prior to the 1994 election. The rate of urbanization that helped to topple the apartheid regime shows no signs of slowing: In the new millennium, the nation's major urban conglomeration will be approaching the size of New York and São Paolo. This urban area will, moreover, display some of the world's starkest contrasts between rich and poor. Under these conditions, urban crime may, as Marais suggests, be a substitute for the civil war that South Africa's peaceful transition has so famously averted.[29]

Mobilizing National Subjects

In its second season, *Ordinary People* returned to the issue of land rights with an episode entitled "Land Affairs." This time, it took a less consensual approach than the one evident in "The Tooth of the Times." The producers decided to cover a land dispute taking place near the town of Weenan in northern Natal/KwaZulu province. The severe drought of the early 1990s that forced Eddie Jacobs into bankruptcy also led to a wave of evictions of farm labor families, creating a rural crisis that the ANC-led Government of National Unity attempted to address with the legislative innovations described above.[30] How successful, this episode of *Ordinary People* asks, have these reforms proved on the ground? To assess government policy, "Land Affairs" focuses on a potential land invasion by a group of labor tenants, who, the narrator explains, have been evicted from the white-owned farms on which they have lived for generations. The three protagonists of the episode are Philip Buys, a white farmer whose property is likely to be seized by the "squatters," Mr. Mzalazi, a black labor tenant who was evicted from one of the farms now owned by Buys, and Derek Hanekom, the new ANC minister of land affairs, who drives in specifically to act as a mediator between the aggrieved parties. The shift in tone and subject matter that characterizes this episode of *Ordinary People* demonstrates the increasing tensions that threaten to rend the ANC's rhetoric of nation building apart.

We are introduced first to the white farmer, Philip Buys. Although the narrator begins the episode by stating that Buys is a descendent of the *voortrekkers* who first colonized the area, Buys is quick to explain that he inherited none of the land he currently owns. According to Buys, he scraped together savings while working in a post office to buy some land. His success over the years has made him the owner of several large, industrially farmed properties in the area. Buys's insistence on the hard work that has brought him to his current prosperous position is a significant move on his part. Faced with imminent land invasions, Buys sets himself up as someone who has been given nothing for free. His hold on the land, Buys argues, has been earned, unlike that of the labor tenants whose infringement of property rights the government seems set to defend. Not much reading between the lines is necessary to understand that Buys is impugning the provisions for social justice embedded in government legislation such as the Land Reform Act.

Although Eddie Jacobs expresses subtle forms of racism in "The Tooth of the Times," speaking about servants who have been working for the family for years more as if they are household objects than sentient human beings, nonetheless at least there is some mutual recognition of shared suffering in the earlier episode. In "Land Affairs," by contrast, the white farmer evinces a paternalism so thoroughgoing that it displaces all possibility of the recognition of black subjectivity. Buys argues that he provides his laborers with everything that they want. When asked whether he is like a father figure to the Africans who are piling into his truck for a day of work in the fields, Buys answers affirmatively with no trace of irony. He also offers a variety of pathologizing explanations for the current plight of former tenant laborers, saying that the protestors have been manipulated by outside agitators, that they've simply reproduced too much on their reservations and now want more land as a result, and that they lack the self-discipline necessary for the wage labor that replaced the tenure labor system after 1969. There is not one moment in this film when Buys recognizes the sufferings of displaced black farmers and the legitimacy of their claims to compensation. One of the final images we have of Philip Buys comes as he gives us a tour of the graveyard where his ancestors are buried. Quick at the outset of his narrative to disavow the idea that he inherited the land he now farms, Buys now stakes his claim for the antiquity of his relation to the land through this tour of the graveyard's time-worn tombstones.

Interspersed throughout Buys's narrative is the story of the displaced tenant laborer Mr. Mzalazi. Mzalazi lives in a "reserve," an arid stretch of unfarmable land to which he was transported after his eviction from one of the farms Buys now owns. As he prepares for his trip to the meeting between fellow displaced farmers and the Minister of Land Affairs, Mzalazi explains that he and his family were driven at gunpoint from the land where they and their ancestors had lived by the white *baas*. Their possessions were flung to the wind. Mzalazi's narrative cuts across Buys's explanations of the motivations of land invaders. These portions of the episode thus provide a subaltern history that disrupts the pathologizing explanations offered by Buys for the plight of former tenant laborers. Walking around the area on Buys's farm where he once lived, Mzalazi extends his hand over the landscape, where not a trace of his people's presence remains. The juxtaposition of this scene with that of Buys's graveyard tour, which follows immediately afterward, underlines the way in which power disparities write themselves into the landscape. Buys's heritage is visible in the enduring lineaments of tombstones, whereas Mzalazi's has been thoroughly erased, its history evident only in the cadences of his voice as he walks across the featureless land.

If "The Tooth of the Times" sought to articulate a new national subjectivity capable of identifying with and reconciling both extremes of South Africa's racialized class structure, "Land Affairs" relentlessly exposes the incommensurability of contemporary social identities in a manner that places national unity under question. These disparities are, of course, embedded in the long history of racial division in South Africa described in the previous section. Not only do the historical narrates of Mzalazi and Buys diverge totally, but the two never actually meet in the flesh. Instead, we witness their separate encounters with the ANC-led negotiation team that is attempting to adjudicate the white farmers' and black laborers' claims to land. In these sections of the episode, the rhetoric of reconciliation and nation building that animates the ANC on a national level rings hollow. Derek Hanekom, the minister of land affairs, is powerless to do more than simply patch over the rancorous animosities and inequalities that manifest themselves at a local level. This episode consequently reveals the increasing differences between the ANC's role as leader of a historic class compromise and its position as leader of extraparliamentary social protest, a dual role that the organization pledged to retain during a congress in the mid-1990s. "Land Affairs" pushes the ANC to recognize the demands of its popular base, if not, ultimately, to live up to those demands.

The chief actor in these segments of the episode is Derek Hanekom. Hanekom shows great sympathy for Mzalazi and his friends. Indeed, we first encounter him dressing nervously for his meeting with the laborers' organization, worrying amiably about which tie would be most suitable for a rural constituency. Perhaps too much should not be made of this relatively human moment. Yet by emphasizing Hanekom's concern with self-presentation, these portions of the film dramatize the significance of the ANC's rhetorical commitment to rural affairs. It is unlikely that the color of Hanekom's tie will make much difference to the dispossessed farmers he is going to meet. But his concern with such issues underlines the gulf that separates him from his constituency. Hanekom extends this sense of a gulf when he talks about the need for a person in his position not just to have a thorough knowledge of farming, but also to have empathy with those who have lost their land. While this perspective certainly contrasts favorably with Buys's paternalism, it does not suggest a very pragmatic commitment to concrete forms of redistribution.

Instead of offering specific forms of redress, Hanekom offers the laborers sympathetic sentiments that veil his role as an ANC spokesman engaged in coopting forms of militant local organization. During his meeting with the evicted, Hanekom again talks about his empathy, describing the years he spent in prison as a result of his opposition to apartheid. Despite such sentiments, however, it becomes clear in the course of the meeting that Hanekom has not come to offer the dispossessed what they want: a firm date for their return to the farmland from which they have been evicted. Indeed, Hanekom offers precious little at the meeting other than a recommendation that the group think through a series of specific measures rather than attempting to reoccupy lands on a piecemeal and individualized basis. The producers cut backward and forward between this meeting and some of Buys's most unsympathetic comments, suggesting that the government policy of market-led redistribution of land based on a philosophy of "willing buyer, willing seller" is unlikely to return the evicted black farmers to their homes. Indeed, during the meeting with white farmers that comes at the end of "Land Affairs," Hanekom's most challenging proposal is simply that no further evictions should be engaged in, since these steps are fanning the discontent of the already evicted. The optimistic statement with which Hanekom closes the episode, suggesting that a community has at least been constituted through these two meetings to address the difficult issue of eviction, is undercut by Buys's final words. In a menacing undertone, Buys says that the white farmers of the area have been doing their best to fit in with the changes that have followed apartheid's collapse, but that their nerves have grown frayed and are likely to break at any moment.

Buys's belligerent comment constitutes a challenge to the ANC's language of nation building, just as does the struggle for social justice engaged in by Mzalazi. "Land Affairs" allows us to witness the unfolding conflict between South Africa's historically dispossessed and those who have benefited from this dispossession and who continue to own the means of production after the demise of apartheid. As Marais has argued, the language of African nationalism that is embedded within the ANC allowed a miraculously bloodless transition from apartheid to its aftermath. It has, however, proven an inadequate vehicle to articulate and resolve the racialized class contradictions in contemporary South Africa. Hanekom's empathetic language in "Land Affairs" suggests that the ANC continues to recognize the claims of its dispossessed constituency but has been unable to generate meaningful forms of entitlement for much of this constituency as a result of the limitations imposed by the negotiated character of the transition. Although the peaceful end of apartheid and the scrapping of its heinous legal infrastructure remain inspiring milestones, the transition prolongs rather than resolves the central contradictions of South African society. Mzalazi's wish for peace and justice at the conclusion of "Land Affairs" is likely to grow more rather than less fragile under such circumstances.

Conclusion: Television as the Angel of History

Ordinary People provides dramatic evidence of the possibilities opened by the SABC's transformation during the years since 1990. The series offers a bold corrective to apartheid-era depictions of South African society. More broadly, the series demonstrates that although South African social movements are confronting a difficult struggle to create meaningful forms of community in the face of enduring inequalities, the recent history of resistance against apartheid has introduced notions of popular power and equality of access into public discourse with an unmatched force. These possibilities will be realized, however, only through continuing initiatives to open the new global conduits of media production and distribution to democratic forces.

While demonstrating the impact of popular struggles for democratic access to the media, *Ordinary People* broaches the question of property rights and of racial ideology without attempting to offer any solutions to these increasingly significant issues. The series thereby demonstrates the ever-increasing strains on the cultures of collectivity developed during the struggle for majority rule. To what extent will increasing forms of mass mobilization in the countryside be seen as a threat to the ANC's politics of reconciliation, to capitalist confidence, and to the government's pledge to deliver order and stability? How will the discourse of nation building shift under the strains produced by the historical class compromise forged by the ANC? The ANC's quick retreat from a policy of growth through redistribution to an orthodox neoliberal strategy of fiscal discipline has raised issues of cardinal significance for the future of the nation. Such policies ramify not simply in the tripartite alliance, with the SACP and COSATU struggling to define a viable oppositional stance to the ANC, but also in the lives of ordinary South Africans. The radical social movements that generated *Ordinary People*'s focus on popular history have long contested state power. The success of such movements in democratizing the media during the transition suggests that popular movements retain a decisive role in rearticulating South Africa's economic and political forces along more egalitarian lines.

Notes

1. Chris McGreal, "South African Media Accused of Racism," *Daily Mail and Guardian,* November 23, 1999.

2. Rachel Swarns, "A Battle in South Africa over Racism and Press Freedom," *New York Times,* March 8, 2000: A3.

3. Neil Lazarus, "Charting Globalization," *Race and Class* 40, nos. 2–3 (1998–1999): 91–106, at 92.

4. This point has been clearly recognized by South African scholars involved in media theory and policy formulation from the outset. For representative early responses to the dilemmas raised in this context, see R. E. Tomaselli, "Public Service Broadcasting in the Age of Information Capitalism," *Communicare* 8, no. 2 (1989): 27–37; and P. E. Louw, "Media, Media Education and the Development of South Africa," *Screen* 32, no. 4 (1991): 32–42.

5. Benedict Anderson, *Imagined Communities: Reflections on the Origin and Spread of Nationalism* (New York: Verso, 1991), 44.

6. The centrality of this question within contemporary South Africa is underlined within a recent volume of the nation's principal journal of cultural studies that is devoted to the subject. See *Critical Arts* 11, nos. 1–2 (1997).

7. For a discussion of the National Party's quite remarkable resistance to the introduction of

television, see Rob Nixon, *Homelands, Harlem, and Hollywood: South African Culture and the World Beyond* (New York: Routledge, 1994), 43–76.

8. Ibid., 46.

9. For a discussion of some of the early programming produced by such collectives, see Jacqueline Maingard, "Television Broadcasting in a Democratic South Africa," *Screen* 38, no. 3 (Autumn 1997): 260–274.

10. Ibid., 262.

11. As Barry Dornfeld has recently argued, "producers' projections about their audiences greatly affect the selection, encoding, and structuring of the media forms these institutions distribute. The multiplicity of audiences' interpretive positions, the various things people do in consuming these texts through dominant, contested, or oppositional readings and the various imagined identities that grow out of these acts are constrained from the start by the way producers prefigure those acts of consumption." Barry Dornfeld, *Producing Public Television, Producing Public Culture* (Princeton: Princeton University Press, 1998), 13–14.

12. Henry Bernstein, "South Africa's Agrarian Question: Extreme or Exceptional?" in *The Agrarian Question in South Africa,* ed. Henry Bernstein (Portland, Ore.: Frank Cass, 1996), 3–4, at 5.

13. Hein Marais, *South Africa, Limits to Change: The Political Economy of Transition* (New York: Zed, 1998).

14. Ibid., 21.

15. Ibid., 8.

16. Richard Levin and Daniel Weiner, "The Politics of Land Reform in South Africa after Apartheid: Perspectives, Problems, Prospects," in *The Agrarian Question in South Africa,* ed. Henry Bernstein (Portland, Ore.: Frank Cass, 1996), 93–117, at 107.

17. Bernstein, "South Africa's Agrarian Question," 12.

18. Levin and Weiner, "The Politics of Land Reform in South Africa after Apartheid," 100.

19. Ibid., 101.

20. Ibid., 108.

21. Ann Eveleth, "Land Reform Targets Are Far, Far Away," *Daily Mail and Guardian,* June 5, 1998.

22. Levin and Weiner, "The Politics of Land Reform in South Africa after Apartheid," 108.

23. Teresa Marcus, Kathy Eales and Adèle Wildschut, *Land Demand in the New South Africa* (Durban, S. Africa: Indicator Press, 1996): 190.

24. Marais, *South Africa, Limits to Change,* 85.

25. Ibid., 245.

26. Ibid., 97.

27. Levin and Weiner, "The Politics of Land Reform in South Africa after Apartheid," 116.

28. David Smith, "Introduction," *The Apartheid City and Beyond: Urbanization and Social Change in South Africa,* ed. David Smith (New York: Routledge, 1992): 1–11 at 2.

29. Marais, *South Africa, Limits to Change,* 110.

30. Bernstein, "South Africa's Agrarian Question," 17.

III | *News and Information in the Digital Age*

16 The Frequencies of Public Writing: Tomb, Tome, and Time as Technologies of the Public

John Hartley

News and Time

Time in communicative life can be understood not merely as sequence but also in terms of *frequency*. A "wavelength" of 1,000 years represents a very low time frequency, whereas the pip-pip-pip of the speaking clock or the up-to-the-second news bulletin represents high-frequency time. Time and news are obviously bound up in each other. The commercial value of news is its timeliness. Simultaneously, for the public, part of the quotidian sense of time in everyday life comes from keeping up with the news. For its devotees, news confirms a sense both of time passing, as stories unfold and new ones emerge, and of the concrete experience of the "nowness" of each day and time of day, as one pays attention to a particular news program or title.

Not surprisingly, therefore, the longest-lasting news outlets tend to be named after time itself, whether their frequency is the hour, day, or week; for instance, the American weekly magazine *Time,* the British daily newspaper *The Times,* and the nightly Soviet/ Russian TV news bulletin *Vremya (Time).* For more than seventy years BBC Radio has used the second-by-second time pips to introduce its most portentous news bulletins. This convention is so naturalized that it has become unthinkable to begin broadcast news bulletins at any other time than "on the hour" (or half-hour): The public simply can't be trained to tune into a news show at, say, seven minutes past the hour.

Clocks and datelines feature prominently in the design of television news programs, such as the British Independent Television News (ITN) *News at Ten.* Indeed, over a thirty-year period, this show and its timeslot became tightly bound together with a widespread sense of British national togetherness. The commercial television network Independent Television (ITV) was allowed to timeshift *News at Ten* only in 1999 (to make room for peak-time movies) after a failed attempt in 1993, a national inquiry by the Independent Television Commission (ITC), and a hostile parliamentary debate. It seemed that messing with the news was tantamount to messing with time itself. The conjunction of time and journalism was thought to be significant to national identity. The "frequency" of news is thus a weighty matter.

Public Writing: From Slow-Mo to Po-Mo

Public writing is produced, circulated, and deciphered or read. Each of these moments in its career has its own frequency:

- the speed of creation: how long a given "text" of public writing takes to produce
- Frequency of circulation: intervals between publication
- The wavelength of consumption: the period a given text spends in the public domain before being superseded by later "pulses" of text from the same source

In news, the frequencies of production and consumption are designed to match that of publication. A premium is set on high-frequency news gathering, on increasing the frequency (i.e., reducing the time lag) between the occurrence of an event and its public narration, although not all public writing shares this imperative. And all news relies on what they used to call built-in obsolescence: a high frequency of consumption. News that is golly-gosh today is chip wrapper tomorrow. There are commercial and even ideological reasons for trying to keep the three wavelengths tightly bundled, although in principle they are not. For instance news can sometimes take much longer to create than its daily rhythm would predict (investigative stories, news from remote locations, stories recovered from the past and rerun); and of course once published, news "texts" continue to exist long after their newsworthiness has expired. Given long enough, their value begins to appreciate once more; a copy of a seventeenth-century newspaper is much more valuable than a copy of this morning's.

   In contrast to news, very low frequency public writing, like an inscription on a public monument, which is designed to remain legible for a very long period, may take longer to create and to transmit than very high frequency writing that is expected to be discarded after a day or two. In other words, carving is slower than speaking, and it also takes a given "interpretive community" longer to pass by a fixed building to read the inscription than it does to broadcast a news bulletin to the same proportion of that population. Low frequency should not be confused with inefficiency: The proportion of Americans who have personally scrutinized fixed inscriptions of the peak national monuments in Washington and New York is likely to be higher than the proportion watching any news show. "Bring me your huddled masses" is written on just one structure, located inconveniently in the middle of a very large harbor, but it is a better-known text than the lead item on the highest-rated news broadcast.

Thus "public writing" displays high to low frequencies right through the process from creation ("writing"), via publication ("text") to consumption ("reading"). For the purposes of this chapter, however, the primary "wavelength" will be that of circulation: the interval between publications, on the model of "journalism" itself (the word derives from the French *jour,* "day").

As already hinted, "public writing" as a term refers not just to alphabetic print but to communication by any means that is designed to address its interlocutor as "the public." Such writing includes contemporary electronic forms of public address from broadcasting to the Internet. Naturally it also includes print, from the tabloid press to book publishing. But public writing is much older than those forms that are currently recognized as "the media," and it extends to much lower frequencies. It certainly includes inscriptions carved into monuments, tombs, temples, and the like.

But to do full justice to the range of "public address" covered by the notion of frequency, it is in fact necessary to expand what is normally understood by the term "writing." Messages "written in stone" are clearly intended to be more permanent and portentous than those breathed into the air; inscription is a mode of public address somewhere along a continuum with speech. However, stone itself may be regarded as a form of writing. Sculpture and architecture are themselves among the earliest forms of public address, the "mass media" of their day, certainly in Western (Egypto-Hellenic) traditions. Tombs and temples, palaces and palisades, statues and sphinxes were all, beyond their functional organization of *space,* also forms of public communication, using familiar codes, conventions, idioms, and styles. They were for their creators, and remain today, forms of public writing in fact. Furthermore they were designed to express long-term, stable meanings, and to communicate very serious messages. They spoke the language of death, eternity, empire, power, and beauty. They took communication from the personal to the collective plane, from individual to imperial. They remain to this day the lowest-frequency forms of public writing.

Indeed, the continued existence of ancient examples of public writing and the re-working of their "idiom" in contemporary buildings demonstrates that "new media technologies," all the way from limestone and granite via print to electronic and digital media, do not supplant but supplement older ones. Writing itself has never been extinguished since the Egyptians and Sumerians first invented it some time before 3000 B.C., despite a number of mass-extinction crises suffered by particular writing systems since then. Individual texts, such as the pyramids at Saqqara and other antiquities dating back to the very earliest periods of public writing, are still belting out complex messages that "speak" to millions of contemporary readers (the Egyptian economy is dependent upon this fact). Such messages survive millennia and communicate to cultures with meaning systems quite different from that of the original builders.

But more significantly, the idiom of ancient public writing in stone survives and is reworked to make new messages; it remains an active "medium" of communication among the many later media. Cities around the world are crammed full of postmodern, high-tech buildings that add their contemporary voice to the low-frequency mode of public writing in stone. Their façades are clad in Portland limestone (quoting St. Paul's Cathedral) or travertine marble (quoting the Roman Forum), even while their occupants are busy producing electronic, virtual, and digital public communication at ever higher frequencies.

Some communicative syntax (for instance, many architectural details understood as "classical" from the portico to the pediment, column to frieze) have been transferred from temples and triumphal arches to the facades of banks and media corporations. Presumably the urge here is to preserve rather than to change the temporal signification of stone. Such uses of architecture have become the very "language" of permanency and power, exploiting the ultralow frequency of architecture and sculpture to "say something" public about commercial institutions, using the idiom of civic and religious communion. The classical temple, tomb and palace, the imperial European city, the art deco American one, and the sprawling megalopolis of the developing world: all rework the low-frequency mode of public writing (see table 16.1).

Paradoxically, the most enduring human creation is the ruin. The ruin may indeed be defined as public writing that has outlived its author's intentions and even the language of public communication in which it was created. It sends what may be termed the "Ozymandias" message. Ruins speak to the unfolding present from "time immemorial," but the message is unintended, a text without an author. The ruin, together with other immemorial texts, such as prehistoric cave paintings and carvings, is the lowest-frequency of all forms of public address.

Some ruins remain semiotically active without a break for millennia: Stonehenge, the pyramids, the Great Wall, the tomb of Augustus in Rome. Although they are not ruins in the same way, even greater communicational longevity may apply to rock carvings and cave paintings. But it would not be safe to associate low-frequency public address with traditional and preindustrial societies. They too make widespread use of high-frequency forms, from the sand art of the Navajo and also of some Aboriginal peoples of Australia, to the painstaking making of the mandala by Buddhist monks who destroy their work on completion. But of course it is the low-frequency communication of traditional societies that tends to survive. Although some "rock art" is perhaps tens of thousands of years old, it remains sacred and significant for the Aboriginal communities who live with it, and it is increasingly revered by official cultures as part of their unique "national" heritage.

Other ruins are intermittent signifiers, being lost or forgotten perhaps for centuries, later to be "reincarnated," as it were, to communicate new meanings with the help of archaeology. Such texts include "rediscovered" temples in Java or Cambodia; Maya, Aztec, and Inca ruins in the Americas; and the tomb of Qin Shi Huang, first emperor of China.

If all media are forms of public writing, then the concept of "media" extends well beyond those forms that are currently recognized as belonging to the media sector of the contemporary economy. Between high-frequency journalism and low-frequency marble there are myriad media of public address, distributed across all frequencies from the moment to the millennium (see table 16.1).

Journalism Frequencies

Over its two- to four-hundred-year history, journalism has shown a consistent tendency to drift upward in frequency. New forms of news, especially those that attract the most intense capital investment and public disquiet, are ever faster. Journalism can range in frequency from the second and faster down to the quarter (e.g., *Fashion Quarterly*), though this frequency (like the once-common biweekly newspaper) is now archaic for news; it has been occupied by academic and scientific journals.

At the very highest wavelengths, instantaneous reporting has appeared on the Internet. This development has caused some commentators to predict the end of journalism (as we know it). The Monica Lewinsky affair was the trigger for such concern, since court decisions and other news-sensitive information were released on the Internet, bypassing the usual journalistic gatekeepers. On the publication of the Starr Report, television viewers around the world enjoyed the spectacle of CNN cameras pointing to a computer screen while the reporter scrolled down pages of Internet text to find newsworthy references to nonstandard uses for cigars. It certainly *looked* as though the form of

Table 16.1
Frequencies of public writing

Before the Event	Previews, Leaks, Briefings, PR, "Spin"
High Frequency	
Instant/Second	Internet, Subscription News: e.g., Matt Drudge, Reuters Financial TV, Bloomberg.com
Minute	"Rolling Update" News: e.g., CNN, BBC-24/Choice, Radio 5-Live
Hour	Broadcast News: e.g., CBS/ABC/NBC, ITN/BBC, Radio 4
Day	Daily Press: e.g., *The Times, New York Times, Sun, New York Post*
Week	Weekly Periodicals: e.g., *Time, New Statesman, Hello!, National Enquirer*
Mid-Frequency	
Month	Monthly Magazines: e.g., *Vogue, Cosmopolitan, The Face, Loaded*
Quarter	Scientific and Academic Journals: e.g., *International Journal of Cultural Studies*
Year	Books, Movies, Television Series: e.g., *Harry Potter, Star Wars, Ally McBeal*
Low Frequency	
Decade	Scholarship, Contemporary Art: e.g, "definitive" works, textbooks, dictionaries, portraiture, fashionable artists
Century	Building, Statue, Canonical Literature: e.g., Sydney Opera House, war memorials, Shakespeare
Millennium	Temple, Tomb: e.g., Parthenon, Pyramids
Eternity	Ruins, Reruns: e.g., Stonehenge, *Star Trek*

journalism that prided itself on its high frequency (i.e., the rolling-update continuous "breaking news" format of cable television) was reduced to the status of mere servant to the instantaneous Internet. Furthermore, CNN got into trouble even for this secondhand timeliness, as commentators expressed discomfort at seeing the unexpurgated facts on a television screen, although they seemed happy for the full text of the Starr Report to appear on the Net itself.

Currently, then, there is a complicated readjustment in progress between the *previously* fastest and *next* fastest news media. Up-to-the-second forms of journalism are concentrated at the premium end of the market for news, targeted at the most highly capitalized sector of the economy with time-sensitive information needs: the financial markets. This is one place where news has attracted new investment and innovative format development. Reuters Financial Television and Bloomberg, for example, are locked in an international competitive struggle for this "narrow-cast" but ultra-high-frequency form of journalism, which can be sold at a premium to corporate clients. Meanwhile, the *look* of the instantaneous format has already been "borrowed" from the Net to give the slightly slower television screen the appearance of instantaneous news. For instance, CNN's on-screen design now resembles the aesthetic of the Internet, with rolling stock prices, text captions that may or may not relate to the pictures being displayed, and inset video frames with pictures that may or may not relate to each other.

It seems journalism can't get any faster than the instant. But with previews, leaks, spin doctoring, news management, and public relations, a good deal of news crosses the time barrier into the strange world of "news *before* the event." This sector too is in a phase of rapid commercial development and expansion. Of course it gives the lie to the old-fashioned notion that news can occur only after some sort of event has occurred, a myth of news making that has never been true.

Just how badly news before the event can tear the normal fabric of the political time-space continuum was demonstrated in 1999 in Britain, with the difficulties experienced by the government after the prerelease of part of the Macpherson Report concerning "institutional racism" in the Metropolitan Police (the Stephen Lawrence inquiry). The government tried to halt by injunction the publication in the daily press of sections of a report it was not due to release to Parliament until two days later. By the time the full report was published, the various players had already taken up their positions in the public domain. But within hours of the official publication the Home Office had to recall the entire print run, as the report contained the identity and addresses of witnesses. Thus, quite apart from its controversial contents, conclusions and recommendations, the report became a political hot potato purely because of its *timing*. Released before their (albeit arbitrary) time of publication, the untimely facts caused unmanageable side effects as they darted about in the public domain before their own release.

More routinely, most morning newspapers and breakfast television or speech radio shows are sustained by giving news of what will be announced, published, and released later in the day. The story, the interview with the minister, the opposition's viewpoint, and the analysis of commentators are all done in advance of the "event" they report.

At the slower end of journalism's frequency range, the glossy fashion and style monthlies hold sway (see table 16.1). *Vogue* and *Elle* have been joined by the "lad mags" for men, like *Loaded*. Some of these have proven so successful that they have crossed the Atlantic. Other booming sectors are lifestyle and "shelter" magazines like *Wallpaper* and a proliferation of titles for teenagers and young women: the *More!* the merrier.

The *monthly* wavelength of the periodicals market is buoyant. The once dominant higher-frequency *weekly* magazines for women, however, such as *Woman* and *Woman's Own*, are in decline. Although their circulation tends to be higher per title than that of the glossies (reaching millions rather than tens or hundreds of thousands), this is no comfort to them. Their sales are steadily trending downward with declining profitability. The reaction to these trends by the top-selling Australian women's magazine, the *Australian Women's Weekly*, is interesting. For some years this magazine has been published as a monthly, despite retaining its title. Recently it has also begun to appear in international editions aimed at a general readership (so it's no longer Australian, women's, or weekly: its descriptive title ought to be the *International General Monthly*).

Whereas news journalism tends to the highest frequencies, nonnews journalism, from the political and gossip weeklies (*New Statesman, Hello*) to the fashion and style monthlies (*Vogue, The Face*), operates at lower frequencies. Weekend newspapers draw on aspects of both of these types. Nonnews journalism on television also tends toward lower frequencies than "hard" news. Whereas news is hourly, current-affairs shows are weekly or daily, and lifestyle journalism (such as holiday, fashion, food, motoring, and consumer watchdog shows) is weekly.

It is also apparent that increases in the speed of journalism are associated with new media. Whereas (five-hundred-year-old) print dominates the wavelengths between the day and the week and below, (eighty-year-old) broadcasting predominates in the frequencies between the day and the hour. Nonbroadcast forms of screen and electronic media (i.e. cable and Internet forms, introduced only in the last two or three decades) have taken over in the wavelengths between the hour and the instant.

Academic Writing

Moving down to the mid-frequency range (see table 16.1), journalism is still present, but it is giving way to other forms. In the nonfiction area, its place is taken by book publishing and by academic, scientific, and scholarly writing. Mid-frequency journalism includes books by journalists on current affairs. Sometimes these can be newsworthy in their own right (Andrew Morton's book on Diana, Princess of Wales), sometimes they can define an event for posterity (John Reed's *Ten Days That Shook the World*), and sometimes they might contribute to the practice of journalism itself (Philip Knightley's *The First Casualty*).

Academic writing is on the same continuum as journalism: It's just public writing at a lower frequency. Its wavelength is counted in months and years (mid) rather than either days (high) or centuries (low). Scholarly writing is mid-frequency. It is of lower frequency than both journalism and much commercial writing (the latter is geared to the financial year and is therefore rarely slower than annual). But it is not as low frequency as canonical big-L Literature, especially "classic" texts that are out of copyright (i.e., with a frequency lower than fifty years). Academic writing that attains classic status, such as Charles Darwin's *Origins of Species,* may be republished *as* literature, even though its value as a scientific text is far from spent.

The time lag between commencing a piece of writing and its publication in academic work is, in the main, much greater than that in journalism. Scholarly articles and books can take months or even years to write. After that, the waiting lists for publication in some academic journals can be counted in years, even after a paper has been reviewed over several months. In the case of books, an academic book takes from nine months to a year to publish after delivery by the author. It is therefore really difficult to achieve topicality in academic writing using print as the means of dissemination (e-journals have begun to change the situation, but as yet only at the margins of academic endeavor). Knowledge of the slow frequency of academic writing has an influence on what is written; topical references and anecdotes have to be treated with care, and arguments or analyses have to anticipate unfamiliar reading contexts. Abstraction is consequently at a premium over immediate local, practical detail. Once published, academic knowledge aspires to stability. Academic books may stay in print for years or even decades. They are available indefinitely in libraries. Influential papers are cited in other people's works long after they are published.

As with other media (see below), there are internal frequency differences within the medium of academic writing. Topographical maps may be expected to be quite stable when published, lasting perhaps decades. Policy documents have a use-by date measured in months. Some academic knowledge is very high frequency at the point of discovery: Witness, for instance, the regularly reported race to publish some new scientific or medical discovery first (and the stakes—a Nobel prize or a lucrative patent—can be very high). But that same knowledge becomes very stable once published, especially in the "natural" sciences such as physics or astronomy. A double helix remains a double helix well after its first announcement, but the people who first announce it can set a very high premium on the timeliness of their work.

Meanwhile, textbooks tend to be much lower in frequency than leading-edge research, becoming more frequent, however, at the most introductory levels. In the teaching context, knowledge can be really low frequency, maintaining theories, methods, and even individual examples or anecdotes long after the scientific field to which they are an introduction has moved on. Not infrequently introductory textbooks will carefully teach ideas, approaches, and even "facts" that have been entirely refuted at higher levels of the same discipline.

Conflict can arise from what may be termed "frequency mistunings." Journalists, habituated to high-frequency public address, and academics, attuned to the rhythms of mid-frequency writing, find it hard to understand one another. They may decode each other's writing as if it should be operating at their own wavelength. The inevitable result is noise, communication breakdown, and bemusement or hostility. Journalists and academics literally (but simply) cannot get on each other's wavelength. If, however, their respective efforts are conceptualized as the *same enterprise,* public writing, done at *different speeds,* then here at least is cause for dialogue, if not common cause.

Public Writing and the Time-Space Axis

Besides the frequency (time) axis of public writing, some consideration of another axis, that of space, is also necessary. Public communication inhabits space as well as time. Just as the very notion of "the public" in contemporary political organization is customarily derived from classical antecedents, so the spatiality of public communication is conventionally associated with the polis—"the city," which in the Western Hellenic tradition equates with "the state." The period of political modernization inaugurated by the American and French Revolutions coincided with the first "virtualization" of a city-based notion of citizenship to the much more abstract concept of the nation, and thence nationality, as the "space" of citizenship.

Combining the concrete spatiality of the city with the abstract idea of national citizenship has resulted in the habitual association of the concept of "nation" with the space occupied by a people. Citizenship is modeled on the spatial idea of assembly of people (in the agora, the forum, or the town square): To perform their role as citizens it seems people must be gathered together in space as well as time. A city's architectural showpieces act as a kind of permanent reminder of that role; they bring together the inhabitants, the place, and the particular ordering of political, religious, commercial, and national arrangements, as manifested through architectural, spatial, and inscribed public writing peculiar to that place.

Contemporary, faster modes of communication based on print and electronic media have radically textualized this association of space and nation. Once virtualized, a sense of civic or national identity is also rendered portable. It can be taken to all corners by contemporary media, which are centrifugal, radiating outward to find spatially dispersed addressees (the "imagined community") at a given moment. The older, slower modes of public address based on stone and sculpture, conversely, are centripetal ("All roads lead to Rome"), drawing the people into the city center to be constituted as the public—as an assembly, congregation, or crowd. Rather than reaching everyone simultaneously, the older modes of communication rely on many people, perhaps all, passing through them sooner or later. Thus frequency and spatiality are related to each other for both very high and very low frequency public communication, albeit in alternating modes.

As it evolved in Britain and France from the late eighteenth and early nineteenth centuries, modern journalism was organized most intensively around a frequency of between a day (the dailies) and a week (the periodicals). In those early days it was not uncommon for titles to be published twice or three times a week, but that intermediate frequency is now empty in the newspaper press. The Sunday paper is still one of journalism's most successful products, even if other weekly formats, especially the political magazine, are in decline. Indeed, the "Sunday" format is expanding. Saturday editions of dailies have taken on many of the characteristics of Sunday papers.

The traditional form of daily/weekly journalism as a whole is undergoing attrition, however, and has been steadily declining for at least fifty years, since the Second World War. Many commentators see this as evidence of changes in *spatial* arrangements. The slow decline of national broadsheet daily newspapers and of weekly political and women's magazines is taken to be a symptom of the globalization of information, the internationalization of trade, and the withering away of individual allegiance to the nation-state.

Questions of identity and citizenship are less easily associated with territorially bounded spatial entities (nations) than was previously taken for granted. Identity is more mobile, indeterminate, and voluntary. Citizenship is "weakened" as sovereignty is shared "upward" and "downward" from the nation-state:

- Upward, sovereignty migrates *formally* to supranational bodies like the United Nations, European Union, World Trade Organization, North American Free Trade Agreement, Asia Pacific Economic Cooperation Forum, North Atlantic Treaty Organization, and International Court of Human Rights, *informally* to "humanity" movements such as the environmental, peace, and various religious, humanitarian, and charity movements.

- Downward, sovereignty is devolved *formally* to subnational regional, state, or federated parliaments, and both formally (by legislation) and *informally* (culturally) to communities based on ethnicity (first peoples), gender (women's rights), age (children's rights), sexual orientation (gay and lesbian rights), virtuality (cyberdemocracy), etc.

Within this context, journalism as a *national* discourse, a discourse of *spatial belonging,* the modern (textualized) equivalent of the agora/forum of the city/polis, is in long, slow decline.

But journalism is no longer confined to the frequencies of the day and the week. Over the whole period of modernity (two to four hundred years) it has tended to drift upward in frequency. Journalism that is *faster* than the day has thrived, both in broadcast and print forms. But also, perhaps counterintuitively, journalism that is *slower* than the week, from monthly magazines to books by journalists on journalistic themes, seems to be in rude good health too.

Thus, as spatial metaphors for large-scale human organization lose their familiar landmarks as they evolve into new configurations, so it may become increasingly important to analyze the temporal axis. What may look like decline or even disaster on the spatial plane may look very different on the temporal plane. Nations and regions may simply be changing speed, at least in communicative terms.

If this does prove to be the case, it is a significant matter, since of course nations are generally perceived to be much more than communicative units. Their culture, custom, and character; law, language, and learning; their very purpose and the power they hold over their citizens are all commonly understood to be unique to each individual nation and one of the main sources of each person's sense of individual identity. There's considerable evidence that national feeling is stronger than ever, despite the decline of the classic, nineteenth-century nation-state (i.e., the self-contained sovereignty of "splendid iso-lation"). Certainly there are literally more nations than ever before, and the logic of self-determination lays claim to ever more locally defined nations.

In such circumstances, in which spatially understood nations are the traditional site for the expression of their people's sovereignty and there are both "strong" and "weak" forces affecting how citizenship is legislated and lived, it is pertinent to ask what is happening to the "technologies" that hold such sites together in some sort of coherence. What, for in-stance, is happening to the technologies of democracy and of the public? Among such "technologies," the mechanisms by which these "imagined communities" are brought into being and sustained, are the media, and diurnal political journalism in particular. This was one of the fundamental "technologies of democracy," being the very means by which the public was brought into being at the outset of political modernity in Britain, America, and continental Europe. Now, this is the form of journalism that seems most in decline. Its decline is far from catastrophic in terms of annual figures, but it is profound in the sense that sales, readers, and titles have all been trending downward for fifty years, across many countries. Does it follow that democracy is trending downward too? Many ob-servers do in fact take this view. But what does the view look like if the changes are ob-served from the perspective of time rather than space?

Technologies of Democracy: "Hunters" and "Gatherers"

To consider the impact of "new technologies" on the space-time axis of public commu-nication, it is necessary to move away from the notion of technology understood as "black boxes" (scientific and technological innovations) and instead move toward ideas like "technologies of democracy" and "technologies of the public." In other words, what are the mechanisms through which democracy and the public are created, sustained, and operated in modern societies?

In this context, black-box technology is not decisive in itself; the French Revolution, for instance, perhaps the most decisive founding moment of political modernity, was promoted and disseminated on the Gutenberg wooden press, a premodern technology that was already three hundred years old at the time. At the lowest frequencies, the same may be argued; the revolutionary form of the Egyptian pyramid was achieved not sui generis but by a novel application of the existing mastaba form of tomb. The Internet may be pointing the direction to change but itself relies on the oldest technology of com-munication (writing) and as yet is not politically or culturally decisive in the way that a newspaper, a book, or even a speech can be. There might even be an argument to suggest that new technologies are less "revolutionary" in their uses than mature ones. It is necessary for a culture or epoch to become familiar enough with a medium to be able to break the rules with it before it can be used for seditious, incendiary, or reformist work. A technology cannot call a public into action before that public has been called into being, and the establishment of a community of readers around a new communicative technology takes time. Books weren't used effectively to spread ideas about science and Enlightenment across Europe until at least a century after Gutenberg. Agitation through the press for popular sovereignty waited centuries after print was invented: two in Britain (the Civil War and the Levellers' pamphlets), three in France, four in Russia, five in South Africa. Similarly, more recent "new" technologies such as television and the Internet ought not to be heralded as revolutionary just because they've been invented. Instead, their social impact needs to be assessed according to their "use" in creating and occasionally mobilizing publics. Their impact is not as "technologies," as such, but as technologies of the public.

Political modernity is itself now over two hundred years old. Despite the spate of bicentennial celebratory pyrotechnics (1976 in the United States, 1989 in France, 1988 in Australia) and a rather muted tercentennial coin issue in the United Kingdom in 1989 (to mark the Glorious Revolution), there is widespread concern about the effectiveness of the aging technology of democracy. It sometimes looks as though it doesn't work any more. Fifty years of Cold War, with its easy-to-understand oppositional structure of friend-and-foe politics, may have masked a growing uncertainty about who "we" are, whether "we" are understood as nations, publics, or even as persons.

A combination of identity politics and entertainment media has grown up in the private sphere and is now sustaining the most vibrant areas of media innovation and expansion, from lad mags and the Internet to spectator sports and sitcoms. Meanwhile the classic technologies of democracy—print media, political parties, parliaments—seem to be atrophying, growing further apart from the people they're supposed to represent, losing credibility and ratings in an inexorable decline that is no less remarkable for the fact that it has been happening for half a century.

It is no longer certain what the public is or where to find it. The classic technology of the democratic public is the daily broadsheet newspaper (*The Times,* the *Washington Post*) and the heavyweight political weekly (*The Spectator, The New Yorker*). Both have given ground to competing media forms, from television to the tabloids. Meanwhile, along with so much else in contemporary deregulating commercial democracies, the public itself has been privatized. People are simultaneously addressed as publics and audiences, citizens and consumers, and the media of democracy have expanded into areas previously thought of as belonging to the private sphere and to commercial entertainment.

Citizen formation is now undertaken by chain stores: Marks & Spencer was named in March 1999 as the sponsor of the "national identity" theme in London's Millennium Dome. The same week, on Wales's national day (March 1), Marks & Spencer's Cardiff store handed out to each customer a daffodil, Wales's national emblem, and a guide to the forthcoming elections to the new National Assembly for Wales. The two-pound commemorative coin that marked the 1989 tercentenary of England's Glorious Revolution was *issued* by the Royal Mint (a privatized public corporation), but it was *circulated* as a gift through supermarkets by the makers of Jif, Frish, and Jif Spray'n'Foam. Teenagers learn ethical comportment, neighborliness, and civic virtues from *Clarissa* and *Clueless*. They avoid the modernist technology of democracy like the plague. Does this mean they are living outside of the political community? Are they incomplete persons, not fully formed as citizens? Or has the technology of democracy migrated to the private sector? Commercial entertainment media and postmodern journalism are new technologies of the public: the new public sphere.

Hence journalism, as the forum in which "we" communities are constructed and "common knowledge" is exchanged, has migrated well beyond news. At the same time, news has evolved generically to accommodate to its media neighbors. Further uncertainty is caused. Doubts about what is fact and what is fiction are now pursued into the very fabric of media communication. News photos are digitally enhanced, public access shows on television are faked by using actors, columnists fake stories, television documentaries feature fake people and situations. Meanwhile, over in the supposedly fictional world of commercial entertainment, you might find much more careful attention to truth.

How do these time frequencies intersect with spatiality? How do technologies of time interact with those of locality, region, nation, and international or global space? The highest-frequency media forms have tended toward transnational markets. Globalization is most commented upon in its commercial, high-speed, information economy guise, even though mid-frequency forms such as science, scholarship, book publishing, and fiction have been international, indeed global, for decades or even centuries. Somehow, high-frequency technologies of public communication seem more threatening to technologies of space than do lower-frequency ones.

Traditional (modernist) journalism and broadcasting have pitched their tent, as it were, in the temporal rhythm of the day and the week. But this is the frequency that seems most under attrition in present developments. There's major investment in very high frequency journalism and also in mid-frequency forms such as magazines. Men's and women's monthlies (lad-mags, style and fashion glossies) are currently the fastest-growing media sector in the United Kingdom, whereas mass-circulation women's weeklies are in decline. Books too remain a significant component of public life and are often extensions of journalism. They are being reinvented for a new generation of reader-citizens by innovative publishers like Dorling Kindersley.

There may be a challenge to traditional daily/weekly journalism and broadcasting in this scenario. But is there a threat to democracy? To public life? For those who worry about the decline of public-service media, the commercialization of the public sphere, and the evacuation of the public domain, perhaps the problem is one of frequency. People are responding to different speeds of public communication, but this doesn't necessarily mean the end of democracy. It's speeding up, not dumbing down.

It may even be argued that the long-standing association of citizenship and nation with space rather than time is nothing more than a constraint on trade, a restrictive practice, a monopolization of the market by those who have trained their readerships to expect information pitched at frequencies these suppliers can accommodate. If all your eggs are in the daily/weekly basket, then you don't want customers wandering off the bandwidth to the nanosecond, the year, or the decade.

People who may suppose themselves entirely explained by spatial coordinates (nation, city, etc.) are nevertheless also attuned to temporal rhythms. The communicative year is divided into seasons marked by sports, television schedules, and annual holidays, weekends, Christmas Day, and once in a while the millennium. In other words "we" communities are identified temporally, via connections that cut across spatial boundaries. Humanity as a whole is in fact a time-based concept, referring to a "we" community of "everyone who is alive today."

Communications media can gather populations, or they can divide them. Some forms, such as sport, drama, and pornography, have proven to be reasonably indifferent to national boundaries. In temporal-spatial terms, they're "gatherers." They gather populations from widely separated places at one time to act as spectators. Others, especially news, seem reluctant to dissolve local, regional, and national boundaries; they insist on differentiation of populations along territorial lines. They're "dividers," if not "hunters." But news media may also be hunters in the sense that they tend to define their "we" communities negatively: "We" are what others (especially other nations, but also criminal negativizations of "we-dom") are *not*. Modern journalism thus has a long history of investment in foe creation and the language of conflict and violence. News media hunt out the alien and the criminal among the home population. Their clumsiness at this task in an era of migration and mobility, in which "we" include ethnicities, identities, and activities routinely marked by the news media as "foreign" or "criminal," is now cause for widespread debate and reformist agitation.

Perhaps this hunter aspect of news journalism is the very technology of democracy that is most in need of reform. Perhaps the higher- and lower-frequency media are establishing new "we" communities via new technologies of the public that are "postmodern," commercial, private, volatile, migratory, dispersed, and aimed at cultural identities not well served by the public sphere—for instance, the young, women, ethnic minorities, and "foreigners" (migrants).

Modern Space, Postmodern Time?

Does a shift in perspective from space to time explain changes in journalistic content? For instance, news has drifted from a "modernist" status as a discourse of power, interested in the decision maker, toward a "postmodern" status as a discourse of identity, interested in celebrity. Citizenship is now struggled over in the name of identity, not territory. There's a shift from discourses of rights to those of ethics, from unionism to individual responsibility. In short, people are identifying with "virtual" communities based on coexistence in time, not coextension in space (see table 16.2).

Comparative Media Frequencies

Moving beyond journalism, it is useful to point out that many different communicative media function to create publics, and they also operate along frequency ranges. The visual arts, drama, fashion (clothing), music, and publishing are all instances of such media. They are indeed technologies of the public.

Internally, each such medium displays different frequencies (see table 16.3):

- In *drama,* soap opera and sitcoms occupy the highest frequency; the telemovie or television miniseries and the feature film dominate the mid-range wavelength; "classic" drama is low frequency. Soap operas operate at a much higher frequency of production than do other forms of screen drama. Many more episodes are made per year, and they are produced on a much tighter schedule (more script pages per day are shot). They are circulated socially at a much higher frequency, being designed for one-pass scanning by a casual audience that is not expected to maintain an interest in the single episode. So it may be that hundreds of episodes of a major soap opera, or dozens of

Table 16.2
Space-time coordinates

Space (modern)	Time (postmodern)
[Coextension]	[Coexistence]
Territory	Community
Actual	Virtual
Power	Identity
Decision-maker	Celebrity
Rights/duties	Ethics/practice
National unity	Individual responsibility

Table 16.3
Frequencies of various media

	Song	Drama	Apparel
High	Single	Sitcom/soap	T-shirt/haute couture
Mid	Album/CD	Movie	Suit/dress
Low	Symphony	Classic theatre	Gown (legal, academic)

episodes of a sitcom, may be made in one year. During the same period, it is unusual nowadays for more than one feature film to be made by any one production team. Assuming it is successful, that movie will be seen over a longer time period than the single episode of an average television serial, and it is more likely to extend its time frequency over several years via the video market, television screenings, and cable television reruns. At the lowest frequency, classic drama, whether film- or stage-based, achieves something close to immortality. People know all the words, moves, characters, and scenes of *Casablanca, Romeo and Juliet,* or *Citizen Kane* (of which a new print was released in 1999, giving the Orson Welles classic a new lease of life, though not very good ratings, for a new generation). Such drama is canonical, "law forming" in relation to its genre, and sometimes even in relation to its time and society: *Apocalypse Now* had this status in the post-Vietnam era in the United States, until this status was "repealed" by the counterrevolutionary film *The Deer Hunter.*

- Recorded *music* ranges from the pop single (high frequency) via the compact disc (mid frequency) to the symphony (low frequency). It would be surprising to find a pop singer such as Britney Spears celebrated on a national currency, but symphonic com-

Table 16.4
Frequencies of culture

High	Popular culture
Mid	Intellectual culture
Low	High culture

posers can be. Sir Edward Elgar, not the Spice Girls, is pictured on the 1999 British twenty-pound note (it was said that Sir Edward's hairy moustache would deter counterfeiters, but the same could be argued in relation to Scary Spice's hair: This was not a "technical" decision). Unlike pop, symphonic music may be taken to express low-frequency, national values. In this context high-frequency music is deemed commercial, ephemeral, global, and "unworthy." No matter how talented, popular, original, or profound a pop act might be, it won't achieve "serious" status until it has released multiple albums—until, that is, its musical frequency is lowered at least to the mid-range (see also table 16.4).

- *Vestimentary* media (i.e., communication via apparel) range from haute couture collections and the T-shirt (both high frequency, though at opposite ends of the pop/high culture scale) through the suit and dress (mid-frequency) to academic, religious, or legal garb (low frequency). Legal wigs and gowns are continuations of eighteenth-century costumes; academic gowns and priestly vestments are medieval. When members of the general public step out of everyday time and into a "timeless" state, as, for instance, during a wedding ceremony, they may signify the same by radically lowering the frequency of their vestimentary communication. The "traditional" bride's wedding dress and the groom's top hat and tails are derived from upper-class Edwardian fashion; "timelessness" is achieved by changing to low-frequency costume. Other vestimentary codes are also tied to time frequencies. For instance, the business suit of the "salaryman" is worn exclusively within the frequency of the working week; holiday fashions follow an annual rhythm; Santa Claus dons his red suit but one day a year (except in Lapland).

- In the *visual arts,* "old master" painting (high-art oils) is low frequency. Portraiture in photography or painting is mid-frequency. Billboard advertising and photojournalism are high frequency (see table 16.4).

- In *publishing,* the book is lower in frequency than the periodical. Within book publishing itself there is a wide range of frequencies, ranging from work that is an extension of journalism in the higher ranges to reference works such as the *Oxford English Dictionary* at the lowest. Some modes of writing, such as canonical Literature, tend to operate socially at a low frequency no matter what their original wavelength, including journalism of a former age (e.g., Samuel Johnson) or political speeches that achieve identity-forming status, from Pericles' funeral oration to Lincoln's Gettysburg Address. Even fiction may be received initially as high-frequency journalistic communication, achieving canonical status later (e.g., Dickens's novels) (see tables 16.1 and 16.4).

The mid-range frequency (see tables 16.1 and 16.4) is developed to the greatest extent not in journalism, but in fiction. The "season" or annual wavelength is occupied by new movies, television series, novels, and comparable productions such as CDs, videos, and computer games. Moving to the lower frequencies of public communication, the so-called serious arts predominate: "classical" music, classic or canonical literature, and "fine" art.

Time and Tide: Frequency in Various Public Contexts

Temporal periodization is itself sensitive to frequency (see table 16.5): postmodern (high frequency), modern (mid-frequency), premodern or classical (low frequency). Whether or not this corresponds to more than the words used in journalism and academic

Table 16.5
Frequencies of historical periods

High	Postmodern
Mid	Modern
Low	Premodern or "classical"

Table 16.6
Frequencies of political economy

High	Commercial
Mid	Professional
Low	Public

colloquy to sort the concepts into coherence is a moot point. Where distinctions are made between, for instance, the modern and postmodern, however, an increase in frequency is clearly an issue, often a cause for concern.

It may be that there is an economic aspect to frequency distribution (see table 16.6): The commercial sector is characterized as high frequency (and high investment), the professional sector as mid-range, and the public sector as low frequency, especially toward the "dignified" part of the constitution (state occasions and courts of law, rather than state enterprises).

It follows that within such a structure, the type of information tends to vary according to frequency (see table 16.7). Rumor, "gossip," and information are "faster" than knowledge, fiction, and science; these in turn are faster than belief, faith, and religion. News, however, ranges across many of these frequencies in its content. News can be a textualization of high-frequency rumor, gossip, and information. But equally news can express much lower frequency rhythms in the guise of quotidian narrative: Myths and beliefs, not to mention fictions, are routinely re-created in the form of daily stories.

As we descend the frequencies from screen via page to stone, it is possible—though far from inevitable—that meanings move from volatile to stable, private to public (see table 16.8). To the extent that this may be so, it may further occur that *volatile* meanings are associated with private affairs and are about identity; meanwhile, *arguable* meanings

Table 16.7
Frequencies of knowledge-type

High	Rumor	"Gossip"	Information
Mid	Knowledge	Fiction	Science
Low	Belief	Myth	Religion

Table 16.8
Frequencies of meaning

Range	*Meanings*	*(Medium)*	*(Location)*	*(About . . .)*
High	Volatile	(Screen)	(Private)	(. . . Identity)
Mid	Arguable	(Page)	(Social)	(. . . Power)
Low	Stable	(Stone)	(Public)	(. . . Nature)

are associated with the collective life of society and are about power. At the same time, *stable* meanings are associated with public life and aspire to the condition of the natural. Thus frequency seems to carry extra import: Low-frequency public communication seems closer to "nature," literally written in stone, when compared with higher-frequency messages.

As it has drifted steadily upward in frequency over the past century and more, journalism has also tended to drift in its meanings. Whereas it was once a discourse about power, focused on the decision maker, it is now (at least as much) a discourse about identity and is focused on the celebrity. Its meanings are now more volatile.

Conclusion

In public address, speed is of the essence. Frequency (rather than ostensible content) may be a major determinant of what a given piece of writing means. Over the *longue durée* of history, public communication has exploited differences in frequency to articulate different types of meaning. Apparently revolutionary periods may be explicable by reference to changes in communicative speed and also by investigating changes in the balance between temporal and spatial coordinates of national and personal identity. To understand what is happening to journalism in the current era of change from spatial (national) to temporal (network) communication, the frequency of public writing is a crucial but somewhat neglected component. It determines what kind of public is called into being for given communicative forms and therefore has a direct bearing on the development of democracy. Changes to technologies of the public have historically tended to increase speed or frequency of communication; democracy itself may be migrating from space-based technologies to faster, time-based ones.

Acknowledgments

I particularly want to thank McKenzie Wark for sparking the ideas expressed in this chapter into life, and William Uricchio, Michael Bromley, and Eva Vieth for straightening some of them out.

Note

This chapter follows journalistic rather than academic practice: There are no scholarly references. The chapter is an attempt to map out (time out?) some ideas, rather than to review an existing field. It is intended as a contribution to an interdisciplinary conversation in the spirit of the MIT Media in Transition theme of comparative media studies; in such a context specialist citations cannot be expected to convey the usual disciplinary sense of place. The chapter is also addressed to those outside the academy who may be interested in public writing. The long-standing convention for that sort of writing is that sources are not formally referenced. Naturally, the lack of references should not be taken to imply that no debts have been incurred to others' ideas in the preparation of this article; indeed, it is brim-full of them.

17 *Journalism in a Digital Age*

Christopher Harper

The current catchphrase in journalism today is the "defining moment." Simply put, the phrase means the way in which a story or an event has defined a specific medium or brand name. For print journalism, the defining moment may have been Vietnam or the Watergate investigation. For radio news, the defining moment may have been the crash of the Hindenburg or Edward R. Murrow's reports from London and Buchenwald. For television news, the defining moment may have been the assassination of John F. Kennedy.

For the Internet and the World Wide Web, pundits have rolled out a variety of defining moments: Pierre Salinger's uneducated use of an apparently bogus document from the Internet about the crash of TWA Flight 800, the public mourning over the death of Princess Diana, the millions of hits on NASA's Web site during the Mars probe, and the report of Web gossip columnist Matthew Drudge about the affair between President Bill Clinton and Monica Lewinsky. A defining moment, however, does not necessary mean that the Internet and the World Wide Web have obtained the power to establish a specific agenda for the rest of the media and the public.

The media play a significant role in what is called "agenda setting." In the 1970s, researchers Max McCombs and Donald Shaw argued that individual media do not determine what one thinks, but what to think about.[1] Simply put, the media emphasize specific events, ideas, and social values. By focusing on these events, ideas, and values, the media provide the issues about which one should think. The media also frame stories in certain ways that affect the way individual readers or listeners may interpret the news.

Only the Mars probe and the Lewinsky case have come close to having a significant impact on the issues of the day. In the Mars case, it was only after the huge interest on the Web that other news organizations prepared extended reports about the scientific venture. The Drudge report clearly established an agenda for reporting on Clinton and Lewinsky, primarily by alerting other news agencies that *Newsweek* had decided not to print the story about the affair between President Clinton and the White House intern.

So far, the Internet and the World Wide Web cannot set an agenda, primarily because the audience remains relatively small when compared with that of newspapers and television, and many online publications depend on major brand names as the primary sources of information. Therefore, the broadcast outlets and newspapers that operate the Web sites still maintain control of the setting of the journalistic agendas and the public debate.

Nevertheless, online journalism stands to alter dramatically the traditional role of the reporter and editor. First, online journalism places far more power in the hands of the user, allowing the user to challenge the traditional role of the publication as the gatekeeper of news and information. The user can depend on the gatekeeper to select and filter the news in the traditional manner, or the user can go to the basic documents of a story. In short, the user can look over the shoulder of the reporter by researching the original documents and easily comparing one reporter's story with those of others by scanning news publications throughout the country. Archives also become easily accessible.

Second, online journalism opens up new ways of storytelling, primarily through the technical components of the new medium. Simply put, online journalists can provide a variety of media—text, audio, video, and photographs—unlike other media. Data searching provides a means of accessing information unavailable in other media.

Third, online journalism can provide outlets for nontraditional means of transmitting news and information. *New Yorker* critic A. J. Liebling once defined freedom of the press as belonging to those who own one. The Internet enables everyone who owns a computer to have his or her own printing press.

Let's look at the audience for news and information on the Internet and the World Wide Web. The audience provides the basis for any journalistic enterprise. As the audience grows, the publication can usually charge more for advertising. As a result, the enterprise becomes more profitable in most cases.

Even though most surveys show an expanding audience for online journalism, the number of users for news and information on the Internet remains relatively small. Television remains Americans' number-one source of news, according to a 1998 poll from Roper Starch Worldwide. When asked where they usually get most of their news, 69 percent of adults cited television versus 37 percent for newspapers, 14 percent for radio, 7 percent for "other people" and 5 percent for magazines, the study noted. Only 2 percent of the general public mentioned online sources for news. Among households that have Internet access, television was still the top source of news (59 percent), with online services mentioned by 15 percent.[2]

A growing number of online users, however, turn to the Web for quick headlines and breaking news. Again, television remains the first source, according to a 1998 survey conducted by Jupiter Communications. The company polled more than 2,000 Internet users and found that television news remains the viewing choice of 39 percent of those surveyed. Online news, however, has begun to outpace radio and newspapers for the first word on breaking news.[3]

Why do people go online? The most important reason for one in three people who use the Internet is to send electronic mail. It is the most popular form of using the Internet. But nearly as many use the Internet and the World Wide Web for research. One in six is looking for specific news and information. One in eight wants business and financial information. One in twelve goes to the Internet for hobbies and entertainment.[4]

A clear division, however, is emerging between younger users and older users online with respect to what they seek on the Internet and how they use the medium. Nearly seven out of ten people think it is important to know what it in the news, mainly those over the age of fifty. That falls to four out of ten for those under the age of thirty, and only three out of ten under the age of thirty follow the news every day.[5]

"A critical segment of the 'news of the future' audience does not have the basic level of interest to be engaged with the news," one survey found. And those who do are turning to the Internet, while the traditional readers of newspapers and viewers of television news are growing increasingly older. "The habit of picking up the daily newspaper religiously is found only among those over fifty," the survey also said. "Network television news is joining newspapers as a medium for older citizens. . . . TV network news may be in danger of becoming an anachronism in the next century."[6]

Michael Kolowich of <www.newsedge.com>, a Boston-based news service, said he believes individuals turn to online services for a variety of reasons:[7]

1. *News consumers want filtering.* "It's defensive. Make sure I don't miss anything important," he said. Newspapers generally do a relatively good job fulfilling this requirement, whereas radio and television do not provide enough specific information.

2. *Finding, or the ability to search for, data is important.* One day some information may be unimportant, but the next month that story may be critical to a decision. Newspapers have archives, but they often are not immediately available to readers except via expensive computer databases.

3. *Browsing.* "I put myself in the hands of someone else whom I trust," Kolowich said. "I trust this editor or this news organization to inform me or tell me what's important

or entertain me. A gatekeeper and a guide." All media can perform this function, depending on the individual.

4. *Communing.* "Put me in a community that shares an interest," Kolowich said. "Sales people almost inevitably use a general interest topic as a conversation starter," such as the weather or a news story.

The role of the gatekeeper, the individual who determines what is news, has been an important component of the media for years. Gatekeepers highlight particular stories, promote trends, sort the journalistic wheat from the chaff, and, some would argue, restrict the flow of information. Will that role change in the digital age?

The original research on journalistic gatekeepers began in 1949 when David Manning White of Boston University persuaded a small city news editor to keep all of the copy from the Associated Press, the United Press, and the International News Service from a one-week period. The editor, who was given the name "Mr. Gates," agreed to provide written explanations as to why he had selected or rejected items from the wire services in making decisions about what to print in the newspaper. About one third of the time, Gates rejected stories because he did not think they were true. Two thirds of the time, he rejected stories because there was not enough space in the newspaper or he had already chosen similar stories for publication.[8] The editor did allow that he had a few personal opinions that could influence his decisions. "I have few prejudices, built-in or otherwise, and there is little I can do about them. I dislike Truman's economics, daylight-saving time, and warm beer, but I go ahead using stories on them and other matters if I feel there is nothing more important to give space to. . . . As far as preferences are concerned, I go for human-interest stories in a big way. My other preferences are for stories well-wrapped up and tailored to suit our needs."[9]

In 1966, a second study showed that Mr. Gates made roughly the same decisions. The editor used fewer human-interest stories in 1966 than in 1949, but he used more international stories. Asked for his definition of news, Mr. Gates replied: "News is the day by day report of events and personalities and comes in variety, which should be presented, as much as possible in variety for a balanced diet."[10]

Researchers found a set of factors that often determine what news gets into the media. Some—but not all—of the gatekeeper's role is applicable to digital journalism:

1. *Intensity of threshold value.* Events are more likely to pass through the media gates if they are of great magnitude or if they have recently increased in magnitude. A digital publication continues this role, particularly with breaking news when stories can be constantly updated.

2. *Unexpectedness.* Again, editors agree that unexpected stories provide interesting material for any medium, including a digital one.

3. *Sociocultural values.* The values of both the gatekeepers and their readership can also influence selection. Once again, the online publication functions much like its printed cousin. But readers of online publications have more power to choose what stories are important to them by filtering in those articles they deem interesting and useful and filtering out those that they do not.

4. *Continuity.* If an event or news story passes through the media gate once, it is likely that it will pass through the gate again. Editors agree that this factor remains true for online publications. Therefore, it is important to assess why a story should get through the gates the first time.

5. *Cultural proximity or relevance.* The media are most likely to accept news events that have close cultural relevance for the audience. Simply put, *Chicago Tribune* gatekeepers are likely to include more stories about Poland in the newspaper because the city has the largest Polish population in the United States. Again, the online editor will continue to follow this pattern.

The following are the gatekeeping roles identified by researchers that do not apply to online publications:

1. *Time span.* Events that coincide with the time frame of publication are more likely to pass through media gates. Digital journalism allows constant updates, so timing plays a limited role in online decisions.

2. *Clarity or lack of ambiguity.* Events whose meaning is in doubt are less likely to pass through media gates. Few stories in the current media fit these categories, so both print and online editions contain stories that may be ambiguous.

3. *Consonance.* Events that are congruent with an expectation are most likely to pass through media gates. Surprises play a significant role in news in today's print and online editions. Therefore, consonance plays a reduced role in both sectors of the media.

4. *Composition.* Because gatekeepers look at the day's news in its entirety, some news items are selected merely because they contrast with others. Because online editions have virtually no limitations on space, this factor has little importance in the realm of online journalism.

Let's take a look at how one newspaper, the *Chicago Tribune,* has put together its digital publication. The *Tribune* has reporters who work exclusively for the Internet edition.

The reporters write stories, take pictures, operate video cameras, and create digital pages. The *Tribune* Internet edition, which debuted in March 1996, contains most of the information from the print version: news, sports, job listings, real estate and automobile advertisements, weather, stocks, and television listings. For its readers, the Internet edition offers in-depth stories, special technology reports, games, and discussion groups. The Internet edition also provides audio interviews and information from the company's radio station and video from the *Tribune*'s twenty-four-hour-a-day news service, Chicagoland Television.

Computer consultant Leah Gentry forged the design of the online edition. Gentry's passion is what she calls nonlinear storytelling. What kind of journalist will make it in this brave new world? The future conjures up an image of a cross between Buck Rogers, Bob Woodward, and Bill Gates, she says. "Buckbobbill is a geek of the first order, who each day intrepidly climbs aboard his spaceship, jets off to probe the inner workings of the high command at Galactic Central, and writes it up in HTML to file it via e-mail," Gentry says. Journalists "see his coming as either the downfall of the free press or the heaven-sent salvation of a dying medium."[11]

Gentry rejects this paradigm and insists that online journalists must embrace traditional news values. "The myth of the new media geek, who has no formal print experience, and who writes computer code in his sleep, scares off many who would otherwise aggressively pursue an exciting new journalistic forum. If you examine the evolution of journalistic mediums, then the Web becomes a much less scary place. It took awhile for radio and TV journalists to discover how to use the strengths of their particular media to tell stories. On the Web, we have that same challenge."

What is nonlinear storytelling? On the World Wide Web, one has the ability to link one computer page location to another. Sometimes, stories must be broken into their component parts. Sometimes, the same story must be told from several points of view. That means the reporter may provide a smorgasbord of viewing options. "Journalists who succeed . . . [online] will do solid reporting, careful editing, compelling writing, and visual storytelling, using the latest tools available. They'll tell their stories in whatever medium people use. But the tenets of the industry will remain the same," Gentry argues.

Before reporting and writing a story, for example, *Tribune* reporter Darnell Little designs a series of storyboards for what each of the main pages will show, a practice used extensively in the film, television, and advertising industries. The storyboard contains an outline of a page's content, graphics, and computer links to other stories. After Little reports a story, he then follows his original storyboards—with adaptations—to make certain that the reporting, photography, headlines, and navigation make the stories easy for the reader to enjoy.

Little tends toward the storytelling style of *Wall Street Journal* feature articles, which he says works well on the Web. The first page uses an anecdotal lead to draw the reader into the story. The second page broadens the story with the "nut graph": the paragraph that explains the main points of the story. The other pages flow from these first two pages to allow the reader to follow a variety of links that expand on each report.

The process is called "layering." Because a computer screen contains much less space than the front page of a newspaper, the first layer, or page, of a digital story contains a headline, a digital photograph, and text that makes the user want to continue to the next layer. The pages are usually less than five hundred words, with the option for the reader with a click of a computer mouse to follow a highlighted path set out as a guide. But the reader may want to follow another path. The layers provide a logical way to proceed, but the layers can also enable the user to read the digital page in any order.

"I write the story in chapters," Little said in an interview with the author. "What works the best is when you have a design on the Web that is the equivalent of the layout of a magazine. Your eye and attention are focused on one part, which is easily digestible, and it flows and leads you into other parts."[12]

Reporter Stephen Henderson noticed a story about the murder rates in the city. He put together all the information about the murders: the times, the neighborhood, the cause of death, and a variety of other statistics. He designed a map of the city and set up the interface so that citizens could look for information about his or her neighborhood, again with a click of the mouse rather than a visit to the record office of the police precinct.

He then devised a database for each Chicago public school, allowing a parent or student to determine how his or her school compares with the rest of the city from spending to reading scores. "The medium really shapes the writing. It makes you write shorter and sharper," Henderson explained in an interview with the author.[13]

"When I worked on the city desk, I would go do my story and I might assign a photographer. Then I'd just pass the thing on. Somebody else edits it. Somebody else copy edits it. Another person would read it and decide whether it would go on page one. Someone would decide where the photos would go. Here it's so much more important for me to be there through the whole process, shaping the thing so that it make sense in the medium."

At the *Tribune* and elsewhere, there are differences among reporters in how they react to digital journalism and the future. Researchers have found that reporters fall into three different groups in regard to their views about the use of computers in the newsroom. The first group, called benevolent revolutionaries, are enthusiastic about new technologies. The second group, described as nervous traditionalists, are not. A third group, known as serene separatists, do not fear technology but see it as having little impact on the role of the journalist.[14]

The survey results are not exactly what one would expect. For example, the so-called revolutionaries strongly support the notion that journalism "will depend on good writing, good interviewing, and thoughtfulness." Among those described as traditionalists, an editor interviewed for the survey said he finds new technology "hardly intoxicating—more a pain in the ass with the constant rush of forcing on journalists more than they possibly need or can use." One traditionalist describes his concern that new media will emphasize presentation over information: "Writing is almost irrelevant now." Another reporter complains: "As media become more dependent on high-tech inventions, speed, I fear, will outweigh quality."

A key aspect to setting any agenda is survival. Simply put, how will new media operations make money? It's difficult to pry much specific financial information from anyone. The *Chicago Tribune's* Internet edition has cost millions of dollars since its inauguration. Owen Youngman, the director of interactive media for the Tribune Company, seems like a high school science teacher behind his glasses, and his nasal-dominated cadence can put some people to sleep. But his zeal for the future makes this son of an evangelical minister come alive. "My neighbor on one side buys the *Tribune* because he's a stockbroker," Youngman told the author in an interview. "My neighbor on the other side doesn't. Why? It's not really fulfilling for someone with two kids in school in suburban Chicago. She cares a lot more about what affects her kids. It's not her fault. It's my fault."[15]

Youngman has a specific business plan that he thinks will make the digital operation a profit center after a few years. "The newspaper business is really good at charging a token amount of money for an expensive product. Fifty cents doesn't cover the paper and ink, let alone the transportation, the gasoline," Youngman says. People won't have to pay for items the newspaper wants them to read; items people want to read may cost them. For example, a report on the city council won't cost a subscriber. A complete year-by-year description of Sammy Sosa's baseball career, however, may cost a subscriber.

At many metropolitan newspapers, about 40 percent of the budget goes for gathering, writing, and editing the news. The other 60 percent goes mainly for printing the news, marketing, and delivering the paper to the subscribers. Many production costs could be eliminated if the story on the computers of the reporters and editors went directly to the computer of the subscribers. "I could see a day rather than run those big old printers out there," says Youngman, pointing to the press room, "that if you want the *Tribune,* I will buy you a laser printer and put it on your kitchen table and deliver a highly customized version on paper every day if you don't want to go online."

Classified advertising, long a key revenue stream for newspapers, may abandon printed publications. Simply put, information can be far more easily found online about the right job, apartment, or roommate than in print. Just go to the classified ads of an online paper and enter a search word like "engineer" or "bus driver." The computer will provide a list of possible jobs by city, state, or even nationwide within seconds. An apartment? Simply type in number of bedrooms, square footage, location, and price range. "Newspaper print classifieds are at their peak," a recent study reports, "and from here on out we can expect to see growth slowed each year as new competitors—fueled by emerging new technologies—chip away at newspapers' long-held lock on the classifieds business."[16] In five years, newspaper classifieds may see no growth. That would have a dramatic impact, because classified advertising accounts for nearly 40 percent of a typical newspaper's revenue. If revenues from classified advertising should fall by 25 percent, Youngman speculates, the industry's profits would drop from today's 15 percent to 9 percent. If revenues drop 50 percent, the profit margin for newspapers would be 3 percent. That means a number of printed newspapers would face serious cutbacks, and some papers would go out of business.

A variety of defining moments lie ahead for online journalism. Even though the expectations for this new medium continue to be high, it remains to be seen whether the Internet can become a true agenda setter in the year ahead. Although online publications have expanded throughout much of the U.S. media, only a few have become profitable. It is likely, however, that the growing trend of young people's using the Internet for information may create a new readership for news on the Web, providing a profitable addition for many publications and broadcast outlets.

Notes

1. Max McCombs and Donald Shaw, "The Agenda-setting Function of Mass Media," *Public Opinion Quarterly 36* (1972), 176–187.

2. Roper Starch Worldwide, "TV Remains Dominant News and Product Information Source, New Poll Reveals" (March 28, 1998), available online at <http://www.roper.com>.

3. Reuters, December 8, 1998.

4. Pew Research Center for the People & the Press "TV News Viewership Declines" (May 13, 1996), available online at <http://www.people-press.org/mediamor.htm>.

5. Radio and Television News Directors Foundation. Washington, D.C., "Profile of the American News Consumer," 1996, 6.

6. Ibid., 24–25.

7. Michael Kolowich, interview with author, March 24, 1997.

8. Pamela Shoemaker, *Gatekeeping* (Newbury Park, Calif.: Sage, 1991).

9. Ibid., 46.

10. Ibid., 11.

11. Leah Gentry, "Buckbobbill," Newspaper Association of America (December 1996), available online at <http://www.naa.com>.

12. Darnell Little, interview with author, August 27, 1996.

13. Stephen Henderson, interview with author, August 27, 1996.

14. Jane Singer, "Changes and Consistencies: Newspaper Journalists Contemplate an Online Future," paper presented at meeting of the Association for Education in Journalism and Mass Communication, Anaheim, California (August 1996).

15. Owen Youngman, interview with author, August 26, 1996.

16. Hoag Levins, "The Online Classified Reports: New Cyberspace Advertising Technologies to Impact Newspaper Revenues in Three Years," *Editor & Publisher Interactive* (November 21, 1996), available online at <http://www.mediainfo.com>.

18 Hypertext and Journalism: Audiences Respond to Competing News Narratives

Robert Huesca and Brenda Dervin

The advent of new communication technologies has brought forth a set of opportunities and challenges for traditional media professions, such as journalism. This challenging new context is evident from the plethora of books and articles that suggest radical changes to human perception, cognition, and expression precipitated by new technologies. For example, a robust literature exploring hypertext suggests that computer technologies spell the end of what has traditionally counted as "good writing" and, in fact, portend the death of print. Although these claims are provocative and somewhat convincing, they lack an empirical dimension that investigates "what these new systems 'do to' reader practices and what the reader can do with the systems."[1] The purpose of this chapter is to explore the particular challenges of hypertext theories to narrative forms and practices of journalism by examining the interactions of news readers and hypertexts. Specifically, it reports the findings of a qualitative study of online news users who read both an original news story that appeared on the *Los Angeles Times* Web site and a redesigned, hypertext version of the same material. By asking readers to think about and explain the differences between these competing forms of news, we hope to begin documenting the viability of hypertext and exploring its implications for journalism practice. The remainder of this chapter explains the theoretical framework guiding this study, methodology and method used, findings generated, and conclusions and implications for future research and professional practice.

New Technology and the Challenge of Hypertext

Within the scholarly literature examining the social and professional impacts of new communication technologies, researchers have drawn contrasting conclusions regarding the implications of electronic media for theory and practice of writing in general, and journalistic writing in particular. On the one hand, scholarship centered largely in the arts and humanities suggests sea changes in narrative form and in the relationships among authors, texts, and audiences. Although this body of work taken as a whole is stimulating, challenging, and evocative, it is guided by highly abstract, theoretical propositions and lacks a solid grounding in empirical evidence. On the other hand, scholarship centered in preprofessional fields, such as journalism education, tends to examine how new technologies are adopted by media producers and adapted to existing industrial routines, needs, and practices. Although this research typically is grounded in some sort of empirical evidence, it tends to lack the experimentation and imagination so vividly suggested by more abstract scholarship. This section briefly outlines the contributions of these contrasting literatures and situates the present chapter as an attempt to address the legitimate concerns brought forth in both of them.

Within the arts and humanities, numerous scholars have suggested that contemporary society is in a period of fundamental transformation in regard to what is considered "good writing" and accepted narrative practices.[2] Characterized as "the late age of print,"[3] this period can be thought of as analogous to the fifty years following the introduction of the Gutenberg press and the invention of typographical and organizational conventions such as typefaces, page numbers, paragraphs, and chapters.[4] Such "incunabular" periods are characterized by experimentation, invention, and struggle to develop new communication conventions. Indeed, numerous scholars are leading vigorous projects to develop a new rhetoric, stylistics, and poetics for the digital age.[5] Much of this development has centered on exploring of the nature and function of hypertext.

Hypertext is a structure that is assumed to be more compatible with the inherent characteristics of digital media than traditional narrative forms, such as journalism's inverted pyramid.[6] When it was introduced by computer visionary Ted Nelson in the 1960s, the concept, "hypertext" was defined simply as nonsequential writing with reader-controlled links. Since then, scholars have refined this general definition beyond a simple visual form to a more abstract notion of "structures for what does not yet exist."[7] That is, hypertext is now defined as a narrative form that does not exist until readers produce it through a series of choices made according to their desires and interests.[8] By refining this definition from one involving a simple textual format to a more abstract notion of structures for making meaning, scholars have opened up a broad area of inquiry with implications for professional information gathering, processing, design, and delivery.

Despite the breadth of the literature examining the qualities of hypertext, certain central characteristics have emerged repeatedly, and they stand in stark contrast to conventional journalistic forms. Modern narrative structures, including journalism, are characterized by a "canon of unity": a singular author exerting an authoritative voice, a fixed order of events, and a developed story line.[9] Hypertexts, by contrast, are in flux, impermanent, and designed to change. Rather than prescribing a fixed, linear reading order, hypertexts exist as networks or metatemplates of potential texts.[10] Furthermore, they do not communicate through a singular voice of authority but incorporate multiple perspectives and expressions to tell the same story. Murray provides an example typical of what could be found in a hypertext newspaper: an account of a suicide told through the form of a "violence hub." Rather than representing the whos, whats, and whys of the suicide through the account of a single author, Murray suggests that hypertext reporters gather complementary and competing accounts. She envisions these accounts as occupying different locations peering in on the same event, much as the outer spokes of a wheel ultimately connect to a central hub. Such reporting results in neither a solution of the incident nor a refusal of resolution, but a "continual deepening in the reader's understanding of what happened."[11] Finally, hypertexts embrace notions of contradiction, fragmentation, juxtaposition, and pluralism, rather than pursuing "truth," which is at the heart of the traditional journalistic enterprise.[12] This approach is described not only as more responsive to the qualities of new, digital media, but as more compatible with challenges from postmodern perspectives that "no longer believe[s] in a single reality, a single integrating view of the world, or even the reliability of a single angle of perception."[13] This sort of interruption in the unified view of reality creates the context for the inviting potentials of hypertext.

Aside from the structural and visual properties that suggest radical changes in narrative form, hypertext theory also posits transformations in the way authors and readers are conceptualized. New communication technologies are considered inherently participatory, which casts readers as active producers of stories. Hypertext readers take on the role of authors, which alters the traditional tasks of reporting and writing. Fredin argues that readers always have been active and self-reflective and that hypertext journalists must provide them with choices that appeal to their interests.[14] This requires not only a specific sense of reader interests, but a more general, theoretical understanding of user expectations and information-seeking strategies. When readers are viewed more as collaborators than as consumers, the tasks of reporting and writing shift from content delivery to information development and design. News reporting and editing undertaken from this perspective must be focused on creating narrative structures that facilitate user navigation through a variety of information resources. Such resources might include a host of "raw data," such as reporter's notes, interview transcripts, government documents, and other materials, that would allow readers to construct their own versions of reality, rather than simply reading a reporter's representation of reality. The resulting hypertexts call attention to the process of narrative construction and enhance the involvement of readers by actually placing them in the role of the creator.[15]

Endowing readers with agency, however, may not be a uniformly desirable production path to be taken by professional communicators. McKnight, Dillon, and Richardson have derived a text classification system to help producers think about the usefulness and applicability of hypertext designs. They introduce a "repertory grid" that captures the perspectives of users along three dimensions: (a) *how* a text is to be used (skimming vs. studying), (b) *why* it is to be used (work vs. pleasure), and (c) *what* it is to be used for (specific vs. general information). Given this classification system, a novel, for example, might not make a good hypertext, unless the user had certain needs. "If we consider the full range of *how* and *why* attributes that emerge as a result of analyzing novels, one can envisage an educational context where various parts of the text are analyzed and compared linguistically, thereby rendering a suitable hypertext version more useful than paper. In other words, a hypertext novel may not be suitable for reading on the train but it may be ideal for the student of English literature."[16] In light of this classification system, many of the uses of news—obtaining quick overviews of events, finding ready reference to context and background on issues, making connections to further information—seem ideally suited to the potentials of hypertext.

The contemporary theories of hypertext outlined in the preceding abbreviated review have enormous implications for journalism education and practice. At the macro end of the spectrum, this literature suggests changes in widely accepted tenets of journalism: the abandonment of truth and accuracy as primary objectives of reporting and the embrace of a conception of the universe as polyvocal and fragmented. Such grand implications are important to contemplate but fall outside of the immediate interests of this chapter. At the micro end of the spectrum, this literature argues that reporters and writers in the online environment must be more intimately concerned with the design of their work. Furthermore, they must be concerned with designs that respond to the reconceptualization of the relationship between authors and readers. In short, this literature implies that communication students, educators, and practitioners should begin exploring alternatives to the traditional journalistic narrative to develop prototypes of hypertext news. Despite this provocative challenge, new media research in journalism studies has been conservative and unimaginative, for the most part, merely suggesting ways to incorporate new technologies into existing norms and practices.

New Technology and Contemporary Journalism

New media researchers in journalism studies reflect, at best, an ambivalent sense of the impact of new technologies on traditional practices. Although scholarly articles generally recognize the significant shift and challenge to traditional norms represented by new communication technologies, most of the literature in this field tends to project images of new media practices that are consistent with the professional status quo. This consistency is reinforced by recent textbooks that are aimed at training journalists to work in the online environment. With the exception of the few studies already noted, most research that explores online journalism ignores the new frontiers implicit in the hypertext theories reviewed above.

For example, researchers have begun to explore the attitudes of media practitioners toward new technologies and to document how online news is being practiced. The attitudes of reporters and editors tend to mix excitement over the potentials afforded by new media with fear of and resistance to the challenges new media present to journalistic traditions.[17] Typical responses to new media include uneasiness and lamentation that traditional demarcations, such as "the firewall between advertising and news," the distinction between news and entertainment, and the separation of objectivity and opinion, are in danger of disappearing.[18] These attitudes are reified in the actual transition from print to online formats. Studies of online newspaper content, for example, have found no difference, other than minor formatting changes, between print and electronic products.[19] Finally, studies of how new technologies are used in reporting and editing indicate that computers and the Internet are used exclusively to extend existing journalistic practices (e.g., fact checking, generating story ideas, gathering background material, and monitoring the competition),[20] rather than in ways that exploit the new opportunities they present. The overwhelming trend portrayed in the scholarly research is that reporters and editors interpret and use new media in ways that conform to traditional tenets of journalism and established, news industry practices.

This tendency in the scholarly literature is reinforced by (and perhaps a by-product of) the guidance offered by online news and computer-assisted reporting textbooks. For the most part, textbooks aimed at news workers and journalism students are atheoretical "how-to" manuals for incorporating new technologies into professional practices. At the most introductory level, textbooks envision the Internet and other electronic resources as faster and bigger tools that primarily expand the range of existing news sources.[21] When placed in the service of talented journalists, this expanded range of sources is considered beneficial to the traditional role of the press. According to one introductory textbook in the field, "The more access to information reporters have, the better reporters will be able to fulfill their mission to inform the public about key issues and interests of the day."[22] Indeed, the use of new technologies advocated in these texts does not question the status quo of journalism but reinforces it with renewed urgency. According to another of these texts, "The job we have as journalists, or gatekeepers, is to present the news as completely and accurately as possible, using our expertise to provide proper emphasis on what is significant and reliable."[23]

Aside from these introductory texts, more advanced books and articles have begun to explore more specific journalistic applications using new technologies. For example, a number of texts provide instruction in "computer-assisted reporting," which aims to harness the power of computers to enhance traditional investigative journalism.[24] These texts provide training on how to use computers to make spreadsheets, manage databases, and access online resources so that reporters can continue to fulfill their watchdog role in society. Bolstering this advanced use of computers in reporting is scholarship aimed at developing professional skills to evaluate online sources. Using criteria from Investigative Reporters and Editors, Inc., Ketterer described a college news project to develop "accurate and credible" online resources to be used by student reporters and editors. The results from the project served to reinforce existing journalistic norms and established power relationships in society, as a majority of the online resources were tied to government sources or other online newspapers. In fact, the project explicitly eschewed much of the expanded information universe—those online sites tied to nonprofit organizations—because they were presumed to "by their nature promote a point of view."[25] This and the other texts noted above have had the ironic effect of shrinking the range of voices and perspectives in the new electronic environment by forcing digital media to conform to existing journalistic norms and practices.

For the most part, studies of new electronic media conducted within the framework of journalism education lack the sense of fundamental change suggested in the hypertext literature. Likewise, these studies convey very little sense that journalism stands at the crossroads of invention and departure from the past, in one direction, and the continuation of the status quo, in the other direction. Nevertheless, the journalism studies literature is grounded in the empirical reality of day-to-day news production, a dimension that is missing from the research on hypertext that advocates sweeping changes in narrative form and function. The hypertext literature in contrast advocates radical invention and change but neglects to bring such change into contact either with working professionals or with actual readers. This chapter aims to explore the challenges hypertext presents to journalism in a way that is inventive and creative, yet is informed by readers' responses to this new narrative form.

Methodology and Method

The completion of the study reported in this chapter involved three basic phases: the selection and design of hypertext news stories; the performance of a reading exercise using volunteers; and the completion of qualitative, Sense-Making interviews with these volunteer readers. Each of these phases will be explained briefly below.

Since hypertext narratives as described above simply do not exist on traditional news sites, we selected existing news stories and redesigned them ourselves using basic principles of hypertext.[26] Because of the multiperspectival, fragmented, polyvocal nature of hypertext, we sought out complex news stories on the Web. Since the *Los Angeles Times* is known for its lengthy treatments of a variety of topics in its "Column One" daily news feature, we monitored its content during a one-month period. In that time we selected three different stories to serve as sample articles in this study. The articles were selected for diverse content, as we wanted readers participating in the study to have a choice of what to read. The articles included a news feature on a trend among immigrants to transfer the remains of their ancestors from their home country to U.S. soil; a news story on the difficulties faced by people living in post-Soviet Siberia; and a recreation story on an adventure sport called "slack-lining," which is similar to walking a tightrope across a mountain gorge. These stories, as well as redesigned, hypertext versions of them, were copied onto a local Web server.[27] The original articles were essentially electronic copies of the printed versions, which, when accessed by computer, had to be read by scrolling down the screen from beginning to end. The redesigned versions contained no new material; rather, they were simply broken into thematic parts that had to be activated by clicking on links running along the left side of the computer screen. Aside from slight changes in transitional phrases, the hypertext content was identical to the original article; only the form was altered—from a unified, linear story to a nonsequential narrative with reader-controlled links.

Once the news stories were installed on the server, twenty volunteers drawn from a liberal arts university setting participated in a reading exercise. Volunteers were recruited from publicity posted around the campus calling for people who "enjoyed reading online news" to participate in study of new forms of online journalism. The participants were scheduled for reading and interview sessions in which they were placed in a quiet office with a computer that was connected to the Internet. After brief

instructions, an explanation of the purpose of the study, and a review of the basic operations of the *Netscape* browser, participants were left alone to select one of the three
articles and to read and compare the original and hypertext versions. Our purpose in
having participants read both versions of the article was to enlist them as new technology theorists in the research act. Each participant was provided with a one-page sheet
that contained the various dimensions of our questionnaire, with blank space to be
used for taking notes during reading. Participants were encouraged to jot down their
thoughts as they related to the various dimensions of the questionnaire while reading and
to use the sheet as a memory aid during the interview that was to follow the reading.
Participants were interrupted after fifteen minutes and asked if they had finished reading the articles. In some cases, readers asked for additional time, which never exceeded
ten minutes.

Following the reading exercise, participants were guided through Sense-Making
interviews, which were tape recorded and transcribed verbatim. Sense-Making is a
methodology and method that is founded on particular communication principles and assumptions of how people actively negotiate and construct meanings from their material
and symbolic environments. Interview protocols developed out of the principles and assumptions of Sense-Making in effect situate participants at the center of determining substantive content, while providing a structure that allows for cross comparison of data.[28]
Participants in this study, for example, discussed how their selected article compared
(original version versus hypertext) in terms of their overall interest, their confusions, the
difficulties they had in reading, the article's usefulness, the level of confidence they felt in
reading the article, their emotions while reading, their satisfaction with the article, and
their level of enjoyment. They also were asked how their experiences with the texts
might inform contemporary journalism in the online environment. Interview transcripts
were analyzed using inductive, qualitative research techniques in which concepts, categories, themes, and relationships emerged from the data set.[29] Each transcript was read
by at least four different persons at least three times before final categories and patterns
were identified. What emerged from the twenty interviews was a rich set of transcripts
in which the participants in essence theorized the relationships among texts, readers, reporting, and writing. These subject-generated theories of hypertext are presented below.

Inductively Derived Themes

During data analysis, the research team worked inductively to identify all concepts present in the transcripts and then to organize them into more abstract categories and themes.

The themes that are reported here were constructed for their heuristic value, rather than for other purposes, such as the creation of a complete user typology or a range of mutually exclusive and exhaustive categories. Because we sought to identify patterns in the data, we required that at least one third of our participants mention or discuss a thematic category in order for us to include it in the discussion that follows.

The most common characteristic of this data set is the presence of multiple contradictions throughout it. On the most general level, the twenty participants in this study were evenly split in their general reactions to the narrative forms: Five preferred the hypertext, five preferred the original, and the remaining ten had mixed responses. Looking more closely at the twenty transcripts, we identified a variety of themes that emerged in the form of paired contradictions. The various themes can be subsumed into three general categories: conceptualizations of the reader/user, characteristics of the narrative form, and self-reflexive hypotheses regarding intentionality and context. The remainder of this section will discuss each of these categories in turn.

Reader Agency

The most robust thematic category that emerged from the data concerned conceptualizations of the reader/user. Specifically, participants talked about the issues of choice, control, work, and labor in terms of their personal satisfaction and edification as readers. Although many readers found the ability to choose a narrative path in a hypertext to be a positive and enjoyable experience, a number of participants identified this as a violation of the author's integrity and an onerous burden placed on the reader. The personal accounts of the participants are summarized below.

Choice/Control versus Author Intention

The most frequent theme that readers in this study discussed concerned the ability to choose that the hypertext form provided. Participants made explicit distinctions between the hypertext's open narrative paths and the original article's prescribed reading order as being at the heart of the provision of choice:

> In the first one [original article], I skipped ahead because I was kinda bored. And in the second one, there was this tiny little snippet at the beginning. So you're kinda forced to skip around. You go to a link, and you skip ahead, and you go back and forth. You play around with the links. But I skipped ahead on the first one, too. The thing about the hypertext one is that I could skip to where I wanted to skip. As opposed to the other one,

where you had to read it like a book and kinda skip like you'd be flipping pages or something. (Luke F.)

On the original article, I had to read though a lot of extraneous information that I did not feel was personally important. I had to read it begrudgingly. I wanted to cut to the chase. I wanted to know what the meat of the story was. The hypertext article allowed me to do that. The original article did not. (David D.)

Users of traditional texts *had* to follow a prescribed order of reading, whereas users of hypertext *had* to make choices. The choices seemed to be facilitated by topical links on the computer screen that were intended to function as metacommunicative "maps" of the stories' contents:

With the original, you have to read the whole story to get it. You piece it together as you read it. And with the hypertext, you can look to the left on the menu and you see all the parts in the story. And you don't have to read it in the order that they wrote it in the original version. (Kelly S.)

Several participants described this aspect of the hypertext as opening up cognitive potential—new modes for thinking and making meaning—for them as readers. Seeing all the parts of the narrative on one screen led them to ask more questions and to notice more facets of the story:

It piqued my interest a little more. It wasn't just "why do it?" it was like "why do they do it? How do they do it? Why is this interesting?" With the different choices on the hypertext article, it spurred more questions in my mind. (David D.)

I saw a lot more in the hypertext than the original, just because it was broken up. I felt that I had an outline to go by. (Sandra M.)

What seemed to be most important to participants discussing positive aspects of choice, however, was that the hypertext form responded to their needs and interests by providing a variety of content paths to follow:

The *Los Angeles Times,* or the original article just seemed to go on and on, and I found myself just skimming the story as a whole. With the hypertext I was able to divide my interests into subcategories and I was able to pick and choose what I was interested in, and eventually I ended up reading the whole article.

I wasn't that interested in the human-interest aspect of the story, I was more interested in the politics and decisions that led to the crisis in Siberia. So that's why I went to the economics portion of the hypertext article. I started with economics and then went to psychology. I went to my interests first, which I enjoyed, and then I went through the whole article. The original article starts off with "this is this person, la, la, la," and I just got confused and bored.

The hypertext, I was able to choose what I wanted to read about. It's kind of empowering because it's what I want to read. I'm choosing. I'm not being told. (Melvin C.)

In contrast to the ten participants who found choice to be a beneficial, empowering, and positive aspect of the stories, about one third of the readers described choice as detrimental, difficult, and objectionable. Several participants, for example, explicitly talked about the hypertext form as violating the efforts and intentions of the author:

I kinda like news articles in the way the journalist wrote them. I figure they're trying to do that, and most of them have been doing that a while, and they know what they're doing. They know how to write a good article for the most part, and it seems like the article should be read as the journalist intended and not as kind of just, you know, the browser skimming little parts here and there, skipping along in the article, unorganized and fragmented. (Jeff T.)

Providing readers with choices, at least for some in this study, violated the traditional authority of the author. Moreover, it truncated their ability to comprehend the material for a several reasons. On the one hand, providing readers with choices placed issues of design into relief, which distracted some readers:

It was simpler to read the original text than to have to think about where would they put it. Where is it in all these links? Why would they put it there? You kind of have to like hop into the designer's mind and figure out where, under which title it would be most appropriate. And with the original text it was all there. You didn't have to worry about anything like that. Just scroll down, scroll down. And enjoy the reading, understand the reading. There wasn't as much thinking involved. (Carrie C.)

In addition to calling attention to the story as a designed object, the hypertext's open order was described as somewhat overwhelming and hard to keep track of:

You had to click on, and you didn't go in, I mean, you're not made to go in any certain order. So you have all these pieces of the story that you, I mean, people aren't really going to fit that into their own heads. They're just going to take it, and it's just going to stick in their heads as different parts of the story, and it's not going to stay up there as well. (Patricia C.)

For several participants, the open order of the hypertext was interpreted as enjoyable and responsive to their interests, whereas its discontinuity was confusing and distracting:

> It was just the distraction of seeing what was coming in the article and choosing what order I wanted to read it in the hypertext article; the article lost continuity that way. It was more fun to choose, but like I said, it lost continuity, and it was a little harder to follow. But the original, at the same time, didn't have that fun aspect. I got to look at what I wanted to look at, like I didn't read the personal stories on the hypertext version because I didn't want to. But then, when I went back and read them in the original article, and was almost forced to read them because it fit in the flow, I enjoyed those. But it wasn't something that I necessarily wanted to do. That's just the way I've learned how to read. It just makes it easier to process it, rather than having to put it together in my mind. (Ellen S.)

Related to this notion of additional burden represented by choice is the theme of general effort, work, and labor required of readers in the hypertext versus original versions.

The Joy / Drudgery of Work

About two thirds of our participants commented that one or the other narrative version required more effort on the part of the reader in general. But these participants were divided in a variety of ways on the significance of the labor required to move through the stories. Many of the readers complained that with the original article, they were forced to read the entire story to gain a complete understanding of the topic. A larger group of participants identified the hypertext as a form that required more effort, but these readers were divided in terms of whether that additional effort was a positive or negative aspect of their experience.

The original narrative required readers to follow a particular order and gave no hints regarding the story's overall content. A number of readers complained that this led them to become bored and/or lost while moving through the story. The most common response among readers was to skim through the original, rather than reading it word for word. One reader, however, eventually abandoned the story altogether:

> It [the original] just seemed to drag on and on, and I think that maybe I have a short attention span, so I like things to be concise. So I just kept skimming, and going back and

forth. I didn't get a lot of the information that I wanted. I didn't understand why the town was being abandoned until I read the hypertext. There was a disagreement between the Russian government and the regional government. That's the information I was not able to get. I was interested in it. I just got tired of looking for it in the original, and I just gave up. (Melvin C.)

Many participants identified the hypertext as a generally more laborious form, but some of the readers interpreted that as a positive quality. Forcing the reader to dig for further information provided fulfillment to certain participants:

> I loved the source listing. I'd love to get more information. In a way, it kind of weeds out people who want to read more and separates them from people who want to just read the first few paragraphs. It weeds out the people who just want to read the story and just forget about it from there. I was certainly more satisfied with the hypertext article. (Bill T.)

Furthermore, a number of participants talked about the hypertext form as something that allowed them to "play around" while looking for information:

> On the hypertext, even though I was slightly bored by the content, at least I could play around with the links and jump around, which is always more entertaining. (Luke F.)

> I spent more time in the hypertext than I did on the original, because I was doing more playing around over here in the hypertext by going to the different links and then getting caught up in one of them. (Maggie S.)

Whereas some participants found the labor of the hypertext satisfying and enjoyable, an equal number identified it as frustrating and bothersome. Because the hypertext links contained only a few words, some participants felt that they had to guess at the contents associated with them, which they found frustrating:

> I was definitely more satisfied with the original text. It was more pleasing for me to read, and I understood it better. Less stress involved with it in a way. I guess that sounds lazy, but I didn't have to worry about finding where else to go get it or would they hide it under this topic or under that topic. Once you got to the main page then went to a link and there were a couple more links on that page so you had to keep searching, like an endless game of hide and seek. Sometimes you got it right, and sometimes you had to keep looking. (Carrie C.)

Aside from the frustration that accompanied the search for information, several participants commented that the cognitive effort of putting a story together was a difficulty for them:

> I think in the original article, I was able to get a better picture of the whole scene and situation and all the background I needed to understand it. And in the second one, I had to move around. It's harder to bring all that information together than it is when it is presented as a whole. The second one required more effort—I sound so lazy—but the effort it took to find the story was frustrating. (Christy S.)

Finally, one participant expressed resentment at what he considered a violation of the author's responsibility to the reader:

> Reading in and of itself is not really that much of a mental strain, but if you have to go hunting for information. It started to feel more like you were trying to research the story than reading about it. I guess I see it as the journalist's job. They're getting paid for that and that's what they do. And for the purpose of reading the news, it's to get all the relevant information and it kinda riled me that it was presented to me as if it was my job to click the links and follow up on the story and look at the list of sources. It seemed like I would be paying for basically doing more work than I would have to do. People don't look at the news where they have to work at it. They just want the story. (Jeff T.)

The sentiments expressed above that are critical of what might be called "active reading" were reinforced and clarified by many of the commentaries that focused on the competing characteristics of the two textual formats.

Textual Qualities

Comments concerning conceptualizations of the reader/user constituted the most robust theme in this study. The next major theme emerging from the data regarded comments related to characteristics of the narrative formats. Specifically, participants identified the texts as either fragmented or linear, novel or conventional. As with previous themes, participants were divided on the benefits and drawbacks of these contrasting forms.

Wholeness versus Fragmentation

Almost half of the participants in the study criticized the hypertext form as being disorganized and difficult to follow. Terms used to describe the hypertext included "fragmented," "choppy," "jumbly," "not cohesive," "butchered," "mutilated," "haphazard," "disjointed," "less complete," "sectioned," "disconnected," and "cut and pasted." For these participants, this format made the hypertext harder to process, understand, and remember:

> I really hated the hypertext. To me it seemed like reading a very detailed outline. It's very choppy, and it's disorganized when it's like that because it doesn't flow logically. (Carol L.)

> I found that the original article in the traditional text form kept my attention and my interest more than the hypertext because the hypertext, you have a piece here, but you have to go to another button to find more information. And just having the process of clicking the button and getting where you need to go broke the continuity of the story. You couldn't think linearly, and the original article just had it all logically proceeding. The hypertext was a lot harder to get. (Carrie C.)

In contrast to the hypertext and its fragmented nature, the original story was praised for the narrative "flow" that it achieved. Participants suggested that the original article "felt more organized," presented the "whole story," and "had it all [the details] right there." The original form was easier to comprehend for these participants, who described the text as having "continuity," "completeness," and "sequence":

> I think because I do some writing and I like to see things that flow in a good way and aren't disjointed. Something that's easy for the reader to get into. (Christy S.)

> I guess I felt more satisfied as a reader when I finished the original article because I looked at that one as a whole, compared to the hypertext article, which seemed like pieces. (Thomas J.)

> I read all the time, and I like doing it. And I think there's a pleasure in just reading and just kind of keeping going. Because if I were just reading the hypertext, I wouldn't remember who was who, or who was from where and which families we're talking about. So there is kind of a continuity that helps when reading the whole article. (Heather S.)

Finally, participants who preferred the original text said that it gave them a satisfying sense of closure that seemed to be missing in the hypertext:

> For me, having the whole entire article as one thing that gave me a sense of closure when I got to the end of it. Whereas when I first read the hypertext, I kept wondering,

"Well, gosh, did I really finish? How do I piece it all together?" I just never felt like I exactly mastered the whole thing because I haven't really, I mean, there's no end. But then, when I went back and read the original, I got a sense of completion when I got to the end. So, because there is no closure in the hypertext, I don't feel as content or satisfied. (Sandra M.)

In contrast to the participants who preferred the original article, a small number of readers preferred the fragmented design of the hypertext. In addition, about one third of the participants spoke both of the benefits and detriments of the hypertext, sometimes in the same sentence. Taken together, these two groups of readers were equivalent in number to the group of participants preferring the original article.

Among those who commented positively on the qualities of the hypertext form, participants explained that it was more organized, focused, and reflective of a greater range of information:

I guess that it makes you more focused on certain things and you know you can always go for more information from there. And it's easier to focus on specifically what it is. You can jump to what you are interested in and in the newspaper article you have to read all of it to find specific things. I think it's more information quicker. The hypertext seemed more organized. I guess, back to the fact that it had specific headings and it was split into different categories, like it would have the information on how it started, whereas the original article just kind of had it all thrown together and it was more of a narrative type that you had to read all the way through. (Helen M.)

The organization of information into categories was valued for its ability to metacommunicate the entire contents of the story:

The opening segment—it gave a great synopsis to the whole article. It was just right there, and I had it. When I'm reading the news, I want it to be boom boom, right there for me to understand and adjust, and in the hypertext, it gave me the whole story in about two paragraphs, and that's all I needed. It was there for me, and if I was interested, I would read more. But just in case I wasn't interested, that was just enough information for me. (Melvin C.)

For one reader, the combination of the synopsis and the links led to the creation of what he termed a textual "flow," but one that was crafted by the reader:

I was reading the hypertext, and I had a couple of questions because I always question when I read. It's kind of annoying, but I do. So I have questions when I read, and I could look to the left and look up and down and not all of my questions were answered, but some of them were, and I could just click on it and then go back to the main page. It wasn't a different flow from the author, it was the flow that I had chosen. I don't perceive it to be a disturbance to the flow of the news because it's going according to the flow that I am choosing. (Melvin C.)

Many readers who commented on textual qualities found the hypertext and original forms to offer competing advantages and disadvantages. While the hypertext presented the reader with choices that responded to specific needs and interests, those choices entailed additional labor:

I liked the traditional one because it was just nice and all right there in one bulk form. I didn't have to go searching for bits and pieces. Of course, in the hypertext, I really enjoyed having the option of being able to find what I wanted. If I wanted to find something more in depth, those links were really nice for that. (Maggie S.)

Despite the added work involved in clicking through a hypertext, this narrative form was "more controllable," which appealed to some readers:

I would say first off that the hypertext article grabbed my attention just a little more because of how it split the information into such short little groups. It seemed to be a little bit more controllable, doable, as far as reading was concerned, in a way because everything was several short little stories, which just appeals to me as a reader. The original article, I kind of liked it more because it had kind of an emotional content that wasn't in the hypertext that held my attention through the whole story. (Henry J.)

Finally, the hypertext, while providing more information through its topical links, constituted a less compelling narrative than the traditional news story and news feature:

Well, in the original text, I was much more drawn into it, and then the hypertext just kind of lays it all out for you. I guess it depends on what you're looking for. If you are looking for a fun story, then first go to the original to hear that, and then the hypertext was more straight facts. It just laid it out for you really quickly. (Anne E.)

Curiosity and Novelty versus Convention

Another significant pattern regarding the competing textual forms focused on either the novel or the conventional nature of the stories and how it related to reader curiosity. For some readers, the novelty and structure of hypertext made them more curious and interested in the story. For others, the novelty was confusing. Many of these readers found it comforting to read "something that I'm used to." Participants were evenly divided in their perspectives regarding these two textual forms, and many readers were internally divided.

For some readers, the mere novelty of the form piqued their interest and propelled them to read further:

> I guess I just saw it as something new that I had never really heard of and didn't know anything about. I just wanted to look a little deeper into and see what it was. (Helen M.)

Aside from the pure novelty, the hypertext seemed to open up cognitive potential that was not possible with the original article. It provided a structure for the "opportunity to be curious":

> On the hypertext, I was curious. The links made me curious to find out what it was. When you see the little . . . on any article, I jump to the links. Just because they're . . . you're tempted by them. It kinda puts you in a different frame of mind. And I read it in that frame of mind, so it was more interesting. (Luke F.)

When contrasted with the traditional, journalistic narrative, this structure for curiosity was what led participants to continue reading:

> If I was flipping through a newspaper and I found this article, I would probably read the first paragraph and skim through the rest of it, maybe even skip to the last two paragraphs. With the hypertext article, I didn't have that desire. I read the first section and decided, "Ooh, I want to know about this." I would go to the link, I would read it, and then I would say, "Oh, this is interesting. I want to go to the next section." (David D.)

About the same number of people who found this novel form beneficial to their curiosity described it in mixed terms. Some readers, for example, found that the hypertext format grabbed their attention at the same time that it confused them:

> The hypertext article was kind of like a novelty, if you will. That caught my attention and that's why I bring that up. It's the first thing that struck me. That was the first time I saw it. This is just my personal opinion, but I'm used to reading news stories all on one page, and I assume that it is written in the order that it is supposed to be read. And because I'm

used to that, I was confused as to why they would lay it out in the way that they did, like a table of contents. (Bill T.)

Other readers spoke of the negotiated tension between the comfort of conventional text and the novelty of the hypertext form:

> The original article, it was pretty straightforward and laid out for me, so it wasn't very adventurous, but it wasn't very tedious. For me, it was cohesive and nice and easy to read. But I spent more time in the hypertext page because there is more stuff to look for and places to go, and you get new ideas as you start reading through. They provoked me to think more about, not even so much the topic of immigrants and their ancestors, but more . . . broader implications of why they do this or who are these people, what kind of religion they practice. (Maggie S.)

Indeed, the most frequent reason participants gave for preferring the original form was related to the comfort they experienced with conventional writing:

> I was annoyed because it's new, and it's something I'm not used to, and I've got to figure it out, and then I have to decide if I like it. And I eventually decided I didn't like it. And I was relieved with the original because I thought, "phew, this is what I know. This is what I'm used to." (Carol L.)

Beyond the recognizable, narrative form, several participants expressed satisfaction with the original article because of the implicit presence of an author:

> The original was more like, I don't know, perhaps it's just a bias towards more traditional news articles, but it was something about it being presented as a reported story. You kind of got a feeling for the person who had written it and the people he was talking about. (Henry J.)

Another factor that seemed to relate to reader satisfaction and competing textual forms was the style of writing in these particular articles. Each of the three stories was written from a human-interest, anecdotal angle, which participants found more engaging than the summary, synopsis style of the hypertext versions:

> Like I said, I was a lot more interested in the original article because it started off with something that was really interesting and kind of emotional because, you know, it

. . . all the human element was pretty much at the beginning. In the other part it was kind of disjointed, there were . . . it didn't read like a story. It was just basic information. So, I thought my feelings were . . . I had more emotional reaction to the original. (Susan D.)

Overall, our participants were evenly divided regarding how the textual forms intersected with their curiosity and interest. These competing textual forms also intersected with readers' evaluations of the credibility of the articles.

High and Low Credibility

About one third of all participants said that they felt the original article was more credible and trustworthy because of textual characteristics. That is, the original article was more what they expected from a journalist and fulfilled their criteria of "good writing," which they then transferred to the quality of the information. Finally, several readers commented that the clear presence of an author in the original version had an impact on how they evaluated the quality of the information:

I kind of trusted, well, trusted might not be the way to put it; I kind of felt like there was an actual writer behind the original article, and so I was inclined to maybe trust that perspective a little bit more than I would, say, the hypertext one. I felt like it could have been written by any group of people. You want to feel like there's somebody who's been out there, who's investigated this, who knows what's going on, and who's trying to convey a story to you. (Henry J.)

On the other hand, about one third of the participants claimed that the hypertext seemed more credible and trustworthy, again, due to textual characteristics. For example, the hypertext listed the sources used in the story for each article. This was commented on repeatedly by participants as a form of accountability in the article that gave them confidence in the reporting. In addition, several readers said that the way the hypertext was divided into categories suggested to them that more care was taken in the construction of the material and that it demonstrated a desire to communicate that to the reader:

It made the reporter in the hypertext article more interested in conveying information to the audience. In other words, the hypertext format said to me the reporter wants to share more information about the story than what's printed in the paper. So the hypertext was better in the sense that it made the reporting seem more confident. Because it wanted to convey more information that we needed, and hopefully, future articles will, you know, use that idea. (Bill T.)

The multiple contradictions running through the themes of reader agency and characteristics of the texts effectively disappeared when participants abandoned the immediate reading experience and made theoretical statements of a hypothetical nature.

Self-Reflexive Theories

Sprinkled throughout the interview transcripts were commentaries that abandoned the participants' immediate experiences and speculated about the uses of these competing forms in different conditions. Rather than clustering into paired contradictions, however, these self-reflexive theories tended to converge around themes regarding reader intentionality and article context.

Regardless of whether they preferred the original or the hypertext article, more than half of the participants explained that their selection of one format over the other would depend on their intended use of the article. Repeatedly, participants said that the hypertext would be a preferred form for fact finding or for conducting "research" in which specific details were being sought. Conversely, the original text would be preferred for leisure or pleasure reading:

> I mean the hypertext, I think the only benefits of it could be if you were doing some sort of very specific research and maybe that would help you get right to what you were looking for. I mean, if you are using it for research reasons it would be beneficial, but if it's just to read it, then I think the original is better. (Carol L.)

Aside from reader intentions, contextual factors, including time constraints and type of story, were identified as playing a role in the appropriateness of narrative format. With few exceptions, participants agreed that the hypertext would be a preferred format in cases in which the reader had little time to read. The hypertext was valued for its speed and convenience by one third of the participants:

> I guess that's something you can only get with this kind of medium because if you're reading a newspaper article, you can't—I mean, it doesn't really break it down like that for you. I preferred it not being broken down, but that's just because I had a set amount of time to sit here and read it, and I wasn't in a hurry or anything like that. But I know that

might be useful if I was just scanning for something specific—if I just wanted to know about dangerous sports. So it can be useful. (Patricia C.)

A smaller number of participants explained that the narrative formats seemed to co-incide with article types. For breaking and hard-news stories, hypertext was identified as a better form, whereas human-interest features were identified as more amenable to linear narratives:

> I didn't really find that in the hypertext because it seemed kind of broken up and I know that was set up to be under subject matter, and I just personally think the story—the type of—since it was a feature story, went better as a chronological story compared to a broke-up-into-subject-matter kind of story. (Thomas J.)

Furthermore, participants repeatedly claimed that the hypertext lacked the emotional, human dimension that came through in all of the original articles, which were soft fea-tures, as opposed to hard news.

Conclusions, Discussion, Implications

The competing patterns that emerged from the data regarding theories of the user, the text, and intention/context begin to fill out some of the theoretical issues raised in the first part of this chapter. The overwhelming pattern that emerged from this data set was the consistent presence of multiple contradictions running throughout the major con-ceptual themes. For educators, students, and practitioners interested in advancing jour-nalism in the new electronic environment, these contradictions imply a mixed set of recommendations that both affirm and negate established values and practices while com-mending the further exploration and invention of routines and conventions that respond to the challenges of digital media.

Ample evidence emerged from the interviews to suggest that journalism in the new electronic environment can occupy an enlarged space in terms of its role in society and its relationship to readers. The repeated comments regarding reader agency and qualities of hypertext as a guide or outline suggest that readers want a dynamic mode of commu-nication that allows them to move through information in ways they find helpful, useful, or otherwise valuable. These dynamic modes should be conceptualized as "verbing" com-munication, which might include traditional journalism paths (*factizing, experting*), as well as less conventional directions (*connecting, empathizing*).[30] In other words, journalism need not abandon traditional forms of narrative presentation, such as factizing, but these forms must be augmented with a greater range of paths that are responsive to readers' ways of making sense of information.

On a higher level of abstraction, this means that journalists will need to rethink and enlarge their professional role from that of arbiters of reality and truth to that of facilitators of social dialogue and cartographers of information and communication resources. Readers who commented positively on the work and play involved in constructing the news story were clearly less interested in receiving the "true" version of events than in being able to select narrative paths that helped them understand events or enjoy the stories. In the future, journalists will be better served by professional skills that emphasize the development of multiple modes of gathering, processing, and presenting information. This will include self-reflexive modes, such as placing reporters' notes and interview questions online, which reveal the constructed nature of news narratives and bring journalists into social dialogue with users. Rethinking the role of the journalist in this way suggests the dismantling of the edifice of expertise, objectivity, and truth and the construction of systems of flexibility, responsiveness, and sense.

This shift in the journalist's role and skills, however, does not spell the end of the author, as suggested in the literature on hypertext, but it does challenge the accepted conventions of "good writing." Indeed, many readers expressed comfort and pleasure in knowing that a living, breathing, thinking author stood behind the text on the screen. The positive response to the human dimension that was present in the original stories but absent from the more mechanical hypertexts suggests that professional writing will continue to be a valued skill in the creation of electronic texts. Furthermore, a number of readers conveyed a high regard and even an expectation for the author's guidance in moving through the stories. This reinforces the need to invent specialized encoding practices that depart from current conventions but continue to be a part of contemporary journalism education and practice.

Just where this invention will occur is not yet clear; however, the literature reviewed in this study suggests that scholars should not expect risk taking or creativity from mainstream news producers. The review of the research into the adoption of new communication technologies in newsrooms earlier in the chapter indicates that journalists are, at best, uneasy about these technologies, having incorporated Internet applications only to the extent that they reinforce existing practices. This tendency to use technologies to reproduce conventions, rather than to alter them, is augmented by textbooks and training manuals in such practices as computer-assisted reporting. Finally, exploring hypertext, not to mention multimedia designs, requires an enormous commitment of energy, thought, and economic resources, based on our experience of preparing the limited number of hyperstories for this study. The media industries today, with their intense focus on bottom-line journalism, strike us as ill prepared to meet the challenges implied by our findings. This should signal scholars and teachers who care about the idea of journalism that, ironically, they likely will have to turn away from the media professions to forge the future of news in the new electronic environment.

Obviously, this study has severe limitations because of its range of readers, artificial design, and limited number of stories. Our intention has not been to generate generalizable conclusions, however, but to explore theoretical challenges and premises through empirically derived, heuristic patterns. These patterns do provide tempered confirmation of assertions that hypertexts function very differently from linear narratives and that such texts suggest a radically different relationship between authors and readers. In fact, given the novelty of hypertext, the literary bias of the participant pool, and the fact that the actual articles were reported, written, and designed using standard journalistic conventions, these findings should be interpreted as erring on the conservative side—that is, the limitations of the study have a built-in bias favoring the original articles. Aside from the implications of this research that have been noted already, this study suggests that empirical research in journalism studies should move beyond collecting data and suggesting practices that merely squeeze established routines and values into the new spaces opened up by electronic media. This study points to a fertile range of research through which scholars and practitioners can and should begin exploring and inventing journalism's future.

Notes

1. T. Rasmussen, "Media Technologies and Practical Action: Notes on Technology, Objectivation and Knowledge," *Nordicom Review* 1 (1994): 105–128, at 105.

2. S. Birkerts, *The Gutenberg Elegies: The Fate of Reading in an Electronic Age* (Boston: Faber and Faber, 1994); J. D. Bolter, *Writing Space: The Computer, Hypertext, and the History of Writing* (Hillsdale, N.J.: Lawrence Erlbaum, 1991); J. D. Bolter and R. Grusin, *Remediation: Understanding the New Media* (Cambridge: MIT Press, 1999); G. P. Landow, *Hypertext 2.0* (Baltimore: Johns Hopkins University Press, 1997); and J. Murray, *Hamlet on the Holodeck: The Future of Narrative in Cyberspace* (New York: Free Press, 1997).

3. Bolter, *Writing Space*.

4. Murray, *Hamlet on the Holodeck.*

5. Bolter, *Writing Space;* W. Condon and W. Butler, *Writing the Information Superhighway* (Boston: Allyn & Bacon, 1997); M. Joyce, *Of Two Minds: Hypertext Pedagogy and Poetics* (Ann Arbor: University of Michigan Press, 1995); Landow, *Hypertext 2.0;* Murray, *Hamlet on the Holodeck;* and V. J. Vitanza, *Writing for the World Wide Web* (Needham Heights, Mass.: Allyn & Bacon, 1998).

6. Bolter, *Writing Space;* E. Fredin, "Rethinking the News Story for the Internet: Hyperstory Prototypes and a Model of the User," *Journalism & Mass Communication Monographs* 163 (1997): 1–47; Joyce, *Of Two Minds:* Murray, *Hamlet on the Holodeck;* and J. Nielsen, *Multimedia and Hypertext: The Internet and Beyond* (Cambridge, Mass.: AP Professional, 1995).

7. Joyce, *Of Two Minds,* 179.

8. The literatures we review rest, for the most part, on a set of related polarities—between order and chaos, truth and ignorance, facts and opinion, the coherent and the incoherent, the real and the interpretive—related to the portrayal of narrative forms (e.g., the encoder controlled versus the decoder controlled). It is beyond the purpose of this chapter to critique and interrupt this set of polarities, although they bear mention as limitations to the advance of theories of new narrative practices. See B. Dervin, "Chaos, Order and Sense-making: A Proposed Theory for Information Design in *Information Design,* ed. R. Jacobson (Cambridge, Mass.: MIT Press, 1999), 35–57, for a fuller explanation.

9. Bolter, *Writing Space;* Joyce, *Of Two Minds;* Landow, *Hypertext 2.0;* and Murray, *Hamlet on the Holodeck.*

10. Fredin, "Rethinking the News Story for the Internet"; Landow, *Hypertext 2.0;* and Murray, *Hamlet on the Holodeck.*

11. Murray, *Hamlet on the Holodeck,* 136.

12. Bolter, *Writing Space:* and Murray, *Hamlet on the Holodeck.*

13. Murray, *Hamlet on the Holodeck,* 161.

14. Fredin, "Rethinking the News Story for the Internet."

15. Murray, *Hamlet on the Holodeck.*

16. C. McKnight, A. Dillon, and J. Richardson, *Hypertext in Context* (Cambridge: Cambridge University Press, 1991), 54.

17. J. B. Singer, "Changes and Consistencies: Newspaper Journalists Contemplate Online Future," *Newspaper Research Journal* 18, nos. 1–2 (1997): 2–18; and W. S. Williams, "The Blurring of the Line between Advertising and Journalism in the On-line Environment," in *The Electronic Grapevine: Rumor, Reputation, and Reporting in the New On-line Environment,* ed. D. Borden and K. Harvey (Mahwah, N.J.: Lawrence Erlbaum, 1998), 31–41.

18. Williams, "The Blurring of the Line," 31.

19. C. Harper, "Online Newspapers: Going Somewhere or Going Nowhere?" *Newspaper Research Journal* 17, nos. 3–4 (1996): 2–13; and S. E. Martin, "How News Gets from Paper to Its Online Counterpart," *Newspaper Research Journal* 19, no. 2 (1998): 64–73.

20. B. Garrison, "Online Services as Reporting Tools: Daily Newspaper Use of Commercial Databases in 1994," *Newspaper Research Journal* 16, no. 4 (1995): 74–86, and "Online Services: Internet in 1995 Newsrooms," *Newspaper Research Journal* 18, nos. 3–4 (1997): 79–93; and S. S. Ross, "Journalists' Use of On-line Technology and Sources," in *The Electronic Grapevine: Rumor, Reputation, and Reporting in the New On-line Environment,* ed. D. Borden and K. Harvey (Mahwah, N.J.: Lawrence Erlbaum, 1998), 143–160.

21. M. McGuire, L. Stilborne, M. McAdams, and L. Hyatt, *The Internet Handbook for Writers, Researchers, and Journalists* (New York: Guilford, 1997); R. Reddick and E. King, *The Online Journ@list: Using the Internet and Other Electronic Resources,* 2nd ed. (Fort Worth, Texas: Harcourt Brace); C. Rich, *Creating Online Media: A Guide to Research, Writing and Design on the Internet* (New York: McGraw-Hill College, 1999); and M. Wendland, *News in the Next Century: Wired Journalist. Newsroom Guide to the Internet* (Washington, D.C.: Radio and Television News Directors Foundation, 1996).

22. Reddick and King, *The Online Journ@list,* 4.

23. Wendland, *News in the Next Century,* 17.

24. M. DeFleur, *Computer-Assisted Investigative Reporting: Development and Methodology* (Mahwah, N.J.: Lawrence Erlbaum, 1997); B. Garrison, *Successful Strategies for Computer-Assisted Reporting* (Mahwah, N.J.: Lawrence Erlbaum, 1996); and B. Houston, *Computer-Assisted Reporting: A Practical Guide,* 2nd ed. (Boston: Bedford/St. Martin's, 1999).

25. S. Ketterer, "Teaching Students How to Evaluate and Use Online Sources," *Journalism Educator* 52, no. 4 (1998): 4–14, at 12.

26. T. Lieb's online supplement ("Creating Compelling Hypertexts," in *Editing for the Web* [1999], available online at <http://www.towson.edu/~lieb/editing/writing.html>), for example, found only one example of a hypertext story <http://cgi.chicago.tribune.com/tech/frobel/frobsum.htm> on a traditional news site. Likewise, Fredin, in "Rethinking the News Story for the Internet," noted that virtually all online news provides links external to the stories themselves to other, related stories, not hypertext links that form part of the internal structure of the narrative.

27. Simple usability principles guided the redesign of the articles. See A. Dillon, "Designing the Human-Computer Interface to Hypermedia Applications," in *Designing Hypermedia for Learning,* ed. D. H. Jonassen and H. Mandl (Berlin: Springer-Verlag, 1990), 185–195; and J. Nielsen, "Evaluating Hypertext Usability," in *Designing Hypermedia for Learning,* ed. D. H.

Jonassen and H. Mandl (Berlin: Springer-Verlag, 1990), 147–168, and *Multimedia and Hypertext.*

28. B. Dervin, "Audience as Listener and Learner, Teacher and Confidante: The Sense-Making Approach," in *Public Communication Campaigns,* 2nd. ed., ed. R. Rice and C. Atkins (Newbury Park, Calif.: Sage, 1989), 67–86, "From the Mind's Eye of the User: The Sense-Making Qualitative-Quantitative Methodology," in *Qualitative Research in Information Management,* ed. J. D. Glazier and R. R. Powell (Englewood, Colo.: Libraries Unlimited), 61–84, and B. Dervin, "On Studying Information Seeking Methodologically: The Implications of Connecting Meta Theory to Method," in *Information Processing and Management* 35 (1999): 727–750.

29. J. M. Corbin and A. L. Strauss, *Basics of Qualitative Research: Grounded Theory Procedures and Techniques* (Newbury Park, Calif.: Sage, 1990); and M. B. Miles and A. M. Huberman, *Qualitative Data Analysis: An Expanded Sourcebook,* 2nd ed. (Thousand Oaks, Calif.: Sage, 1994).

30. See B. Dervin, "Verbing Communication: A Mandate for Disciplinary Invention," *Journal of Communication* 43, no. 3 (1993): 45–54, for a fuller discussion of the notion of "verbing" communication.

liverpool
JMU

Loan Receipt
Liverpool John Moores University
Library and Student Support

Borrower Name: Jones-Kelly,Meaghan
Borrower ID: **********0112

Technology in human communication /
31111005785801
Due Date: 28/09/2012 23:59

New media :
31111011388368
Due Date: 19/07/2012 23:59

Democracy and new media /
31111010761433
Due Date: 28/09/2012 23:59

Total Items: 3
12/07/2012 16:08

Please keep your receipt in case of
dispute.

Beyond the Global and the Local: Media Systems
and Journalism in the Global Network Paradigm

Ingrid Volkmer

The Internet, with around 407 million users worldwide, has shaped the idea of a global community and has, in its early days, inspired new visions of "world peace" through digital communication,[1] notions of "being" in the formats of new cyberbodies in a new "prosthetic consciousness,"[2] and varying identity modes.[3] In terms of communication and journalism, however, approaches (and visions) that would define new categories and relationships on a global scale, as well as theories of global communication, are still rare. One reason for this lack of inspiration might be the fact that imbalances of Internet access, for which the Organisation for Economic Cooperation and Development (OECD) has coined the term "digital divide," are too profound: the fact that approximately 182.7 million of the 580.7 million Internet users worldwide are located in North America, 185.8 million in Europe, 167.8 million in Asia and the Pacific, 32.7 million in Latin America, and 5.5 million in Africa[4] seems to prove for many critical realists that the Net is dominated by the Western industrialized nations. Utopians who believe in a new global communication infrastructure, a global communication forum, require "hard" data (i.e., facts in addition to visions) for their line of argumentation—and these are hard to find. Although numbers of Internet users have increased tremendously in a variety of world regions, these numbers are still small in relation to the North American Internet-user base. These very basic figures tend to overlook the relationship of the number of Internet users and total population statistics, which reveal "facts" of a different nature: Given these figures, Singapore has the highest Internet-penetration rate worldwide, with 53 percent of households being connected (as opposed to 50 percent in the United States). Korea (42 percent), Taiwan (36.4 percent), Hong Kong (29.2 percent), and China (23 percent) have the highest rate of Internet access per household in Asia.[5] One market showing a sharp increase is China, with around 45.8 million Internet users in 2003. Since the Internet will in the future be accessed not only via home PC but also via mobile gadgets (i.e., mobile phones and Palm Pilots), these analyses ignore completely the potential of the advanced wireless application protocol (WAP) mobile-phone market, which will be available through a Universal Mobile Telecommunications System (UMTS). This non-PC Internet market, so far a small fragment of the overall market, could easily become dominant in those regions where PC usage is limited by a low degree of telecommunication landline infrastructure. Particularly in these so called peripheral countries, mobile phones might (again, in the near future) provide the major access to the global cyberworld, simply because new technology (i.e., satellite Internet distribution) allows an easy convergence to these new emerging mobile or (to use the television terminology) "out-of-home" markets. Given the fact that there are a billion mobile-phone users worldwide[6] (as opposed to the 250 million PC Internet users), it becomes obvious that Internet accessibility will increase tremendously as soon as the out-of-home UMTS market unfolds.

One step toward understanding this new global communication architecture could be to replace the conceptual framework of modern international (i.e., between nations) communication with a new globalized perspective that permits a construction of new communication formats in the global context of interrelated communication structures. In terms of communication and journalism, these do not so much consist in new "cybersocietal" modes or "imperialism," as Herbert Schiller would argue,[7] but in a process of globalizing communication, with new spaces of power and, as Slevin argues, "shifts in the global flow of symbolic goods and in the concentration of symbolic power."[8] Slevin and other critics of globalization, such as Anthony Giddens,[9] claim that "globalization" is a three-way process: "pulling away," "pushing down," and "squeezing sideways."[10] "Globalization," according to Slevin, "'pulls away,' for example, in the sense that the powers once held by agencies of state or large economic organizations have been weakened by global developments. Globalization 'pushes down' in the sense that it creates new burdens and new options for local identities and interaction. Finally, globalization 'squeezes sideways' in that it reorders time and space, cutting across old boundaries and creating new horizontal alliances."[11] Such an approach to modern globalization forgets, that, however, "pulling away," "pushing down," and "squeezing sideways" and other "risk" factors of globalization can, in terms of communication and journalism, involve new opportunities. Giddens's and Slevin's pessimistic perspective is embedded more in a theory of modernization and less in a new globalization approach. This new globalization approach is "intimately related to modernity and modernization, as well as to postmodernity and 'postmodernization'" and concerned with "the concrete structuration of the world as a whole"[12] and I might add, its re-structuring (i.e., by media). It is from this perspective that a new global communication infrastructure becomes visible, one that includes the "global" and "local" as an interesting parallel (or dialectic) globalizing process, which Wilson and Dissanayake describe as "intertextuality"[13] and Featherstone as a new "spatial continuum" between "small relatively isolated integrated communities based upon primary relationships and strong associations of the modern metropolis."[14] In terms of the Internet, these "small communities" are elements of a global communication sphere as well as of a worldwide audience of globally operating (new and old) media monopolies. It is quite interesting to note that aspects of this new global media infrastructure of the Internet were already visible in the push-and-mass-medium television. One example of this paradigm of "intertextuality" in terms of television news journalism is the Cable News Network's (CNN's) *World Report,* a globalized program to which worldwide broadcasters contribute "their viewpoints."

World Report, launched in 1987, is a globally unique news program that consists of reports produced by worldwide broadcasting companies and organizations. CNN airs all programs that are sent in unedited and uncensored. The initial idea was to develop a news program in which many voices around the world could be heard. *World Report* is therefore an interesting open global platform, a microcosm of the "global public sphere" initiated by the push-medium television. The program offers developing nations, still today, in the age of the Internet, the chance to present their points of view on international political and social issues or present topics that are not on the gatekeeping agenda of the big news agencies. Many critics argue that CNN, as a U.S.-based commercial company, uses CNN-style news formats to which contributions have to be adjusted and that the proclaimed "global diversity" is just illusionary. I claim, however, that this program model has inaugurated a unique and interesting news strategy that presents the chance of opening up the otherwise nationally dominated political discourse internationally.

In my content analysis of 397 reports aired on the program,[15] I found that *World Report* is used in crisis regions (such as Cyprus) not only as a global newscast but also as a communication platform to communicate bilaterally with the opposing party (such as on Antenna TV Greece and TRT Turkey). *World Report* is also used as a propaganda forum for totalitaristic nations (Cuba, China), bringing press conferences of national affairs to a global audience. The program is used as a marketing medium and as a communication tool between expatriates and their home countries. My study also revealed that national, regional, international, public, state-owned, commercial, and private broadcasters from all world regions use *World Report* as a carrier program to deliver their reports to "the world." The majority of programs cover political, economic, or military issues, followed by topics in the areas of international aid, human rights, liberation, agriculture/environment, culture, and education.

World Report also reveals new international journalism styles, such as "interactive journalism," in which one report reacts to another news report on the same issue: clearly biased, not objective "reciprocal journalism," in which reports are transmitted back into countries of origin and avoid censorship by airing a report via *World Report* rather than via the station that originally produced it; and finally, "showcase journalism," which includes presentation and marketing of regional cultures.

Players in this microcosm are otherwise unknown news organizations of global political organizations (e.g., UNESCO-TV of the United Nations Educational, Scientific, and Cultural Organization), news bureaus of regional and continental political organizations, and partisan political organizations (PLO-TV, Afghan Media Center, South Africa Now), as well as publicly funded national broadcasters, political and private broadcasters (such as TRT, a Turkish television channel that is owned by Türkye, a Turkish right-wing fundamentalist newspaper), news organizations that operate on the agency level, and also local broadcasters.

Whereas *World Report* can be regarded as a new type of global journalism, the "global" and "local" paradigm of globalization is also represented in other models of international television programming that were developed in the era of new C- and K-band satellite technologies in an increased satellite bandwidth spectrum in the early 1990s. It is the enlargement of program platforms that has been made possible by these technologies that has finally shaped the basic architecture for new programming strategies (in many cases, modeled on CNN's innovative strategy), targeting not international, but a diffuse transnational audience along fragmented special-interest channels.

Not "intertextuality," but "translocality" became the new slogan of television program strategists in the mid-1980s. The global extension of "locality" promised to develop new program markets that were not only for U.S.-based companies, which were then criticized for "imperialism" of the global popular culture. All of a sudden, translocality turned out to be a program strategy for larger national television companies not only in western but also in eastern Europe, in Asia, and in the Arab nations, which began to distribute their "local" programming to communities in western Europe. Their "local" audiences, living worldwide, were able to watch original national Polish or Russian television transmitted via Eutelsat, a noncommercial satellite organization, part of the Eurovision organization and available in Europe and Northern Africa. Italians in the United States are served by original RAI news footage via the Public Broadcasting System (PBS) or DirecTV; Indians worldwide favor Zee-TV, one of the most successful "expatriate" networks worldwide, which offers news and entertainment; Arab communities in the United Kingdom tune in to MBC, the Middle East Broadcasting Centre (the only network that airs prime-time commercials for Lear Jets); most Turkish communities in Germany receive a Turkish state television, TRT, transmitted via Astra, the commercial direct satellite service based in Luxembourg.

Besides providing expatriates with current information on their home countries, translocal television has had a tremendous influence on national politics in a variety of world regions. The impact on the national-statist public sphere of extending political news and information beyond national borders has been obvious in China as well as in the fall of the Eastern bloc. This important impact has been less obvious when TRT encourages Turkish communities in Germany to engage in large-scale demonstrations concerning Turkish Kurd issues or when Al-Jazeera <www.aljazeera.net>, an Arabic, noncensored, CNN-type news channel based in Qatar, one of the most democratic and modern Arab emirates, seems to challenge the conservative politics (and censorship) of neighboring Arab League nations. Being available in Algeria's casbahs, Cairo's slums, and in the suburbs of Damascus, Al-Jazeera, modeled on the BBC, has become a new political voice with Arab nations. As the *Financial Times* commented, "Broadcasting the truth, or the nearest approximation to it, is a new development in the region, shunned by more or less repressive governments from Morocco to the Gulf, but embraced by a steadily growing audience, which reportedly stands at 35 million."[16] The channel is available via satellite in the United States, Europe, North Africa, and the Middle East. Based on these observations, the global and translocal reach of CNN, Zee-TV, and Al-Jazeera and the translocality of a variety of national news programs are changing the conventional terminology of communication theory. The traditional meanings of "gatekeeper" and "news factors" become obsolete. A new translocal reference system of news selection and presentation replaces the domestic and foreign news angle with a global juxtaposition of internal and external perspectives. One could argue that a substantial new "extrasocietal sphere" has been shaped that today influences political and economical processes. This extra-societal new communication structure has been transferred to the push-pull medium the Internet, on which it has gained pace—and autonomy.

The Internet transfers every content segment, each local article into a global arena, in a wide, somewhat diffuse global public sphere. Whereas CNN, Zee-TV, and MBC select particular programs for international distribution in the push-medium television, the push-pull medium makes all content globally available. Such a global forum delineates former borders of news production, which were restricted to local and/or national borders. A local newspaper from Anchorage, Alaska, can be read online in Sydney, Australia, even before the hard copy is dropped on the doorsteps of suburban households in the Anchorage area. This example not only illustrates the insignificance of geographical space but indicates the new potential roles of journalism in such a translocal global public sphere.

Today, globalization goes far beyond the "global" and the "local." I argue that the Net paradigm of the Internet has become a metaphor for a new perspective of globalization. The global network paradigm, a new parallelism of supranational and subnational within a global network of economy, politics, and media, influences media organization and regulation. As Castells argues, "In this realm, the nation-state confronts three major, interrelated challenges: globalization and interlocking of ownership; flexibility and pervasiveness of technology; autonomy and diversity of the media. In fact, it has already surrendered to them in most countries."[17] The environment of this global media network paradigm is fully visible with the Internet, on which regulation and "control" is no longer a matter of nation-states (such as it was for television, at least in some world regions) or even of international organizations, such as the International Telecommunications Union (ITU), which assigns national satellite slots. Organizations such as the Internet Corporation for Assigned Names and Numbers (ICANN) might become a prototype for future extranational and extrasocietal regulatory bodies of the otherwise wide-open field of global communication flow. It is this network paradigm that has created confusion when legislators (of different political systems) have attempted to apply conventional legislative terminology in the context of the global media market and economy, (trans)national content regulation, and censorship practices.

The longitudes and latitudes of this global network have developed new parameters that are relevant for journalism. For a first analysis and definition of media systems and journalism in this global network infrastructure, I suggest the following four models: convergence and coorientation of formats, dialectics of content, self-reference of networks, and mediation of communication flow.

Longitudes in the Global Network: Parameters of Journalism

Convergence Coorientation of Formats

Whereas in 1994, the Internet was regarded either as a peripheral medium in industrialized nations or as an unaffordable medium in developing nations, as well as in the Perestroika Eastern Europe, today almost all countries have began to adapt at least a number of offline media (in most cases print media) to the Internet. This is the case in all European countries, as well as in Asia, Africa, and South America.

According to Netsizer, as of July 2001, 126 million Internet hosts were registered worldwide (as compared with 59 million in July 1999 and 85 million in 2000). Those regions that show the largest numbers of hosts are the United States, Japan, Canada, the United Kingdom, Germany, Italy, the Netherlands, Taiwan, and France. In these countries, convergence has already been completed. Convergence implies in these regions not only the transition of content to a new technology platform, but also different "convergence strategies," that is, methods of reaching particular audiences or user communities (along the lines of "net gain")[18] as well as the organizational transformation of the entire news or program organization.

Whereas in the first years of the Internet, a Net outlet was viewed in the United States as an additional marketing tool for programming, an "ugly sibling," as one *New York Times* journalist reflects, convergence strategies have today become major consultancy fields and require differentiated approaches. In the United States, the *New York Times,* CNN, and major networks have already transformed their entire news production (and news archive) to accommodate digital outlets. Similar developments have commenced in Germany, another country among the top ten host countries. The news magazine *Focus,* the major competitor of *Der Spiegel,* published in Munich, has, similarly to the *New York Times,* built an entire digital company branch. This institutional change seems to pay off and has brought Focus <www.focus.de> to a position as the top news site (in terms of page visits) in Germany. Also in Germany, the MTV-like music channel Viva <www.viva.tv> has launched a fully integrated Web TV program strategy in which the Web is the clear centerpiece and the television channel just one related outlet. Convergence has also developed more differentiated aspects, such as "divergence," which involves a more differentiated, independent content from the original medium, a "vertical" approach into one content segment. This model could apply to NBC, which focuses on sports in its cyberoutlet. Another process within this convergence model can be described as "reciprocal convergence," in which the Internet and the Web influence programs of the original medium. A first step in this process is the inclusion of e-mail in programming (such as CNN's *Q&A*); a more advanced model could be NBC's *Giga* <www.giga.de>, a program that combines MTV-style program segments with the Net and provides information about Web sites, interacts via the Net with its young audience, and reviews Net music and games.

Convergence has, in mature Internet markets, created new competitive fields. Television competes with print media (in both cases text dominates the Web content). Print media (such as the *Boston Globe*) offer video material. Additionally sites that I describe as "micro" news outlets, such as One World <www.oneworld.net> compete with "macro" outlets (i.e., major [commercial] print and television media) in terms of breaking news and "authentic" news coverage. News agencies begin to extend their revenues not just by marketing to news organizations but by tailoring news segments for particular professional customers, such as Reuters <www.reuters.com>. In many cases, audiences and journalists have access to the same authentic material. This applies not only to Western agencies, but also to those of the former Eastern bloc. The news agency TASS, founded in 1904, was renamed in 1992 the Information Telegraphy Agency of Russia (ITAR). ITAR-TASS offers a photo service and a multimedia databank <www.itar-tass.com>. Apart from ITAR-TASS, TASS.net, a special Net branch news agency, was founded during the reform period in Russia, and funded by Sevend, Germany, Poland, and other nations. TASS.net provides three product lines to subscribers worldwide: TASS Infoweek; TASS Newswire, which serves large corporations; and TASS Informatics, an individual message service, which delivers a "discreet" message to "some very hard to reach person" <www.tass.net>.

Those countries where the Internet is currently unfolding in terms of number of hosts, such as Uruguay, Mexico, Poland, Brazil, China, Estonia, Romania, Austria, Malaysia, and Japan, are in an initial convergence stage. Uruguay, with a population of around three million, located between Brazil and Argentina, lists currently only one site in the category "news and media," whereas Uruguay's newspapers and television are still absent on the Web. The only media site available is Falkland Islands and Mercosur News, published by a local news agency called Merco Press.

Mexico, listed by Netsizer as a country with a considerable growth in number of hosts worldwide, represents another model of an "unfolding convergence" region. Television (eight stations have a Web outlet) and radio (four stations use the Web) as well as print media have developed sites. Although eight print media outlets are listed, almost all of them (except one financial service) target tourism. For instance, one online publication, *Novedades de Quintana Roo,* offers a variety of links to various news (local, international) as well as a very detailed list of links for tourists and weather information. Austria lists only five newspapers, one of which, *Der Standard* <www.derstandard.at> can be easily considered a high-quality online version of a newspaper in a conventional information-rich format.

Whereas television, radio, and newspapers in Brazil are not yet fully represented online, magazines in that country seem to use the Internet as a new market. Of the fourteen Brazilian magazines with an online presence, almost half cover cultural and media issues, one focuses on tourism, and only two cover political issues. Another model of convergence might be that presented by the *Times of India* <www.timesofindia.com>, one of fifty-four Indian newspapers online, and Doordarshan <www.ddindia.net>, the national broadcaster, which provide Internet content, targeting primarily expatriates and less the audience in India, where television and film are still clearly the mass media. In countries where the Internet is unfolding, convergence is geared toward a potential international audience, either tourists or expatriates.

Dialectics of Content

Within the framework of the global network, content that represents a variety of view-points can be accessed. In Western, democratic societies, whose political systems believe in "freedom of expression," the global content discourse provides an additional information source that is composed under different circumstances. The possibility that critical content that is suppressed in one country can be located on worldwide servers provides a new political network that began to unfold in the transnational television era (see the discussion of translocal television above) but has been fully unfolded on the Internet.

One example in which these dialectics of content are playing an important role is China. The Chinese government carefully monitors Web sites in Chinese; however, it monitors English-language sites less. This political strategy on the part of the government is already reflected in the topography of Chinese Web sites: Of 11,373 sites dealing with China, the majority (7,360) represent "provinces and regions" and 2,572 cover the topi-cal section "business and economy." Only eighty are related to "news and media." Critical political issues, however, are covered by international organizations (particularly non-governmental organizations) such as Action works <www.actionworks.org>. In such a restricted context, in which access to communication infrastructure is extremely limited and closely monitored, Web sites that allow true interactivity and information exchange have been set up outside the region, for instance, in the United States and Hong Kong, where the Information Center for Democracy and Human Rights is located. One of these sites, that of the Digital Freedom Network <http://www.dfn.org>, publishes the writ-ings of Chinese political prisoners and monitors human rights abuse not only in China, but also in Burma and Bangladesh. "Reciprocal communication" also applies to the use of the Internet by political minorities or opposition groups within a restricted media envi-ronment (Singapore, Malaysia).

Another example in which dialectics of content play an important role involves Ger-many. Right-wing political extremists who are banned from German servers locate their sites on servers in the United States and elsewhere, which shows that conventional regulation of the push medium cannot be applied to the global network arena; nationally blocked sites can be accessed through internationally operating Internet service providers (ISPs) such as America Online (AOL).

Self-Reference of Networks

The Internet has already established dominating networks, or powerful digital networks, as Saskia Sassen would phrase it, that seem somehow to "format" the global public sphere by means of their "branded" presentation mode, their topical selection, their content categories, and the language they use: "Suddenly, over the last few years, the two major actors in electronic space—the corporate sector and civil society—which until recently had little to do with one another in electronic space, are running into each other."[19] It is interesting to note that almost all networks that serve as global models are located in the United States. I describe as "self-reference networks" those networks or media systems that have localized content internationally and are leading models in their markets. These networks have gained their global status by following a variety of different strategies. One strategy is to focus on audience shares in major markets where the networks "anchor" their products, and to expand selected products into peripheral regions. CNN's online edition is a model for this strategy. CNN's online reputation is closely related to its television profile as a twenty-four-hour news machine.

Other networks have developed a strategy for global market dominance that involves localizing content in homogenous formats. One example of a network using such a strategy is Yahoo, which has established itself as a leading global network. Yahoo's portal not only serves as a search engine but combines information sources (for private use and also as business services) with a variety of community and interactive formats. Yahoo's content is locally adjusted (i.e. it provides local links in a global format) and is available in eight European languages (Dutch, English, French, German, Italian, Norwegian, Spanish, and Swedish), as well as in Chinese, Indian, Japanese, and Korean. Local-content sites are also available in Argentina, Brazil, Canada, and Mexico. Another facet of the Yahoo strategy includes "localization" for the prime Internet market, the United States, where Yahoo offers local services in major cities.

AOL, with twenty-six million users worldwide, can be considered another global network; it offers local services in eleven countries. These include the core markets in Europe (Sweden, the United Kingdom, France, and Germany), Australia, Japan, and Hong Kong with a developed Internet infrastructure and the developing regions in South America (such as Mexico and Argentina). Yahoo and AOL, as major global networks, serve as "natural" models for local start-ups, particularly in those regions where the Internet has been developed and is still regulated. In China, for instance, where international investors in the Internet business sector have to cooperate with local companies, these local companies develop sites similar to those of global networks in order to be picked by international businesses as the ideal (i.e., the "natural" partner).

A third strategy employed by global networks to establish market dominance consists in distributing a particular content worldwide. This is the model of news agencies and financial services, such as Bloomberg <www.bloomberg.com> and Reuters. This market niche is currently the most competitive and lucrative journalism sector. The self-reference of these networks is revealed in the fact that their sites are copied in many world regions. In Africa, a portal called "WoYaa!" is modeled after Yahoo; AOL serves as a model for other ISPs, such as "Africa Online" <www.africaonline.com>. Amazon has a Russian counterpart, called "Ozon" <www.Ozon.ru>.

Mediation of Communication Flow

Mediation—the presentation of local content for a world community—can be regarded as another parameter of global journalism and content organization. Mediation journalism seems to provide a new market niche for audiences interested in emerging economies and political transformation processes. Particularly when regions with such economies or undergoing such transformations cannot provide content that meets a globally comprehensible standard, a new type of content fills this niche. One example of such a "mediator" media system is the European Internet Network (EIN), based in Prague, Czech Republic, and Bethesda, Maryland. EIN provides ten online publications that "mediate' politics and the economy in eastern Europe and China for a global audience. Among these online publications are *Russia Today* <www.russiatoday.com>, *Central Europe Online* <www.centraleurope.com> and *Inside China Today* <www.insidechina.com>. The site for each publication contains mostly original and local content, presented in a globally homogenous format. According to user demographics available on its Web site, *Russia Today* is accessed mainly by users in North America (68 percent), less so by those in Europe (19 percent) and in Asia (9 percent), and the least of all by those in Russia (4 percent). *Russia Today*'s users are international professionals interested in information on events in Russia presented in an internationally comprehensible form. Another example of a mediated system is China.com, an Asian transnational portal network based in Hong Kong that provides political and economical information for China, Hong Kong, and Taiwan. Sina.com is yet another example of a mediating site within the global communication infrastructure. Sina.com, founded by Chinese students from Stanford University, regards itself as the provider of news and information about China for the global Chinese audience (including China). The Sina.com portal provides local sites for Taiwan, China, Hong Kong, and the United States. In Africa, WoYaa <www.woyaa. com>, modeled on Yahoo, views itself as a transnational "African internet portal," and its mission is to increase "the visibility of African Web sites and resources." WoYaa's content sections are very similar to Yahoo's, and it offers additional links to all African nations. WoYaa was established by the African Banner Network, a company based in five African capitals and also in three European cities.

Latitudes in the Global Network: Internet Environments

A closer analysis of the different world regions in terms of their Internet use (and their idea of a global public sphere) helps us understand the relevance of the Internet in different media cultures. I propose to characterize these environments in light of overall media structures to determine specific Internet profiles within the specific media setting. Based on this model, at least four basic environments can be identified, each of which reveals a different approach to this technology as well as to its "globality": statist regulatory environments, local-communication environments, hybrid environments, and pluralist-commercial environments.

Statist Regulatory Environments

In statist regulatory environments, the push mass media, such as television and radio, are undergoing the transition from communism to democracy, which requires a transformation of journalistic approaches. Ideas of the "public sphere" are not clearly defined, and the role of media in a democratic society seems to be ambiguous.

This type of Internet environment can be characterized by still strong statist regulation and political influence on media organizations, commerce and content. Russia is an example of a country with this type of environment. Although the Internet market is growing exponentially in Russia, the Russian government attempts to define new strategies for regulation and control. Vladimir Putin's government has already drafted a bill for tight statist regulation of domain name registration. Another bill currently under debate would require the registration of "Internet mass media," targeting those sites "with periodic updating of communications and materials intended for an undetermined group of people." The term "periodic" here refers to updating that occurs more often than once a year.[20] A third strategy of control employed in Russia is the monitoring of e-mail communications.

A second example of profound statist regulation and content surveillance for protectionist reasons is offered by China (as already mentioned above; see "Dialectics of Content"). China exercises a radical protectionism in conjunction with strong state control in its attempts to "regulate" the Internet. The Chinese government restricts access to major international Web sites that contain political news and originate in the United States, such as CNN, *Time,* and the *Wall Street Journal,* among others. (It also restricts access to university Web sites, such as that of the New School for Social Research in New York). Many sites of dissident groups that discuss Hong Kong- and Taiwan-related issues, particularly those located on servers in the United States, are also blocked from access. Chinese news sites (as well as Internet portals) are permitted to use only official sources for political news and information. These are monitored by the Propaganda Department, which bans all original content online and prohibits the use of cyber-reporters. Sites that post other material that has not previously been published are subject to prosecution. The goal of the Chinese government, according to Fravel, is "to push private and foreign web companies out of the content business," which not only is regulated by the government, but—by the same token—is financially supported by it, which demonstrates the "dual" political system at work in the country. In addition to providing this support, the Communist Party (on the local as well as national level) has stakes in online media. The strategy of the Chinese government includes a "double shock of the new"; as Laperrouza remarks, "[T]he technology that China needs to build the most powerful country on earth in the 21st century could also undermine the monolith state itself."[21]

Local-Communication Environments

Local-communication environments can be identified by the low level of technical infrastructure they exhibit. Such environments are located within or on the border of relay satellite footprints of major media environments. The reason that local communication on the Internet has become dominant in these regions is that regular media in the regions do not sufficiently serve these needs. Many of these regions, chiefly located in Africa, are so-called spillover regions, in which television-satellite feeds, targeting major media markets, such as Europe, are available. The feeds contain almost no African content, since they are tailored for Western nations.

Since August 2000, when the last national ISP in Africa was launched in Somalia, all of the fifty-four African countries have had national Internet access. In most African countries the Internet is available at least in the capital cities, and of these only a minority have full Internet connectivity. (In contrast, at the end of 1996, only eleven African countries had Internet access.) Jensen estimates that the total number of permanently connected computers in Africa is about 30,000,[22] and the number of Internet users is thought to be around two million, including the one million estimated users in South Africa.[23] These estimates incorporate the fact that each computer serves roughly three users. The average African computer user is male, English speaking, and educated. Jensen also assumes that "the highest number of users . . . belong[ed] to nongovernmental organizations, private companies and universities."

The local aspect of Internet use in this environment can be ascribed to several circumstances. One is that gaps within communication systems can be bridged by the Internet. This is particularly relevant for professional journalism and community communication, as phone calls to neighboring countries are expensive and, because of the "colonial" routing system, time consuming. Another reason for the role of the Internet in serving local communication needs is the available technology. As Jensen states, "The pricing for international bandwidth has dropped because of greater competition in the sector caused by new supplies from satellite providers and the establishment of new marine fiber cable along West Africa connecting to Europe and Asia."[24] The increased demand for outgoing bandwidth is served (and this might become the crucial technology) by satellite and less by telecommunication. Of the five direct satellite systems available, four are based in Zambia (for example, <www.infosat.co.za> and <www.siyanda.co.za>). As Jensen remarks, "With the exception of some ISPs in Southern Africa, almost all of the international Internet circuits in Africa connect to the USA, with a few to the United Kingdom, Italy and France. However, Internet Service Providers in countries with borders shared with South Africa benefit from the low-tariff policies instituted by the South African telecom operator for international links to neighboring countries. As a result, South Africa acts as a hub for some of its neighboring countries—Lesotho, Namibia, and Swaziland."[25]

E-mail is the major segment of Internet use in Africa. Whereas in the statist regulatory environment, online journalism is regulated by governmental monitoring of original content, media in the local-communication environment have to overcome a variety of technical hurdles, and one major goal is to be represented on the Web at all. Almost every African country has at least one media Web site, the most advanced being those of Cote d'Ivoire, Egypt, Ghana, Kenya, Senegal, South Africa, Tanzania, Zambia, and Zimbabwe. Currently, the Internet is developing increasingly in Kenya, where ten newspapers are already online. South Africa is the most advanced Internet nation on the African continent, bridging the industrial Internet perception with that of developing countries. Whereas South Africa's media have advanced Internet sites, the technical infrastructure supports media in less-developed neighboring countries as well. In addition to national Internet providers, commercially operating transnational providers have been launched. One of the major commercial ISPs is Africa Online, which was founded in 1994 by two former MIT students and operates today in seven countries in southern Africa. Africa Online views itself as a gateway to African Internet content. Each of the content categories it offers, such as "news," "health," "business," "computing," "travel," and "education," lists African sites. Eighty percent of Africa Online users are located in the United States and Europe, which shows that this site serves a "global community" and can be categorized as a mediation system (see above). The "news" section of Africa Online does not offer original news content or content from major news sources (America Online does) but provides a list of those nineteen African countries where at least one media outlet is online. Only the Africa Online home page offers original stories, in some cases written by Africa Online reporters.

To increase Internet access in towns and rural areas of Africa, the International Telecommunications Union (ITU) has developed plans to launch "telecentres," so called shared facilities that will also serve as "multipurpose community telecentres" that will provide Internet access to people in rural and remote areas.[26]

Hybrid Environments

In hybrid environments, media are viewed as part of the national culture, as in Europe. For this reason, nations with hybrid environments regulate their media infrastructure individually. The Internet in European countries is so far unregulated, with commercialization of providers, so that transnational providers are gaining large stakes (AOL is the second-largest ISP in Germany, behind the commercial outlet T-Online of the national provider Deutsche Telekom). Whereas in postcommunist environments, regulation attempts target content, in hybrid environments, the state exercises basic control of content (in terms of banning pornography and politically extremist sites and taking measures for the protection of minors) and also of the new commercial market infrastructure. In many hybrid models, statist regulation also includes other, more technical (i.e., distributional) aspects of the Internet. Five years ago, telecommunication in Europe was entirely a state monopoly. Accordingly, high Internet access rates have slowed the Internet development of the markets in European nations tremendously. With the breakup of the postal, telephone, and telegraph monopoly (for instance, in Germany), commercial telecommunications providers have created technical circumstances that have also influenced the sharp rate of Internet development in Germany, to around eighteen million households being online. An attempt by the German government to raise the copyright fee for makers of equipment that can be used to duplicate "protected works"[27] can be regarded as a new attempt to integrate the Internet somehow into a regulation structure.

Pluralist-Commercial Environments

As opposed to other environments, the pluralist-commercial environment can be characterized as having only basic media regulation. Media in these environments are regarded less as cultural goods and more as commercial enterprises and means to exercise freedom of expression. Because of this approach, the Internet (and related technologies) are commercially exploited and offer a high degree of freedom of information flow. The United States is one example of a pluralist-commercial environment. The technologically available "superhighway" in the United States has initiated a new space for interaction and information as well as commerce. It is interesting to see that on one hand, the commercialization of the Internet in the United States is advanced (all self-reference networks originate in this environment and play a leading role worldwide); on the other hand, information space for political communication is also provided (many of the dialectical sites are located on servers in this environment as well). Online journalism has also been extremely professionalized, given the 6,721 U.S. newspapers and newsweeklies on the Net, as well as 2,378 magazines. In addition to these forms of online journalism, Internet broadcasting, which rarely appears in other environments, is well developed in the United States, thanks to the highly developed technological infrastructure. Newspapers as well as television and radio stations have become strong competitors on the Web. Recent statistics reveal that newspaper Web pages receive more visits than online versions of television networks and stations. It is less the particular online journalism of newspapers that attracts more visits to their Web sites than the access those sites provide to local classified ads. Regulation is also an issue in pluralist-commercial environments; however, "regulation" in this content refers more to commercial regulation via licensing requirements than to content regulation. Pluralist-commercial environments are also characterized by a specific depth of Internet use. This means that the Internet is not only exploited for conventional journalism (such as the television, radio, newspapers that are online): A variety of online-media outlets as well as informal newsgroups are also available. Examples of these are *Slate* and *Salon* as well as "egroups," <www.egroups.com>; the majority of the listed political newsgroups on the latter originate in the United States.

Online Journalism—Global Journalism

Given the global supranational longitude and subnational latitude infrastructure of the Internet, online journalism gains a new role within global networks. Within each of the various Internet environments described, journalism faces specific challenges and obstacles: In the protectionist environment, journalism is censored, and journalists have to develop particular cooperation models between off- and online media. Journalists in the local environment have to overcome technical shortcomings to provide any online outlet at all. In the hybrid environment, privacy protection and other ethical questions are important issues. In the pluralist environment, as the most advanced and multilayered model, issues seem to revolve around detailed and specific aspects of online journalism, such as developing new technical platforms (Web-TV, streaming video) and also around the wider societal impact of online journalism. In both the hybrid and pluralist environments, there is additional competition through news media "layers" of online sites and e-zines. In both of these environments, commercial pressure is high, since online versions are in most cases accessible free and rely solely on the sale of advertising for revenue. To maintain a competitive site on an increasing technical level depends on a high level of investment, which has to be covered by revenues through commercialization.

Yeshua and Deuze detect a variety of ethical dilemmas confronting journalists, particularly with the parallelism of "new" media versus "old" media in the hybrid environment of the Netherlands.[28] The main issues, for the journalists they interviewed, are commercial pressure (i.e., the relationship and overlapping of commercial and editorial content), the use of hyperlinks (i.e., the awareness of hyperlink content and its relation to the editorial content), and accuracy/credibility (given the constant pressure of deadlines). Yeshua and Deuze describe a general mentality among online news outlets than can be characterized as "first we put it online and when it appears to be wrong we take it out." Other issues cited by the journalists they interviewed are sources (i.e., the awareness of source credibility), and privacy, regulation, and newsgathering methods (under the pressure of high competition).[29]

It can be stated that online journalism is global journalism and constitutes a dynamic "global public sphere" in which conventional reference systems of national news presentation, of so-called domestic and foreign angles, are mixed with or exchanged for other topical or political news angles, since each story is distributed worldwide and forms a substantial new extrasocietal public sphere. It is not the globalization of news flow, of converging media and the reformatting of programs to "content," that transforms the global communication infrastructure: Content itself becomes the independent variable in a (global) cybersociety,[30] subsequently replacing the "local," community material and developing communication segments within the global context of interrelating communication structures. This global level is rich in new cross-cultural, cross-societal and cross-national implications. The integration of national public spheres into an extrasocietal global public sphere that requires not only a new terminology of communication analysis but also new modes of "online journalism" marks the transformation into global journalism. Global journalism applies in the network paradigm to a local journalist in Cancun, Mexico, or in St. Petersburg, Russia, as well as to a journalist in Orlando, Florida, or in Cologne, Germany, who provides a small content segment of the global Internet platform. Tools have not yet been developed to connect these segments and defining a new global journalism, of developing a theory of journalism as well of the organization of media systems that provide support. Given the global network infrastructure, as described above, the new "global sphere of mediation," the role of journalists seems to have changed. I suggest the following modes of global online journalism:

- *Contextualization.*   Contextualization involves the presentation of a story in the local context of where it originates, by providing links to the region where the story takes place and presenting opposing local viewpoints. In addition to providing hyperlinks, journalists of the regions in question could contribute their views and moderate subsequent debates.

- *Guidance.*   Given the sometimes ambiguous origin of sources and the need sometimes to rely on unverified sources under the heavy time pressure of instant publication, global journalism should guide used through the sources consulted in constructing a particular story and explain the circumstances of news gathering. Online news is not as authoritative as news of push media. For this reason, a guide through the news-gathering process (and the circumstances under which "authentic" sources operate in crisis regions and protectionist environments) will support the competence of the user to develop her own modes of "truth."

- *Cooperation.*   Parallel to local viewpoints and local online journalism, other formats of content presentation and organization could be developed. For instance, leading international stories could be provided in a portal format that includes all online sources covering the story as well as newsgroups and other interactive platforms. In this model, content becomes the independent variable, and less so the news organization covering the story.

It can be argued that the public (and its opinion) is no longer a substantial element of the political system of one society but has entered into a more or less autonomous global public sphere, a global sphere of mediation, which can be considered not as a space between the "public" and the state but between the state and an extrasocietal global "imagined" community, giving shape to the concept of "being in the world" and of world citizenship. As system theorists assert, the growing density and complexity of communication are signs of a growing "world community." Understanding the new global sphere, its autonomy, its interdependency, and its "mediation" will support the transition into a world community in the twenty-first century: This is the vision.

This approach has to be distinguished from ideas of "internationality," which has its own history. International "public" communication was invented by the regular print of newspapers as early as the seventeenth century in Europe and the United States. This process was accompanied by the rise of the "citizenry," of an informed public, which was interested in international news. The steam engine and Morse's telegraph brought about the professional journalist and the international correspondent, who covered specific international regions. The increasing commercialization and wider circulation subsequently called for a new infrastructure to provide newspaper editors with the commodity "news." The first news "wholesale" agencies, such as Havas (the predecessor of today's Agence France Presse) and Reuter's, were founded in the century. In the second half of the nineteenth century, these agencies quickly entered specific continental markets. The German agency Wolff'sche Telegraphenbureau spread through northern Europe to Denmark, Finland, Sweden, and Russia; Havas expanded into Portugal, Spain, Italy, Romania, and Serbia; Reuter's expanded into Belgium, the Netherlands, Bulgaria, the British Empire, Egypt, Australia, New Zealand, Japan, China and Malaysia.[31]

World wire and cable systems were established in the late nineteenth and early twentieth century by Britain and Germany. By 1912 Great Britain already dominated the world cable system. Transnational media organizations such as Intelsat and Eurovision, founded in the middle of the twentieth century, were the starting point for a now new idea of international communication. International and global commercial media systems characterized the second part of the twentieth century. News and program pools of

national broadcasters of a specific region have formed models of international cooperation, Eurovision, Asiavision (in Asia) and Intervision (in the former Soviet Union) increased transborder exchange of programs. In 1962, the Union of Radio and Television
of African Nations (URTNA) was formed; the Arab States Broadcasting Union was established in 1969; the Caribbean Broadcasting Union was established in 1970; and the
Asia Pacific Broadcasting Union, formed in 1971, supported closer cooperation among
34 Asian nations. International services of the BBC and Deutsche Welle entered into the
field of television.

It was the establishment of internationally operating media systems, such as CNN and
MTV, established not by national broadcasters, but by commercial companies, that finally inaugurated a new age of global communication by distributing the same program
"around the world in thirty minutes," as a CNN slogan impressively stated.

Notes

1. "Negroponte: Internet Is Way to World Peace" (1997), available online at <http://www.
   cnn.com/TECH/9711/25/internet.peace.reut>.

2. Robert Rawdon Wilson, "Cyber(body) Parts: Prosthetic Consciousness," in *Cyberspace, Cyberbodies, Cyberpunk,* ed. Mike Featherstone and Roger Burrows (Newbury Park, Calif.: Sage,
   1995), 239–260.

3. Sherry Turkle, *Life on the Screen: Identity in the Age of the Internet* (New York: Simon and Schus-
   ter, 1995).

4. "How Many Online?" available online at <www.nua.com>.

5. "Internet Users in China Reach 45.8 Million: CNNIC Report," *People's Daily,* July 23,
   2002, available online at <http://english.peopledaily.com.cn/200207/22/eng20020722_
   100150.shtml>.

6. "Mobile Phones To Reach 1 Billion Within 2 Years," *Mobile News,* May 10, 2000, available
   online at <http://uk.gsmbox.com/news/mobile_news/all/809.gsmbox>.

7. Herbert I. Schiller, *Communication and Cultural Domination* (White Plains, N.Y.: International
   Arts and Science Press, 1976).

8. James Slevin, *The Internet and Society* (Malden, Mass.: Polity, 2000).

9. Anthony Giddens, *The Consequences of Modernity* (Cambridge, Mass.: Polity, 1990).

10. Giddens, quoted in Slevin, *The Internet and Society,* 200.

11. Slevin, *The Internet and Society,* 200.

12. Roland Robertson, "Mapping the Global Condition: Globalization as the Central Concept," in *Global Culture: Nationalism, Globalization and Modernity,* ed. Mike Featherstone (Newbury Park, Calif.: Sage, 1990), 15–30, at 20.

13. Rob Wilson and Wimal Dissanayake, eds., *Global/Local: Cultural Production and the Transnational Imaginary* (Durham and London: Duke University Press, 1996).

14. Mike Featherstone, "Localism, Globalism, and Cultural Identity," in *Cultural Production and the Transnational Imaginary,* ed. Rob Wilson and Wimal Dissanayake (Durham and London: Duke University Press, 1996), 46–77, at 48.

15. Ingrid Volkmer, *News in the Global Sphere: A Study of CNN and Its Impact on Global Communication* (Luton, U.K.: University of Luton Press, 1999).

16. "Get the Message from the Gulf," *Financial Times,* Sept. 14/15, 2002.

17. Manuel Castells, "The Power of Identity," in *The Information Age: Economy, Society and Culture,* vol. 2 (Oxford: Blackwell), 254.

18. John Hagel III and Arthur G. Armstrong. *Net Gain: Expanding Markets through Virtual Communities* (Boston: Harvard Business School Press, 1997).

19. Saskia Sassen, "Digital Networks and Power," in *Spaces of Culture, City-Nation-World,* ed. Mike Featherstone and Scott Lash (Newbury Park, Calif.: Sage, 1999), 52.

20. "Russia's Online Media Alarmed by Pending Internet Regulation," *Russian Weekly Journal,* Feb. 14, 2000, available online at <http://www.therussiajournal.com/index.htm?obj=2260>.

21. Mark Laperrouza, online commentary originally posted at <http://www.eviangroup.org>, no longer available.

22. M. Jensen, "The African Internet—A Status Report," Association for Progressive Communications, July 2002, available online at <http://www3.sn.apc.org/africa/afstat.htm>.

23. United Nations Economic Commission for Africa available online at <http://www.un.org/DPT/eca/it.htm>.

24. Jensen, "The African Internet."

25. Ibid.

26. Johan Ernberg, "Universal Access for Rural Development: From Action to Strategies," paper presented at the First International Conference on Rural Telecommunications (Washington, D.C., November 30–December 2, 1998), available online at <http://www.itu.net/ITU-D-UniversalAccess/johan/papers/NTCA_johan.htm>.

27. "Germany Considering Copyright Fee," *New York Times,* September 9, 2000.

28. Daphna Yeshua and Mark Deuze, "Online Journalists Face New Ethical Dilemmas: Report from the Netherlands" (2000), available online at <http://home.pcsw.uva.nl/deuze/publ15.htm>.

29. Ibid.

30. Steve Jones, *Cybersociety 2.0* (London: Sage, 1998).

31. Hansjoachim Hoehne, *Die Geschichte der Nachricht und ihrer Verbreiter* (*History of News and its Distribution*) (Baden-Baden: Nomos Verlag, 1977).

20 Resource Journalism: A Model for New Media

Ellen Hume

The State of Democracy in the Digital Age

In the formerly communist Czech Republic, where democracy is struggling to be born, life is "incomparably better and richer now than it was in times when almost everything was forbidden, and almost everyone was afraid to say aloud what he or she really thought," Czech President Vaclav Havel observed. But "the life of our society . . . has another face," he emphasized, "which we might describe as the relationship of citizens to their state, to the social system, to the climate of public life, to politics. It is our primary responsibility to concern ourselves with this second face, to try to understand why it is so gloomy and to think about ways to brighten it up—at least a little."[1]

The new media technologies, which hold so much promise for empowering citizens, are building new stresses into our democratic discourse. If they were used differently, these technologies could do democracies significant good. More people than ever could get access to information and make their own views heard.

And in a media culture dominated by journalists, some are doing important and coura-geous work, such as the international reporting from Bosnia during the ethnic cleansing of 1993–1996. The use of faxes, videocassettes, and the Internet help keep outlawed democracy movements alive in repressive countries like China.

But in the United States, the world's most important incubator for democracy, these tools are largely squandered. It is the message, not the medium, which is the problem. If the content is wrong, it is wrong in all of its media forms. All the gorgeous streaming video and razzle-dazzle delivery systems won't make it any better for our civic culture. America's media-driven culture is saturated with entertainment, much of it violent. We've cleaned up the air but toxified the airwaves. A mounting body of scholarship demonstrates the deleterious impact some of this material is having on children and on democracy in general.[2]

When it comes to information, citizens now are overwhelmed with its quantity and skeptical of its quality. Fewer journalists and media consumers are separating the important information from the false diversions, and fewer still seem ready to reward the truth. Across the country, a constant stream of issue and candidate advertising on television, on radio, on the Internet, in telephone "push polls" and in the mails deliberately distorts the facts. More media noise has not created more melody. Appearances have become more important than facts. Heaven help the policymaker who doesn't know how to surf the airwaves; officials' effectiveness these days is measured by their media performance.[3]

More sources of information have not improved our "civic face," the joint enterprise we call democracy. In fact, the opposite has happened.

Democratizing the Wrong Information

The easier access provided by today's mass media, particularly radio, television, and the Internet, has democratized extreme hate speech and pornography, making the worst content more prevalent and thus more legitimate. Noxious material that once was walled off in small cul-de-sacs on the information highway—music lyrics, films, and video games that glorify violence and pornography, including sexual attacks on women and children; sadistic and racist comedy routines; talk radio that calls blacks "primates," praises violence against the government, and vilifies Jews and others—all are now available to a mass audience through the old and new media technologies. In some countries, including Bosnia and Rwanda, this kind of material has been used to incite genocide.

But in America, the problem is usually subtler than the direct damage done elsewhere by such extreme messages. American journalists seem to have lost their footing in the new media landscape. When they do navigate the important democratic issues of public or government policy, they often talk in code, concentrating more on strategies and who is winning or losing politically than on what difference it might make to the average American.[4]

Just when we need them the most, journalists who purport to offer veracity and relevance standards for the news seem to be abandoning their mission.[5] With a falsely placed sense of responsibility to report any rumor because it is "in play" in cyberspace, news organizations offer legitimacy to intentionally false attacks that spring up through the Internet and talk radio.[6]

A scandal—any scandal—tends to take priority now over other news, as the networks run in tabloid panic after their fragmenting audiences.[7] Although investigative reporting on real abuses is vital to democracy and journalism, real scandals today seem to be buried in an avalanche of meaningless gossip and unverified attacks. This can be harmful to democracy in at least two ways. First, a frivolous scandal wastes everyone's time and attention. Policymakers, who need to find some public resonance for their work, must divert their attention to fielding whatever rumor might be dominating the day's news. Second, excessive scandal coverage can actually reduce the government's accountability to the public. It is likely that the American people were cool to the Clinton sex allegations not just because the economy was strong and the public wanted to restore a distinction between private and public behavior, but because they were suffering from "scandal fatigue."

Ironically, many journalists genuinely are trying to serve the public interest, reporting the "tough stories" and "difficult facts" in each new scandal. Yet too few editors and producers recognize that serving the public interest is not the same as simply serving what the public is interested in. Just because sex scandals and celebrities are interesting doesn't mean they should replace other news. Similarly, just because the new media technologies enable television to go "live" to show the unfolding drama of a man's freeway suicide, it does not mean that journalists are serving the public interest by doing so.[8]

News organizations that should know better are constantly choosing entertainment, violence, and scandal news priorities over more substantive political discourse—as in, for example, the networks' decision to cut away from the live broadcast of President Clinton's State of the Union address in 1996 to cover reactions to the O. J. Simpson civil-trial verdict.[9] Americans may want to tune in to all the salacious gossip, but they also know that there is more to democracy than celebrity and sex. It's not surprising that the lowest poll ratings these days are the journalists'.

What is lost when all the news arteries are clogged with muck is a flow of information to the public about what their government is actually doing from day to day, as well as information about what real choices they have to shape the nation's future. Most news organizations simply are not trying hard enough to offer political news that is meaningful to people. When offered encrypted political news interrupted by hysterical feeding frenzies, citizens conclude that the political system belongs to someone else and doesn't have any real need for them.[10]

There are notable exceptions to this sorry picture. Television-news executive Carole Kneeland[11] was widely admired for holding her local Austin, Texas, television-news division to a higher standard. She determined that crime coverage wouldn't depend on "can you go live at five?" which had been the previous test at her station. Under Kneeland's management, KVUE reporters got crime and accident news on the air only when it genuinely was relevant to the public. Thus a private tragedy involving a suicide, accident, court case or family violence that did not involve any threat to the public would not normally make it to air. A crime that the public should know about in order to increase its own safety, news about a public figure, or news about patterns, responses, or solutions to crime would meet her broadcast test. Under her leadership, KVUE was number one in its market.

Similarly, many "civic journalism" experiments have helped, in their finest moments, to inform voters and draw communities together to tackle racism, crime, and other problems. Studies of civic-journalism projects in Charlotte, North Carolina, Madison, Wisconsin, San Francisco, California, and Binghamton, New York, concluded that these localized efforts to cover relevant issues from a citizen's perspective made people "think more about politics, gave them a better idea about important community problems, made them want to be more involved in the community, and made them feel more strongly they should vote."[12]

These civic-journalism projects create a critical mass of multimedia coverage and even a temporary "public square" in which citizens can face common problems. In the summer of 1994, for example, the *Charlotte Observer* teamed up with competitors WSOC-TV, the local ABC affiliate, and two local radio stations, WPEG and WBAV, on a project called Taking Back Our Neighborhoods/Carolina Crime Solutions. After using crime statistics to identify neighborhoods that had been hard hit by crime, the news organizations held joint town hall meetings and produced special-issue coverage featuring citizens' proposed solutions. They reported "success stories" about fighting crime. Their collective efforts inspired a burst of civic activity: About 500 people volunteered to help out in targeted neighborhoods. Eighteen law firms helped to file pro bono public-nuisance suits to close down crack houses; a local bank even donated $50,000 to build a recreation center. Crime rates decreased in the wake of all of this civic activity.[13]

The Technology Could Help

The new technologies should make it easier for journalists and others to improve—not weaken—their service to democracy. We journalists used to shrug when people complained about the shallowness of our work by saying "I ran out of space" or "I was on deadline and ran out of time." Now, thanks to the Internet, there are no deadlines, space constraints, or excuses. Journalism can be much more accurate, thoughtful, and complete. A constant deadline means no deadline, so a journalist now has whatever time is needed to check out the facts. And whatever can't fit into the old media container (the print news story or newscast) can be put onto the companion Web site. There is a bottomless news hole.[14]

Yet the new technologies are not being used this way by most news organizations. Instead, we get even more raw "instant" information now that has not been tested for accuracy and relevance. It is time consuming to seek additional information to assess the meaning of a news story and even harder to discover one's options for affecting future developments. Since anyone can throw half-baked material onto her Web site in order to be "first," why do we need journalists at all, if they aren't going to offer the benefits of verification, relevance, and context?

And what, finally, is the marketplace value of that precious "scoop" that so often now trumps the traditional two-source rule? Who broke the Paula Jones story first? The story about O. J.'s bloody glove? The Kathleen Willey story? The fact that Linda Tripp taped Monica Lewinsky's conversations with her? Nobody in the audience remembers. Scoops, which may have mattered when newspapers competed side by side on street corners for each customer through multiple editions a day, have no marketplace meaning to the audience in a constant-deadline, twenty-four-hour news environment.[15]

Scoops matter only to other journalists, as a way of keeping score. This makes no sense in terms of the journalist's long-term survival, and in fact it often has the opposite effect. Throwing accuracy to the winds undermines the credibility of the news brand. Better to build the brand by offering a consistently trustworthy, accessible place to go for news.

There are, of course, all the "quality" channels emerging on cable, from CNN and MSNBC to A&E and Discovery. Do they have a "public service" mission or just a neat marketing niche? Test the democracy quotient by asking: How much of this new channel is taken up with pundit score keeping, celebrity gossip, and voyeur crime news, issue-free animal features, sports, entertainment, and weather programs? The transformation in particular of MSNBC from a promising television/Internet laboratory into a scandal news service has been disheartening. Neil Postman's lament that we are "amusing ourselves to death" has never seemed more accurate.

David Fanning, senior executive producer of PBS's *Frontline* documentary series, described recently to the *New York Times* how difficult it is to place a hard-hitting documentary these days: "I was once told by someone at Discovery that they would not do a film on human rights in China because then they would not be able to film pandas there," he said. In response, Michael Quattrone, the Discovery Channel's senior vice president and general manager, said that a film on Chinese human rights would not fit with Discovery's mix of programs. He said he found it unlikely that anyone at Discovery would use the panda excuse. "We make programming which is as credible and informative as possible, while being entertaining, but with a subject matter that people expect to find on Discovery. I make no apologies for concentrating on science and natural history. There is some great stuff in there."[16]

Public and Private Are Reversed

One reason that democracy isn't being served well by the new media outlets is that our popular culture has been turned inside out. What should be private is now becoming public, and what should be public is being privatized. Our recent obsession with the president's sex life, for example, is an intrusion into something most people believe should remain his own business. Journalists' self-righteous "outing" of officials' sexual adventures has to be blamed to some extent on the falseness of politics to date (the phony "family values" candidates who can't wait to run off with their mistresses) and on the broader culture in which the journalists are operating. Thanks to the confessional Jerry Springer and Laura Schlessinger talk shows on television and radio, we now have a culture saturated with perverse revelations exposed as voyeur entertainment. If there were commensurate reporting on the sex histories of prominent Washington journalists and media executives, it would reveal a fair number of boss-employee adulterous affairs and perhaps even a few intern seductions.

Veteran newsman Robert MacNeil argued before 9/11 that substantive "issue" news was less interesting to people because there were no major overriding public policy problems such as the nuclear threat during the Cold War. Now, however, we face far-reaching shifts in foreign policy, domestic surveillance, and other anti-terrorist activities, and in our own posture toward the rest of the world. Why isn't there a better public debate about all of these deep challenges to America's traditions?

The private has taken on too much national importance, whereas the public has lost the attention it deserves. Antigovernment activists use the word "public" as a pejorative, equating it with the word "government." The word "public" actually means "of the people." It would be helpful to restore this core definition if we are to build digital public squares and honor democracy as a common responsibility and goal.

Getting the Point: Resource Journalism

It is time for a new model for news, a multimedia model relying on objective, independent journalism that better serves democracy than today's journalists normally do. My proposed new model—"resource journalism"—draws especially on the flexibility offered by the new digital technologies and on lessons learned from watching local and national television news, the magazine and pundit shows, the Internet, and the civic journalism experiments.[17]

Resource journalism attempts to offer thorough but unbiased reporting, assembling for citizens the authentic information they need to make civic choices. It seeks to enlist not only the traditional charms of television, radio, and print, but also the interactivity and depth afforded by the Internet. Resource journalism provides historical context as well as local, national, and international reference points and tries to answer the question "Compared to what?" It tries to respond to the question "Why does this matter to the average American?" Resource journalism works to combine news about problems with news about a range of potential solutions to those problems, but it does not seek to encourage any particular action. Through carefully curated Web sites, resource journalism tries to offer a relevant selection of deeper information resources, a range of clearly labeled, diverse opinions, and interactive access points for citizens who may want to get involved.

Clearly, not every breaking news story can be spun into all of these forms. But a thoughtful news organization could divert some of the time, talent, and money now spent on chasing the entertainment side of politics and culture to assembling an updatable set of interactive multimedia resources about the top ten issues that will shape our nation's future.

It doesn't have to cost a lot of money. In fact, resource journalism was developed by PBS's Democracy Project in the spring of 1997, when the project was presented with the need to cover, with limited resources, the prospect of unlimited daily congressional campaign finance hearings in both the Senate and House. If PBS offered the traditional live daily feeds of the hearings to its participating stations, C-SPAN-style, few stations would have preempted what has become very important daytime programming for families and schools: *Sesame Street, Magic School Bus, Arthur, Wishbone,* etc. More importantly, few people would actually have watched these hearings as they stretched through the entire workday. (C-SPAN and MSNBC were expected to offer daily hearings feeds for the tiny minority who might do so.)

What could be a better way for PBS to serve the busy adult who should have access to more than the brief nightly news coverage of the hearings? We determined that a weekly highlights show would be the most accessible and cost-effective approach. But we wanted to be sure the content was truly useful, that the series was more than just insider scorekeeping or theater criticism. We saw our news colleagues assessing the opening hearings according to the wrong measurements—by whether or not Senate Committee Chairman Fred Thompson had a smoking gun, a great television show, or a presidential campaign.

Our different approach, a twenty-four-week half-hour series, *Follow the Money,* started each broadcast Friday night with a documentary-style highlights tape of the week's hearings in both houses. We had "tour guides" who were encouraged not to prattle as pundits, but rather to provide citizen-oriented insights into what the hearings were telling us about money and politics in America. We surrounded this news summary with history minidocumentaries (George Washington plying his voters with rum-laced bumbo), field reports on what citizens were thinking and doing about the issues the hearings were raising, news about a range of reform efforts, a soapbox of citizen and expert viewpoints, and other features.

We reached out to partners to expand the impact of the project and offer more resources to our viewers. There were spin off radio discussions on National Public Radio's *Talk of the Nation,* thanks to Ray Suarez, who was host of both the television and radio shows. Our Web site created much of the series' interactivity, providing viewers with a chance to make their comments for others to see online and to answer the "question of the week" posed by the television hosts, who then reported back some responses on the next television program. It also assembled an archeological trove of related resources, providing not just the transcripts of all the programs in the series, but HTML point-and-click access to layers and layers of specific information about money and politics generated by such research groups as Public Campaign and the Center for Responsive Politics. There was a reform game, Destination Democracy, invented by the Benton Foundation, to navigate each Web visitor through the likely changes each reform option would entail. For those viewers who wanted to know how they could get involved, we offered click-through access to the Web sites of such groups as Common Cause, which favored the McCain-Feingold reform legislation, and the Cato Institute, which opposed it. We offered insights from historians, including a congressional expert from the Library of Congress, and signed opinion columns. The Capitol Steps comedy troupe provided real-audio comic relief.

Lacking any advertising funds or coverage in the "free media," we generated a core audience for the television show and Web site through national civic groups. At a series of hastily organized meetings, we invited the Washington representatives of those grassroots organizations that had some interest in the issues of campaign finance to use their list-servs, e-mail, Web sites, newsletters, and phone banks to invite their members to watch and critique the show.

Ultimately, our *Follow the Money* audiences were relatively small but actively engaged in feedback and Web discussions prompted by the series—a desirable audience model for the niched media landscape. We had compliments from all across the political spectrum: the National Rifle Association as well as liberal groups and ordinary citizens who don't align themselves with any particular ideological camp. They liked the efforts at fairness and comprehensiveness. They liked the doors we opened for citizens to put themselves into the action. They loved the attempt to bring history and humor into the unfolding scandals and also the pairing of problem news with solution news.

There has been some concern, as PBS has experimented with such multimedia projects, that the Internet Web sites might divert audiences from the television programs. But PBS has found that many viewers are online at the same time as they are watching television, using both at once. *Frontline,* PBS's documentary series, has pioneered separate but complementary "webumentaries,"[18] as well as a moving Webmarker bug along the bottom of the screen that prompts viewers to go to PBSOnline for more information about the subject of the program. When *Frontline*'s Whitewater documentary program "Once Upon a Time in Arkansas . . ." used the Webmarker bug just as it was getting into the details of the Castle Grande investments, thousands of people hit the Web site at that particular moment. *Frontline*'s "Jesus to Christ" series in 1998 similarly drew so much Internet traffic that it temporarily overwhelmed the PBS server.

For the fall 1998 elections, PBS applied the "resource journalism" model to two special projects. In early October we had PBS Debate Night, featuring a live national congressional leadership debate hosted by Jim Lehrer, broadcast from the historic House of Burgesses in Colonial Williamsburg. Before and after that debate, on the same night, local PBS stations conducted local congressional candidate debates. The Web sites offered voting records, interest group scorecards, issue summaries, biographies, campaign donation information, and other background on the candidates.

A week later, we had a one-hour national PBS documentary, "The 30-Second Candidate," on the history of political advertising in America, including a look at how ads were shaping some 1998 campaigns. Participating local stations did "ad watches" during regular news programs or as interstitial messages between programs, providing fact checks, funding sources, and other contextual information. Perhaps most valuable were the "ad watch" Web sites, which offered the information that voters needed to get beyond the ads, including voting records, issue positions, financial backing, and news coverage of the races. Educational materials were developed so that schools could use the "ad watch" project as a critical viewing tool as well as a political science project. These projects all carried the hallmarks of resource journalism, including complementary local and national news, interactive background information that is useful to citizens, a citizen soapbox, and educational tools.

PBS is not the only media provider making efforts to harness new media technologies to serve democracy. But at the national level, it remains a lonely fight. The television cable channels and broadcast networks seem to be retreating from their moral responsibility to offer bread as well as circuses. "Our national adventure is taking a wide and dangerous turn. We are entering an age when problems are deep-set and government cannot necessarily provide the answer, when citizens need to claim a place at the table or watch the table get spirited away, when democracy will either become a willed achievement or a sentimental dream," concludes Jay Rosen of New York University. "Journalists should not huddle together in the press box, wondering how the story will come out. They need to rejoin the American experiment."[19]

PBS's Democracy Project invites others to offer models for news that better serve our nation's civic life. We hope that many will join the attempt to create a multimedia "public square" for American democracy, a source of updated information, discussion and decision-making that offers citizens real opportunities to participate in their own governance.

Even modest efforts can have ripple effects. As James Baldwin once observed, "Words like 'freedom,' 'justice' and 'democracy' are not common concepts; on the contrary, they are rare. People are not born knowing what these are. It takes enormous and, above all, individual effort to arrive at the respect for other people that these words imply."[20]

Notes

1. Vaclav Havel, "State of the Republic," address to the Czech Parliament, February 1998.

2. See Kathleen Hall Jamieson's works and Sissela Bok, *Mayhem* (Reading, Mass.: Addison-Wesley, 1998).

3. Harvard sociologist Kiku Adatto recounts, for example, how during the 1988 campaign, Sam Donaldson of ABC News faulted Democratic candidate Michael Dukakis for not playing his

trumpet in camera range, measuring this as an example of his unfitness as a presidential candidate. See Kiku Adatto, "Sound Bite Democracy," research paper, Shorenstein Center on Press, Politics and Public Policy, Harvard University, June 1990.

4. Kathleen Hall Jamieson has written extensively about this problem. In particular, she has mapped the way this "strategy" formula distorted network television and newspaper coverage of the Clinton health-care debate in 1994. Kathleen Hall Jamieson and Joseph N. Cappella, "Newspaper and Television Coverage of the Health Care Debate," Annenberg Public Policy Center paper, August 12, 1994.

5. For a lengthy examination of this point, see my "Tabloids, Talk Radio and the Future of News," monograph, Annenberg Washington Program, 1996.

6. Examples are rampant. The *Miami Herald's* Tom Fiedler recalled, at a June 10, 1988, conference at Harvard's Shorenstein Center on the Press, Politics and Public Policy, how during the 1988 campaign, a *Newsweek* editor justified the printing of rumors about Gary Hart's sex life (before the celebrated Donna Rice townhouse story, which the *Herald* broke): "When *Newsweek* was asked about that later, why they chose to report the rumor which they hadn't substantiated, the answer was . . . that the rumor itself reached such crescendo level that it had achieved a critical mass of its own. It had somehow become reality. The rumor had gotten so large that it was reality. So therefore the press was justified in printing it."

7. Even scandals that prove to be untrue make big news stories. The syndicated television magazine *Inside Edition* on May 4, 1998, featured charges that Cristy Zercher, a former flight attendant, was groped by President Clinton on a 1992 campaign flight. On May 5, the show offered a "world television exclusive," outlining how Zercher "failed miserably" a lie detector test administered on behalf of *Inside Edition*. The King World vice president in charge of the show concluded, "There's a 99 percent probability that she's not telling the truth." In a last-minute change, he decided to reveal in the final minute of the May 4 report that the next program, on the following night, would show the charges to be false. As Howard Kurtz of the *Washington Post* asked, in reporting on this, "Why air the story at all?" The answer from King World Vice President Marc Rosenweig: "You have to set up the premise of what her story is in order to thoroughly examine the results."

8. When this gory incident was shown on live television in Los Angeles on May 1, 1998, preempting cartoons watched by children, one Los Angeles television station representative compared the criticism of his live broadcast to support for "censorship." Others argued that the unfolding suicide had tied up freeway traffic and that this justified the high-priority live news coverage.

9. At least ABC's Sam Donaldson regretted his network's decision on May 4, 1998, not to carry President Clinton's last news conference live, the way CBS and NBC did: "There are some events that major news organizations have to cover, even if it's unlikely that news will happen," he said in Howard Kurtz, "Flight Attendant Tale Lands with a Thud," *Washington Post,* May 5,

1998, C1. One wonders what the president would have had to do to meet Donaldson's standard for "news." Donaldson covered the Clintons' then-recent trip to Africa by implying that they were there only to "duck the executive privilege controversy." Thus the sex scandal was his news frame for even this historic and long-planned presidential trip.

10. Markle Commission on the Media and the Electorate, New York, "Key Findings," May 6, 1990.

11. Kneeland, who also helped to innovate television "ad watches," died of cancer in 1998 in the prime of her career.

12. "New Civic Journalism Research," *Civic Catalyst* (Winter 1997), available online at <http://www.pewcenter.org/doingcj/civiccat/displayCivcat.php?id=107>.

13. Ed Fouhy, "The Dawn of Public Journalism," *The National Civic Review* (Summer–Fall 1994): 263.

14. When PBS's *Frontline* runs a moving "bug" prompting viewers to go to the PBS Web site for more information, the flood of hits is enormous. At least twice, the instantaneous response has crashed the overwhelmed PBS server.

15. One could argue that there is still a place in financial and weather news for timely "scoops," since each is so time sensitive.

16. Louise McElvogue, "Tough Documentaries Are a Tough Sell on TV," *New York Times,* April 13, 1998.

17. The Pew Center for Civic Journalism in Washington, D.C., has numerous publications and studies that map the positive civic impacts, the pitfalls, and the still uncertain effects of "civic journalism" experiments around the country.

18. David Fanning, the impresario who created *Frontline* and led it to win the Gold Baton at the duPont Columbia Awards in January 1998, has copyrighted this wonderful term.

19. Jay Rosen, *Getting the Connections Right* (New York: Twentieth Century Fund, 1996), 6.

20. James Baldwin, "The Crusade of Indignation," in *The Nation,* July 7, 1956.

21 What Is Information? The Flow of Bits and the Control of Chaos

David Sholle

The social sense making surrounding the new information technologies is diverse and contested, but the terms of this debate are becoming circumscribed within the general notion that we have become an "information society." This discourse, in all its varieties, is shaping our very conception of the new technologies. At first glance there seems to be a set of beliefs that underpin this discourse: an economic philosophy that posits information as the source of value in a global economy; a business logic that focuses on the accumulation, production, and management of data; media claims that availability and access to information technologies represent an increase in choice and freedom; political projections that computer-mediated communication networks can solve the problems of democracy in the United States; and a quasi-religious hope that technology can save us from our own excesses.[1] Although this discourse is rooted in the mythos of democracy, at the same time powerful interests are producing an immense infrastructure of technologies that will determine access to the new media and the manner in which information resources are allocated.

Pronouncements on the promises and dangers of the new information technologies (the information infrastructure, Internet, digital imaging, virtual reality, etc.) now saturate our society's public discussion, and the ideological debates surrounding the use of these technologies will be instrumental in determining the direction that public and private agencies take in developing an information infrastructure. This discourse does not circulate in the sphere of "culture" as a disarticulated set of ideologies but rather is linked with the material practices of technological, scientific, and economic formations. These material practices and discourses are significantly tied together in the attempt to define and explain the contemporary social formation as "an information society." This chapter is part of a larger project that will attempt to analyze this discourse in its various locations. I do not propose to present a comprehensive analysis of the discourse of the "information society" in all of its locations and trajectories. Here I will examine this "information society" discourse in its contemporary manifestations through analyzing the particular construction of the concept of "information" itself within the particular institutions of the information sciences and economic theory, not in order to examine the concept of "information" as a purely scientific term, but rather to trace how this concept of "information" is taken up in the discourse on "the information society."

Theories of the information society propose various analyses for why this designation fits contemporary society: the widespread development of informational technologies, the percentage of economic activity devoted to the processing and distribution of information, the shift to an occupational structure dominated by information work, the emergence of networks that redefine spatial arrangements through the flow of information, the saturation of the cultural environment with media representations, etc. None of these theories can do entirely without a conception of information and the construction of knowledge as meaningful activities that provide for decision making, symbolic representation, emotional intensity, and conceptual analysis.

In fact, the information society is being sold to the average citizen as providing access to knowledge, meaningful dialogue, and information essential to everyday decision making. But at the same time, even within the marketing of the information society, the actual nature of the information and knowledge produced and distributed by information technology remains abstract and underdefined. Instead, government and corporate pronouncements focus on the sheer power of the network, on the technological magic of information machines, on the overall capacity of the system, on the abstract phenomenon of "being digital." One needs only to examine the shift in advertising about the Net to see this. When interest in the Internet first developed, corporations such as Microsoft ran ads depicting kids learning and playing, people emoting and connecting. In a few short years, Net ads have shifted to depictions of complex circuitry with information represented as a glowing dot traveling through space and time within the networks of global capitalism. As a Sprint ad claims, the point of contact is upping one's profits through the control of abstract flows of information.

The argument of this chapter is that both academic and political/economic discourses on the information society are fed into the instrumental projects of developing a technological infrastructure and instituting economic practices for controlling the exchange of informational products. As such, these projects operate with a conception of information that brackets its meaning, while allowing "information as meaning" to remain as an unspoken background that seeps into their discourse. This discourse and the practices to which it is connected have profound implications for how the new technologies will be utilized.

"Information" as Keyword

The use of the word "information" as a descriptive adjective has exploded to the point of near absurdity: information age, information society, information economy, information superhighway, information millennium, information revolution. But what does this word "information" mean in these constructions, and how did it become the new keyword of our social formation's self-definition? At first, it appears that the definition of "information" is clear and unproblematic: we all know, in common sense, what it is. But immediately it becomes evident that we can't exactly specify the term in its everyday usage and that the term is being used in some other way when attached to the words "society," "age," etc. In fact, it appears that "information" is either used too ambiguously, as a collection place for multiple significations that are generated in the application of the term to a bewildering range of different practices, or that "information" is used too precisely, that is, that its meaning becomes attached to narrowly specific technological functions, such as those generated in the field of information science or engineering.

As Machlup has noted, the original meaning of the word "information" derives from the Latin *informare,* which means "to put into form." "Informing" therefore carries the sense of "imparting learning or instruction" or more generally conveys the sense "to tell (one) of something."[2] Thus, "information" refers to the action of informing or to that which is told. These meanings of the term are carried along with it wherever it occurs and are the basis of our commonsense notions of "information." As Webster points out, the semantic definition of information conveys that "information is meaningful, it has a subject, it is intelligence or instruction about something or someone."[3] When we talk of an "information society," it is these connotations of "information" that we would expect to be discussing. It is this commonsense definition of information, however, that is sidestepped in the fields of cognitive science, information theory, cybernetics, and the like. Here, information does not have a semantic content. In other words, the dominant conception of information within the technical, scientific, and economic institutions that are instrumental in defining "the information society" is one in which information is emptied of any relation to "meaning." Within the limits of specific disciplines, this nonsemantic use of the term "information" is, at times, carefully circumscribed, but each of these fields undergoes an extension in which it applies itself to processes in which the semantic definition of information normally holds sway. This creates a confusion of levels, one in which meaningful activities are reduced to nonmeaningful ones. In each of these disciplines the term "information" is applied metaphorically to processes that involve a flow, an impulse, and so on. But it seems unavoidable that some of the "meaning" component of the term "information" carries over into the characterization of the processes. This can be compared to the circular reasoning that occurs in some work in artificial intelligence. The mind and computer are defined in a circular loop: The computer thinks like the human mind, the human mind is like a computer. Just so, in the information sciences, phenomena such as activating impulses and signal transmissions are analyzed as informational. Then the feedback loops, binary switching, etc., of these machine actions are used to analyze the semantic informational processes of human communication. I want to be clear that I am not claiming that there are no interconnections between these phenomena, nor that the commonsense definition of "information" is somehow superior. Rather, the problem is the way in which "information" itself becomes a master concept. I will argue that these definitional ruminations are not insignificant quibbling but rather are crucial to the formation of the "information society," since the very conception and forging of this construction is rooted in the technological and economic formation of a conjuncture of sciences united through the model of information processing. Again, I am not proposing that all informational sciences can be lumped into a corporate-driven project, nor that abstract or metaphorical applications of the term "information" are not useful. After all, the extension of concepts into new domains can fruitfully open up unseen connections that advance the diversity of knowledge. What I am examining is how easy it is to elide the metaphorical nature of concepts and to begin to unreflectively apply them to diverse phenomena in a way that truncates rather than expands our understanding.

To get a handle on the usage of "information," we need to situate the term historically within the forces of technology and language that have constructed it as the linchpin of our present social, political, and economic terrain. We first need to recognize that historically, "information" holds little significance in Western history as a term of broad definitional power. Western philosophy, for instance, foregrounds "knowledge" as its keyword within the broader project of epistemological grounding (tied to the material projects of the domination of nature and the conceptualization of the human individual as juridical, political, and economic subject). "Information" emerges as a keyword only in the mid-twentieth century as industrial capitalism grapples with the incorporation of "intelligence" into its machine tools and the production of consumption through the "intelligence gathering" of marketing and as modern scientific thought re-forms itself around the technology of the computing machine. Within the context of these economic and technological developments, the stance toward epistemological questions shifts away from preoccupations with referentiality, transcendental grounds, and rational synthesis toward the project of building a cognitive science in which the concern is not with representation *by* knowledge but representation *of* knowledge.[4] Although, as we will see, there are connections between cognitive science, information theory, and cybernetics and philosophies of mind dating as far back as Descartes, we should not underestimate the significance of the influence of these "information processing" fields on the reconceptualization of information and knowledge.

Defining Information

Why have we become an "information" society? Why not a "knowledge" society, an "intelligence" society, an "understanding" society, a "communication" society? We should consider that it may not be helpful at all to distinguish among these terms in the first place. It may be that the territory that they enclose is better seen from another territory outside of this sphere of the projection and reflection of the mind. That being said, the information sciences have continually distinguished between information and knowledge. Generally, "information" and "knowledge" are distinguished along three axes:

1. *Multiplicity.*   Information is piecemeal, fragmented, particular. Knowledge is structured, coherent and universal.
2. *The temporal.*   Information is timely, transitory, even ephemeral. Knowledge is enduring and temporally expansive.
3. *The spatial.*   Information is a flow across spaces. Knowledge is a stock, specifically located, yet spatially expansive.

In summary, information is conceived of as a process, whereas knowledge is a state.[5]

It can be seen that within this model the assumption is that information is the building block underlying the process of knowledge construction. Information is elemental and takes up a position akin to energy in the discipline of physics. It is this discovery of the elemental nature of information within a complex range of phenomena that serves as the self-defined originary moment of the development of the information sciences.

The Conjunction of Sciences

Sometime in the period immediately following the Second World War, "information" became the key term that united a diverse number of technical and scientific disciplines: biology, cognitive science, information science, computer science, the psychology of the brain, physics, economics, etc. The exact historical development of the conjuncture of sciences around the term "information" has not yet been precisely located. Some scholars believe that the origins of this conjuncture were first formulated (in the 1930s) within the discipline of symbolic logic, which reoriented logic away from concerns with the material representation of reality toward a focus on purely formal criteria and rules. As Pylyshyn notes "this work made precise the notion of formal mechanism or a mechanism or process that functions without the intervention of an intelligence or any natural being and yet can be understood without knowing about any of its physical properties. In making this notion precise, these studies laid the foundations for a way of conceptualizing a wide range of problems in many different areas of intellectual endeavor—from philosophy of mind and mathematics to engineering, and including almost every facet of social and biological science."[6]

But the real takeoff of these disciplines required the intervening necessity generated by economic and political forces surrounding World War II and its aftermath. It is no coincidence that the same scientists who formulated the various information sciences and proposed the primacy of information as the linking element within all formal mechanisms were directly or indirectly involved in the war effort and in the development of the resulting technologies for peacetime economic practices. It is to these pivotal disciplines that I now turn.

Cybernetics   Cybernetics, as conceived by Norbert Wiener in the 1940s, is a master science founded on the issues of control and communication. It is concerned with self-correcting and self-regulating systems, be they mechanical or human, and most importantly posits that the functioning of the living organism and the operation of the new communication machines exhibit crucial parallels in feedback, control, and the processing of information.[7] Cybernetics has evolved into a field of competing interpretations, some of which attempt to construct open systems. The strain of cybernetics taken up by the dominant economic and scientific institutions, however, has produced, at best, a contradictory stance toward open systems. The glowing utopian image of this cybernetics, with its claim of two-way reciprocal interaction, is belied by its conceptualization within "human engineering," "focusing on mechanisms of steering, governing, or control."[8]

This shift to an emphasis on control is evidenced in the success of cybernetic conceptualizations in the development of military targeting and communication machines that were extended to other spheres of broader significance. For example, cyberneticist C. H. Waddington, "facilitated a general transference of methods associated with operations research in military organizations to the emergent field of molecular biology, where a new image of the body as an information-driven communications system was already beginning to take hold."[9] This extension of cybernetics fit well with Wiener's overall goals. As Roszak notes, "Wiener was claiming nothing less than that, in perfecting feedback and the means of rapid data manipulation, the science of cybernetics was gaining a deeper understanding of life itself as being, at its core, the processing of information."[10]

To serve as the basis of cybernetics, information must be conceived as discrete bundles, physically decontextualized and fluidly moving. For ultimately the control processes of complex systems are a matter of regulated feedback, which requires that processes of communication be conceived of as exchanges. (This serves as the basis for the notion of a cybernetic capitalism, a capitalism dependent on the control of exchanges at their molecular level.) Within this cybernetic model, feedback is not free and equal; rather it is governed by the system's constant battle with entropy, chaotic disorganization, or noise.[11] Thus, information becomes a means of mapping space and time through the control of communicative feedback, a defining characteristic of information that we will see repeated in other disciplines such as economics and communication science. Further, economic and life processes are brought together as formally ruled by the same information processes, equally part of a natural system of spatial and temporal flows.

Systems Theory   Systems theory begins in application to mathematical modeling but eventually is proposed as an extensive model encompassing cybernetics, information science, and indeed all other disciplines. Most significant for this analysis is the manner in which systems theory has been applied to the social sciences. Within the systems theory view, one major model of information is what Langlois calls the "oil-flow" model.[12] In this model, information is seen as an undifferentiated fluid that courses through society's communication circuits. This fluid gets stored in a tank, the contents of which we can then measure as the amount of knowledge a society has. This tank then serves as a reservoir for control.

Within systems theory (as within cybernetics), information and control are closely related concepts. As Finley notes, "the role of systems knowledge practices is to find order in the world, to find universal laws that circumscribe the system, and never to yield to the appearance of chaos."[13] This view obviously has resonated with those who see information infrastructure as a means of increasing the capacities of corporations to monitor and control the market (the measure of their knowledge). In fact, we shall see that information economics derives its terms from systems theory and the other information sciences.

In contradistinction to its model of information as commodity, it also treats information as a lubricant that functions within the feedback mechanism through which markets are controlled. But as Giddens notes, the model of feedback derived from general systems theory is inadequate for dealing with the self-regulation of human action: "A specific version of cybernetic information control has quite recently been introduced into the social sciences by Parsons. Here it is assumed that hierarchies of control can be discerned in social systems, in which the controlling elements are values, with social, economic relations. . . . But, values cannot anyway serve as 'information regulators' in the sense which is demanded in systems theory: as control centers which process information so as to regulate feedback."[14] For Giddens, systems theory reduces the self-reflexive monitoring of action among human agents to principles of teleology that function within mechanistic systems.

As Langlois points out, this reduction in systems theory is tied to the oil-flow model of information. Contrary to this model, he posits that information is not homogeneous: "meaning is a matter of form not of amount; and the value or significance of a message depends as much on the preexisting form of the receiver as on the message itself. Information is stored as knowledge in a system not as oil is stored in a tank, but by virtue of the change that information makes in the very organization of the system itself."[15] Such a model of information would imply that disorganization is an integral process within the very formation of knowledge, because if nonmechanistic change is an inherent factor in organization itself, then the disruptive potential of chaos is also ever-present in the system.

Computer Sciences   A similar approach to information has developed within the parallel fields of computer science, informatics, and the specific areas of cognitive science that approach artificial intelligence from the perspective of computation. Cognitive science is "the domain of inquiry that seeks to understand intelligent systems and the nature of intelligence," and it does so through an analysis of the human mind in terms of information process.[16] Philosophical arguments about the nature of knowledge are mirrored in the cognitive sciences. As Gardner notes, the classic arguments between rationalists (for whom the mind exhibits powers of reasoning that it imposes on the world) and empiricists (for whom mental processes either reflect, or are constructed on the basis of, external sensory impressions) are revived in the debate between cognitivists and behaviorists. Cognitivists generally embrace some form of rationalism.[17] The problem for rationalists since Descartes has been bridging the gap between the rational mind and the mechanical body. As Gardner posits, Descartes was arguably the first cognitivist, basing his theory on an "information processing" device: "Descartes' diagram showed how visual sensations are conveyed, through the retinas, along nerve filaments, into the brain, with signals from the two eyes being reinverted and fused into a single image on the pineal gland. There, at an all-crucial juncture, the mind (or soul) could interact with the body, yielding a complete representation of external reality."[18] From this, we can move rather easily to interpreting the information flows within a machine to those that circulate in the mind/body.

Thus, the current wave of information science is not so far away from the traditional logic of science, in which "the input of data, the raw material, is worked over by the axiomatic of the system, yielding an output of truths, goods or wealth."[19] All of this occurs outside of the inhabited world of human action; it is a process in which information can be handled as the formal expression of knowledge and thus as something that can exist independent of human beings.[20] As Machlup and Mansfield show, the computer science model of information treats information in the same manner as physics treats energy: It focuses on the representation, storage, manipulation, and presentation of information within automatic processing systems. "As physics uses energy transforming devices," Machlup and Mansfield argue, "computer science uses information transforming devices."[21]

Under this model, computer science is able to transpose terms that apply to computers with those that apply to the human brain and vice versa. Thus, terms such as "memory," "storage," "thinking," "bit," "content," and "transmission" are applied with no distinction to communication between machines, between humans, or between humans and machines.[22] The model of communication applied within this information-transforming process is the basic sender-signal-channel-receiver model. Lakoff refers to this as the conduit metaphor of communication, which is based in a general metaphor for mind "in which ideas are taken as objects and thought as the manipulation of objects. An important part of this metaphor is that memory is 'storage.' Communication in that metaphor is the following: ideas are objects that you can put into words (or store as bits), so that language is seen as a container for ideas, and you send ideas in words over a circuit, a channel of communication to someone else who then extracts the ideas from the words."[23]

Again, this implies that the ideas can be extracted and can exist independent of people, in a computer, for example. As a result, information and its processing (information worked up through manipulations, reorderings, hierarchies) can exist in a disembodied form. (It should be noted that such a conception is belied by other strains of cognitive science itself that have shown how reasoning processes are embodied, that in fact, human beings think through schemas that are spatially mapped in accordance with body orientations.)

Once again, the computer science model of information separates information and knowledge on the three axes I noted earlier. Information is present in discrete transitory bits that flow across spatial domains. But in this model, not only is knowledge the output of the system, it is built into the system, in the form of programs. Thus, knowledge is encoded into bits in a form that works with the hardware and software of the computer system, the implication being that the knowledge stored in the computer processes raw data and turns it into information. The computer's processor becomes, in effect, Descartes' pineal gland.

Information Theory   In the late 1930s, Claude Shannon, usually credited as the founder of information theory, "saw that the principles of logic (in terms of true and false propositions) can be used to describe the two states (on and off) of electromechanical relay switches. Shannon suggested that electrical circuits (of the kind in a computer) could embody fundamental operations of thought."[24] In the 1940s, working on the engineering problems of signal transmission, Shannon and Weaver further developed the key notion of information theory: that information can be thought of as divorced from the specific content of a message. Instead, information can be defined as simply the "single decision between two equally plausible alternatives."[25] As a result, the basic unit of information is designated as "the bit." This conception of information becomes crucial within the other information sciences in that it exceptionalizes information. As Wiener explains, "Information is information, not matter or energy."[26]

This content-blind conception of information is clearly evident in the thinking of those general theorists who have attempted to define "the information society" (Bell, Toffler, Piore, Porat, etc.). As Webster describes it, "searching for quantitative evidence of the growth of information, a wide range of thinkers have conceived it in the classic terms of Claude Shannon and Warren Weaver's (1964) information theory. In this theory, information is a quantity that is measured in bits and defined in terms of the probabilities of occurrence of symbols. This approach allows the otherwise vexatious concept of information to be mathematically tractable."[27] Information, again, takes on an elemental quality akin to matter or energy. As Stonier puts it, "information exists. It does not need to be perceived to exist. It does not need to be understood to exist. It requires no intelligence to interpret it. It does not have to have meaning to exist. It exists."[28]

It should be noted that Shannon and Weaver never intended their model to be extended into characterizations of information in domains in which its content was in question. In fact, they suggested that "communication" might be the better term, since it did not necessarily imply a sender and receiver of a message, as in the usage "communicable disease." But "information" stuck and became the keyword across the disciplines we have been discussing. Information, so defined, has become a singular element with unique properties that can thus be separated from the social processes underlying it. As Webster points out, "If this definition of information is the one which pertains in technological and spatial approaches to the "information society" (where the quantities stored, processed and transmitted are indicative of the sort of indexes produced) we come across a similar elision of meaning from economists' definitions. Here it may not be in terms of 'bits,' but at the same time the semantic qualities are evacuated and replaced by the common denominator of price."[29] Thus there is a definitional isomorphism between information as the flow of discrete bits and information as commodity.

As scientific and technical fields converge around "information," its spatial-temporal location is further and further displaced as it becomes conceived of as a sheer "existence," a form or process evident across phenomena as diverse as electronic signal flows, human brain functions, and the genetic code of DNA. As Roszak notes, "In the course of the 1950's, information had come to be identified with the secret of life. By the 1970's, it had achieved an even more exalted status. It had become a commodity—the most valuable commodity in business."[30]

Information Economics

In parallel with these developments in the information sciences, neoclassical economic theory has attempted to incorporate "information" into the lexicon of its discipline. In fact, unbeknownst to most communication scholars, the neoclassical economic tradition has attempted to claim that information and communication processes are best explained using the categories of neoclassical economics and are, in fact, subsets of these economic processes. Babe characterizes this as economic imperialism, in which a diverse set of phenomena are grafted into economic analysis, because, in the economist's reasoning, "all behavior involving scarce resources can be illuminated by neoclassical price theory."[31]

Ultimately, it is claimed that information activity is a transactional activity, one that, at its core, can be defined as simply coterminous with commodity exchange. To carry out this grafting of information into the logic of exchange processes, economics needs a definition of information that can be dealt with under the terms of equivalency and that can yield measurements in terms of exchange and price. The commonsense definition of information, in which information is a heterogeneous object or process, does not comply with these needs.

As a result, neoclassical theory actually begins with the notion of information as defined within the information sciences and transmutes it into economic terms. As we have already noted, economists empty information of its semantic content. In this regard, price becomes equivalent to "the bit," in that information is reduced to a homogeneous form characterized as discrete atomic units. Thus, the meaning (content) of information is set aside as extraneous to the determination of its value in terms of quantitative measures. Further, as in cybernetics, information is at the same time conceived of as a flow; but here, this is seen within spatial and temporal dimensions defined in terms of the market. Information is the "energy" in the system that functions within the control processes of cybernetic capitalism. As in systems theory, information is conceived as an element of control within a complex system. The enemy of the smoothly functioning market system is disorganization, noise, chaos.

Economics focuses on the exceptional nature of information, an "exceptionalism" that is defined in terms of the preceding concepts. Information is so distinct, so unique within the processes of capitalism that it requires a different form of analysis and, in fact, takes up a unique existence within capitalism. The positing of a set of "inherent characteristics" of information leads to the notion that information production is radically different from all other forms of production. Thus, information supplants capital and labor.[32] Kenneth Boulding extends this claim in "substituting the triad know-how, energy and matter for the traditional land, labor and capital as basic factors of production. He contends that similarities become evident in developmental processes of biological, societal and physical systems."[33] The information present in the coded patterns of DNA is the same information that directs energy in the transformation of materials into products. Information is the secret of life—genetic and economic. As we shall see, however, information, though exceptional, is also simply a commodity. So information is unique enough to displace Marx's categories of analysis of capitalism, but not so unique as to fall outside of the purview of neoclassical categories of price, supply and demand, and exchange. (We will see in a moment why information has this double existence in neoclassical economic theory.)

Two Forms of Information in Information Economics

Information takes up at least two functions in contemporary economic processes:

1. It is a resource that provides input into the production process of other commodities and into the control of the market itself.
2. It is an output that is materialized and sold as a commodity.

Within both incarnations, information is taken as a nonsemantic entity or activity whose "work" can be priced.

Information and the Reduction of Uncertainty   One of the preeminent "information society" proponents, Daniel Bell, has declared that information, for him, means "data processing in the broadest sense; the storage, retrieval, and processing of data becomes the essential resource for all economic and social exchanges. These include: data processing of records . . . data processing for scheduling . . . data bases."[34] Bell is pointing to the function of information in providing the basis for knowledge of the market, one of the key components of cybernetic capitalism. Up until the 1970s, this was the key focus of information economics: determining information's place in market performance. As Lamberton notes, information "reduced uncertainty for the firm and for the consumer, both of whom could therefore make decisions. This was basically the information-as-oil viewpoint."[35] Here, information is the lubricant in the market. This notion of reducing uncertainty fit well with the information science viewpoint of information as defined by its existence as a bit—in Shannon's formulation, a single decision between two equally plausible alternatives.

The uncertainty referred to in these formulations is the uncertainty of price. Babe documents how the neoclassical economists grafted information into the price system: "Hayek (1945) too lauded the informational properties of the price system, viewing prices as 'quantitative indices' (or 'values'). Each index or price Hayek contended should be understood as concentrated information reflecting the significance of any particular scarce resource relative to all others. The index of price borne by each commodity, Hayek enthused, permits autonomous economic agents to adjust their strategies 'without having to solve the whole puzzle [input-output matrix] ab initio.'"[36]

Prices, then, are information. Here, information is reduced to the sphere of problem solving and decisionistics, a sphere that obviously points to the computer as the processing device that promises to impose order and hierarchy on quantities of atomized items. Krippendorf, discussing information in the context of general communication processes, defines information in much the same way: it is a change in an observer's state of uncertainty. He then makes the same move we have seen time and time again:——Information is compared to energy: "Energy and information are measures of work. But whereas energy is a measure of the physical work required to transform matter of one form into matter of another, information is a measure of the (intellectual) work required to distinguish, to a degree better than chance, among a set of initially uncertain possibilities."[37]

Reducing the uncertainty of a situation involves delimiting the possible choices by considering them in terms of the probabilities of outcomes. For information economists this means that information is only information when it reduces the complexity of the decision-making process. Thus, business depends upon the preprocessing of information, controlling the amount of information by eliminating the unnecessary. As Gandy notes, for Beniger, this serves as a definition of rationalization within economic bureaucracy, "that is, rationalization, as preprocessing might be defined as the destruction or ignoring of information in order to facilitate its processing."[38] Once again, information is linked to control, but this time through a process of standardization that closes off certain paths through which the information might flow. If information still has a semantic content, which it does appear to in this case, then the preprocessing of information shuts off certain paths of meaning; it territorializes and closes off certain possible forces and practices. In economic practices this facilitates routinization, the reduction of skills, stereotyped reactions, the preformation of demand, and the channeling of information resources into methods for structuring production, distribution, and consumption.

Information as Commodity   In the second economic definition of information, it is conceptualized as a commodity. This is a key element within the discourse of the "information society," for the dominant conceptualization of this new form of sociality is described as one in which information work and information products have replaced the industrial form. In addition, it is the vast array of information commodities produced within the information economy that is the key selling point of this digital age. The selling of information commodities requires considerations of their value as "meaning" to the consumer (whether corporate or private individual). The originality, innovation, and power of particular information commodities, as well as their packaging, seems to be a major part of marketing these products. Ironically, however, it is these very claims that produce problems for information economics, for its homogeneous conception of information falls flat when confronted with the heterogeneous qualities of information commodities. The economic rationality behind the information society/economy discourse would like to conceive of all forms of information as homologous "in the monetary sense of easy conversion from one form into another."[39] The impetus is for information commodities to escape any particular form, that is, for the informational message to float free of any specific medium and thus to become transferable into as many contexts as possible. Thus the information society/economy promises a convergence of technologies in which print, audio, video, film, and graphic representation appear and reappear in various forms and formats. The first form of economic information, the reduction of uncertainty, creates the conditions for the production of such commodities. This is what Boyle calls "perfect information": free, complete, instantaneous, and universally available—an uninhibited flow of information that serves as the lubricant for market activity. In addition, information also needs to be treated in a second way: "As a good within the perfect market, something that will not be produced without incentives—expensive incentives," according to Boyle. This requires a restriction on the form of information: It must be conceived as a finite good, one whose exchange value can be determined and one whose availability can be purposely restricted.[40]

As Morris-Suzuki explains, "the special properties of knowledge (its lack of material substance; the ease with which it can be copied and transmitted) mean that it can only acquire exchange value where institutional arrangements confer a degree of monopoly power on its owner."[41] The problems for information economics are further laid out by Morris-Suzuki: Information can be copied and reproduced at low cost; it is never consumed; its price is nearly impossible to calculate, because the buyer cannot know the content until she has bought it; and the monopoly of particular information is extremely difficult to maintain (it tends to "flow back into the public domain").[42] These properties are clearly illustrated by the example of software, in which the lines between the public stock of social knowledge, the originary "intelligence" behind the design, and the encoding of this onto a "hard" object are nearly completely blurred.

For the producer of a commodity, the meaning of the product is inessential within the exchange process itself; its existence as information consists of the fact that it can be encoded, reproduced, and exchanged as a commodity. The producer would sell each bit of information at the same price if he could and, in fact, producers attempt to do just this in certain sectors of the information economy. From the consumer's perspective, however, it is the meaning of the information that is being purchased (at least this is a major factor in the demand for consumer entertainment/information products), and so the distinction among products in terms of the knowledge they contain is always pertinent to the producer. But ultimately, the use value of commodities in terms of their meaning complicates the measurement of value in terms of price. Thus the producer must come up with strategies to control the exchange of these information commodities. A number of strategies are possible in this regard:

1. *Standardize the various products and make them equivalent.* The modern video store illustrates this principle, in which the information's value seems to be determined by its ability to occupy a certain amount of the consumer's disposable time. The only distinction made in the pricing of products is that the most recent information is given a slightly higher value.

2. *Sell the information flow, not the specific contents.* The World Wide Web, at the present time, illustrates this strategy. The consumer purchases access to information as an abstraction (in most cases). It is this vision of having access to a flow of information that encourages society as a whole to conceive of information along the same lines as the information scientists and economists: information as a flow of discrete bundles (bits)—thus, the pay-per-call, pay-per-view, pay-per-bit model.[43]

3. *Produce ephemeral information that must be consumed over and over.* In digital networks, information appears, disappears, and re-forms, requiring a continual return on the part of the consumer. A reverse way of looking at this is through the lens of the "perpetual innovation" economy.

4. *Redistribute the information in as many forms as possible.* Once produced, the meaning of the product (such as a film) becomes secondary; its exchange value is determined by its reproducibility within a variety of packages and in a variety of markets. This repackaging makes calculating value much more manageable.

5. *Equalize, standardize (yet marginally individuate), and format the content.* Information processing enhances the ability to reduce information to schemas and predetermined patterns, again serving to bracket the significance of the information's value as meaning.

6. *Process the consumer's behavior.* The information industry automates the process of marketing, enabling the production of personal behavior databases. The use of infor-

mation processing and modeling to predetermine audience response is an example of this process.

None of these strategies, in themselves, can solve the problems of determining the value of information or the problems of producing profit in a "knowledge economy." As Davis and Stack note, "the easy replicability of the digital product poses a quandary for capitalists—how to deliver digital products while still enforcing ownership and control of distribution when copying is virtually free and exact."[44] The answer currently lies in the reworking of the laws of "intellectual property," a reworking of the notion of the ownership of content that is based in the definitions of information that we have been examining. The ownership rights must be shifted from the content as "idea" (the meaning constructed within and through the social knowledge of the public) to the content as "expression" (the reworking and reordering of that knowledge).[45]

Through this process accumulated social knowledge is privately appropriated for profit. As Morris-Suzuki explains, out of informal and formal social knowledge (publicly paid for), "corporations produce private knowledge, from which they extract monopoly profits. Eventually, the monopoly is eroded as patents and copyright expire, or as new products and techniques become widely known and imitable. Information seeps back into the expanding pool of social knowledge, but, in the meanwhile, the corporation has accumulated increased resources which enable it to move forward into a new cycle of private knowledge creation."[46]

The emerging copyright and intellectual-property laws will help cement this process and extend its scope. The juridical formation of property rights will depend on a legal translation of the contradictory definitions of information that we have analyzed.

Disorganizing Information

Ultimately, the complex processes and problems of the information economy are clouded in a veil of fetishism. Digital information is conceived of as an inexorable force that will finally enable a faithful representation of reality, both the reality of the external world and the reality of the processes of the market. Information, as the digital rendering of the skills and social knowledge of laborers, is programmed into automatic machinery. Information, as consumer data, is input into "the difference machine that sorts individuals into categories and classifications on the basis of routine measurements."[47] Information, as measurement of the rise and fall of market fluctuations, is encoded and processed as feedback crucial for the control of market chaos. Just as Descartes's pineal gland provided a space for the merging of soul and body, thus enabling the complete representation of external reality, the computer bridges the gap between the physical body of actual material relations and exchanges and the invisible hand (soul) of the market. The computer is the pineal gland of cybernetic capitalism.

The humanistic critique of information theory would emphasize the destruction of meaning that it engenders; the reduction of human thought to binary switching, when it should instead be thought of as a public activity, a social accomplishment; the deemphasis on knowledge in favor of information, which blocks critical and conceptual thinking, for information cannot make sense of that which has lost it; and the reduction of information to the status of commodity, leading to the appropriation of socially produced knowledge and further, to the modeling of all human practices within the logic of exchange. These are all valid criticisms and evaluations of information science and information economics, but they are limited to the sphere of the projection and reflection of the mind. These analyses need then to be connected to the sphere of mobility and fluidity, particularly in relation to the processes of labor. As Negri put it, informatics becomes accentuated as capital develops a need for "innovation in the instruments and processes controlling the circulation and reproduction of the factors of capital" and the "diffuse mechanization involved in the technological control of socialised work."[48] Thus, information becomes the control mechanism within the "workerless factory"; it enables operations to disperse in search of cheap sources of labor; it enables surveillance of the workplace and automation of formerly skilled tasks through the implementation of "intelligent agents." In short, "the stark goals of control and reduction in the costs of labor" are central to the "information society."[49]

But the information economy is not simply an extension of capital in a smooth transition from its industrial mode of production; it is as much a response to loss of control, to disorganization and noise endemic to the process of accumulation. As Witheford states, "To coordinate its diffused operations and activate its huge technological apparatus, capital must interlink computers, telecommunications and media in ever-more convergent systems, automating labor, monitoring production cycles, streamlining turnover times, tracking financial exchanges, scanning and stimulating consumption in the attempt to synchronize and smooth the flow of value through its expanded circuits.[50] This trajectory of information in the disposition of labor and material organization does not overturn or simply lie beside the analysis of the trajectory of information as projection of mind; rather it can be seen to redirect it toward a third trajectory: a spatial and temporal logic.

Information science operates with a binary logic of reflection that results in multiple paths, but these paths are always circumscribed by laws of combination.[51] In this manner the fragmented space and time of information flows is reordered and directed toward specific objectives. But the objectives of information processing within the capitalist dynamic are not end points: They are aimed at an accumulation of knowledge that is always an impetus for further accumulation, for multiplying the flow, opening out into every horizon. But this flow is at the same time stored in a central memory that traces the exact paths of this flow, connecting geographic spaces and matching up the temporal locations of dispersed market centers. This central memory system functions through command trees, centered systems, and hierarchical structures that attempt to fix possible pathways of the network and thus to limit the possible variations immanent in the network. The definitions of information formulated within information science and information economics derive from and serve this modeling of the system. As we have seen, information defined as nonsemantic discrete bits flowing across space and then directed and stored substantiates information as the object of control. Thus, the enemy of the information scientists and economists is heterogeneity, disorganization, noise, chaos. They want an uninterrupted flow, but at the same time a destruction of the unnecessary. This encloses or territorializes information; it becomes a part of capitalism's mapping of space and time. But what I have shown in this chapter is that information's function is precisely to disorganize, interrupt, to remain itself and at the same time to disperse. Information may, in fact, be a keyword connecting the phenomena we have examined, but not as an element, and not as a content, but as a heterogeneous remapping of space and time. If the information society is to be our society, let it be disorganized.

Notes

1. A. Balsamo, "Myths of Information: The Cultural Impact of New Information," in *The Information Revolution: Current and Future Consequences,* ed. A. L. Porter and W. H. Read (Greenwich, Conn.: Ablex, 1998), 225–235, at 226.

2. F. Machlup, "Semantic Quirks in Studies of Information," in *The Study of Information: Interdisciplinary Messages,* ed. F. Machlup and U. Mansfield (New York: John Wiley and Sons, 1983), 641–671, at 642.

3. F. Webster, *Theories of the Information Society* (New York: Routledge, 1995), 26–27.

4. F. Machlup and U. Mansfield, "Cultural Diversity in Studies of Information," in *The Study of Information: Interdisciplinary Messages,* ed. F. Machlup and U. Mansfield (New York: John Wiley and Sons, 1983), Prologue, at 34.

5. Machlup, "Semantic Quirks in Studies of Information," 642.

6. Z. W. Pylyshyn, "Information Science, Its Roots and Relations as Viewed from the Perspective of Cognitive Science," in *The Study of Information: Interdisciplinary Messages,* ed. F. Machlup and U. Mansfield (New York: John Wiley and Sons, 1983), 63–80, at 64.

7. H. Gardner, *The Mind's New Science: A History of the Cognitive Revolution* (New York: Basic Books, 1987), 20–21.

8. S. Pfohl, "The Cybernetic Delirium of Norbert Wiener," in *Digital Delirium,* ed. A. Kroker and M. Kroker (New York: St. Martin's, 1997), 114–131, at 116.

9. Ibid., 121.

10. T. Roszak, *The Cult of Information* (New York: Pantheon, 1986), 9.

11. Pfohl, "The Cybernetic Delirium of Norbert Wiener," 126.

12. R. Langlois, "Systems Theory, Knowledge and the Social Sciences," in *The Study of Information: Interdisciplinary Messages,* ed. F. Machlup and U. Mansfield (New York: John Wiley and Sons, 1983), 581–600, at 586.

13. M. Finley, *Powermatics: A Discursive Critique of New Communication Technology* (New York: Routledge, 1987), 163.

14. A. Giddens, *Studies in Social and Political Theory* (New York: Basic Books, 1977), 116.

15. Langlois, "Systems Theory, Knowledge and the Social Sciences," 593.

16. H. A. Simon, "Cognitive Science: The Newest Science of the Artificial," *Cognitive Science* 4, no. 33 (1980): 33–46, at 35.

17. Gardner, *The Mind's New Science,* 53.

18. Ibid., 51.

19. A. Feenberg, *Critical Theory of Technology* (New York: Oxford University Press, 1991), 111.

20. C. Leeuwis, *Of Computers, Myths, and Modeling* (The Netherlands: Agricultural University Wageningen), 29.

21. Machlup and Mansfield, "Cultural Diversity," 23.

22. Leeuwis, *Of Computers, Myths, and Modeling,* 31.

23. G. Lakoff, "Body, Brain and Communication," in *Resisting the Virtual Life,* ed. J. Brook and I. Boal (San Francisco: City Lights), 115–130, at 116.

24. Gardner, *The Mind's New Science,* 21.

25. Ibid.

26. N. Wiener, *Cybernetics, or Control and Communication in Animal and Machine,* 2nd ed. (Cambridge: MIT Press, 1961), 132.

27. Webster, *Theories of the Information Society,* 27.

28. T. Stonier, *Information and the Internal Structure of the Universe: An Exploration into Information Physics* (Heidelberg: Springer-Verlag, 1990), 21.

29. Webster, *Theories of the Information Society,* 28.

30. Roszak, *The Cult of Information,* 20.

31. R. E. Babe, "The Place of Information in Economics," in *Information and Communication in Economics,* ed. R. E. Babe (Boston: Kluwer, 1994), 41–67, at 41.

32. D. Schiller, *Theorizing Communication* (New York: Oxford University Press, 1996), 167.

33. R. E. Babe, "Preface," in *Information and Communication in Economics,* ed. R. E. Babe (Boston: Kluwer, 1994), xi.

34. Daniel Bell, quoted in Schilller, *Theorizing Communication,* 168.

35. D. M. Lamberton, "The Information Economy Revisited," in *Information and Communication in Economics,* ed. R. E. Babe (Boston: Kluwer, 1994), 1–33, at 12.

36. Babe, "The Place of Information," 47.

37. K. Krippendorf, "Paradox and Information," in *Progress in Communication Sciences,* vol. 5, ed. B. Dervin and M. Voight (Norwood, N.J.: Ablex, 1984), 45–72, at 50.

38. O. Gandy, *The Panoptic Sort* (Boulder, Colo.: Westview, 1993), 42.

39. J. Boyle, *Shamans, Software and Spleens: Law and the Construction of the Information Society* (Cambridge: Harvard University Press, 1996), 7.

40. Ibid., 29.

41. T. Morris-Suzuki, "Robots and Capitalism," in *Cutting Edge: Technology, Information Capitalism and Social Revolution,* ed. J. Davis et al. (London: Verso, 1997), 13–28, at 17.

42. T. Morris-Suzuki, "Capitalism in the Computer Age and Afterward," in *Cutting Edge: Technology, Information Capitalism and Social Revolution,* ed. J. Davis et al. (London: Verso, 1997), 57–72, at 62.

43. V. Mosco, *The Pay-Per Society* (Toronto: Garamond Press, 1989).

44. J. Davis and M. Stack, "The Digital Advantage," in *Cutting Edge: Technology, Information Capitalism and Social Revolution,* ed. J. Davis et al. (London: Verso, 1997), 121–144, at 132.

45. See Boyle, *Shamans, Software and Spleens,* 57.

46. Morris-Suzuki, "Capitalism in the Computer Age and Afterward," 66.

47. Gandy, *The Panoptic Sort,* 15.

48. A. Negri, *La classe ouvriere contre l'etat* [The Working Class Against the State] (Paris: Edition Galilee, 1978), 235, 254.

49. Ibid., 254.

50. N. Witheford, "Autonomist Marxism and the Information Society," *Capital & Class* 52 (1994): 85–125, at 101.

51. G. Deleuze and F. Guattari, *A Thousand Plateaus* (Minneapolis: University of Minnesota Press, 1987).

22 That Withered Paradigm: The Web, the Expert, and the Information Hegemony

Peter Walsh

The title of this chapter is taken from a comment posted on the online discussion group for an art museum project. The original message, which was apparently from a Web artist, was "That withered, disreputable, often laughable 'expert' paradigm is what the Net now displaces."

This comment had the ring of truth about it: There is something about the Web that makes the idea of the expert seem withered, even disreputable and laughable. But why does this happen? And what exactly is the "expert paradigm"?

I concluded that the list-serv message probably was not referring to the expert in the individual sense. A single person might make him- or herself an expert in flower arranging or Japanese medieval armor, but that does not constitute a paradigm. Instead, the "expert paradigm" must be a social construct, a dialogue between the experts and the rest of society.

I suspect that the expert paradigm goes back to the beginnings of human culture. It probably evolved as a counter to brute force in human societies. It was a way of creating a value and use for intellectual activity and insights.

At its basic and most ancient form, the expert paradigm was an undifferentiated variety of what we now call religion. All members of the "expert class" are still in some sense priests, practitioners of a hermetic cult giving access to divine knowledge. And as members of a priestly class, all experts still have special, quasi-religious status.

As part of our cultural evolution, this undifferentiated expert form developed into many kinds of expert knowledge: astrology, astronomy, philosophy, natural science, medicine, law, and so on. All of these types still bear the marks of their protoreligious origins and follow the expert paradigm.

What, then, are the elements of the expert paradigm?[1] I propose these five basic characteristics:

1.   The expert paradigm requires a body of knowledge. This can really be any body of knowledge, but abstract knowledge tends to have higher prestige than practical knowledge. Predictive knowledge—that is, knowledge like astrology or economics that helps predict future important events—has even higher status.

      This body of knowledge, however, need not be objectively true to be valuable or prestigious.[2] The paradigm requires only that the experts convince a certain number (not necessarily even a very large number) of those outside the group that the knowledge the experts control is both true and useful. That the expert class really has such a true and useful body of knowledge always tends to be suspect to outsiders, even in expert paradigms that are long and well established.

      Even the best (that is, the most objectively truthful) body of expert knowledge is wrong some of the time. Thanks to the laws of coincidences and averages, even the worst is right some of the time.[3] These facts of the limits human understanding can be used either to support or to attack any body of expert knowledge.

2.   The expert paradigm creates an "exterior" and an "interior," an outer group of laypersons and an inner group of experts. This is neatly symbolized in the classic Greek temple form. There, the columned exterior was for the public. Only the priests—the experts—were allowed in the cramped and dimly lit interior. This differentiation between interior and exterior, between insider and outsider, is an essential feature of the expert paradigm. If there are no insiders, no experts, the entire structure begins to crumble.

3.   The expert paradigm uses rules. The paradigm has external rules for the access to and use of its base of knowledge. There are also internal rules, usually kept hidden from outsiders, that regulate the internal affairs of the group, its membership, and its interface with the outside world.

      A self-appointing, self-regulating hierarchy typically manages both sets of rules. The expert hierarchy is usually jealous of its privileges and suspicious of outside attempts to control it. The hierarchy often uses its influence in the outside world to pass laws that help enforce its rules. The hierarchy uses the rules and supporting laws to manage the recruitment, initiation, promotion, and (when necessary) the expulsion of expert insiders. This set of rules and their organizational application is what I will call the "knowledge hegemony."

4.   The expert paradigm uses ritualistic ways to define the expert group from outsiders. These include initiation ceremonies of various kinds, the use of symbols, rituals, and monuments with particular meanings for the insiders, and special uniforms and costumes to identify the experts to outsiders. Expert-insiders also typically use a spe-

cialized language that tends to make their utterances incomprehensible—yet impressive—to the uninitiated. "What a delightful thing is the conversation of specialists!" the painter Edgar Degas remarked on this phenomenon. "One understands absolutely nothing and it's charming."[4]

5. The expert paradigm is inherently unstable. It is constantly threatened by factions and turf battles from within and by skepticism or jealously of its privileged status from without. Expert paradigms thus tend to break down, fragment, or change dramatically, as Thomas Kuhn reminds us,[5] over time. The expert paradigm continues to have a tense relationship ("conflicts of church and state") with political power. As British Prime Minister Harold MacMillan put it in a speech given at Strasbourg, France on August 16, 1950, "We have not overthrown the divine right of kings to fall down to the divine right of experts."

One of the main premises of this chapter is that innovations in technology tend to break down and transform existing expert paradigms. Take, for example, the Christian Church in the western Europe of the Renaissance. This was, I think, a prime example of the expert paradigm. The church claimed privileged access to an extraordinarily valuable body of knowledge. It claimed to know the will of an omnipotent and omniscient God. Most especially valuable, the Church understood the rules for establishing residency in the better neighborhoods of the afterlife.[6]

The medieval church had developed an elaborate hierarchy, set of rituals, costumes, rules, and methods for recruiting, controlling, and separating its members from the outside world.[7] It had, moreover, the usual instabilities of all expert paradigms. It was heavily factionalized within, had to deal with challenges to its knowledge hegemony called "heresies," and was locked in continual power struggles with temporal authorities in western Europe.[8]

We are accustomed to think that the Protestant Reformation started in 1517 when Martin Luther nailed his ninety-five theses to the door of Wittenburg's castle church. Actually, far more important to the Reformation was the fact that Luther made use of a developing new technology and printed his views.

The printing press thoroughly undermined one of the key elements of the medieval church's knowledge hegemony: the control of book production and libraries. Before the printing press, church members copied books by hand for church-managed libraries. Books were not only expensive and time-consuming to produce, they were written in special languages such as Latin and Greek known primarily to members of the church hierarchy.

The printing press ended all this.[9] Cheap pamphlets ridiculing the church flooded Europe. Translations of the Bible, one by Luther himself, into common languages ended the church's control of sacred texts. These printed texts turned the very elements of the expert paradigm against the church to ridicule its pretensions and privileges. Thus the expert paradigm of the church lost its credibility, and the church itself soon shattered into hundreds of fragments.

Today's new communication technology, the World Wide Web, also promises to make profound changes in the knowledge hegemony of a number of fields. I will outline here a few examples from three areas with which I am somewhat familiar: journalism, the art world, and intellectual property.

It is easy to see that the Web tends to eliminate a number of the characteristic defining points of the knowledge hegemony. It is quite easy to set up an official-looking knowledge base on the World Wide Web. A major newspaper like the *New York Times* can do it. So can an individual.

Thus one of the first undermining aspects of the Web is the elimination of the inside-outside distinction. On the Web, it becomes impossible to differentiate the expert from the nonexpert. The rules essential to maintaining the distinction between the expert paradigm and the rest of the world can no longer be enforced.

At the time he created the Web site The Drudge Report, Matt Drudge was a convenience-store clerk working out of his tiny Hollywood apartment. Drudge worked entirely outside the expert paradigm of journalism. He bypassed the hierarchies of editor and publisher and ignored the internal journalistic laws of verifiable sources and standards of privacy. By challenging the expert rules that govern what is and is not news, Drudge was able to scoop the world on the White House sex scandal that became the Lewinsky affair.[10]

Newsweek reporter Michael Isikoff, who had spent months trying to pin down the various rumors of presidential extramarital affairs, was particularly furious at Drudge's behavior. Isikoff later attacked Drudge for breaking the inner rules of journalism. "While ignoring the question of whether something actually happened in the White House . . . ," Isikoff wrote, "commentators were fascinated by the role of Drudge in briefly creating a media firestorm. Not surprisingly, a few called me for comment—and I jumped at the chance to publicly slam him. 'He's a menace to honest, responsible journalism,' I told *The New York Times*'s Todd Purdum. He was digging through unverified reporting— 'like raw FBI files'—and shoveling it onto the Internet, I told *The Washington Post*'s Howard Kurtz."[11]

In the process of exposing the scandal, Drudge also created paranoia and consternation among the various witnesses in the Lewinsky affair and shook the entire knowledge hegemony of journalism. In particular, Drudge indirectly exposed journalism's secret, internal methods to public scrutiny. Once the "news," which journalism traditionally presents as the objective truth, was revealed to be a manufactured product—a product manufactured, moreover, by methods that seemed cynical and manipulative to many outsiders—the knowledge hegemony of journalism began to show cracks.

The Web is beginning to have the same kinds of effects in the art world. Norman Bryson, borrowing an analogy from Foucault, has compared art museums to prisons, "panopticons" in which the inmates (or artwork) are both confined and constantly observed by their keepers, the curators. By locking up most of the world's great art in private collections and in guarded art museums, the insiders of the art world have, to an amazing extent, been able to control discourse about art in general.

For example, before allowing works of art from their collections to be published, most art museums not only demand a fee but also require signed contracts that control, in various ways, how the work is reproduced and described. Their physical control of the art also allows art museums to control which artists are presented to the public, the context in which they are seen, the public's interaction with the art, and the sorts of discourses about art that are considered "appropriate."

Museum curators typically think of themselves as acting on behalf of the artists themselves. Curators generally turn down requests to publish art works in ways they consider demeaning (for example, in commercial advertising). They often forbid the use of details, electronic manipulation and distortion of images, and the like on the grounds that they are contrary to the original intent of the artist.[12]

With the advent of the World Wide Web, cheap color image scanners, and easy ways to copy and transmit digitized images, this sort of control is rapidly beginning to wane. The Web site Artchive appears to be a normal art museum Web site, with floor plans, a collection catalogue, a museum shop, and the like. In fact, this site was created and is managed by an individual—a non-art historian living in Texas named Mark Harden—who uses it to present his own views about art. His art images are gathered, via various quasi-legal means, from around the world and furnish his virtual galleries.

Lately, large corporations like Intel have also gotten into this act, creating their own museum sites. Some insiders of the art world are quite up in arms about this development—and with good reason. The idea that anyone can manipulate art, present it, and comment on it in their own way is a deep threat to the art world's knowledge hegemony.

Harden's use of images without permission raises my third example, the assault via the Web on the traditional controls over intellectual property. Except in a legal sense, intellectual property is not an expert paradigm in itself. Rather, as a product of technology and law, intellectual property is most often a managing tool of expert paradigms, as we have just seen in the case of art museums.

Contrary to some popular opinion, copyright and intellectual property were not invented to protect the rights of individual authors. The ancestors of the copyright laws were first used, in the wake of the creation of the printing press, to control the destabilizing effects of the new technology on established hierarchies, especially the church and the monarchical state. Thus the proto–copyright laws granted monopoly rights over certain titles to publishers in return for a royal right to censor all that was published.

These early copyright laws later came to be used to provide ways for business entrepreneurs to derive a profit from that new technology.[13] After all, the fiscal beneficiary of the invention of the printing press was not Gutenberg. He evidently went bankrupt. Nor did the profit go to the first authors printed, who generally were long dead.

Instead, it was the early entrepreneurs of printing who figured how to turn profits from the combination of laws and technology. A contemporary example of this process is Microsoft's Bill Gates. Gates's business empire (and knowledge hegemony) was created, I submit, almost entirely from his astute understanding and exploitation of intellectual property laws and not on any special insight into software technology.[14]

Not only did the World Wide Web's ability to bypass the status quo of intellectual property shake the confidence of Mr. Gates, it also threatens to destroy the entire established order of such things as the music industry. Now that music recordings can be downloaded directly from Web sites, normal distribution methods for recorded music are effectively made obsolete, and with them the ability to control the music people hear and enjoy. Since such downloaded recordings are also so easy to pirate, the Web also threatens the industry's ability to make a profit.

Has the Web, then, "withered" the entire "expert paradigm"? It is too soon to tell. Radio and sound recordings once had the potential to undermine the old music publishing industry, which was based on printed sheet music. But the Federal Communications Commission and such music rights agencies as BMI and ASCAP put a sudden end to that. There are already considerable efforts to put similar controls on the World Wide Web.

In the end, I think it is unlikely that the Web will destroy the expert paradigm. It will, however, continue to alter existing paradigms, to push them in new directions and into new forms, just as the printing press did in the past. In this, it will be yet another chapter in the evolution—in the adventure—of human consciousness.

Notes

1. The literature on the expert is largely to be found in such fields as organizational behavior and sociology, the latter being an expert paradigm under some stress in recent years. See, for example, Erving Goffman, *The Presentation of Self in Everyday Life* (Woodstock, N.Y.: Overlook, 1973); and Richard M. Hall, *Organizations: Structures, Processes, and Outcomes* (Englewood Cliffs, N.J.: Prentice-Hall, 1987).

2. Scientists, in particular, have trouble accepting that any body of knowledge that cannot claim to be objectively true can be worthy of serious consideration. They do not understand that the value of the expert paradigm is in its social functions, not in its quotient of truthfulness. The long history of religion in human societies, with competing and incompatible dogmas that cannot be scientifically verified, suggests that, on the contrary, the social value of the expert paradigm has little or nothing to do with "truth" as the scientist views it.

3. Often, the popularity of an expert body of knowledge seems to be inversely proportional to its objective verifiability. For example, astrology and astronomy both grew up together as predictive sciences. Today, astronomers' ability to predict future astronomical events is, for all everyday intents and purposes, flawless. Astrological predictions remain far less precise. Yet daily media coverage of astrology and astronomy suggests that astrology remains far more popular than astronomy.

4. Daniel Halévy, "Notes on Degas," in Edgar Degas, *Letters,* Marcel Guérin, ed., Marguerite Kay, trans., (Oxford: Bruno Cassirer, 1947), 246.

5. Thomas S. Kuhn, *The Structure of Scientific Revolutions,* vol. 2, International Encyclopedia of Unified Science, no. 2 (Chicago: University of Chicago Press, 1970). Kuhn, of course, gave "paradigm" and "paradigm shift" to the postmodern glossary. It should be noted, however, that his use of the word is somewhat different than mine. For Kuhn, a paradigm is a kind of resting point in the progressive development of a body of knowledge. Once the natural inertia of the knowledge base has been overcome, according to Kuhn, it in effect rolls to a higher place. My use of the word "paradigm" is closer to its pre-Kuhn sense of "model" or "pattern." In my estimation, changes in the knowledge base (which are not necessarily "improvements") are less important than shifts and alterations in the entire expert paradigm.

6. Outrage at the church's sale of indulgences—in effect, providing access to heaven in return for contributions to such projects as the creation of the new basilica of St. Peter's in Rome—was one of the leading causes of the Reformation.

7. Among the methods the church developed were monasteries and celibacy. Both separated its expert members from the outside world and allowed the church to control its expert membership, since one could not be born into membership.

8. The church's claim to temporal power in Western Europe was the source of constant friction with secular authority well into the twentieth century.

9. See, for example, Mark U. Edwards, Jr., *Printing, Propaganda, and Martin Luther* (Berkeley and Los Angeles: University of California Press, 1994).

10. For a profile on Drudge, see D. McClintock, "Matt Drudge, Town Crier for the New Age," *Brill's Content* (November 1998), 112–127.

11. Michael Isikoff, *Uncovering Clinton: A Reporter's Story* (New York: Crown, 1999), 167. Elsewhere in his book, Isikoff is a particularly eloquent and insightful commentator on the inner rules of journalism and their internal contradictions, which perhaps suggests one source of the inherent instability of the expert paradigm in that field.

12. Curators ignore, in holding these positions, that the history of art is much longer than the history of art museums and that art itself has generally progressed by each generation's appropriating the images of its predecessors and altering them, often beyond all recognition.

13. See, for example, Ronald U. Bettig, *Copyrighting Culture: The Political Economy of Intellectual Property* (Boulder, Colo.: Westview, 1996); and Anne Wells Branscomb, *Who Owns Information? From Privacy to Public Access* (New York: Basic Books, 1994).

14. Gates founded his fortunes by contracting to provide IBM with a disk-operating system for its new personal computer. At the time of the arrangement, Gates did not possess such a system. He purchased the rights to what became MS-DOS from another company for a nominal sum. Since Gates understood intellectual property better than IBM's executives did, he retained the right to license MS-DOS to manufacturers making IBM-compatible machines. Thanks to IBM's dominance in hardware, MS-DOS and Windows gained dominance in operating software, but IBM's lack of control over its own operating system meant that Microsoft's fortunes and power grew at IBM's expense. IBM saw power in hardware. With considerable foresight, Gates saw the coming shift in power toward software and intellectual property.

Contributors

Philip E. Agre is the author of *Computation and Human Experience* and coeditor of *Reinventing Technology, Rediscovering Community: Critical Studies in Computing as a Social Practice*. He is an associate professor of information studies at the University of California, Los Angeles, and edits an Internet mailing list called the Red Rock Eater News Service about the social and political aspects of networking and computing.

Benjamin Barber holds the Kekst Chair of Civil Society at the University of Maryland and directs the New York offiice of the Democracy Collaborative. Among his fourteen books are *Strong Democracy* and *Jihad versus McWorld*.

Nolan A. Bowie is a senior fellow and adjunct lecturer in public policy at Harvard University's Kennedy School of Government. He has served on a number of advisory panels, including the U.S. Congress's Office of Technology Assessment, and is currently a board member of Citizens for Independent Public Broadcasting and an advisor to the Center for Media Education.

Ashley Dawson is an assistant professor of English at the University of Iowa, where he teaches cultural studies, postcolonial theory, and contemporary literature. He is completing a book on geographies of identity among diasporic groups in postimperial Britain.

Brenda Dervin is a professor of communication at the Ohio State University. Her articles on information and democracy and alternative communication practice have appeared in *Journal of Communication* and *Journal of American Society for Information Science*. Dervin is past president of the International Communication Association.

Peter S. Donaldson is head of the literature section at the Massachusetts Institute of Technology, the author of *Machiavelli and Mystery of State* and *Shakespearean Films / Shakespearean Directors,* and director of the Shakespeare Electronic Archive.

Amitai Etzioni, a professor at George Washington University, is the author of *The Mono-chrome Society* and *The Limits of Privacy* and numerous other books and articles. Etzioni has served as president of the American Sociological Association and as a senior adviser to the White House.

Christopher Harper is the author of *And That's the Way It Will Be: News and Information in a Digital World* and editor of *What's Next in Mass Communication: Readings on Media and Culture.* Harper, who spent more than twenty years in journalism with the Associated Press, *Newsweek* and ABC News, holds the Roy H. Park Distinguished Chair at Ithaca College.

John Hartley is dean of the creative industries faculty at Queensland University of Tech-nology in Australia. He has published several books and articles on media, journalism, and popular culture, including *The Indigenous Public Sphere* and *Uses of Television.*

Robert Huesca is an associate professor of communication at Trinity University in San Antonio, where his research centers on alternative media, Internet journalism, and the uses of communication for social change. He is currently the regional editor for Latin America for *Communication Booknotes Quarterly.*

Ellen Hume was the founding executive director of PBS's Democracy Project from 1996 to 1998, during which she also oversaw PBS's election coverage. Prior to that, she was a political correspondent for the *Wall Street Journal* and a reporter with the *Los Angeles Times* and served as executive director and senior fellow at Harvard University's Shorenstein Center on the Press, Politics and Public Policy.

Roger Hurwitz is a research scientist at the Massachusetts Institute of Technology's Artificial Intelligence Laboratory and a developer of systems for electronic publication, intelligent routing, and wide-area collaboration. His publications include *Communication Flows,* a study of media development in the United States and Japan, co-authored with Ithiel de Sola Pool and Hiroshi Inose.

Andrew Jakubowicz is a professor of sociology at the University of Technology in Sydney, Australia. He has been a consultant to the Australian government on new media and the cultural industries and produced *Making Multicultural Australia—A Multimedia Documentary.*

Henry Jenkins is the Ann Fetter Friedlaender Professor of Humanities and director of the Program in Comparative Media Studies at the Massachusetts Institute of Technology where he writes "Digital Renaissance," a monthly column on media and culture for *Technology Review*. He is the author of *Textual Poachers: Television Fans and Participatory Culture* and editor of *The Children's Culture Reader:*

Ira Magaziner served as senior advisor to the president for policy development during the Clinton administration. His responsibilities included charting government policy concerning the Internet. Before joining the Clinton administration, he was a corporate strategist and consultant, directing policy analysis for major corporations.

Lloyd Morrisett was president of the Markle Foundation from 1969 to 1998, during which time he initiated the foundation's program in communications and information technology. He cofounded the Children's Television Workshop (now Sesame Workshop), producer of *Sesame Street* and other television programs for children.

Adam Clayton Powell III recently retired as vice president of technology and programs at the Freedom Forum, where he supervised forums and programs on information technologies and new media. Prior to joining the Freedom Forum, he was vice president in charge of news at National Public Radio, a producer and manager at CBS News in New York, and news director of Satellite News Channels.

Michael Schudson is the author of *The Good Citizen: A History of American Public Life* and *The Power of News*. A professor of communication at the University of California, San Diego, Schudson has been the recipient of a Guggenheim fellowship, a MacArthur Foundation fellowship, and a residential fellowship at the Center for Advanced Study in the Behavioral Sciences.

Doug Schuler, cofounder of the Seattle Community Network, teaches at Evergreen State College in Washington. He is the author of *New Community Networks: Wired for Change* and coeditor of several books on cyberspace and community, including *Reinventing Technology, Rediscovering Community: Critical Explorations of Computing as a Social Practice.*

David Sholle is an associate professor in mass communication at Miami University in Ohio, where he teaches classes in media production, critical theory, and technology and culture. He is working on a book about cultural and critical approaches to the study of the information society.

David Thorburn is a professor of literature at the Massachusetts Institute of Technology and director of the MIT Communications Forum. He is the author of *Conrad's Romanticism* and many essays and reviews on literary, cultural, and media topics.

Cristina Venegas is assistant professor in film studies at the University of California, Santa Barbara, where she teaches film and media with a focus on Latin American, Latino media and digital technologies. She is currently completing a book titled *Digital Dilemma: New Media Relations in Contemporary Cuba.*

Ingrid Volkmer is a fellow in the Shorenstein Center on the Press, Politics and Public Policy at Harvard University. She is the author of *News in the Global Sphere,* a study of CNN.

Peter Walsh is chairman of the Massachusetts Art Commission and a consultant to Dartmouth College, the Metropolitan Museum of Art, the Museum of Fine Arts in Boston, and the Art Museum Image Consortium. He serves as chair of the Committee on Intellectual Property of the College Art Association.

David Winston was the director of planning for former House Speaker Newt Gingrich and a senior fellow at The Heritage Foundation, where he helped develop the award-winning townhall.com Internet site. He is president of the Winston Group, a consulting and market research company.

Index